OG MANDINO'S
University
of Success

OG MANDINO'S
UNIVERSITY OF SUCCESS

by Og Mandino

BANTAM BOOKS
Toronto • New York • London • Sydney • Auckland

OG MANDINO'S UNIVERSITY OF SUCCESS

A Bantam Book / August 1982

38: From *The Three Keys To Success* by Baron Beaverbrook; Copyright 1954, 1956 by Sir William Maxwell Aiken, 1st Baron Beaverbrook. Reprinted by permission of Hawthorn Books, Elsevier-Dutton Publishing Co., Inc.

40: From GETTING TO THE TOP FAST by Auren Uris and Jack Tarrant; Copyright © 1976 by Auren Uris and Jack Tarrant by permission of Contemporary Books, Inc., Chicago and Arthur Pine Associates, Inc., Literary Services.

41: From THE NEW ART OF LIVING by Norman Vincent Peale; Copyright © 1971, 1973. Reprinted by permissions of Hawthorn Books, Elsevier-Dutton Publishing Co., Inc.

43: "For Better Beginnings" from THE GOLDEN AGE by John Paul Getty; Copyright © 1968 by Simon & Schuster, Inc. Reprinted by permission of Simon & Schuster, Inc., a Division of Gulf & Western Corporation and permission granted by Roslyn Targ Literary Agency, Inc. New York, N.Y.

44: "Control Your Enemies" from THE ART OF SELFISHNESS by David Seabury; Copyright © 1937 by David Seabury. Renewed 1964 by Evelyn Seabury. Reprinted by permission of Simon & Schuster, a Division of Gulf & Western Corporation.

46: Reprinted by permission of Farrar, Straus and Giroux, Inc. "Love and Status" from THE ABILITY TO LOVE by Allan Fromme; Copyright © 1963, 1965 by Allan Fromme.

47: Reprinted by permission of The Sterling Lord Agency, from the book EXCELLENCE by John W. Gardner; Copyright © 1961.

48: "You Raise Carrots But You Don't Raise Kids" from I AIN'T WELL—BUT I SURE AM BETTER by Jess Lair, Ph.D.; Copyright © 1975 by Jesse K. Lair. Reprinted by permission of Doubleday & Company, Inc. and Richard Curtis.

49: "You and Your Happiness" from THE POWER OF MATURITY by Louis Binstock; Copyright © 1969 by Hawthorn Books, Inc. Published by Hawthorn Books. Reprinted by permission of Ruth Atlas Binstock.

50: "Success is Still Success" from the book SUCCESS IS WITHIN YOU by Howard Whitman; Copyright © 1956 by Howard Whitman. Reprinted by permission of Doubleday & Co., Inc.

(Note: Every effort has been made to locate the copyright owner of material reproduced in this book. Omissions brought to our attention will be corrected in subsequent editions.)

Library of Congress Cataloging in Publication Data
Main entry under title:
Og Mandino's University of Success.

Bibliography: p. 523
1. Success—Addresses, essays, lecture. I. Mandino,
Og. II. Title: University of success.
BF637.S8035   158'.1   81-17561
ISBN 0-553-34535-4 (pbk.)   AACR2

Published simultaneously in the United States and Canada

*Dedicated, with humility and love,
to the more than ten million readers,
worldwide, who have welcomed my books into
their homes ... and into their hearts.*

"I am convinced," Zacchaeus said, "that life is just a game, here on Earth, a game where no one need be a loser, no matter what his plight or condition may be. I believe that everyone can enjoy the fruits of victory but I am equally as certain that, like all other games, one cannot participate in this mysterious act of living with any hope of satisfaction unless one understands a few simple rules."

From *Og Mandino*'s
The Greatest Success In the World

WELCOME TO
The University
of Success

Congratulations!

If you have been wearily attending the "school of hard knocks" up to now, I have great news for you.

You have just been transferred!

Your life is about to change—for the better!

Forget yesterday and last month and last year, with their gloomy diary of failures and disappointments. All that is in the past. This is the day you were beginning to believe would never arrive and yet it is here! This is the day you begin to turn your life around. This is the day you commence learning the greatest secrets of success from experts and, more important, *how to use what you learn* to make a better world for yourself and those you love.

Henry David Thoreau once wrote, "It is time that we had uncommon schools, that we did not leave off our education when we begin to be men and women." Through the pages of this book you are about to enter an "uncommon school," one designed to provide you with valuable information that will fill a large gap in your life and your instructors are, without question, the greatest faculty ever assembled to teach the subject of success and how to achieve it.

Dale Carnegie, J. Paul Getty, Dr. Maxwell Maltz, Napoleon Hill, P. T. Barnum, Norman Vincent Peale, Dr. Wayne W. Dyer, W. Clement Stone, Dorothea Brande, Richard DeVos, Benjamin Franklin, Lord Beaverbrook, Joyce Brothers—these are only some of the fifty brilliant minds who have been gathered together for the first time in history in the fulfillment of a dream I have had for many years—to publish the *ultimate success book* where only the acknowledged masters of that subject were made available to counsel and teach and guide you.

Undoubtedly those years you spent in school taught you many things. But during all those hours spent in all those classes, *never*, not even for a single fifty-minute period, were you taught or shown how to apply what you were learning in order to achieve a life filled with happiness, accomplishment, and success. That is the sole purpose of this book and with your potential we will succeed together.

Success! Such a magical word—like gold or love or Shangri-la, it conjures up different but always enticing visions in the minds of all of us. Has it been missing from your life? Even if it has, you still daydream don't you, about how wonderful things might be if only fate would smile in your direction and bestow upon you a more generous portion of money, position, power, freedom, and perhaps even a touch of fame?

WHY SUCCESS IS SO DIFFICULT

We are, each of us, a miracle. Within every one of us, the pilot light of hope never dies. Mechanics, executives, salespeople, students, models, writers, carpenters, computer operators, store owners, entrepreneurs, fruit pickers, stockbrokers, housewives—all of us, to some degree, indulge in the same dreams and wishes—to be free from want, to live in a finer home, to owe no one, to drive that sleek new automobile, to eat in an elegant restaurant now and then, to vacation in exotic places, to have a few items of designer clothing in our wardrobe, to send our children to the best of schools.

Why not? Haven't we been told, since birth, that we live in a land of unlimited opportunity?

Why not? The answer is obvious, but painful. The vast majority of us have absolutely no idea how to begin to make our dreams come true! Undoubtedly you already have all the tools necessary to create a magnificent life, but what good are they ... if you don't know how to *use* them? And how can you build a life worth living without any plans or blueprints?

Not once—neither in primary school nor junior high school nor high school, not even in the most hallowed halls of higher learning—were you ever instructed on the simple techniques of setting goals, of motivating yourself and others, of dealing with adversity, of eliminating self-defeating habits, of using time profitably, of practicing the power of choice, of developing self-confidence, of doing the things you are afraid to do, of generating enthusiasm at will, of organizing your life, of accumulating wealth, of getting people to give you what you want, of looking like a winner, of guiding your children, of handling stress, of counting your blessings ... and so much more. That you have managed to survive at all is a tribute to your courage and faith.

And yet, though we hang on, our shortcomings haunt us. We are made vividly and painfully aware of them every time we turn on a television set or pick up a newspaper or magazine. Bravely we try to ignore the affluence and success of so many others but we are forced to admit, if only in our darkest moments of introspection, that Hendrik van Loon was correct when he wrote, "In history as in life, it is success that counts."

Well—is it too late for you to reach for that brass ring or make a run for the roses? Should you crawl into your dusty little corner of self-pity and just let the world pass you by? No! Never!

YOUR GREATEST ASSET

Let us take inventory. Did you possibly learn anything during those formative years of schooling that might help you to change your life for the better, if you were to begin today, regardless of your age, your skills, your background, your color, your financial condition, or your opinion of yourself? Just one thing, if you stop to think about it *and that one thing may be all you need!*

Listen carefully as the great English essayist, historian, biographer, and philosopher, Thomas Carlyle, explains.

If we think about it, all that a university or final highest school can do for us, is still but what the first school began doing—teach us to *read*. We learn to read in various languages, in various sciences; we learn the alphabet and letters of all manners of books. But the place where we are to get knowledge, even theoretic knowledge, is the books themselves. It depends on what we read, after all manners of professors have done their best for us. *The true university of these days is a collection of books!*

According to Carlyle's specifications this volume you are holding is a "university of success" since it contains a choice collection of the wisdom, techniques, and principles from the greatest books in the world of success literature. Here you will discover nuggets of pure gold, waiting only for you to reach out and claim them as your own. Here you will be taught by men and women whose messages have withstood the tests of time and practicality and whose principles *work.*

Please remember, you need not accept or attempt to use all of the hundreds of success ideas and techniques you are about to learn. Just one may be all you need to work wonders in your life and career. All that is required of you, in this place of learning, is an ability to read plus—a burning desire to make something more of your life. And don't even be too concerned if the flames of that desire give off little heat as you begin your studies. Their temperature will rise, gradually, as you begin to realize how much you can still accomplish in the years ahead.

HOW TO GET THE MOST
FROM THIS BOOK

Read it from beginning to end. Do not skip any of the lessons. They were arranged in the order they are presented, after much deliberation, in order to assist you in making a gradual transition from the person you are today to the person you can become.

Because you are about to be exposed to a wealth of knowledge, it might be easier for you to assimilate if you take it in small bites. For maximum effect I would suggest that you read only one lesson each day, and try to make that reading as close to your bedtime as possible. Marvelous things happen when you put your subconscious mind to work, and when you awake you will be amazed at how much of the material you have retained. Don't hurry. You will be guided patiently through eight semesters, as in a normal university career, plus two additional semesters of graduate work so that you will even be able to cope with success, once you have it.

If you are a woman, an overemphasis of the masculine tense in a few of the lessons may disturb you. Don't let that prevent you from extracting the good in each. Usually those particular segments were written long before the happy emancipation that has taken place in the second half of this century. Just remind yourself that the bias, if it shows at all, was an innocent product of another age. Success is no longer restricted, thank God, to either gender.

One more thing. Avoid, if at all possible, falling into the trap of reading this book in the same casual manner that you might read most volumes of fiction or even nonfiction. Your teachers are all highly motivated and dynamic individuals and there is an ever-present danger that you may become fascinated by their personalities, delivery, and charm, enjoy their words as entertainment, and *forget* that your main purpose for being here, attending these lectures, is to acquire the tools necessary for success.

How do you avoid this danger? Simple. Whenever you open this book, be certain that you have a pen or pencil in your hand. When you read a line or paragraph that is meaningful to you— underline it! This simple act, alone, will triple your retention of that thought or principle and also make it easier for you to find it again, later on. You might also wish to draw a star next to certain powerful suggestions or methods that catch your fancy, or an exclamation mark, or a question mark if you don't agree. After all, this is your own personal textbook for a brighter tomorrow.

IT'S ALL UP TO YOU

Unlike most higher schools of learning, this university will have no graduation ceremonies, no diplomas signifying you have survived the system, nor will there be any final exams or degrees conferred. The only reward you will receive, because of your efforts here, will be how much you manage to change your life for the better—in terms of peace and contentment and pride as well as material gain.

History is filled with stories of individuals who dated a new era in their lives from the reading of a single book. May your name eventually be added to that already impressive and glorious list. But—it's all up to you. No one else can live your life for you. No one else can succeed for you!

It's your move.

Og Mandino

YOUR UNIVERSITY'S CURRICULA

SEMESTER ONE

SEMESTER TWO

SEMESTER THREE

SEMESTER FOUR

SEMESTER FIVE

SEMESTER
ONE

Beware of no one more than of yourself;
we carry our worst enemies within us.

Charles Spurgeon

In order to plan your future wisely,
it is necessary that you
understand and appreciate your past.

Jo Coudert

LESSON 1

HOW TO LOOK BACK
ON WHERE YOU HAVE BEEN

Are you ready to take that first step toward a better life?

If you are, I sincerely hope that two sentences from the welcoming chapter are still ringing in your head. "No one else can live your life for you. No one else can succeed for you!"

As Jo Coudert wrote, in her marvelous classic, *Advice from a Failure,* from which this opening lesson is taken, "It is not an easy world to live in. It is not an easy world to be decent in. It is not an easy world to understand oneself in, nor to like oneself in. But it must be lived in, and in the living there is one person you absolutely have to be with."

That person, of course, is *you.* But who are you? What are you? How sad that most of us know more about how and why our automobile functions than we know about ourselves.

If someone asked you, for example, what business you are in, you might respond that you were a salesperson, a computer operator, a model, a stockbroker, a truck driver, a carpenter, or whatever your vocation may be. You would be wrong!

The business you are in, the business we are all in, is the business of *living*—and the sooner you learn who you are and how you became the person you are—the sooner you will be able to deal with challenges that may have frustrated your success, up to now. So, let us hasten to begin ...

I call him X because, when his story starts, X was a victim of total amnesia. He did not remember his name nor his previous life nor how he had gotten where he was. The best guess was that he had been a flyer and there had been an accident. When he came to, he seemed to be in a dark cave, and apparently there were no broken bones because he could move his limbs, but his brain was barely functioning and he soon slipped back into unconsciousness. How long he remained in the cave he had no idea. Weak and helpless, he dozed, moved a little, dozed again. Since he was warm, not hungry, and perfectly comfortable, he made no effort to rouse himself. He was content to let things be as they were.

But paradise is lost as well as gained, and one day he woke to find himself being hauled unceremoniously into the light. Anxiety flooded through him, and he screamed in terror. For the first time since the accident, he feared for his life. It was a primitive, consuming fear that washed through every cell, every capillary. Coming out of darkness, his brain was seared with glare and his eyes blinded. Sounds beat at his ears. Cold penetrated every pore. For all he knew, the natives who had yanked him from his hiding place had yanked him into hell.

Apparently, though, they did not intend to kill him. They covered him and laid him down, and, exhausted, X fell asleep. He slept most of the next days and weeks. He was too weak even to lift his head; all his energy was concentrated inward on the effort to stay alive. Unable to speak and at the mercy of the natives for his every need, he called out when he woke, cried helplessly when no one came. This may not seem very admirable behavior, but put yourself in his shoes: he was feeble and helpless; he was surrounded by strangers whose ways and intentions he did not know; his mind was barely working; his eyes scarcely saw; he knew little beyond that he was alive and totally dependent.

But gradually his panic began to subside and his mind emerged fitfully from its haze. As he gained a little strength, his attention flickered outward for brief moments, and he tried to gather some clues as to where he was and whether the natives were friendly. He noticed that apparently one native in particular had been deputized to look after him and that it was usually she who came when he needed something, although occasionally it was her assistant, a man. Since she was gentle enough in handling him and even seemed to be rather fond of him, he began to feel somewhat reassured about his situation. His longing for the serenity and simplicity of the cave did not end, but it grew less intense. His new environment more and more engaged his attention. And he had one success, which encouraged him to believe he might be able to learn to get along. He noticed the woman smiling at him, and he smiled back. This seemed to delight her, and she called other natives to come to see. He obligingly smiled at them, figuring that if this was what they wanted, this was what he would do.

As the time went on, X gained strength, but it was a slow business and he still did little but sleep. In his waking moments, lying on his back and looking at the ceiling, he speculated about what kind of place he had landed in and what sort of people he would encounter when he was able to be up and around. He took it for granted that the woman who cared for him was typical of the natives, so he stored up every clue he could glean from her behavior. He listened to her tone of voice for hints as to whether she was happy or discontent. He noted how she handled him so as to guess whether he must be prepared to deal with a hostile people or a peaceful one. He counted how long it was after he signaled he was hungry before she came with food, so he would know whether, later, he would have to battle for sustenance or would obtain what he needed quite readily. He eavesdropped on the talk around him, although he could not understand the language, to learn whether this was a place where the people quarreled a good deal among themselves, or whether they got along equably and enjoyed each other's company. He watched the woman's expression as she tended to his needs to find out whether they were a puritanical or a natural people.

Knowing that his life depended on whether or not the people would accept him once he was able to move about among them, he was most intensely interested in what the woman thought of him. He evaluated her behavior for clues as to whether he would be liked, whether he would be found personable and attractive, whether he would elicit sympathy and interest or be ignored. So preoccupied was he with this that he began to find acceptable in himself anything that she found acceptable and to dislike anything about himself that she disliked. Without realizing it, he came to use her as a mirror to reflect back what sort of person he was.

Being so dependent on her, when she went away he wondered desperately if she would ever return. Some of the early anxiety flooded back when he feared she had deserted him. He had so much of her attention that it took a long time for him to realize that she was a person with a life of her own, that her life did not center exclusively on his, that they were two different people. He had viewed her, at first, just as an extension of himself, the legs that could fetch for him, the arms that could bring things to his mouth. His weakness had made him terribly self-centered, as people who are ill are self-centered.

Being together so much, a closeness grew between X and the woman. They developed a language of their own of signs and sounds. She had always been empathic to his needs, but now he began to understand her better, to know her moods and read her expressions. They laughed quite a bit sometimes, and sometimes they were just quiet together. They played small games, and they teased each other. Once, when they were playing, he nipped her to show his increasing strength. He was startled when she pulled back and frowned and spoke sharply. He had not meant to hurt her. He decided it meant that the natives did not like aggressive behavior and that he had best keep any impulses in that direction under wraps.

With the man, whom he was also coming to like and trust as he saw more of him, he could play more roughly, and he enjoyed this because it gave him needed exercise. From them both, he learned how love was expressed in this culture, and he tried to imitate them, for he realized that it was their loving behavior that meant the difference between life and death for him. If he could not make these people who knew him most intimately care about him, he would have to expect little goodwill from the other inhabitants, and so he was alert to any clues and he tried hard to please them.

It was clear by now both that he would survive and that he would be spending a long time among these people, so X set about learning the language. This had both welcome and unwelcome consequences: the increased ease in communicating was satisfying, but he had a sense of loss that the direct, wordless communication between himself and the woman was gone. He was nostalgic for that, as he had been nostalgic for the cave and as he was to be for other warm closeness as he grew more competent and better able to look after himself, but he knew he could not remain helpless and dependent always.

The woman knew it too, and she began to point out his responsibility for keeping himself clean. For the first time since he had been with them, X found that he had the upper hand, that he could choose to comply or not. There was some pleasure in testing out this area of autonomy, and a battle of wills seemed to be in the offing. But the woman made an effort to remain good-humored and relaxed, and X, valuing her affection and approval, decided to do his best to meet her wishes.

It is not surprising that, with X becoming more of a person, one of his first acts as a person was to fall in love with the woman. He asked her to marry him, but she pointed out that, not only did he still need a long period of care before he would be able to be on his own, but that she was already married to the man. He considered the first objection no more of a drawback than does the patient who decides to marry his nurse. As for the second, he settled on a straightforward approach. He told the man he planned to marry the woman and that he would appreciate it if he did not come to the house anymore. The man laughed and went right on returning each evening. Brooding on the problem and wondering if he would have to resort to violent means to get the man out of the way, X considered the possibilities. A most unexpected realization was that the man, being far more powerful and perhaps able to divine his intentions, would strike first and render X impotent to take his place. This threat of castration, although existing entirely in X's mind, so frightened him that he abandoned any plan to take the man's place. Indeed, he went somewhat to the opposite extreme. On the theory that if you cannot beat them, join them, he set about identifying with the man and attempted to become more like him. This episode ended with their becoming good friends and joint admirers of the woman.

X had been with them for about four years at the time of this contretemps, and he learned from it that he had best begin to widen his horizons. Accordingly, he began to venture farther from the woman's side. Initially, of course, he had not been able to walk at all, but as his muscles strengthened, he had tried short steps with the woman's help, and now he was walking fairly well without her aid. He sallied forth to see something of the village, but still stayed close enough to call for help if he needed it. He became acquainted with the natives in the surrounding houses, observed their mores, increased his vocabulary, and acquired some new skills. As far as he could see, he had been right to assume the woman was typical of the other inhabitants, and he confirmed many of the conclusions he had drawn when he had had only her to go on. One of the most pleasing ones was that other people also found him attractive and likable, and this gave him a happy confidence in himself. He made friends easily with the natives. They liked his smile and his sturdiness. They approved of his efforts to learn and to master the world he found himself in.

Each success gave him courage to try for a further success, and the man and woman had taught him well enough so that when he failed, he learned from it and went on. It was satisfying to X to be increasingly self-reliant after his long period of helplessness, and because his problems were few, it was a tranquil time. His keepers were proud that he was learning the ropes and they did not try to hold him back. But they were there when he exceeded his strength or his capacities, and thus he had the best of both independence and dependence.

The culture was not the simple one X had expected. He tended at first to make easy generalizations about the people and their life, but eventually he became able to accept complexity and contradiction. He stopped looking solely for answers and became interested in the questions. He realized that it was more useful to draw inferences than conclusions. He became an avid collector of facts.

And so time passed, and X got along very well. If he remembered the early time at all, it was only on the rare occasions when something threatened to go wrong and some of the anxiety came seeping back. Having learned so much in the twelve years he had been there, X began to feel that he had learned everything, and he was startled to discover that the woman and man, who had once seemed to him to be omniscient, really did not know so much after all. It was clear that he had grown beyond them and they had outlived their usefulness to him. He found his strength and his enthusiasm, not in them now, but in friends. His friends understood him, understood his moodiness, his rapidly changing interests, his concerns, his impatience. He felt guilty that he was turning his back on the man and woman who had saved his life, but he told himself that he had not asked them to bring him into their world.

As tranquil as the previous time had been, this one was stormy. It was not until after it was over and he looked back on it that X knew it had had to be this way. The stirrings within him that had given rise to his rebelliousness were the promptings of knowledge that he must turn outward, must leave this home, must wean himself from this woman and this man if he were ever to find who he really was and where he belonged. It had been a trial time of sailing while still tied to the dock. His old gratitude to the man and the woman came back. He saw that they were wise, and when not wise, they were generous. He saw that they had done their best and that they loved him. He saw that he loved them, and it did not lessen him but enrich him. They had sheltered him for twenty-one years, and now they knew they must let him go. Their job was over. It was up to him now to find his own people.

X never did anything harder in his life than leave them.

Until you acquire five essential ingredients,
success will never be success.

Howard Whitman

LESSON 2

HOW TO FASHION
YOUR OWN BRAND OF SUCCESS

Today, there are as many different definitions of success as there are human beings, and there are those who claim, with considerable proof, that the greatest failure of our times is success since we have come, more and more, to equate success solely with material possessions.

"I've been rich and I've been poor—and rich is better!" chants one show business personality after another, and we all smile and nod our heads in envious agreement.

But is that all there is to success? Was Howard Hughes any happier or more at peace with himself when he doubled his first million dollars? Is that movie star, her safety-deposit box stuffed with diamonds, more content with life after she sheds her fourth husband for number five?

How do you define success? Perhaps you have been too busy at making a living to ever give it more than a passing thought. Still, if you are attending this university in order to improve your life, and I hope you are, it's not too early to give you some guidelines to think about and perhaps adopt for yourself.

You *did* take my advice didn't you, and you *are* reading this book with a pen or pencil in your hand? I hope so, for there is much of value to learn and remember from the brilliant Howard Whitman as he unveils the ingredients for true success from his book, *Success Is Within You . . .*

9

There are two main criteria of success: 1. Do others think you are a success? 2. Do you think so?

These two are related as the straw is related to the ice cream soda. If you want fully to enjoy an ice-cream soda it is nice to have both. But if you are to have one only, it is certainly far better to have the ice-cream soda than to have only the straw, for the straw is quite worthless alone. And it is quite worthless, and futile too, to have the whole world thinking that you are a success if you do not think so yourself. The ice cream of success is your own inward knowledge of it. Given that, you do not necessarily need the acknowledgment of the outside world.

The trouble comes when we try to fashion our success to the outside world's specifications even though these are not the specifications drawn up in our own hearts. For whom are we succeeding, for ourselves or for somebody else? Success, if it is to be meaningful, must be a personal thing. It varies from individual to individual as personality varies; indeed, it springs from the very depths where personality itself arises, and often it takes insightful probing to find out for ourselves what our own ideas of success actually are. Too often we conform to the outside world in our success patterns without thought or analysis, just as we conform in other departments of living. But a few brave ones among us have had the courage to think on this and have occasionally spelled out patterns of success which are at once honest, courageous, and individual.

William Faulkner, the Nobel prize novelist, has said, "I was born to be a tramp. I was happiest when I had nothing. I had a trench coat then with big pockets. It would carry a pair of socks, a condensed Shakespeare, and a bottle of whiskey. Then I was happy and I wanted nothing and I had no responsibility."

One may reject this definition of success. That is, one may reject it for himself, but he cannot reject it for Faulkner. It is a forthright statement, typical of the honest Mississippian.

I personally get a little tired of seeing the name of Albert Schweitzer every time someone wants to raise the image of a deity on earth. And it is interesting to note that even Schweitzer tired of it. On his eightieth birthday in 1955 celebrations were held all over the world by Schweitzer admirers. Funds were raised (over twenty thousand dollars in the United States and more elsewhere) to send as birthday presents to the mild-mannered little doctor who gave up worldly fame for the seclusion of darkest Africa, where he could minister to the natives. At his hospital at Lambaréné in French Equatorial Africa, five hundred singing, bell-ringing, flower-bearing admirers gathered to greet him on his birthday, for fame shone on the good doctor more brightly in dark Africa than it ever had in the luminous cities of Europe. Schweitzer's birthday comment: "How I regret all this fuss. How tired I am."

Here's a man with his own great idea of success—but the world just won't let him pursue it.

In the turbulent Europe of the mid-nineteenth century the convention-flouting, incurably romantic George Sand wrote in one of her famous letters a quite remarkable definition of success:

> One is happy as a result of one's own efforts, once one knows the necessary ingredients of happiness—simple tastes, a certain degree of courage, self-denial to a point, love of work, and, above all, a clear conscience. Happiness is no vague dream, of that I now feel certain. By the proper use of experience and thought one can draw much from oneself, by determination and patience one can even restore one's health . . . so let us live life as it is, and not be ungrateful.

The most thoughtful among us conclude at last that personal success must exist inside if it is to exist at all. It cannot be composed of outward signs or appearances, but only of intangible personal values stemming from a mature philosophy. One of the things which impressed the world most about Mahatma Gandhi was the published photograph of all his earthly possessions at the time he died: a pair of spectacles, a pair of sandals, a few simple garments, a spinning wheel, and a book. Yet the world knew that here had passed one of the richest of men. Perhaps the world in the wells of its consciousness was somehow aware of what Henry David Thoreau had put into this simple sentence: "A man is rich in the proportions of things he can let alone." Gandhi himself often had spoken of the reduction of needs. Life to him seemed a process of gradual divestment of needs, so that from a squalling infant in the cradle who needs everything, the human being, if he lives successfully, gradually matures into an adult who needs virtually nothing. Gandhi was himself an example of such growth, so rare an example that his life dramatized for the rest of us how short we fall of the human growth potential.

This is not to say that poverty should be the goal, or that an ascetic denial of material progress or possessions makes one a *mahatma*, a great soul. Many a great soul has been vastly surrounded by material possessions and formidably wealthy: Andrew Carnegie, Jacob Riis, Julius Rosenwald, Samuel Mather, the Guggenheims, and Russell Sage, to name a few. All these men achieved true personal success, in these cases, outward as well as inward. They managed to have the ice-cream soda and the straw as well.

There are certain constant factors to be found in true success whether it be the success of an Andrew Carnegie or of a Mahatma Gandhi. These are the essential factors, independent of wealth or achievement, poverty or asceticism. These are the dynamic factors in success, the very bone and sinew of it.

The first constant factor is *purpose*. One must know that in whatever he does he is moving forward toward a goal. Aimlessness is the worst enemy of success. One can hardly feel successful in a bog. But as long as one has purpose he feels that his energies and creative thought are taking him *somewhere,* and there is satisfaction in the journey just as there is despair whenever we feel, as we often insightfully put it, that we are "getting nowhere."

A recent news report from Biloxi, Mississippi, powerfully illustrates the role of purpose in making life worth living. A young woman, a dancer twenty-four years old, jumped from a wharf in the colorful little town in an attempt to commit suicide. As she later put it, she was "tired of living."

A young man saw her jump from the wharf and splash into the water. Forgetting that he himself didn't know how to swim, he stripped off his coat and leaped from the wharf after her in a blind attempt to save a fellow human being. He began to thresh about in the water and was in serious danger of drowning when the young dancer, her own despair momentarily forgotten, began to paddle her way toward him. As he was gulping water and gasping for breath, she grabbed hold of him and pulled him safely ashore. Instead of ending her own life she had saved the life of another.

In that crucial moment when she saw the young man struggling for life, her own life suddenly gained something it had lacked before: *purpose*. And so what was drowned there in the waters beneath the wharf was merely her despair and not her spirit. She had known in a dramatic flash the difference between having nothing to live for and something to live for, and having pulled the young man to safety, she was herself taken to the hospital, treated for exposure, and released with a new lease on life.

Not all of us have such stark encounters with purpose or the lack of it. But each of us has known occasions when life was suddenly vibrant and alive because we were going somewhere, and contrastingly bleak occasions when life seemed like the wooden horse at the end of the road which says Dead End. Success to be true must have an abiding sense of purpose; otherwise, though one may vegetate successfully, one cannot live successfully.

Secondly, success has the intrinsic character of a *batting average*. It is not all of a piece; not every hour nor every day is uniformly successful. Rather there are upturns in success separated by valleys of failure. Recently I met a successful television producer, responsible for turning out an intensely complex and difficult program every day. He remarked,

I'd go crazy if I tried to judge every day's performance against an absolute standard of perfection. All I try for is a good batting average. I know very well that sometimes I'm going to foul out, but so long as I get my share of singles and doubles, perhaps an occasional home run, I don't mind the inevitable errors and strikeouts.

So, too, a successful life will have its days or even years of failure. It will certainly have its moments of utter washout. These are not blights upon such a life but merely the inevitable failings which bear testimony to the fact that success isn't easy.

The psychiatrists tell us of "compulsive" types of individuals who cannot bear a moment of failure. Actually such people never taste real success. They rather have the constant flavor of mediocrity upon their tongues. They fear even the slightest failure lest it topple their trembling confidence in themselves. With more firmly anchored confidence a person is able to absorb occasional failure; in fact, with close touch to reality the mature individual knows that occasional failure is inevitable and he wastes less energy in fretting over it so that he may have more energy with which to bid for the success he seeks.

In growing up each of us must learn sooner or later that every day isn't Christmas, and so in courting success we must learn, too, that every effort cannot be crowned with glory.

A third constant ingredient of success is the *price* of it. There is no success for free. One of the wondrous aspects of these lives of ours, a somewhat mystical aspect, is our constitutional inability to enjoy what we have not earned. Psychiatrists' couches are deeply shaped by the contours of coddled middle-aged women who have been given just about everything they ever have asked for but find themselves strangely unable to discover any joy in life. Some psychiatrist someday should explore the human personality for a subtle little balance scale which I'm sure exists there, and if he finds it and closely examines it, I believe he will note that *joy* is written upon the poise and *effort* upon the counterpoise. The joy of success, it seems, must be counterbalanced by the effort to achieve it—and that's a mystical little aspect of human character which exists in all of us.

During a recent commencement week at Oberlin College I especially noted, among the conferrals of honorary degrees, the citation appended to an LL.D. awarded to Theodore E. Steinway, president of Steinway & Sons. It noted that the Steinways "had produced 342,000 pianos, used and abused by pianists from Liszt to Rubinstein the Second." And the citation also observed, "In one of their concert grands 243 taut strings exert a pull of 40,000 pounds on an iron frame. Theodore E. Steinway gives constant proof that out of great tension may come great harmony."

Perhaps this is the yin and the yang of existence in the Western world. The hooked half circle of joy nestles against the half circle of effort; thus tension and harmony share their oneness within the all-embracing arc, and in quite the same relationship success and the price of it coexist as an inseparable whole.

A fourth essential ingredient, without which success is not success, is *satisfaction*. One man's meat is, of course, another man's poison, and so satisfaction to one man may stem from the amassing of a fortune, while to another man it may come from the writing of a poem. But certainly neither man can claim success at all if there is no satisfaction in either the fortune or the poem.

Success must be enjoyed. It may be won with tears but it must be crowned with laughter. Otherwise the effort may be worthwhile—it may be good or even great—but for the individual without the inner laughter, which is known by another name as satisfaction, there can hardly be success. This has become one of the strange anomalies of our time: that so many have all the outward trappings of success without the essential inner trappings of it. They don't *feel* success. Instead of warmth inside there is barrenness. "I've worked and slaved and knocked myself out—for what?" has become the refrain.

The satisfaction of success need not be identifiable by anyone else or to anyone else so long as the person himself knows it is there. A schoolteacher working on a meager salary and with the diminished respect that schoolteachers command these days might not be regarded as very successful by the community at large, but if in his own heart there is a good feeling, a conviction that he is doing well at work he loves, then an essential ingredient of success is his whether anyone knows it or not. So much of this ingredient depends upon the individual's own attitude rather than upon overt evidence. For example, one carpenter might feel an utter failure because he must ply a trade with his hands and take orders from a boss while other men sit in offices and dictate to secretaries, yet another carpenter on the very same job might feel the satisfaction of the master craftsman because of his skill at shaping the board and fitting the joint. I know a carpenter of this latter stamp, a man who need bow to no one for he has the mastery of a trade, and, for all our lives of modern gadgetry and the tube-metal glass-brick fronts of our existence, such mastery is still a mark of virtue.

A pastor may feel the inner satisfaction of success if in his quiet rounds he brings a touch of God to fellow beings; so may a manufacturer if he feels his product is the best of its kind, a source of pride to him; so may a professional baseball player if he loves the game; so may a housewife if her daily chores are purposeful and creative, not just irksome. Satisfaction, stemming largely from an attitude, is available to all in that it begins inside, a kind of central nugget deep in the strata of our souls.

A final basic element of success is *spirituality*. It is hard to imagine anyone feeling successful without also feeling related somehow to the greater purposes of life and to the Author of those purposes. Whether one is a successful hobo or a successful banker he must, if he is to sense the full bouquet of success, have a conviction, however subtle, that he is in tune with God. He must sense somehow the pervasive currents of God's existence and recognize his own existence in those currents, too.

Again, this is personal. The spirituality of the successful hobo and the spirituality of the successful banker hardly could be sounded in the same octave, yet, though far apart in the scale, they form a harmony. It is not the disparity of outlook or vocation which counts, but rather the fact that both are in tune with life and its Maker.

Success is no straitjacket. It is no mold into which all must be poured. It is no rigid stamp. It is as individual as our fingerprints or the look in our eyes. All we need is the courage to be—and realize—ourselves.

> *Feeling sorry for yourself, and your
> present condition, is not only a waste of energy
> but the worst habit you could possibly have.*

Dale Carnegie

LESSON 3

HOW TO
COUNT YOUR BLESSINGS

Any university's greatest asset, including this one, is the credentials of its faculty.

In Lesson 1 you met Jo Coudert, who has edited many textbooks in the fields of psychiatry and medicine and has a special talent for presenting complex and personal material, as you have seen. Her book, *Advice from a Failure,* has been a constant bestseller ever since its publication in 1965.

In Lesson 2 it was Howard Whitman, war correspondent, syndicated columnist, television commentator, producer, and author of hundreds of articles dealing with family life and human relations. He has also been the recipient of three Freedoms Foundation awards.

Now you are about to hear from a man whose name has been a household word in most of the civilized world for almost half a century. His book, *How to Win Friends and Influence People,* with sales long past the ten-million mark, was at first a textbook that Dale Carnegie prepared to supplement the adult courses he was teaching (at five dollars a night in the beginning) to YMCA classes. His subject: self-confidence and how to develop it in order to deal with others.

However, there was far more to Dale Carnegie's philosophy than merely learning how to influence others for personal gain. His wisdom, his common sense, his ability to reduce success to its barest essentials, rescued countless thousands from lives of failure and self-pity.

Feeling sorry for yourself and your present condition? Listen to Dale Carnegie, from his other best-seller, *How to Stop Worrying and Start Living . . .*

I have known Harold Abbott for years. He used to be my lecture manager. One day he and I met in Kansas City and he drove me down to my farm at Belton, Missouri. During that drive, I asked him how he kept from worrying; and he told me an inspiring story that I shall never forget.

"I used to worry a lot," he said, "but one spring day in 1934, I was walking down West Dougherty Street in Webb City when I saw a sight that banished all my worries. It all happened in ten seconds, but during those ten seconds I learned more about how to live than I had learned in the previous ten years. For two years I had been running a grocery store in Webb City," Harold Abbott said, as he told me the story. "I had not only lost all my savings, but I had incurred debts that took me seven years to pay back. My grocery store had been closed the previous Saturday; and now I was going to the Merchants and Miners Bank to borrow money so I could go to Kansas City to look for a job. I walked like a beaten man. I had lost all my fight and faith. Then suddenly I saw coming down the street a man who had no legs. He was sitting on a little wooden platform equipped with wheels from roller skates. He propelled himself along the street with a block of wood in each hand. I met him just after he had crossed the street and was starting to lift himself up a few inches over the curb to the sidewalk. As he tilted his little wooden platform to an angle, his eyes met mine. He greeted me with a grand smile. 'Good morning, sir. It is a fine morning, isn't it?' he said with spirit. As I stood looking at him, I realized how rich I was. I had two legs. I could walk. I felt ashamed of my self-pity. I said to myself if he can be happy, cheerful, and confident without legs, I certainly can with legs. I could already feel my chest lifting. I had intended to ask the Merchants and Miners Bank for only one hundred dollars. But now I had courage to ask for *two* hundred. I had intended to say that I wanted to go to Kansas City to *try* to get a job. But now I announced confidently that I wanted to go to Kansas City to *get* a job. I got the loan; and I got the job.

"I now have the following words pasted on my bathroom mirror, and I read them every morning as I shave:

I had the blues because I had no shoes,
Until upon the street, I met a man who had no feet.

I once asked Eddie Rickenbacker what was the biggest lesson he had learned from drifting about with his companions in life rafts for twenty-one days, hopelessly lost in the Pacific. "The biggest lesson I learned from that experience," he said, "was that if you have all the fresh water you want to drink and all the food you want to eat, you ought never to complain about anything."

Time ran an article about a sergeant who had been wounded on Guadalcanal. Hit in the throat by a shell fragment, this sergeant had had seven blood transfusions. Writing a note to his doctor, he asked: "Will I live?" The doctor replied: "Yes." He wrote another note, asking: "Will I be able to talk?" Again the answer was yes. He then wrote another note, saying: *"Then what in the hell am I worrying about?"*

Why don't you stop right now and ask yourself: "What in the hell am I worrying about?" You will probably find that it is comparatively unimportant and insignificant.

About 90 percent of the things in our lives are right, and about 10 percent are wrong. If we want to be happy, all we have to do is to concentrate on the 90 percent that are right, and ignore the 10 percent that are wrong. If we want to be worried and bitter and have stomach ulcers, all we have to do is to concentrate on the 10 percent that are wrong and ignore the 90 percent that are glorious.

The words Think and Thank are inscribed in many of the Cromwellian churches of England. These words ought to be inscribed on our hearts, too: Think and Thank. Think of all we have to be grateful for, and thank God for all our boons and bounties.

Jonathan Swift, author of *Gulliver's Travels*, was the most devastating pessimist in English literature. He was so sorry that he had been born that he wore black and fasted on his birthdays; yet, in his despair, this supreme pessimist of English literature praised the great health-giving powers of cheerfulness and happiness. "The best doctors in the world," he declared, "are Doctor Diet, Doctor Quiet, and Doctor Merryman."

You and I may have the services of "Doctor Merryman" free every hour of the day by keeping our attention fixed on all the incredible riches we possess—riches exceeding by far the fabled treasures of Ali Baba. Would you sell both your eyes for a billion dollars? What would you take for your two legs? Your hands? Your hearing? Your children? Your family? Add up your assets, and you will find that you won't sell what you have for all the gold ever amassed by the Rockefellers, the Fords, and the Morgans combined.

But do we appreciate all this? Ah, no. As Schopenhauer said: "We seldom think of what we have but always of what we lack." Yes, the tendency to "seldom think of what we have but always of what we lack" is the greatest tragedy on earth. It has probably caused more misery than all the wars and diseases in history.

It caused John Palmer to turn "from a regular guy into an old grouch," and almost wrecked his home. I know because he told me so.

"Shortly after I returned from the army," he said, "I started in business for myself. I worked hard day and night. Things were going nicely. Then trouble started. I couldn't get parts and materials. I was afraid I would have to give up my business. I worried so much that I changed from a regular guy into an old grouch. I became so sour and cross that—well, I didn't know it then; but I now realize that I came very near to losing my happy home. Then one day a young, disabled veteran who works for me said, 'Johnny, you ought to be ashamed of yourself. You take on as if you were the only person in the world with troubles. Suppose you do have to shut up shop for a while—so what? You can start up again when things get normal. You've got a lot to be thankful for. Yet you are always growling. Boy, how I wish I were in your shoes! Look at me. I've got only one arm, and half of my face is shot away, and yet I am not complaining. If you don't stop your growling and grumbling, you will lose not only your business, but also your health, your home, and your friends!'

"Those remarks stopped me dead in my tracks. They made me realize how well off I was. I resolved then and there that I would change and be my old self again—and I did."

A friend of mine, Lucile Blake, had to tremble on the edge of tragedy before she learned to be happy about what she had instead of worrying over what she lacked.

I met Lucile years ago, when we were both studying short-story writing in the Columbia University School of Journalism. Nine years ago, she got the shock of her life. She was living then in Tucson, Arizona. She had—well, here is the story as she told it to me:

"I had been living in a whirl: studying the organ at the University of Arizona, conducting a speech clinic in town, and teaching a class in musical appreciation at the Desert Willow Ranch, where I was staying. I was going in for parties, dances, horseback rides under the stars. One morning I collapsed. My heart! 'You will have to lie in bed for a year of complete rest,' the doctor said. He didn't encourage me to believe I would ever be strong again.

"In bed for a year! To be an invalid—perhaps to die! I was terror-stricken! Why did all this have to happen to me? What had I done to deserve it? I wept and wailed. I was bitter and rebellious. But I did go to bed as the doctor advised. A neighbor of mine, Mr. Rudolf, an artist, said to me, 'You think now that spending a year in bed will be a tragedy. But it won't be. You will have time to think and get acquainted with yourself. You will make more spiritual growth in these next few months than you have made during all your previous life!' I became calmer, and tried to develop a new sense of values. I read books of inspiration. One day I heard a radio commentator say: 'You can express only what is in your own consciousness.' I had heard words like these many times before, but now they reached down inside me and took root. I resolved to think only the thoughts I wanted to live by: thoughts of joy, happiness, health. I forced myself each morning, as soon as I awoke, to go over all the things I had to be grateful for. No pain. A lovely young daughter. My eyesight. My hearing. Lovely music on the radio. Time to read. Good food. Good friends. I was so cheerful and had so many visitors that the doctor put up a sign saying that only one visitor at a time would be allowed in my cabin—and only at certain hours.

"Nine years have passed since then, and I now lead a full, active life. I am deeply grateful now for that year I spent in bed. It was the most valuable and the happiest year I spent in Arizona. The habit I formed then of counting my blessings each morning still remains with me. It is one of my most precious possessions. I am ashamed to realize that I never really learned to live until I feared I was going to die."

My dear Lucile Blake, you may not realize it, but you learned the same lesson that Dr. Samuel Johnson learned two hundred years ago. "The habit of looking on the best side of every event," said Dr. Johnson, "is worth more than a thousand pounds a year."

Those words were uttered, mind you, not by a professional optimist, but by a man who had known anxiety, rags, and hunger for twenty years—and finally became one of the most eminent writers of his generation and the most celebrated conversationalist of all time.

Logan Pearsall Smith packed a lot of wisdom into a few words when he said: "There are two things to aim at in life: first, to get what you want; and, after that, to enjoy it. Only the wisest of mankind achieve the second."

Would you like to know how to make even dishwashing at the kitchen sink a thrilling experience? If so, read an inspiring book of incredible courage by Borghild Dahl. It is called *I Wanted to See*.

This book was written by a woman who was practically blind for half a century. "I had only one eye," she writes, "and it was so covered with dense scars that I had to do all my seeing through one small opening in the left of the eye. I could see a book only by holding it up close to my face and by straining my one eye as hard as I could to the left."

But she refused to be pitied, refused to be considered "different." As a child, she wanted to play hopscotch with other children, but she couldn't see the markings. So after the other children had gone home, she got down on the ground and crawled along with her eye near to the marks. She memorized every bit of the ground where she and her friends played and soon became an expert at running games. She did her reading at home, holding a book of large print so close to her eye that her eyelashes brushed the pages. She earned two college degrees: a B.A. from the University of Minnesota and an M.A. from Columbia University.

She started teaching in the tiny village of Twin Valley, Minnesota, and rose until she became professor of journalism and literature at Augustana College in Sioux Falls, South Dakota. She taught there for thirteen years, lecturing before women's clubs and giving radio talks about books and authors. "In the back of my mind," she writes, "there had always lurked a fear of total blindness. In order to overcome this, I had adopted a cheerful, almost hilarious, attitude toward life."

Then in 1943, when she was fifty-two years old, a miracle happened: an operation at the famous Mayo Clinic. She could now see forty times as well as she had ever been able to see before.

A new and exciting world of loveliness opened before her. She now found it thrilling even to wash dishes in the kitchen sink. "I begin to play with the white fluffy suds in the dishpan," she writes. "I dip my hands into them and I pick up a ball of tiny soap bubbles. I hold them up against the light, and in each of them I can see the brilliant colors of a miniature rainbow."

As she looked through the window above the kitchen sink, she saw "the flapping gray-black wings of the sparrows flying through the thick, falling snow."

She found such ecstasy looking at the soap bubbles and sparrows that she closed her book with these words: " 'Dear Lord,'

I whisper, 'Our Father in Heaven, I thank Thee. I thank Thee.' "

Imagine thanking God because you can wash dishes and see rainbows in bubbles and sparrows flying through the snow!

You and I ought to be ashamed of ourselves. All the days of our years we have been living in a fairyland of beauty, but we have been too blind to see, too satiated to enjoy.

If you want to stop worrying and start living:

Count your blessings—not your troubles!

LESSON 4

HOW TO RECOGNIZE YOUR FAILURE SYMPTOMS

This lesson may be painful to you. You might even find yourself squirming a little, especially if you recognize a few traits in your personality that you thought were quite harmless and suddenly are made to realize that they are destroying any opportunity you have to succeed—to achieve your true potential.

When your automobile malfunctions it can only be repaired after a mechanic has determined the cause of the trouble. When you are ill you can only be made healthy again after a physician has diagnosed your sickness through its signs and symptoms. However, you could be a failure all of your life and no one would be able to help you simply because you have managed to camouflage the reasons you are failing, often unconsciously, *even from yourself!*

Dorothea Brande's *Wake Up and Live!* was published in 1936, during the very depths of the depression. It was a life preserver to a nation drowning in its own despair and its message is as meaningful today as it was during those dark years.

Pay careful attention to this amazing woman who learned how to turn her own life around after she discovered some shocking truths about herself, and about all of us. And, if the truth hurts, be grateful. That's why you're here, aren't you? To learn about yourself. To cure yourself of failure . . .

25

From the disciples of Schopenhauer and Freud, of Nietzsche and Adler, we have all become conversant with such phrases as the Will to Live and the Will to Power. These phrases, representing— sometimes to the verge of overstatement—drives of the organism toward fulfillment and growth, correspond to truths of experience with which each of us is familiar. We have seen children struggle to make themselves and their personalities felt; as young people we have contended for a chance to try our own emerging forces; after long illness we have felt the tide of returning strength in our veins. We know that any average man caught in unfortunate circumstances will put up with poverty, distress, humiliation, with conditions which an onlooker will sometimes consider as much worse than death; and that only the presence of a will to continue living can account for the tenacity with which a man in such circumstances clings to the mere right to breathe and exist.

Furthermore, we first experience and then later turn to realize the process of growth in ourselves. The individual emerges from childhood into adolescence, from adolescence into maturity; and at each of these crises we find that the activities and interests of the old period are being replaced by those of the new, that Nature is preparing the organism for its new role in the world, is actually reconciling us to the new demands on us by showing us pleasures and rewards in the oncoming state which will replace those we must abandon.

But the idea of another will, a counterbalancing will, the Will to Fail, the Will to Death, is not so readily accepted. For a while it was one of the tenets of psychoanalysis, for instance, that no individual could actually imaginatively encompass the idea that he might *cease to be*. Even the death-dreams and suicide-threats of deeply morbid patients were held to be grounded solely in ideas of revenge: the explanation was that the patient thought of himself as living on, invisible, but able to see the remorse and regret caused by his death in those by whom he thought himself ill-treated.

Freud, indeed, analyzing shell-shocked patients after World War I, issued a monograph in which he stated that he had occasionally found dreams that indicated sincere death wishes. This monograph is full of some of the best of Freud's speculations and suggestions; but as for the appearance in popular psychologies of the idea that there could logically be a deathward current running through our lives, it is as though the thesis had never been suggested.

Yet death is as much a fact of experience as birth and growth; and if Nature prepares us for each new phase of life by closing off old desires and opening new vistas, it does not seem too difficult to think that we are, always, being slowly, gently reconciled to our eventual relinquishment of all we hold dear as living creatures. And withdrawal from struggle, abandonment of effort, releasing of desire and ambition would be normal movements in an organism which was being gently wooed away from its preoccupation with life.

It is for this reason that we are entitled to look upon the Will to Fail as a reality.

Now, if inertia, timorousness, substitute activity, effortless effort, quiescence, and resignation were found only at the end of life, or when we were drained by sickness or fatigue, if they never handicapped us when we should be in the full flood of our vital powers, there would be no reason at all for attacking this Will to Fail as if it were—as indeed it is—the arch-enemy of all that is good and effective in us. But when it appears in youth or full maturity it is as symptomatic of something wrong—deeply, internally wrong— with one's life as untimely drowsiness is symptomatic of ordinary bodily ill health.

And if it were easily seen for the black-hearted villain it is, when it arrives out of its due time, it would be easy to fight. But almost always we are well within its power before we do more than suspect rarely and vaguely that all is not as it should be with us. We are so accustomed to speak of failure, frustration, timidity, as negative things, that it is like being invited to fight windmills when we are urged to fight the symptoms of failure.

In youth we seldom recognize the symptoms in ourselves. We explain our reluctance to getting started as the natural timidity of the tyro; but the reluctance stays, the years go, and we wake in dismay to find that what was once a charming youthful diffidence in us is now something quite different, sickly, and repellent. Or we find a convenient domestic situation to bear the brunt of excusing us for never having got to work in earnest. We could not leave this or that relative lonely and defenseless. Then the family grows, scatters, and we are left alone, the substitute activity at which we had been so busy is taken remorselessly away from us, and we are sick and terrified at the idea of turning back to take up the long abandoned plans.

Or we have the best of all reasons for not doing as well as we might. Most of us are under the necessity of choosing between work and starvation, and the employment we were able to find when it was imperative that we should begin earning is not work for which we are ideally suited. When marriage and the raising of a family have been undertaken, the necessity is all the more urgent. We might be willing to wait through a few thin years if no one but ourselves would suffer, but to ask others to do so takes more selfishness, and more courage, than most of us can muster.

Especially in America, where marriages for love are the rule, most young people start out on their married life with little more than their health, youth, and intelligence as capital. We are accustomed to think of the European idea of asking a *dot*, a dower, from the bride's family as somehow ignoble and mercenary. Yet insisting on that little reserve fund of money with which to meet the demands of establishing a new household has much to recommend it, and the fact that we have no such custom in this country may be one reason why America, the much-vaunted Land of Opportunity, can show so many men and women of middle age wasting themselves in drudgery, filling positions which bring them no joy, and looking forward to a future which at its happiest promises years of monotony, and at its worst the nightmare of poverty-ridden unemployment.

This necessity to fall upon the first work we can find is alone enough to explain why so few of us ever manage to bring our plans to fruition. Often, at first, we have a firm intention of not losing sight of our real goal, in spite of the fact that we must make a living at uncongenial work. We plan to keep an eye on our ambitions, and to work at them by hook or crook—evenings, weekends, on vacations. But the nine-to-five work is tiring and exacting; it takes superhuman strength of character to go on working alone when the rest of the world is at play, and when we have never had any evidence that we should be successful if we continued, anyway. And so without realizing it we are swept into the current of the Will to Fail. We are still moving, and we do not see that our motion is downstream.

Most of us disguise our failure in public; we disguise it most successfully from ourselves. It is not hard to ignore the fact that we are doing much less than we are able to do, very little of what we had planned even modestly to accomplish before a certain age, and never, probably, all that we had hoped. One reason it is so easy to deceive ourselves is that somewhere along the way we seem silently to enter into a sort of gentleman's agreement with our friends and acquaintances. "Don't mention my failure to me," we tacitly plead, "and I will never let the hint that you are not doing quite all I should expect of you cross my lips."

This tactful silence is seldom broken in youth or in the early middle years. Until then, the convention is that at any moment we may get into our stride. A little later and the silence is relaxed. There comes a time when it is safe to smile ruefully and admit that the hopes we went out to meet the world with were too high and much too rosy, particularly those hopes we had held for our own performance. In the fifties—and sometimes earlier—it is usually safe enough to do a little disarming and semihumorous grumbling; after all, few of our contemporaries are in a position to say "Why can't you start now?" And yet some of the greatest work in the world, many of the world's irreplaceable masterpieces, were done by men and women well past what we too superficially consider their prime.

So we slip through the world without making our contribution, without discovering all that there was in us to do, without using the most minute fraction of our abilities, either native or acquired. If we manage to be fairly comfortable, to get some respect and admiration, a taste of "a little brief authority" and some love, we think we have made a good bargain, we acquiesce in the Will to Fail. We even pride ourselves on our shrewdness, not suspecting how badly we have been cheated, that we have settled for the compensations of death, not the rewards of life.

If the elaborate game that we all play with ourselves and each other never came to an end—never ran down for a moment so that we suddenly saw that it was only a game after all—the Will to Fail might urge us all gently downhill till we came to rest at its foot, and no one would dream of protesting. But the game has such a way of breaking off sometimes, right at its most amusing spot; and we suddenly wonder why we are running about like this, how we happen to be playing away at hide-and-seek as if our lives depended on it, what became of the real life we meant to lead while we have been off doing nothing, or busy at the work that provides us with no more than our bread and butter.

Sometimes the moment passes and is forgotten until long after, if ever remembered at all. But some of us never forget it. If we go on with the game, it turns into a nightmare, and how to wake out of it and get back into reality becomes our whole preoccupation. Then sometimes the nightmare seems to deepen; we try one turn after another which looks as if it led to freedom, only to find ourselves back in the middle of Alice's Looking Glass Garden, beginning the hunt all over again.

Yet we can escape; and again, rather like Alice, by seeming

at first to go backward: by admitting that there may be a real Will
to Fail, and next, that we may be its victims.

VICTIMS OF THE WILL TO FAIL

If the Will to Fail announced its presence with symptoms as
uniform and unmistakable as those which indicate measles or a bad
cold, it would probably have been eradicated, or a technique for
combatting it would have been worked out, long ago.

But unfortunately its symptoms are varied and legion. If you
were to drag a dining, dancing, theater-going, middle-aged metropolitan playboy away from his merry-go-round and introduce him
to an unshaven, ill-clad cracker-box philosopher dreaming in the
sun, saying, "I want you two to know each other; you have so
much in common," you would be thought mad, yet you would be
right. The dreaming idler, the introvert, and the dancing extrovert—
at the antipodes from the point of view of worldly circumstance—
are motivated by the same impulse; unconsciously they are both
trying to fail.

Their lives have a common denominator. "Do not act as if
you had a thousand years to live," Marcus Aurelius warned himself
in his maxims. All those in the grip of the Will to Fail act as if they
had a thousand years before them. Whether they dream or dance,
they spend their precious hours as though the store of them were
inexhaustible.

But since there are as many ways of failing as there are
divisions and subdivisions of the psychological types, we often do
not recognize the presence of the Will to Fail in others or in
ourselves. Here are a few of the innumerable ways of "acting as
though you had a thousand years to live":

There are, for instance, those who sleep from two to six
hours a day more than they need to sleep to keep in perfect
physical health. In any individual case, unless the sleeping hours
far exceed the normal quota, it is very hard to be sure one has not
to do with merely an unusually long sleeper. But when the note of
compulsion enters, one can be sure of having found a true victim
of failure. Those who are bad-tempered or only half alive if an
early bedtime must be postponed, those who anxiously count each
morning the exact number of hours spent in sleep the night
before, mourning inconsolably any interruption, every hour of
insomnia, every untimely doorbell, are looking to sleep for more
than its normal restorative function. When an adult extends even
this, making a nap or two a day a matter of routine, the diagnosis
becomes simple.

Next, still among the inconspicuous failures, the "introverts," are the waking sleepers: persons who allow some activity to pass before them almost without participation, or indulge in time-killing pursuits in which they take only the most minor and unconstructive parts: the solitaire-players, the pathological bookworms, the endless crossword puzzlers, the jigsaw puzzle contingent. The line between recreation and obsession is not hard to see once we know it is there.

Easiest of all to recognize as lovers of failure are the heavy drinkers. A volume could be written on them, but too many volumes have. Where drinking is so constant as to bring on a waking sleep, or, deeper, a kind of death in life, the presence of the Will to Fail is obvious to any observer. But there are thousands who show the symptoms in so faint a form that they pass almost unnoticed: all those who drink knowing that it means a bad morning the next day, a vague and woolly approach to every problem until the effects have passed off; those to whom any drinking means physical discomfort, whether acute or trifling. Anyone who has learned to expect these consequences and yet continues to lay himself open to them stands convicted of the desire to handicap himself, at least to that extent. It makes very little difference what the drink in question may be. If coffee disturbs you, if you cannot digest milk, and you nevertheless continue to drink it, you may escape the disapproval which is meted out to the highball drinker, but you are in the same class. And, plainly, unwise eating comes under the same head.

Turning to the active type, it may be said that the extroverts who pursue failure as their primary career find so many ways of doing it that the attempt to tabulate them all would be hopeless. But, as examples, there are the relentless movie- and theatergoers, the nightly dancers, all those who count the day lost which has not a tea or dinner or cocktail party in it. . . . No, of course there is nothing against relaxation and recreation when they are really called for, after a period of contributory activity. But those who enter an objection to this classification too early and too angrily, crying that one *must* have recreation, give themselves dead away as setting an abnormal value on release.

Then there are the half-and-half failures, difficult to place, such as the embroiderers and knitters, although it is only fair to say here that sometimes a light task calling for only manual dexterity may go on while the mind is usefully engaged in solving a real problem. Complete honesty with oneself is all that is necessary to discover whether the rhythmical activity is being used in one way or the other. If a dull stupor sets in, or if, on the other hand, the work is just elaborate enough, calls for just enough conscious attention so that no automatic rhythm can be established, then it is rare indeed that this kind of motion can be put in the category of true creative activity, or that of being accessory to creative action.

As to aimless conversationalists, we can more easily see that others fall in that group than that we are included ourselves. Sometimes we are startled into realizing that we have repeated the same anecdote to the same friend and for a few days go warily. That is a minor slip. No reminiscent ring, no forced smile on our auditor's lips will stop us when we are habitually marking time with words—when we have the same unevolving round of topics, the same opinions to repeat mechanically, the same half-aimless observations to make on the same recurring situations, the same automatic indignation at the same old abuses, the same illustrations to prove the same points, and a few lukewarm arguments to bolster up what may once have been opinions but are now seldom more than prejudices.

Sometimes we ride a verbal mannerism so hard that a hearer objects irritably. It is probably a great piece of luck to rouse a friend to this extent. If you learn with shocking suddenness that you are forever saying "I mean," "Of course," "I imagine," "Do you see?" "You know," "As a matter of fact," you are likely to listen to your own voice for a period and discover that not only do these tag-words occur over and over in your conversation, but that there is nothing particularly fresh or valuable about the ideas they have served to embellish. Here, as in the other categories, it is very easy to see that there is something wrong when one meets gross examples of the difficulty; an hysterical talker is obviously mentally ill. But that there are subtler forms of the same trouble, often hidden for years because we do our repeating to constantly changing audiences, seldom dawns on us.

There are still more obscure and unnoticeable ways of falling victim to the Will to Fail, ways to which introverts and extroverts are almost equally susceptible. Consider the innumerable persons, for instance, who deliberately undertake work which calls for only a small part of their abilities and training, and who then drive themselves relentlessly, exhausting themselves over useless details. There are the takers of eternal postgraduate courses, turning up on the campus year after year like so many Flying Dutchmen. There are the "devoted" daughters and sons and mothers and wives (fathers are seldom found here, for some reason, although there may be an occasional husband) who pour out their lives into the lives of other adults, but whose offering, since they have never truly developed what was most valuable in themselves, adds no richness and only unimportant comfort to the objects of their "self-sacrifice." There are those who undertake a task known by them to be beyond their powers, or engage in a specious "research" problem: there is a man in New York, for example, who has been gathering biographical details about an obscure Italian statesman since his sophomore year in college. This pseudobiographer is now in his late forties, and not one word of that definitive *Life* has been written.

Perhaps the greatest class of all those whose goal is failure is that of the Universal Charmers.

When you find yourself in the presence of more charm than the situation calls for, you are safe in saying to yourself, "Ah, a failure!" This is no diatribe against genuine warmheartedness, against friendliness, or true sweetness of character. We are talking now about the Harold Skimpoles of the world, about the cajoling, winsome adult, either man or woman, who insists on being accepted by his contemporaries as just a great, big, delightful child— irresponsible, perhaps, not very thoughtful, but so exceedingly lovable, even to strangers! There are the whimsical teases and the humorous complainers, and if they are good to look at, quick-witted or amusing, they are more likely than not to be successful in arousing a momentary indulgence, a tolerant tenderness. It is only in retrospect that one realizes there was no valid reason for the moment's emotion. A healthy adult does not need the tenderness or indulgence of every casual acquaintance. Except for a guilty conscience, no one would ever dream of making a play for this kind of response. These victims are under the hard necessity of working at charm as convicts work at stone-crushing; they must go on being more and more charming to offset their waning attractions, or face the truth—admit that they have not adequately discharged their responsibilities. As long as their inadequacy is never seen except mirrored in the indulgent eyes of another they can go on without admitting the fact that they are failing. So on they go, cheating their way through life—unless by good fortune they can come to see who really suffers most from the exercise of their charm.

So there are all these ways, and innumerable others, of filling one's time with seemingly purposeless activity, or a falsely purposeful routine, and they are all the result of submitting to the Will to Fail.

For, remember, these activities are only *apparently* purposeless. There is in every case a deep intention, which may be stated in many ways.

We may say that the most obvious intention is to beguile the world into believing that we are living up to our fullest capacity. This is particularly true of those cases where the outward life is full of a thousand little matters, or one big job of drudgery conscientiously done. No one surely, could ask us to do *more* than we are doing! Are we not plainly so busy that we have not one minute or a grain of strength to do anything more? Is it not our duty to do the dull, insignificant, unsatisfying task thoroughly? Those are questions which only the individual can answer honestly for himself, usually in the hours of insomnia or convalescence, when the mind which is usually so engrossed about trivial affairs finds time to stop and consider. In the long run it makes little difference how cleverly others are deceived; if we are not doing what we are best equipped to do, or doing well what we have undertaken as our *personal* contribution to the world's work, at least by way of an earnestly followed avocation, there will be a core of unhappiness in our lives which will be more and more difficult to ignore as the years pass.

The fritterers and players and the drudging workers are bent mainly on deceiving themselves, on filling every nook and cranny of their waking hours so that there is no spot where a suspicion of futility can leak through. And at night, of course, they are either still hard at play or too exhausted to consider realities. Yet such victims present a dreadful spectacle when once they are plainly seen—seen as insane misers, stuffing a senseless accumulation of trash, odds and ends of sensations, experiences, fads and enthusiasms, synthetic emotions, into the priceless coffer of their one irreplaceable lifetime.

Whatever the ostensible purpose may be, it is plain that one motive is at work in all these cases: *the intention, often unconscious, to fill life so full of secondary activities or substitute activities that there will be no time in which to perform the best work of which one is capable.*

The intention, in short, is to fail.

Very often we are our own worst enemy as we foolishly build stumbling blocks on the path that leads to success and happiness.

Louis Binstock

LESSON 5

HOW TO CONQUER THE TEN MOST COMMON CAUSES OF FAILURE

To help you to "know thyself" a little better has been the prime purpose of this first semester. It is always a difficult indoctrination because most of us, unfortunately, are unable to capitalize on our abilities. We overestimate them; we underestimate them; we become complacent; we allow them to decay. Occasionally we are unaware that they exist.

There are those who may dream of some exotic career like acting, singing, painting, writing, and who feel that only persistence is necessary, who are never able to reconcile themselves to a lack of genius—or even talent; who will never admit that true success for them may lie in other fields.

John Keats, the English poet, once wrote, "Failure is, in a sense, the highway to success, inasmuch as every discovery of what is false leads us to seek earnestly after what is true, and every fresh experience points out some form of error which we shall afterward carefully avoid."

Regrettably, Keats was not describing how most of us deal with adversity. We *do not* all learn from our failures, nor are we quick to perceive the errors we commit so that they are not repeated. To do these things effectively, we need direction.

From his widely acclaimed book, *The Road to Successful Living,* Louis Binstock, the late and beloved rabbi of famed Temple Shalom in Chicago, introduces you to the major stumbling blocks you may have unknowingly erected in your life, errors you may be making, again and again, that are hurting you every day. After you've taken this inventory of yourself you'll be better prepared to advance into Semester Two ...

The causes of failure lie within a wide and confusing area: the culture we live in, our definitions of the two words, *success* and *failure*, our personal psychological makeup. But often failure, and the approach of failure, take more common and obvious forms. We are not all scholars; we are not all godly; we are not all psychoanalysts: we must deal with the world as it presents itself to us.

There are, in terms of our everyday reactions, ten common causes of failure. These ten are basic. Know them, conquer them—even a few of them—and you will have removed the most stubborn obstacles from the path of true success. No one else can handle them for you. You must clear your own path. Others may help; but the job is really yours alone.

The first stumbling block is the age-old trick of blaming others. This is not the same as worrying about what others think (or have, or do). It is the actual fastening of responsibility onto another. (The difference between witchcraft and medicine, we are informed by a man who has spent twenty-five years as a doctor in Africa, is that when a man falls sick, witchcraft makes him ask, "Who did this to me?" while medicine makes him ask, "What did this to me?") It is the primitive or juvenile mind that seeks the cause of fears and failures outside itself. And almost always the primitive mind seeks a "who"; if it suspects a "what," it believes it to be animate, to have a "who" inside it. We sometimes credit success and failure to good and bad luck, as though luck were a god or goddess intervening in the affairs of men. Rarely does the primitive mind look inside itself and ask, "What in me is responsible for this?" The more sophisticated mind, educated and civilized, learns to ask, "What is there within me that caused me to think (or not) that thought, to feel (or not) that emotion, to do (or not) that deed?"

But even now very few of us are ready to admit immediately, "Maybe it's my fault." Most of us respond initially in a primitive, or childish, way to any situation involving fault or failure. It is almost instinctive for the child to blame a brother or sister; "He made me do it," or even "He did it," are common reactions when punishment is in the offing. A schoolboy may blame his teacher for his own deficiencies-in learning or conduct ("She's always picking on me"); the motorist claims it was "the other guy's fault"; a husband shouts at a wife, "Why do you always pick quarrels?"; the employee claims, "The company doesn't appreciate me." Mankind's great bewildered cry has always been, "Who did this to me?"

The practice of blaming others accounts not only for perhaps half our failures, but also for our failure to cash in on failures. We do not recognize failure for what it is, and consequently we cannot deal with it. Instead we set up straw men, knock them down several times, and waste days in a battle which we cannot win. The battle we ought to be fighting is within ourselves; that battle, if we bring valor to it, we cannot lose.

A second stumbling block is the opposite of the first: the ready tendency to blame oneself, in private anyway. Why was I such a fool? What an easy mark I am! Why do I always put my foot in it? Why do I always say the wrong thing? What a dope I was!

We do not believe, really, that we are fools or easy marks. This is a quick, easy way to brush off a failure that probably runs much deeper and requires more consideration than we are willing to admit to ourselves.

Instead of wrestling with the problem behind the failure and struggling to resolve it—to prevent its recurrence—we blame ourselves (as though we were congenital failures!) and let it go at that.

This is pernicious thinking and dangerous practice. It plants deep the feelings of inferiority and insecurity which will later spring up like weeds to dominate "the well-ordered garden of the mind." Abraham Lincoln, who failed in many things but was far from being a failure, once said, "My great concern is not whether you have failed, but whether you are content with your failure." This contentment is paralyzing. You may see yourself as happy in failure; and you will tend to fail everywhere.

When Major General William F. Dean was released by his Communist captors, a newsman, it is reported, asked what sustained him during his three years of misery. "I never felt sorry for myself," the general replied, "and that's what licked it." Self-pity whips more people than anything else; and I would say that self-blame is even worse, because it is one of the prime causes of self-pity. Or we may proceed from self-blame to self-deprecation to self-contempt, and thence even to self-destruction.

Excessive self-blame opens the door to guilt feelings. In the habit of blaming yourself for your apparent failures, you may come in time to seek the blame for the failure of others. In my own study many a wife has cried, "It was my fault!" when clearly it was her husband's. Many a mother has wept, "Where did I fail?" when obviously a child's failure had brought destructive tension to the family.

And self-blame closes the door to self-development. Behind the closed door one's personality may withdraw permanently; it may languish in extreme melancholia. Like a deer blinded by a bright light, it may stand paralyzed in feeling and will, lacking the nerve and the drive that would carry it to safety.

It has been often observed that the Great Wall, centuries old, stretching eighteen hundred miles across plains and deserts, is one of history's monumental structures—and a symbol of China's failure to progress as a nation. The wall was a barrier; the Chinese isolated themselves behind it and turned inward. Self-blame can be the Chinese Wall of our lives. Stone after stone of self-criticism, self-contempt, self-deprecation, falls into place; and one day we find ourselves so restricted and inhibited that we are isolated from family, friend, and community. We become companions of death.

A *third stumbling block is having no goals*. Dr. William Menninger opines,

> A fellow must know where he wants to go, if he is going to get anywhere. It is so easy just to drift along. Some people go through school as if they thought they were doing their families a favor. On a job, they work along in a humdrum way, interested only in their salary check. They don't have a goal. When anyone crosses them up, they take their marbles and walk out. The people who go places and do things make the most of every situation. They are ready for the next thing that comes along on the road to their goal. They know what they want and are willing to go an extra mile.

William Saroyan has provided us with a character—Willy, in *The Time of Your Life*—who personifies man without a real goal. Willy has a mania for pinball. Throughout the play Willy fights the machine. In the last scene he wins a game—finally. Red and green lights flash, a bell rings six times, an American flag leaps out of the machine, Willy salutes, collects six nickels from the bartender, and says, "I knew I could do it!"

Success.

No goal is bad enough; but low goals are worse.

Probably there is no such thing as *no* goal. Willy had a goal. To beat the machine. He succeeded. But at the cost of failure in everything else. His story is like the old one of the dog who bragged that he could outrun anything on four legs. He gave chase to a rabbit soon afterward, but fell behind. The other dogs laughed derisively. He shrugged it off: "Don't forget, the rabbit was running for his life. I was just running for the fun of catching him."

We rarely see them in their pure form, but there *are* those whose only goal in life is fun; who do nothing but amuse themselves, often at the expense of others, and always at the expense of their real selves. They waste their God-given talents on worthless pleasures; they spread the salt of their energies over the meat of their life, and they find that the salt has lost its savor. Or—to change the metaphor—they aim simultaneously at a number of targets, scattering their talent like buckshot and exaggerating the value of whatever they happen to nick. The shooting and shouting are all that their hearts desire.

Then there are a few whose goal is an undefined "break" somewhere in the future. Like Micawber, they wait for something to turn up; meanwhile they turn everything down. It's beneath them, beyond them, not what they're suited for, they don't like it. They wait for the Fairy Prince, the Dream Boat. And their instincts for life atrophy; their minds dull and their bodies grow flabby, and when the Prince comes, when the Boat docks, they are not ready. In the end, all is vanity.

According to Richard L. Evans of the Detroit *Times*, it isn't always clear—perhaps it's seldom clear—just what we are waiting for, but some of us persist in waiting so chronically that youth slips by, opportunities slip by, and life slips by—finding us still waiting for something that has been going on all the time. . . . But when in the world are we going to begin to live as though we understood the urgency of life? This is our time, our day, our generation . . . not some golden age of the past, not some Utopia of the future. . . . This is it . . . whether we are thrilled or disappointed, busy or bored. This is life . . . and it is passing. . . . What are we waiting for?

But care is needed: a fourth stumbling block is choosing the wrong goals. The Chinese tell of a man of Beijing who dreamed of gold, much gold, his heart's desire. He rose one day and when the sun was high he dressed in his finest garments and went to the crowded marketplace. He stepped directly to the booth of a gold dealer, snatched a bag full of gold coins, and walked calmly away. The officials who arrested him were puzzled: "Why did you rob the gold dealer in broad daylight?" they asked. "And in the presence of so many people?"

"I did not see any people," the man replied. "I saw only gold."

When gold or glory, power or place, become a fixed idea, we are usually blinded not only to the needs of others—in the home as well as in the marketplace—but also to our own needs, to the needs of our inner selves. I have met and talked with hundreds of men and women who were accounted great successes, but who, within the sanctity of my study, confessed to a devastating sense of failure. They had set their sights upon one goal and allowed it to represent self-fulfillment; they had attained the goal, and found that it was not what their souls required. It was often one that destroyed their souls.

This is a great sadness: to discover after many years of struggle that attaining the object of your efforts will not bring happiness. Often it is a question of professional displacement: the practice of medicine, or of the law, or of management, which once promised all success and all happiness, may leave the practitioner weary and disillusioned, empty of hope. And when he has reached his fifth or sixth decade, he knows that it is too late to turn back, to find contentment in another life. (There are rare souls who have gathered their courage, faced the truth, and turned away from a lifetime of "achievement" to a calling that brought them peace. But most of us, I am afraid, would carry dissatisfaction with us. Even Tolstoi was not entirely happy when he had renounced the life of a count and gone back to the land.) Most of us, dissatisfied or not, realize that we must go on to the end of the trail. We have begun badly, and compounded the error through the years, but no further choice is possible.

Here is a dangerous paradox: most of our choices, vocational and domestic, are made when we are young; and yet the responsible man cannot easily take advice; he must find out for himself what life is all about. Often he is beyond the possibility of change when he comes to realize what happiness consists of. It takes great honesty and serious thought to be able to make a firm and confident choice before it is too late. Too many of us allow the choice to be made for us—by family or circumstance—and regret it later.

A great preacher, Phillips Brooks, once commented:

> There is a young man droning and drowsing along at what he calls the practice of law. It amounts to nothing. The profession does not want him any more than he wants it. He is there because it is an honorable and respectable employment; because the tradition of his family or a little set of people put him there. Let him once get some moral courage; let him once briefly ask what he is really here for, what he can really do well and with love, what is his duty, and such

questions would carry him perhaps to the carpenter's bench, perhaps to the blacksmith's forge.

Chuang-tzu, a disciple of Confucius, was fishing one day in the P'u River. The prince of Ch'u sent two high officials to ask him if he would take over the administration of the state of Ch'u. Chuang-tzu ignored them, and went on fishing. Pressed for an answer, he said, "I have heard that in Ch'u there is a sacred tortoise, dead now these three thousand years. The Prince keeps this tortoise locked in a chest on the altar of his ancestral temple. I ask you: Would this tortoise rather be dead and venerated, or alive wagging its tail in the mud?"

"Alive, wagging its tail in the mud," the officials said quickly.

"Begone!" said Chuang-tzu. "I too will wag my tail in the mud!"

A fifth stumbling block is the short cut. "Out at Forest Hills last week," reported the late sports columnist Arch Ward, "sixteen-year-old Maureen Connolly had just defeated Doris Hart in the semifinals of the Women's National Singles. Her opponent, according to expert testimony, had never played better. But the Wimbledon champion and tournament favorite had been no match for the teenage Californian and she went out in straight sets. Mary Hardwick Hare, former British champion and Wightman Cup veteran, rushed to the dining room to congratulate Miss Connolly. 'Mary,' said Maureen, 'if you can be ready in thirty minutes I'd like to practice!' They worked for more than an hour. The next day Maureen won the National Championship. Most of us could profit," Ward commented, "by rereading the story of the San Diego miss who, in the hour of her greatest triumph, said: 'I'd like to practice.'"

An electric current will follow the line of least resistance; but a bulb glows precisely because there *is* resistance. Many of us instinctively choose the shortest, easiest, quickest way to success, only to discover that the success was illusory; that the bulb did not glow. There have been too many platitudes about hard work; we shall try not to add to them. Hard work is only rarely pleasurable. But conquest—of matter, mind, or soul—is pleasurable; it is conducive to well-being, to happiness. And no conquest can be achieved without hard work—no conquest can give true pleasure if it has not required hard work.

Too often the shortcut, the line of least resistance, is responsible for evanescent and unsatisfactory success. Too often the shortcut is responsible for the choice of unsuitable goals we discussed a moment ago. I know of a man who is a magazine editor, and a good one; but he has known for fifteen years that he was born to be a teacher. Teaching meant first the acquisition of a master's degree; then a slow start in a small school; a long period of hard work and low salary. He had a flair for writing and rewriting; it paid off quickly and opened a good future to him in magazine work. He took his choice consciously, and he is not miserable; he is a competent and respected man. But he is not entirely happy; he cannot feel successful. He is good-natured about it, and views his failure quite sensibly; but it remains a failure.

There are other shortcuts. One is the refusal to observe established rules of decency and honesty. A good many of our higher-bracket businessmen might have been just as rich, just as powerful, but more respected and infinitely happier, if they had taken the slower and longer road of absolute ethical integrity and moral decency. The habit of sharp dealing, hard driving, seemed necessary to success; it was certainly quicker and more profitable. Some part of them is now forever cut off from happiness. Can this be called success? Sharp practices and immorality often "succeed"— precisely because the vast majority of mankind senses intuitively that decency and honor are necessary to happiness; they are therefore relatively innocent, and to some extent at the mercy of the liar and swindler. Barnum was right, in a way: there is a sucker born every minute. And thank God for the suckers of decency: they are the salt of the earth. They are those in whom the possibility of happiness has not been killed.

A sixth stumbling block is the exact opposite of the fifth: taking the long road. There's an old saying that the longest way round is the shortest (and sweetest) way home. That may often be true in love but not always in life. It is told that once Einstein, when asked to explain his theory of relativity, replied that perhaps the simplest example he could offer was the following: when a boy spends an hour with the girl he loves it seems like a minute, but that same boy compelled to sit on a hot stove for a minute would feel that it was an hour. We're talking, however, about reality and not relativity.

The ancient biblical commentators in explaining why God did not lead the children of Israel to the Promised Land via the short straight route, up through the land of the Philistines, requiring only an eleven-day jaunt, but instead led them over a long circuitous route through the wilderness for forty years, said that it was in order that the slavery-conditioned people might gradually prepare themselves for the wise use and enjoyment of freedom. But we learn that they (the entire adult generation that left Egypt) died in that wilderness. They took so long in getting to the Promised Land that they never got there.

From time to time, I officiate at the last rites of a man in his fifties or early sixties who has suddenly died, just as he was making plans to use his hard-earned wealth and his remaining years in the doing and enjoying of all the things of which he dreamed when he first started to carve out his career. With tears in their eyes the family tell me of the long difficult road of toil and trouble, of struggle and sacrifice, he has traveled to achieve his great success, and how their hearts ache when they realize that at the very time when he could have taken it easy and "lived it up" he was taken away. "What a pity," they cry. And I think, what a pity he hadn't stopped on the road sooner; hadn't been satisfied with less material success and fulfilled himself earlier. The longest way round is not always the shortest way home. Too often if you wait or travel too long, you never reach home.

The seventh stumbling block is neglecting little things. An anecdote about President McKinley—the story is possibly apocryphal but perfectly relevant—illustrates the point. He was in a dilemma; he had to choose one of two equally capable men for a high diplomatic post. Both were old friends. He reminisced, and recollected an incident that helped him to make his decision. One stormy night McKinley had boarded a streetcar and taken the last available seat, toward the rear, when an old washerwoman climbed aboard with a heavy basket of clothes. She stood in the aisle; despite her age and forlorn appearance, no one offered her a seat. One of McKinley's two candidates, then much younger, was seated near her; he was immersed in a newspaper, and took care to remain immersed in it so that he could ignore the old woman. McKinley went down the aisle, picked up the basket, and led the woman to his seat. The man never looked up, never knew what had happened; nor did he ever know that this act of minor selfishness later deprived him of an embassy, the crown of his ambition.

There are hundreds of stories stressing the importance of little things. A door left unopen, a document unsigned, a few live coals left upon a hearth; Edison losing a patent because of a misplaced decimal point. Vital battles have been lost for the "want of a nail." We grow sentimental over songs that tell us "It's the little things that count," but we go right on disregarding the little things.

At a prayer meeting in an old country church, a pious member was overheard imploring fervently, "Use me, O Lord, use me—but in an executive capacity." Big ideas, big money, big events, big shots: we feel we want to be in and around them; little things (so-called) are for little people (so-called). The truth is that no man, no job, is little. Men and jobs are different: easier to handle, or easier to approach, or with a less significant result. But everything that requires noticing or doing is big. "Without sharp knives," a French chef once said, "I am just another cook." It was good news to the apprentice who sharpened his knives.

The good executive keeps his finger on the little things: he knows that they may, if mishandled, become big problems. To an operating surgeon there are no little things: every slightest detail is a matter of life and death. To a lawyer, an obscure and minute legal confusion may cost a client liberty, even life. To a clergyman there are no small problems: in a human soul there is nothing unimportant.

We must appreciate the details; we must *care* for them. Oscar Hammerstein II once saw a close-up of the Statue of Liberty, taken from a helicopter. The head of the statue was revealed in fine detail, and Hammerstein noticed that the sculptor had done a painstaking job with the lady's coiffure. Every strand of hair was in its proper place. In his day he could hardly have known that anyone—save possibly a seagull—would ever see that hair. But he gave it as much care as he had the face, the arm, the torch.

And the New Testament tells the parable of a nobleman who, finding that a servant had handled a small assignment with unusual success, said to him, "Well done, thou good servant; because thou wast found faithful in a very little, have thou authority over ten cities."

The eighth stumbling block is quitting too soon. Recently I read a magazine story (the author claims it to be true) called "The Pebble of Success." Discouraged, physically exhausted, Rafael Solano sat on a boulder in the dry river bed and made an announcement to his two companions. "I'm through," he said. "There's no use going on any longer. See this pebble? It makes about 999,999 I've picked up, and not a diamond so far. If I pick up another, it will be a million—but what's the use? I'm quitting."

It was 1942; the three men had spent months prospecting for diamonds in a Venezuelan watercourse. They had worked stooping, gathering pebbles, wishing, and hoping for one sign of a diamond. Their clothes were ragged, their sombreros tattered; but they had never thought seriously of quitting until Solano said, "I'm through." Glumly, one of them said, "Pick up another and make it a million."

"All right," Solano said, and stooped, put his hand on a pile of pebbles, pulled one forth. It was almost the size of a hen's egg.

"Here it is," he said, "the last one." But it was heavy—too heavy. He looked. "Boys, it's a diamond!" he shouted. Harry Winston, a New York jewel dealer, paid Rafael Solano $200,000 for that millionth pebble. Named the Liberator, it was the largest and purest diamond ever found.

Perhaps Rafael Solano needed no other reward; but I think he must have known a happiness that went beyond the financial. He had set his course; the odds were against him; he had persevered; he had won. He had not only done what he had set out to do—which is a reward in itself—but he had done it in the face of failure and obscurity.

An old hunter's aphorism teaches us that half the failures in life come from pulling in the horse in the midst of his leap. Elihu Root once said, "Men don't fail; they give up trying." Often it is not the wrong start but the wrong stop that makes the difference between success and failure. To quit while we're ahead would be silly; to quit when we're behind is even sillier. It requires will to hold on a little longer. It requires wit to know that the measure of success is not the luck, the breaks of the game, but the conquest of failure.

"The trouble with most of us," it has been said, "is that we stop trying in trying times." There is wisdom even in puns.

The ninth stumbling block is the burden of the past. We can never free ourselves from memories; we can only face them honestly. Somewhere I have read, and noted, this wise observation:

> All our lives we have to live with our memories, and as we grow older we depend upon them more and more, until one day they may be all we have left. Either they can be depressing, embittering, humiliating, tormenting, or they can be cheering, sympathizing, self-respecting, comforting. The things that went in are the things that will come out, whether we put them there or we're forced to receive them.

Memories of the past can infuse us with courage and confidence and creative power; or they can bind us in a dark shroud of dejection and defeat. Even the joys of the past can shackle us: I know men and women so proud of their ancestors' names, achievements, or accumulations, that they are unable to strike out in new directions for themselves. I know men so spoiled by one early success that there remains no further impulse to accomplishment.

But discouraging memories are more common. The memory of pain, of loss, of previous failure, can make life seem not worth the living. Often this is temporary—we see it among the bereaved, or among suddenly liberated prisoners, or among refugees who have been through all the horrors of modern life and have never known its joys. And depressing memories tend to congeal, to harden; we carry them like weights, and we lose our ability to transform them into creative energies.

A distinguished psychiatrist reports that a disturbed patient conceded, after several sessions, "It's easier to lie on a couch digging into the past than it is to sit on a chair facing the present." It is even harder to get up and walk toward the future. Preoccupation with the past is always a retreat. An old hunting joke makes the point: two hunters on a safari cornered a lion, who, instead of attacking, turned tail and disappeared into the underbrush. One terrified hunter stammered to the other, "You go ahead and see where he went to. I'll go back and see where he came from."

We react often like that hunter. Tomorrow's problems are unknown; they may cause new pain. Yesterday's are over with; they are still painful, but the pain is familiar, almost comfortable. It is easier, less risky, to be static, to take what comfort we can out of our accustomed miseries. And sooner or later we find ourselves incapable of moving forward; we are trapped in the quicksand of our own regrets. David Livingstone, the great explorer, once explained: "I will go anywhere so long as it is forward." This is an ideal not always possible in practice. There are times when we must take a step or two backward to orient ourselves. But our drives should be forward, our instincts should be for advancement. Remember that life is growth, and in ceasing to grow, in fearing the new, we deny life.

The tenth stumbling block is the illusion of success. Success is a fickle goddess; we think we have her, but she knows better. One of modern literature's favorite themes is the tragedy of the easy success, the quick success, the near-success, the *ersatz* success. Many of us are deceived by an event, an accomplishment; it has all the marks of success, and others act as though it were a success, but it fails to satisfy us. We shrug off our doubts; we agree that we have arrived; we don a mask and accept the high popular opinion of ourselves.

At that point we have stopped trying to be ourselves. We have accepted praise or money, identified it with happiness, and assumed that success was ours. Further accomplishment seems unnecessary. We have abjured the right to go on to true success.

Napoleon knew this (little good it did him!); he said once, "The most dangerous moment comes with victory." The achievement of success is most precarious when it appears to be permanent. Overconfidence sets in; and when a new problem rises we are puzzled and bitter: how can I have troubles now, when I have already succeeded? The answer is that success, being fickle, must be continuously wooed; she can never be won forever and ever. Victory loses its value unless we use it as a means to even greater ends. Of itself it is only a temporary, *and essentially useless,* triumph. Talleyrand once commented, "A man can do everything with a sword but sit on it." The same is true of success.

And when we have lost the habit of constant striving, success can do us more harm than good when it comes to us again. Horseplayers like to tell the story of Broadway Ltd. (a son of Man o' War), who cost his owner $65,000 in 1928. Broadway Ltd. never won a race (he might have preferred hunting, we should remember, or even a milk wagon, but of course he was not consulted); his heart was not in his work. Finally, in 1930, running for a $900-purse, he rounded the stretch turn out in front. Alone and ahead for the first time in his life, he dropped dead.

We cannot suffer from illusory success unless we are so foolish as to consider public success an end in itself. The trouble is that most of us have not learned to disentangle the notions of vulgar success and personal success: we constantly aim for goals of which we think others will approve, and we are pained to find that they have little to do with true happiness.

Tolstoi has left us a striking parable, an allegory for the twentieth century, in his "How Much Land Does a Man Need?" The Russian peasant Pakhom is convinced that he will be a success when he owns as much land as that contained in the vast estates possessed by Russian noblemen. The time comes when he is offered free as much land as he himself can encircle by running at top speed from sunrise to sunset. He sacrifices all he has in order to move to the far-distant place where this generous offer has been made. After many hardships, he arrives and arranges for his great opportunity the next day. A starting point is fixed. Pakhom is off like a shot with the breaking dawn. Running with the morning sun, he looks neither to the left nor to the right; feverishly he runs into the blinding light and the burning heat. Without stopping to eat or rest, he continues his grinding, grueling round. And as the sun sets, he staggeringly completes the circle. Victory! Success! The realization of the dream of a lifetime!

But with his last step, he drops dead. All the land he will need now is six feet of earth.

SEMESTER
TWO

Begin to be now
what you will be hereafter.

St. Jerome

To succeed means that you
may have to step out of line and march
to the sound of your own drummer.

Keith DeGreen

LESSON 6

HOW TO ACCEPT
THE CHALLENGE OF SUCCESS

"Compared to what we ought to be, we are only half awake. Our fires are dampened, our drafts are checked, we are making use of only a small part of our mental and physical resources."

Those somber words of William James, psychologist and philosopher, were written more than fifty years ago and they are still a haunting rebuke to all of us who do little more than exist in a sea of mediocrity.

We live in an age that has come to accept "average" as a standard of performance and then we watch, in amazement tinged with chagrin, when someone we know moves out from our crowd to receive all the rewards that are his or her due for excellence.

"Safety" and "security" have become ideals, in this world of future shock, almost completely submerging our desire for growth. And yet we must grow, we must be willing to take risks, we must be willing to take advantage of the ninety percent of our potential that James said we never use. We were not placed on this earth to be little more than walking vegetables.

Dr. Abraham Maslow, another eminent psychologist, wrote, "One can choose to go back toward safety or forward toward growth. Growth must be chosen again and again; fear must be overcome again and again."

Forward or backward? Which will it be for you? Your answer should ring out loud and clear after one of America's most compelling authors and speakers, Keith DeGreen, has introduced you to someone from his powerful book, *Creating a Success Environment*, someone who may be painfully familiar to you ...

W hen Calvin awoke, he was, pardon the expression, scared to death.

"This must be it," he thought. "I must have died and gone to heaven."

He looked around. Everything was so vast and white and hazy that it was hard to tell for sure. But it looked like, well, it looked like a big garage.

"Calvin Cautious?" a voice asked from behind him.

Calvin was startled. He spun around. Behind him stood a large, bearded man, wearing white overalls. He was carrying a clipboard.

"Where did you come from?" Calvin asked.

"I work here," the man said.

"But a moment ago you weren't here."

"We travel differently up here," the man said.

"Up here?" Calvin asked. "Where is this place? Where am I? Am I dead? Is this heaven?"

"No, no," said the man. "You're not dead, and this isn't heaven. This is simply a way station, a checkpoint. You're here for warranty service and to answer some questions on a new survey we're conducting."

"A survey?" Calvin asked.

"Yes. It's a new policy. Ever since we sent the Ralph Nader model down, we have to keep closer track of consumer satisfaction. The Manufacturer says we better clean up our act before we get sued."

"Are you . . . are you? . . ." Calvin asked.

"No. I'm not Him. I'm just one of the Engineers. My job is to ask you some tough questions, Calvin."

Calvin kept looking around. "When can I go back?" he asked.

"When you answer the questions."

"Just any answer?" Calvin asked.

"No. You must provide me with the correct answers, Calvin." Suddenly The Engineer had Calvin's full attention. "You see, *it's a new policy. We see no sense wasting space down there on equipment that won't be used properly."*

"Do . . . do you mean," Calvin stuttered, "that if I can't answer the questions the way you want me to, I'll be dea . . . I'll be dea? . . ." Calvin couldn't quite bring himself to say the word.

"That is correct," The Engineer said. "Your warranty will be revoked, and you will be permanently recalled. Are you ready for your questions, Calvin?"

"I guess so," Calvin nervously answered.

"Very well, sit down, and we'll begin."

DO YOU REALLY BELIEVE YOU WERE PUT HERE TO FAIL?

The Engineer examined his clipboard. "Tell me, Calvin, what is your purpose down there?"

"Well, I . . . um . . . you know," Calvin mumbled, "I want to work hard and not hurt anyone, and I want to get along with folks and stay out of trouble."

"But what about your talents, Calvin, your talents?"

"Well, what talents I have—and they're not much—I take good care of. I kind of pace myself, you know."

"No! No! No!" The Engineer shouted. "Your answer is all wrong. Don't you remember the story of the talents?"

"Yes, I think so," said Calvin. "The Manufacturer gave each of three men a different set of talents. To one man He gave five talents. To another man He gave two talents. And to the third He gave but one talent."

"That's right," The Engineer said. "And some years later The Manufacturer checked up on each of those three men. He checked with the man who had five talents, and was pleased to find that he had multiplied his five talents many times by working hard, and by applying each one. He checked with the man to whom He had given two talents, and was equally pleased to see that he had labored hard, used his talents, and multiplied them. But when He checked with the man to whom He had only given one talent, He became very angry. For that man had buried his talent in the name of protecting it. And it was then that The Manufacturer uttered some of the harshest words He was ever to utter. 'Thou wicked and slothful servant!' He shouted. 'How dare you not use the gifts that I gave you!' Do you get the point of the story, Calvin?"

"I think so," Calvin said. "I think so."

"I don't know what we're going to do with you, Calvin. I just don't know."

IS IT WRONG TO BE RICH?

The notion has been with us for thousands of years: poverty either produces or proves purity. The notion may be correct, but there is nothing inherent in it that implies that poverty is the only road to salvation, however we personally define the term.

I suspect that the belief that wealth is wrong is more social than scriptural. It is a rationalization imposed upon as by many of those who choose not to earn much wealth. It is a philosophy with which we have all had to live at some level during our lifetimes. Is it inherently wrong to be rich? Of course not. It is no more inherently wrong to acquire material wealth than it is wrong not to acquire wealth if we truly don't desire it. It's what we do with money that matters. It's how we get it that counts.

To the extent that money is a measure of the services we perform for others, its accumulation is noble. To the extent that we press our money into the service of those we love, to provide them with as warm and as comfortable and as secure an existence as possible, its disbursement is inspired and divine.

DO YOU HAVE TO GO THROUGH HELL TO GET TO HEAVEN?

Each Sunday he sits on a red velvet throne, on a gold stage, in an ornate old theater in the heart of Harlem.

As he expounds his message to the faithful, the hearts of his listeners are *filled with hope*. He is "the Reverend Ike."

He is immensely popular with his followers because he hits, time and again, upon a theme with which they all agree. Those who are genuinely poor know, much better than the rest of us ever will, the truth of the statement which, through repetition, the Reverend Ike has made famous: *You don't have to go through hell to get to heaven.*

Incredibly, large portions of the human race still believe that for an individual to experience an eternity of happiness, he must first experience a lifetime of unhappiness. We must suffer, they say, to earn our reward. Yet, how tremendously inconsistent it would be to accept such a philosophy. On the one hand, we find ourselves placed upon this planet, fully equipped to contribute significantly to our own individual success. Yet the psychology of suffering would require us not to use the very tools and talents we were given.

If our being here proves anything, it is that we must accept the challenge of using the tools and talents that we possess. Our purpose is to make our lives as successful and as happy as we possibly can. Rather than being a mantle of suffering, we should view our existence here as a dress rehearsal for the eternity of happiness we deserve.

ISN'T BEING HERE ALL THE PERMISSION YOU NEED?

An old Jesuit saying provides, "It is better to ask forgiveness than permission."

Mediocrity, you will recall, is at all times expected without someone else's permission. But excellence, it frequently seems, requires another's expressed approval. This phenomenon seems to spring from our belief that somehow we are not individually worthy of success, without someone else's expressed permission.

The belief may stem from the conformity which is thrust upon us from childhood. Educators call it the "socialization" process. It is the time it takes for a child to learn to stand quietly in line, to answer his name when it is called alphabetically, to speak only when called upon, and to otherwise conform to the codes and expectations imposed upon him.

But to succeed requires that we step out of line, away from the pack, and march to the sound of our personal distant drummer. So we wait for the voice of some subconscious teacher to excuse us from the room before we begin. Yet that voice will never come—unless it comes from us.

Although being here is all the permission we need to succeed, we still feel unworthy because we see others who seem inherently more deserving of success. Yet no one is *inherently* more deserving of success than another. Others may do more to earn it. They may work harder at it. But no one begins more entitled to it than another. Being here is all the permission we need.

We find ourselves in a world filled with challenges just waiting to be taken on. We find ourselves equipped with the talents necessary to meet those challenges. Does not that combination of challenges, and the abilities to meet them, tell us something about why we're here? Doesn't it confirm, finally, once and for all, that no other voice will be forthcoming, and that our existence alone is all the permission we will ever need to succeed?

WHO WILL CONTROL YOUR LIFE?

The Engineer jotted a few notes on his clipboard. Then he looked at Calvin.

"Calvin," he asked, "who is in charge of your life?"

Calvin knew he had the right answer to this question. "I am!" he said. "I'm in charge of my life."

The Chief Engineer remained expressionless. He made another note on his clipboard. There was a long pause. Calvin grew nervous.

"With, of course, a few exceptions," he finally said. "I mean, it's not my fault the way my parents treated me when I was a kid. You know, one time I came home and I wanted to tell them I had made the football team and gotten an A on a test, and I couldn't get either of them to listen to me. And I'm not responsible for the fact that my boss is a real bear. He won't allow me to accept much responsibility. Once I proposed a new sales plan, and he assigned a younger man to administer it. Yeah, I'm responsible for my life—but with a few exceptions. I mean, sometimes you just don't get the breaks, you know? Sometimes things just don't come your way. But that's the way the ball bounces. That's the way the cookie crumbles. That's the way the mop flops."

The Engineer jumped to his feet. He threw his clipboard to the floor. "No! No! No!" he shouted. "When will you learn, Calvin? You're hopeless, I say! Hopeless! There are no exceptions. You must control your life, Calvin. You are totally responsible for the results that you obtain. It's you, Calvin, you, not your mother, not your father, not your boss. It's not the breaks, Calvin, that control your life. It's you. Don't ever say, 'That's the way the ball bounces. That's the way the cookie crumbles. That's the way the mop flops.' Don't you understand, Calvin? You must bounce your own ball. Crumble your own cookies. Flop your own mop. It's totally up to you. I don't know what we're going to do with you, Calvin. I just don't know."

WERE YOU DESIGNED TO BE LED?

We were not equipped with minds of our own so that we could abdicate control of our destiny to someone else.

It makes no sense to believe that we are in any way designed to be kept under the care and control of another. We were not

designed to be led. We were not designed to follow. We were
designed to achieve, to strive, to build.

We were never intended to act, for example, as does the
pine caterpillar. Place a series of pine caterpillars end-to-end in a
circle until the circle is closed, and each will follow the caterpillar
in front of it around the circle indefinitely. Place food in the center
of the circle, and the caterpillars will continue to follow each other
around that food until they die from starvation. The pine caterpillar is an insect without imagination. It lacks the ability to seek any
form of independent success on its own. It blindly adheres to a
herd instinct, often to its detriment, and even to its demise.

We must control our lives. To do otherwise is to, quite
literally, waste them. Papillon, the French prisoner who was condemned to life imprisonment on Devil's Island, was disturbed by a
recurring nightmare. Repeatedly, he would dream that he stood
before a harsh tribunal.

"You are charged," they would shout, "with a wasted life.
How do you plead?"

"Guilty," he would say. "I plead guilty."

Papillon, the prisoner, knew the meaning of waste. For him,
waste was to permit his life to be spent under the control of
someone else. Yet, we too, each in his own way, are prisoners. We
must break through the bars of conformity that we have constructed around ourselves. We must not permit our lives to be
spent trudging in circles behind another, who follows another, who
follows another, who might ultimately be following us.

We are equipped with the ability to lead our own lives. To do
otherwise is, as Papillon might have attested, quite simply a waste.

DO YOU PREFER MEDIOCRITY?

Too many of us try to right the world's wrongs from the
outside-in. Rather than worrying about what is happening in our
own backyard, we attempt to reform the entire world, or, at least,
portions of it thousands of miles away.

The outside-in approach lends itself to what might be called
official mediocrity. In the name of alleviating poverty, for example, we do not work on specifically equipping the person who is
poor with the tools necessary to compete. Rather, we simply
redistribute wealth, generally. It is an outside-in solution. Yet,
most of us know at a gut level that the long-term solution to the
type of poverty we most often encounter in our industrialized
society cannot be found in the text of any book on macroeconom-

ics. The solution is micro in nature. It must begin inside the affected individual and work its way out. A Chinese proverb says, "Give a man a fish and you feed him for a day. Teach a man to fish and you feed him for life."

Communism is the clearest example mankind has of official mediocrity. It presumes that if the *system* is made right, the individuals living within it will ultimately benefit. All things, the system dictates, will be evenly shared. But that type of system consistently neglects the inside-out approach so necessary for positively motivating individuals to produce the items that the system needs. Consequently, the only things that are, in fact, evenly distributed by the system are scarcity and misery.

Man, generally, is not equipped for mediocrity. His imagination, for example, is merciful. Generally, we cannot imagine those things that we cannot accomplish. In the classic self-help volume *Think and Grow Rich,* by Napoleon Hill, it is written, "Whatever the mind of man can conceive and believe, he can achieve." We would not be equipped with the ability to imagine future accomplishment and conditions if we were not correspondingly equipped with the ability to turn those imaginings into reality.

But mediocrity may look comfortable. We all know those who have settled into a routine job at a routine salary, and who live in a routine home, in a routine neighborhood. They seem routinely comfortable and happy, at least from the outside. But on the inside they must contend daily with the rationalizations they have accepted, and the nonuse of the abilities that they possess. The tension thus created is anything but comfortable.

As the great cartoon philosopher Ziggy has said: "Security is knowing what tomorrow will bring. Boredom is knowing what the day after tomorrow will bring."

DO YOU ACCEPT RESPONSIBILITY FOR YOU?

EST (Erhard Seminar Training) has survived attempts by many to characterize it as irresponsible, faddish, and as a typically Californian self-help gimmick.

The popularity of EST stems in part from the discipline it imposes upon the participants. Smoking is not permitted. Discussions between participants are not permitted. Restroom breaks are infrequent. Seating accommodations are Spartan. Yet, most of the participants agree that the discipline (or, as it is called in EST, "the agreements") imposed upon them is necessary, for it helps each participant avoid the tendency to escape from himself.

When the dialogue becomes too real, or too hard-hitting,

and when the participant feels that little man inside trying to sneak out, the tendency is natural to reach for a cigarette, to talk to another person, to get up and walk around, or to go to the restroom—anything to divert attention from that little man inside.

But EST, as well as many other responsible self-help philosophies, strips these diversions away from an individual and forces him to confront his innermost self directly and unabashedly. In short, EST forces participants to accept responsibility for themselves.

We frequently use diversion in our lives as a tool to avoid direct confrontation with our innermost feelings, and to avoid accepting total responsibility for who we are and what we do. Our approach is somewhat as we described above—outside-in. Instead of working on what is going on inside us, we try to rearrange things around us.

A familiar phenomenon among couples seeking divorce, for example, is that they will often have recently worked together at remodeling their home. They might even have recently added a child to the family. This is not to intimate that individuals who remodel their homes and have children are prime candidates for divorce. It is simply to say that in many instances such activities are utilized as a diversion by unhappy couples to keep them from confronting the essence of their problems.

It is always more convenient to assume the answer lies elsewhere, with others. But, of course, it does not. There is an old fable about the wise river barge captain who operated a ferry between two towns. Occasionally, an individual on one side would come to him and ask, "How are the people in the other town? I am thinking of moving there."

The captain, in his wisdom, would always ask, "How do you find the people in the town where you live now?" If the person would respond by saying that they were warm and kind and friendly, then the captain, in turn, would say that the people in the other town were warm and kind and friendly. But if the person would respond by saying that they were cruel and cold and unfriendly, then the captain would describe the people of the other town as being the same. The fable, of course, emphasizes that, while we're not responsible for every action and deed of another, we are responsible for how we react to others and, for that matter, for how we react to ourselves.

The responsibility for us is ours.

WILL YOU PREVENT YOUR OWN SUCCESS?

The Engineer had grown impatient. He tapped his pen against his clipboard and stared at Calvin.

"What are you now, Calvin," he asked, *"and what will you become?"*

Calvin shuddered at the question. How could he know what he should say? His very life on earth hung in the balance. "Humility," he thought. "I must be humble."

"I'm just a working stiff," Calvin said. *"I'm just an average guy. I work hard, but of course I only have so much to work with. I try as best I can to get along with those around me. But I'm, you know, just me."*

Again, The Engineer jumped from his chair. He began thrashing the air with his clipboard.

"No! No! No! A thousand times no!" he shouted. *"Humility does not require mediocrity. By insisting that you are just this, or just that, or that you will never amount to much, in the name of humility you talk yourself down to a state of nonaccomplishment. You program yourself for mediocrity. Humility requires no such sacrifice! It requires no such waste of life. Humility requires only that no matter what you do, you always recognize that it might have been done better. That you remain aware that your life on earth is temporary, and that those who occupy the planet with you have as much a right to be here as you do. I'm afraid there's very little hope, Calvin. This may be the end . . ."*

DO YOU FEEL THAT YOU DESERVE SUCCESS?

Secretly, you may know you're a klutz.

"I'm the guy who can't even remember his car keys and wallet," you say. "I'm a stumblebum, a schlock. My father said I was clumsy. My mother said I was accident-prone. My wife just laughs and says I'm cute. How can I deserve success?"

But how can you not deserve success? Your success is not measured relative to what others say or do or accomplish. It is merely the extent to which you utilize the potential that you possess. If part of your Personal Potential Package includes a tendency to be forgetful or clumsy, or whatever, that element makes you no less deserving of success. It is merely part of the total you. It is a characteristic that must, in its own way, be made to work for you when at all possible.

But others, you think, are obviously smarter, or younger, or harder working, or more educated, or better looking. "They deserve success more than I do," you think. But the characteristics of others remain irrelevant to your success. While the tendency to compare ourselves to others may be overwhelming, it is not against them we compete.

It is only our tendency not to utilize all the potential we possess against which we must constantly fight. Success is not something that must be deserved or earned. It is more an inherent right—an inherent responsibility. The only qualification for success is that you be *you*, that you utilize whatever combination of talent you possess to the fullest extent possible.

Do you deserve success? Of course. You deserve no less.

WILL YOU WAIT FOR THE WORLD TO COME TO YOU?

We all have a natural tendency to daydream. Perhaps among the most common of such dreams is the fantasy that in some way, and at some time, the world will beat a path to our door.

But the next time you catch yourself daydreaming about someone or something coming to you, stop yourself and resolve to do whatever is necessary to go to him or it. If, indeed, the world ever does beat a path to your door, it will do so only after it first discovers who you are and where you can be reached. You must supply the world with this information. You must let it know that you are here, that you are eager to do business, and that you offer to the world something of value to it.

We must resist our tendency to believe that the world will come to us, that things will happen to us. We must go to it. We must happen to things. There is nothing as sad as the man who spends his entire life waiting for his ship to come in, when he never sent one out. Don't spend your life waiting for that "big break." Don't rely upon luck. Make your own.

Your talent may be enormous. Your potential may be great. But talent and potential unannounced to the rest of the world is wasted.

WILL YOU ACT NOW?

It is always easier to act tomorrow.

The world is filled with tomorrow people: those who will tell us in no uncertain terms that they're going to get started tomorrow, and tomorrow, and tomorrow.

The fact is, no matter what we do, where we do it, or when we start, we'll never do it perfectly. There will never be just that right combination of circumstances that will make each and every major undertaking of our lives come off without a hitch.

Before an author writes a book worth reading, he usually writes several that aren't. Before a speaker learns to bring audiences to their feet, he usually makes a complete jerk out of himself more than once. Before a salesman closes that big sale that puts him on top of the world for weeks, months, or even years, he suffers dozens of disappointments, rejections, and refusals.

It will never be done perfectly no matter what it is, who you are, or what you're doing. All that we can ever do is our best, imperfect though it may be. But it is better to attempt to reach a goal and to reach an imperfect result than not to attempt at all. As has been said many times: *I would rather try to succeed and fail than try to do nothing and succeed.*

As we act now to reach our full potential, we must not permit ourselves to be deterred by the critics around us. There will always be that percentage of the population that takes pleasure, indeed delight, in pointing out to the rest of us the imperfection of what we do. Yet we need only remember that we are, by nature, imperfect. We claim to be nothing more. As such, the results that we obtain are bound to be imperfect as well. But most results, imperfect though they may be, are better than no results at all.

There are few who have the right to criticize. Only those who stand by our side on the firing line, and who suffer the same challenges as we do, possess the right; only those who, as Theodore Roosevelt said, are with us in the arena, with soiled hands and sweaty brows and a sense of purpose and daring and dedication, may critique us.

For now is the only time that we have. It is our only negotiable currency. Yesterday is a canceled check. Tomorrow is a promissory note. It is only today that we may spend in the noble effort of using all the gifts that God gave us.

"If none of this is sinking in, Calvin," The Engineer was saying, *"then I'm afraid we'll. . . ."*

"But wait!" Calvin said. "But wait!"

Calvin was not looking at The Engineer. He was staring intensely into the hazy distance.

"I think I see," he said. "I think I see. The fact is I must have been put on earth to succeed. I don't have to apologize to anyone for being a success, or for trying to succeed, since I have an obligation, a responsibility, to use my abilities to the fullest. I can see, too, that wealth, honestly earned and well spent, is inherently good, not evil. I don't have to suffer now to prove my right to eternal happiness. If anything, I should use my experience on earth to practice being happy, to let my soul rejoice at the thrill and exaltation of life.

"Being here is all the permission I need to succeed! I must

control my life, for I wasn't designed to be led. Not at all. I prefer excellence to mediocrity, and I accept total responsibility for me. I won't prevent my own success. I won't. I deserve success, for all success requires is that I am here, and that I use my talents to the fullest. I will bring my message and my talents to the world, and not wait for the world to come to me. And I'll act now, no matter how convenient waiting may seem, no matter how imperfect might be the results I obtain."

Tears welled in The Engineer's eyes. A smile creased his face.

"Yes, of course," he said. "Of course, Calvin. There is hope for you yet! You must return to the world from which you came, to make constructive use of the equipment with which you are blessed. Take with you all the love and energy and talent and hope that you have, and share it. Share it with all whom you meet, until it seems that you have no more to give. And when it seems that you have exhausted your supply of all the gifts you have been given, I promise there will always be more and more and more in reserve.

"For you are infinite, Calvin. Your potential extends beyond your wildest imaginings. And The Manufacturer wants you to know that the only limitations you will ever face will be those you place upon yourself."

> *The easiest thing to find on God's green earth is someone to tell you all the things you cannot do.*

Richard M. DeVos

LESSON 7

HOW TO GIVE YOUR DREAMS A CHANCE TO COME TRUE

A simple two-word phrase, if you have uttered it very often, has probably wreaked more havoc in your life than all your enemies combined.

"I can't!"

Do you use it frequently? Did you learn, when you were very young, that by screaming, "I can't!" at the top of your voice you could manage to avoid most things that appeared to be unpleasant like eating spinach, or taking your cough medicine, or doing the chores?

It still works, doesn't it? How many tasks and challenges and opportunities have you managed to brush aside, in the past five years, or ten, with just those two words?

No need to hang your head. Everyone of us is guilty of that same act far more times than we care to admit. But for you, that sort of behavior is in the past. Before Amway Corporation's dynamic president, Rich DeVos, has finished reasoning with you in this lesson, taken from his inspiring book, *Believe!,* you will have learned a truth, introduced in the previous lesson, that is older than Solomon—*your only limitations are those you set up in your own mind, or permit others to set up for you!*

Free yourself of the chains stamped "I can't!" and you will be able to achieve any height you desire. You can do anything ... if you believe you can! Easy? Of course not. Nothing in life worth achieving is easy. Can you pull it off? Yes, but you will never know, unless you *try* and keep *trying* ...

Those people whose aim is always low generally hit what they shoot at: they aim for nothing and hit it.

Life need not be lived that way. I believe that one of the most powerful forces in the world is the will of the man who believes in himself, who dares to aim high, to go confidently after the things that he wants from life.

"I can." It is a powerful sentence: I can. It is amazing how many people can use that sentence realistically. For the overwhelming majority of people, that sentence can be a true one. It works. People can do what they believe they can do. Apart from the few people in the world who are deluded in a psychotic sense, the gap between what a man thinks he can achieve and what is actually possible to him is very, very small. But first he must believe that he can.

Let's get one thing straight: I do not pretend to be an expert on the subject of motivation. I have no more knowledge of what motivates men than does the average person. Since Amway has grown so rapidly, and since its success has depended on five hundred thousand self-employed distributors, I am often asked for my notions of motivation. "What makes some people succeed when others fail?" they want to know. Or they ask for my "secrets" on motivation, as if I can deliver some profound bit of wisdom about why one man sets new sales records while another folds up and quits. I hate to disappoint these people, but the simple fact is that I have no gimmicks or tricks or magic words to make people succeed.

But although I cannot claim any special knowledge of motivational technique, I do have a firm conviction that almost anyone can do whatever he really believes he can do.

The nature of the goal really makes little difference. When I was a young man, I had an ambition to go into business for myself and succeed at it. That was "my thing," as the current expression has it. I was not particularly interested in finishing college, or traveling around the world, or becoming the leading golfer on the PGA tour, or the top man in the Michigan legislature. There is nothing wrong with those things—they all are legitimate goals—but they just didn't happen to appeal to me at the time. My goal was to succeed in my own business, and I believed that I could do it.

There is no way ever to know for sure, of course, but I believe the result would have been much the same whatever my goal had been. The point is that there are no areas of life which are immune to the combination of faith and effort. The personal philosophy of "I can" does not apply just to business but to politics, education, church work, athletics, the arts, you name it. It cuts across all lines. It can be the greatest common factor in such diverse accomplishments as earning a Ph.D., making a million dollars, becoming a five-star general, or riding a winner at Churchill Downs.

I look back at the forty-odd years of my life, and it seems that, more than any other single lesson, my experiences have conspired to teach me the value of determined, confident effort. For most of my life, I have been associated with Jay Van Andel. We started the Amway company together in 1959, but long before that—since we were teenagers in high school, in fact—we were sharing experiences that taught us forcibly the excitement of "I can."

When World War II ended, Jay and I came home convinced that the aviation business was the hot item of the future. We had visions of airplanes in every garage, millions of people learning to fly, that sort of thing. So we wanted to go into the aviation business. We had a few hundred dollars, bought a little Piper Cub airplane, and got ready to open an aviation school. There was a minor problem: neither of us knew how to fly an airplane!

We didn't let that stop us. We simply hired experienced pilots to give the flying lessons, while we stayed busy with the work of selling those lessons to the public. The point is that we had decided to operate a flying service, and we refused to let anything dampen our enthusiasm—not even a small detail like not knowing how to fly.

We hit another snag—when we got our customers signed up and our instructors hired, we discovered that the runways at the little airport had not been completed yet. They were still nothing but giant streaks of mud. We improvised. A river ran alongside the airport, so we bought some floats for our Piper Cub and flew right off the water, taking off and landing on those bloated pontoon floats. (We eventually had two students who graduated from our course who had never landed an airplane on dry land!)

We were supposed to have offices there at the little airstrip, but the time came to open our business and the offices were still not built. Something had to be done. A chicken coop was bought from a farmer down the road, hauled over to the airstrip, white-washed, a padlock put on the door, and a sign hung that read grandly: WOLVERINE AIR SERVICE. We had set out to get into the aviation business and we were in it.

The end of that story is that we built a thriving business, bought a dozen airplanes, and eventually had one of the biggest aviation services in town. But we made it only because from the very start, we believed in ourselves. We felt in our bones that we could do it, and we did, despite those early roadblocks. If we had launched the project halfheartedly, not quite believing in it, always looking over our shoulders for an excuse to lie down and quit, the first plane would never have made the first flight—there never would have been a Wolverine Air Service.

That story illustrates a basic point: one never knows what he might accomplish until he tries. That is so simple that some people completely overlook it. If we had listened to all the logical arguments against our air service in those days, we would never have attempted it. We would have given up before we started, and to this day we would assume that we could not have made a go of it. We would still sit around and talk about that great idea that didn't work. But it did work, because we believed in it and committed ourselves enough to try it.

Also, after that we decided to try our hands at the restaurant business. Not that we knew anything at all about the restaurant business—we didn't—but we had been out to California and seen drive-in restaurants for the first time. Grand Rapids had nothing like that, we thought, and we believed we could make a drive-in restaurant go in our hometown. So we tried it. We bought a prefabricated building, put a one-man kitchen inside, and were all ready for the grand opening. When opening night came, the power company had not connected the electricity. Temporary panic. But we never once entertained the idea of postponing the opening. We rented a generator at the last minute, set it up in that squatty little building, and cranked out our own electricity. The restaurant opened right on schedule.

That little restaurant never became the biggest money-maker in the world, but it was a going venture. One day Jay would cook while I hopped cars; the next day we would reverse roles. (It was a terrible way to try to make a living!) But the important thing is that we put our minds to doing the thing we had set out to do, instead of just sitting around and talking about it. We could have talked about it for years. We could have worried about all the problems and reflected on the obstacles and never gotten around to *doing* it. So we would never have known whether or not we could succeed in the restaurant business.

What does all this say? Give things a chance to happen! Give success a chance to happen! It is impossible to win the race unless you venture to run, impossible to win the victory unless you dare to battle. No life is more tragic than that of the individual who nurses a dream, an ambition, always wishing and hoping, but never giving it a chance to happen. He nurses the flickering dream, but never lets it break out into flame. Millions of people are that way about having a second income, or owning their own business, and Amway is designed somewhat in response to that need. There are millions more who nurture private, almost secret dreams in other areas: the schoolteacher who wants to go back for that master's degree; the small businessman who dreams of expanding his business; the couple who has intended to make that trip to Europe; the housewife whose ambition is to write short stories for the free-lance market. The list could go on and on. People dreaming but never daring, never willing to say, "I can," never trusting their dreams to the real world of action and effort—people, in short, who are so afraid of failure that they fail.

For the individual in that position, there is only one thing left after all the arguments are weighed and all the costs measured. Do it. Try it. Quit talking about it and do it. How will you ever know if you can paint that picture, run that business, sell that vacuum cleaner, earn that degree, hold that office, make that speech, win that game, marry that girl, write that book, bake that soufflé, build that house—unless you try it!

My early experiences with Jay were so dominated with this kind of attitude that we did things which, looking back, seem almost foolhardy. But we were so eager to try our hand at new things and so confident that they would come out right that we just floated along on a cloud of "I can." And usually we found that we could! But to know that, first we had to try.

We read a book—before either of us was married—that really turned us on to sailing. The book was written by a fellow who had sailed around the Caribbean, and it was filled with the adventures of the high seas. So we decided to sail to South America. We had worked hard and deserved a break, a vacation. We bought an old thirty-eight-foot schooner in Connecticut and got ready for a big trip. We planned to sail down the eastern coast of the United States to Florida and then over to Cuba, then down through the Caribbean to see all the exotic islands, and eventually wind up in South America. We were going to have a wonderful time. The only problem was that neither of us had ever been on a sailboat in our lives. Never.

I remember going to Holland, Michigan, one day and asking

a fellow in a sailboat to give us a ride. "Why should I give you a ride?" he asked.

I said, "Well, we just bought a thirty-eight-footer and we've never sailed in our lives."

"Where are you planning to go in it?" he asked. And when we told him South America he almost passed out right on the dock.

But we believed we could.

We picked up our boat, got a few quick lessons, and set sail with the book in one hand and the tiller in the other. We got lost immediately. We got lost so badly in New Jersey that even the Coast Guard couldn't find us. We missed two turns at night and got way back up in the inland marshes someplace. When the Coast Guard finally found us after an all-day search, they couldn't believe where we were. "Nobody has ever been this far inland in a boat this size before," they declared, and hauled us unceremoniously back out to the ocean with a rope.

That was a wonderful old boat, except for a habit it developed of leaking, which might be considered a rather bad habit for a boat. We finally got to Florida, pumping water out of the bottom of that boat all the way. We would set the alarm for three o'clock every morning to get up and put the pump on, or by five o'clock we would practically be bailing water out by hand. By the time we got to Havana, the situation improved and we hoped our troubles were over. We turned down the northern coast of Cuba, and one dark night the old schooner just gave up and began to sink in fifteen hundred feet of water, ten miles off the coast. The first ship that came in sight was a big Dutch ship—which would have made a beautiful ending to the story, since Jay and I are both of Dutch ancestry, except that this Dutch ship wouldn't pick us up. The men on board just radioed and reported that they had spotted a crummy old Cuban boat in distress and went on their way. An hour later an American ship from New Orleans picked us up and deposited us in Puerto Rico.

Did we give up then and go home?

We didn't even consider it. We had arrived in Puerto Rico in a fashion different from our plans, to be sure, but we were there nevertheless. Back home in Michigan our folks thought, "Oh well, now those two young boys will be coming home." The thought never occurred to us. We notified our insurance company, told them where to send the money, and kept right on traveling. We went all through the Caribbean, through the major countries of South America, and eventually returned to Michigan right on schedule.

That trip was not a matter of life-or-death importance; it wasn't as significant as a career or a family; it was just a trip, a lark, a time for two young guys to get out and see a little piece of the world. But it came at a meaningful time for me, because it reinforced this growing conviction that the only thing that stands between a man and what he wants from life is often merely the will to try it and the faith to believe that it is possible. After thirty years in business nothing I have learned has weakened that conviction.

Why do so many people let their dreams die unlived? The biggest reason, I suppose, is the negative, cynical attitudes of other people. Those other people are not enemies—they are friends, even family members. Our enemies never bother us greatly; we can usually handle them with little trouble. But our friends—if they are naysayers, constantly punching holes in our dreams with a cynical smile here, a put-down there, a constant stream of negative vibrations—our friends can kill us! A man gets excited about the possibility of a new job. He sees the opportunity to make more money, do more meaningful work, rise to a personal challenge; the old heart starts pounding and the juices begin to flow and he feels himself revving up for this stimulating new prospect. But then he tells his neighbor about it over the back fence one evening. He gets a smirk, a laugh that says, "You can't do that," a foot-long list of all the problems and obstacles, and fifty reasons why he never will make it and is better off to stay where he is.

Before he knows it, his enthusiasm falls down to near zero. He goes back into the house like a whipped pup with his tail dragging the ground and all the fire and self-confidence is gone and he begins to second-guess himself. Now he is thinking of all the reasons that he *can't* make it instead of the reasons that he can. He lets one five-minute spiel of negativism or ridicule or just plain disbelief from a dream-nothing, do-nothing neighbor take the steam right out of his engine. Friends like that can do more damage than a dozen enemies.

A young housewife decides to take knitting lessons so she can knit sweaters, afghans, all sorts of things. She gets a book and the needles and yarn and starts to learn the simplest knitting steps, full of visions of brightly colored mittens and clothes. Then her husband comes home from work and tells her how hard it is to knit, how she'll have to work years to be any good at it, how many women have started and quit. He gives her one of those patented, patronizing smiles that says, "You'll never learn to knit very well, you poor thing." And before he has left the room she is believing more in his cynicism than in her faith.

Remember that the easiest thing to find on God's green earth is someone to tell you all the things you cannot do. Someone will always be eager to point out to you—perhaps merely with a look or a tone of voice—that anything new or daring which you try is hopelessly doomed to failure. Don't listen to them! It is always the fellow who has never made ten thousand dollars a year who knows all the reasons why you can't make thirty thousand. In the Boy Scouts, it is always the tenderfoot who can recite the reasons that you can't make Eagle Scout. It is the college flunk-out who can explain why you are too dumb to get that degree; the fellow who never ran a business who can best describe the obstacles that make it impossible to get started; the girl who never entered a golf tournament who can most convincingly tell you why you don't have a chance to win. Don't listen to them! If you have a dream, whatever it is, dare to believe it and to try it. Give it a chance to happen! Don't let your brother-in-law or your plumber or your husband's fishing buddy or the guy in the next office rob you of that faith in yourself that makes things happen. Don't let the guys who lie on the couch and watch television every night tell you how futile life is. If you have that flame of a dream down inside you somewhere, thank God for it, and do something about it. And don't let anyone else blow it out.

My father was a great believer in the potential of individual effort. Every time he heard me say the word "can't" as a boy, he would say, "There is no such word as 'can't,' and if you say it one more time I'll knock your block right through that wall!" He never did that, but I never forgot the point he was making. I learned that there really are no good uses of the word "can't."

Believe you can, and you'll find that you can! Try! You'll be surprised at how many good things can happen.

> *You may live in an imperfect*
> *world but the frontiers are not all closed*
> *and the doors are not all shut.*

Dr. Maxwell Maltz

LESSON 8

HOW TO DEVELOP YOUR STRENGTH TO SEIZE OPPORTUNITIES

Who among us, with our marvelous "20-20" vision called hindsight, cannot compile a lengthy list of missed opportunities?

Did you miss them because they were unrecognizable to you, at the time?

Or did you know they were there but felt that you had neither the ability nor the strength to deal with them?

In retrospect, it makes little difference, doesn't it? The truth of the matter is that your plane lifted off the runway and you were still standing at the boarding gate. As George Eliot wrote, "The golden moments in the stream of life rush past us, and we see nothing but sand; the angels come to visit us, and we only know them when they are gone."

Actually, if you stop to think about it, you are working your way through these semesters, not only to learn how to succeed, but to learn to be prepared to capitalize on the next opportunity that presents itself, or, better still, to *make your own opportunities*—with a confident, positive mental attitude that will almost certainly guarantee your success.

There have been few, in the field of achievement and success, whose lectures and writings have affected more lives than the gifted plastic surgeon, Maxwell Maltz. His magnificent style of delivery made the complicated subject of one's "self-image" easy to understand, convincing legions of his followers that life can be lived with pride and joy when it is lived to its fullest.

Here, from his book, *The Search for Self-Respect,* Dr. Maltz shares with you five secrets that will better equip you to handle any opportunity . . .

What is opportunity, and when does it knock? It never knocks. You can wait a whole lifetime, listening, hoping, and you will hear no knocking. None at all.

You are opportunity, and you must knock on the door leading to your destiny. You prepare yourself to recognize opportunity, to pursue and seize opportunity as you develop the strength of your personality, and build a self-image with which you are able to live—with your self-respect alive and growing.

Opportunity covers a wide area: some people may constrict the totality of its meaning and apply it only to work or financial success, but your opportunities in living are really much wider than this. Opportunity may also mean warding off negative feelings. It may also mean functioning under pressure. It may also mean rising above vanity, bigotry, and deceit as you strive to live with dignity. It is your opportunity to be an archaeologist digging under the debris of tension and conflict to uncover for yourself a sense of self-acceptance that will give you inner peace and comfort in our swiftly paced, always troubled world.

Accessible to you may be the exciting opportunity of steering yourself to a productive goal through your growing awareness of who you are and what you can be and how you can channel your assets in practical terms toward achieving your ends. Developing your strength as you build your self-respect, you mobilize yourself for action and place yourself—practically, in an external sense, and emotionally, in an internal sense—in a position to seize opportunities at the proper times. You build the caliber of your thinking, propelling your thoughts into and through your imagination. Then with internal strength, you move toward your goals of fulfillment and happiness.

You create opportunity. *You* develop the capacities for moving toward opportunity. *You* turn crises into creative opportunities and defeats into successes and frustration into fulfillment.

With what? With your great invisible weapons: your good feelings about yourself, your determination to live the best life you can, and your feeling—that only you can give yourself—that you are a worthwhile, deserving person.

You must fight for your right to fulfill the opportunity that God gave you to use your life well. You do this when, in your mind, you support yourself instead of undermining yourself. You do this when, in your mind, you develop your creative and imaginative powers instead of worrying about what other people think or foreseeing endless disasters.

What are explorers? Men alive to opportunity and adventure. Men unafraid to challenge uncertainty and seek new horizons. Men alive to possibilities of expansion and innovation. Suppose, in 1492, Columbus had said to himself, "But the weather may be stormy," or "I'd better not go. I might get scurvy."

What are inventors? Men who see opportunity in things where others see none. Men whose senses are alive to creative possibilities. Where would the world be today if Thomas Edison had been unable to see opportunity where others saw nothing— and then to seize it?

You must stop complaining about your unfortunate past or your bad luck and open your eyes to the opportunities that exist for you. You have limitations, sure, and no matter who you are, you will sometimes meet frustrations—but you have opportunities too, and you must search for your creative powers so that you can move toward them. In a sense, you become Columbus; you become Edison; you explore and invent and originate and adapt.

Who gives you this right? You give it to yourself because you respect yourself.

OPPORTUNITY IS NOT
JUST FOR THE OTHER GUY

From New York to California, I have gone back and forth lecturing for quite a few years now, and I have talked to thousands of people about things that worry them—so let me anticipate a few thoughts of many people reading this:

"The other guy gets opportunities. I know that. But I'm just unlucky."
Or, "I have this handicap, so you can see that I'm licked before I start."
Or, "I have no right to try something like that. Who am I, just a nobody."

This is self-defeating; you must fight to overcome this type of negative thinking or you block yourself off from opportunity as an eclipse blocks off the sun.

You must understand that opportunity is not just for "the other guy." Opportunity is a possibility for you, too—if you can accept it and make it welcome. A plant may wither and die if you don't water it and give it enough sunshine. So will opportunity.

Don't let opportunity die for you! Don't kill it with negative feelings!

There is much concern in education today about "disadvantaged" children in our schools and in many communities university teams are helping public school teachers to improve communication between school, students, and parents and thereby to give the "disadvantaged" children more of a chance to climb up the educational and vocational ladder.

Well, as adults, we all have disadvantages—and limitations. If we get help—as these children are getting today—wonderful. If we don't, we must nevertheless move toward whatever opportunities are realistic for us anyway.

Many people sit around moping, envying others, complaining, resentful. If they hear about people like Helen Keller, who overcame drastic handicaps to seize her opportunities for achievement, they say that this is an isolated case.

Indeed, in the case of Helen Keller, her handicaps were so severe that perhaps she is an isolated case.

Still, in general, many people who have pursued and seized their opportunities and risen to prominent positions in our world have had no easy road.

A study was made of four hundred eminent men and women of this century, and the researchers concluded that three fourths of these celebrated people had been handicapped in their youth by tragedies, disabilities, or great frustrations, and had overcome these problems to achieve their position of renown and make their contributions to others. Three fourths of these four hundred people fought through their handicaps; an important statistic. Thomas Edison and Eleanor Roosevelt were included among those who had risen above handicaps to achievement and opportunity.

Opportunity is not just for others. But you must make opportunity for you.

DON'T CLOSE THE DOOR ON OPPORTUNITY!

Opportunity won't knock on your door; nevertheless you must not close the door on opportunity.

To close the door on opportunity is, unfortunately, common. You must guard against this type of tendency in yourself. Let me tell you an illustrative story:

It's about a doctor who shut the door on an opportunity to advance himself.

He was already a doctor; and he wanted to become a plastic surgeon.

"Can I watch you operate?" he asked me.

"Tomorrow," I said. "Eight A.M. Okay?"

I wasn't sure the "eight A.M." pleased him, but I figured I was probably imagining this. He nodded his head. "I'll be there," he said. "Eight A.M."

He was as good as his word. He was there at eight A.M. and he watched me operate. He said he was fascinated. Could he be my pupil? I agreed that I would teach him.

The doctor came a few times, expressing fascination with plastic surgery and for the opportunity for fulfillment that this work could be for him.

I was delighted with his enthusiasm.

But one morning he was not there.

The morning after that he was also absent.

Finally, a few days later, I walked into my office and there he was. "Where have you been?" I said.

"I overslept a few times," he answered, rather sheepishly. "When I woke up, I looked at the time and it was too late to come."

"You won't learn this way," I said mildly.

"I know. Tell me, do you operate in the afternoon? I like to sleep, and it would be easier for me."

"Sorry. I always operate in the morning. The patient has just awakened, and I feel it is best for the patient psychologically."

"Oh," he said.

And, fascinated as he was with plastic surgery (it represented a creative opportunity for him, and I do not believe he faked his interest) he didn't follow up. He couldn't get up early in the morning. He shut the door on his own opportunity. He was qualified to succeed, but he denied himself success in his own terms.

Learn from this story. Are you, without knowing it, blocking yourself from opportunity? You have this great gift of life, and you must make the most of it. When you fail—and sometimes you will—let it be after you have done your best, not as a result of your own inertia.

Now let me tell you a story about a scrubwoman who found opportunity.

A SONG OF HAPPINESS

I met her, this scrubwoman, in the elevator one evening. I had enjoyed my dinner in a nearby restaurant, returned home about eight o'clock, and stepped into the elevator to go up to the eighteenth floor, where I live. She was armed with mop and pail. A small woman, in her late forties, she had worked about ten years in the building, but we didn't know each other any better than to nod our heads and say hello. That's what we did this night: we nodded our heads, and murmured "hello."

She came up with me to my place, with mop and pail, ready to empty the wastepaper basket and mop the floors. While she started on a front room, I walked to the living room.

I made myself comfortable. I was smoking my pipe; my feet were up; I was reading a play. I had forgotten about the scrubwoman's presence. She might have been on another planet.

Then I heard singing from another room—no, humming. Someone was humming a lullaby. It was soft and sweet and happy-sounding, a song of happiness.

I got out of my chair. In another room the woman was mopping the floor, humming her lullaby. She looked up as I entered the room and we exchanged greetings again.

"Did you have a busy day?" she asked me.

"Yes. And you?"

"About the same as usual."

"But today is different, isn't it?"

"How?"

"You're smiling, and you're humming a song."

"I often do. It makes my work more pleasant. I'm cleaning up, and I'm singing while I work, so I'm happy."

"I never heard you before," I said.

"Perhaps not."

"And," I said, "we never talked before."

"That's true."

I asked her about herself. Her life had been a difficult one—enough to crush many an individual who could not endure grief and rise above it to regain herself. Her husband, a truck driver for the government, had been killed in a car accident twelve years earlier. She had one child, a daughter—nine at the time of the accident—now twenty-one, unmarried, a college student. She and her daughter were in the car with her husband when it crashed and he died; by some miracle the woman and her daughter had survived.

Grief stricken at her husband's sudden and horrible death,

consoling her daughter who at such a young age had seen such a frightening tragedy and suffered such a catastrophic loss, she had nevertheless found in herself the courage to go on. She had for many years supported herself and her daughter, who was soon to graduate from college in Wisconsin.

"What will she do then?" I asked her.

"She majored in psychology. She'll go for her master's degree and then she's going to get a job teaching underprivileged children."

"May I congratulate you?"

"Do you want to?"

"I do. I think you deserve it. I think you should be very proud of yourself."

"I am proud."

"You should be."

"And I'm happy."

"Good."

"About my daughter."

"That's fine," I said. "But I feel also that you should be proud of your great achievement—of the way you came through for your daughter when she was a little girl and you didn't let her down."

"Thanks, Doctor."

"You know, we've never talked before—all these years—but I've seen you now and then and you look different somehow. What is it?"

"My wig?"

"Oh." I looked at her hair. "Oh. That's it. Yes."

"Do you like it?" She was suddenly shy, almost a little sensitive; in a flash, she seemed waiting, depending on my opinion, hoping for my approval.

"I like it."

"Does it make me look like a lady?"

"You always were." I hate to flatter people, but I felt an honest respect for her that made me enjoy complimenting her.

She stood there with mop and pail, her eyes gleaming with pleasure. No princess or countess on the French Riviera ever gleamed with more inner pride. "I wanted to look better for my daughter. I'm so proud of what she's learning and what she's planning to do with her life. She wants to contribute to the children of the world—she is sincere in this—and then she wants to have children of her own and teach them to lead useful lives and to assume responsibility as human beings."

I went back into the other room to continue my reading; strange, all these years, coming and going, nodding hello as people whose lives meet on no level at all—and suddenly I knew so much about the woman who scrubbed my floors and cleaned up. Some people might look down on her because they thought her work demeaning: I could only respect her for her courage in rising above misfortune and maintaining her self-respect in the face of a tragedy that would have crushed many people.

Humming again, soft and sweet. Happy. A song of happiness from a scrubwoman. She wore a wig to cover her hair, but she needed no artificial aid to cover her sense of purpose. It was there.

Husband alive, husband dead—just like that—but she had overcome her grief and terror to find opportunity once more. Still, she had reached out to find opportunity in helping her daughter toward a life hopefully easier than her own had been.

Even while working—tiring, painstaking, ill-rewarded work— she found opportunity to sing a song of happiness.

HOW TO MOVE TOWARD OPPORTUNITY

This world is far from perfect—you don't have to be brilliant to perceive that—but it nevertheless contains many opportunities for fulfillment and achievement.

Some people spend all their time criticizing the American culture and, while some of their criticism may be quite valid, still we must be pragmatists. We must ask: "Where have men grouped together in civilizations and behaved like angels, with absolute justice and absolute constructive effort and absolute brotherhood and peace of mind?"

Even ancient Athens, home of so many great philosophers whose thoughts have lived through the ages, even ancient Athens had serious defects as a culture. The worst of which was its lack of an adequate sanitary system. The lack of a sanitary system helped spread a terrible plague which was largely instrumental in destroying ancient Athens.

All right, we live in an imperfect world, in an imperfect culture, and as you settle in your easy chair after a hard day's work to read your newspaper all the frightening headlines upset you further and finally, thoroughly irritated, you throw the newspaper at your cat. But the cat slinks away. Even the cat doesn't want to read about all the world's troubles.

Yet ours is a world of opportunity, too. The frontiers are not all closed, and the doors are not all shut. We can still look forward and move forward—toward exciting new opportunities.

How?

1. Keep an eye on the red light. I mean the red light on your mental dashboard, with which you stop yourself from moving toward your opportunities. Red lights on our streets are necessary for safety, of course. But when you stop yourself, you must ask yourself this: am I stopping myself for realistic reasons, because I am moving into a danger area, or am I just stopping myself because my opinion of myself is too low, and I do not believe I deserve success?

Stop wasting fuel worrying about yesterday. Just as you would take care of your car, oil it, and check it out—take care of your emotional car, so that it moves you toward your objectives.

Stop when the red light on your mental dashboard signals a necessary slowdown—but change it to green when, for no real reason except negative feelings, you would keep yourself from moving forward down the main highway toward opportunity.

Stop and start—this is the way to move toward your goals. As you formulate them and move toward them, remember your past successes and, even more important, see them in your mind as if they were happening *now*. Thus your success lives again, in your imagination, so that you live and breathe the success of the past and project it into the present.

Stop, but then start again.

2. Live in the present. The past is gone; the future is unknown—but the present is real, and your opportunities are now. You must see these opportunities; they must be real for you.

The catch is that they can't seem real if your mind is buried in past failures, if you keep reliving old mistakes, old guilts, old tragedies.

Fight your way above the many inevitable traumatizations of your ego, escape damnation by the past, and look to the opportunities of the present. I don't mean some vague moment in the present—next week or next month, perhaps. I mean today, this minute.

The past may not be your only obstacle; tomorrow-type thinking can also block you from your goals. Yearning for a new tomorrow may often be unrealistic and negative—especially if you foresee some angel coming to your rescue and pressing a magic button for you. There is no magic button—just your own resources, your own determination, your own feeling that you have the right to succeed.

3. Stop belittling yourself. Too many people do this. Maybe you're not a celebrity or a millionaire or a football hero or an astronaut hero. You can be great if you're a sales clerk or a housewife, or a car washer or a dishwasher, or a garbage collector, or a bill collector. Learn from my story about the scrubwoman with pride and courage. A scrubwoman can be a great human being.

Stop belittling yourself. If we were all movie stars, there would be no food on our tables, no production in our factories—and maybe no one to watch movies.

Accept yourself as you are. Otherwise you will never see opportunity. You will not feel free to move toward it; you will feel you are not deserving.

4. Try to set constructive goals. We have enough negativism these days, enough violence, enough cynicism.

Experiments in Australia have indicated that kangaroos do not like loud noises. Well, I'm with the kangaroos. I'm in favor of quiet, purposeful, constructive people who move toward their goals without unnecessarily loud fanfare.

I know of some people who have adopted a child; the youngster's parents died and he was needy. He needed affection; he needed a home. This couple wanted to help him, and so they adopted him. But they did it quietly. They did not boast loudly about how great they were. They just did it. I admire them as much for the way they handled themselves as I do for what they did.

I feel proud of my nephew Joe also; his goals are quietly, modestly constructive. He seeks opportunity—the opportunity to help other people lead longer, more secure lives.

I went with my wife Anne to Cambridge, Massachusetts, to see the Commencement Exercises. Our nephew was graduating from Harvard. Thousands of people had come to attend. We sat with Joe's parents in the rear, under a tree near a dirt roadway. The sun was shining and it was hot; waiting for the formal exercises to begin, I thought about my talk with my nephew the night before.

He had told me about his plans. He had been on a scholarship at Harvard, in organic chemistry; now he was about to go on to his master's in biological chemistry. He told me that some research on wound healing that I published many years ago had excited him very deeply and had influenced his thinking to the point that he was determined to pursue research in chemistry, on the life of the cell. He told me of his determination to do research, to find a clue to the cure of cancer, to make a serum that would prevent it.

This was no wild-eyed boasting, no loud conceit. We discussed some technical points; we exchanged opinions. His feet were on the ground; his goal was straight ahead.

I was most pleased with his quiet purposefulness. That night I couldn't sleep. I was excited by his determination, by the wonder of his youthful belief in himself, by the thrill of the Commencement Exercises next day.

The Commencement Exercises were stormy. A student was allowed to criticize the learning process in a ten-minute lecture to the audience and following his talk one hundred students—boys and girls—walked out.

Still, the Commencement Exercises proceeded and our nephew Joe, along with many others, received his degree. An important step toward the implementation of his constructive goals.

A move toward opportunity.

5. *Stand up to crises*. Don't let them throw you! Fight to stay calm. As I've written in other books, even surmount the crisis completely and turn a crisis into a creative opportunity.

Refuse to renounce your self-image. No matter what happens, you must keep your good opinion of yourself. No matter what happens, you must hold your past successes in your imagination, ready for showing in the motion picture screen of your mind. No matter what happens, no matter what you lose, no matter what failures you must endure, you must keep faith in yourself. Then you can stand up to crises, with calm and courage, refusing to buckle; then you will not fall through the floor. You will be able to support yourself.

Look in the mirror. That's you. You must like yourself; you must accept yourself; you must be your own friend. In crises, especially, you must give yourself support. That is you in the mirror. Don't look at yourself narcissistically, telling yourself you're the most perfect, wonderful, godlike individual on earth, but give yourself appreciation. Remember other crises you've lived through. See in your mind the ones you handled successfully, the ones you turned into opportunities for growth. Don't let yourself down!

OPPORTUNITY AND SELF-RESPECT

Five suggestions for moving toward exciting new opportunities. I hope they help you. I think they will.

In a physical sense, the American frontier and many other frontiers throughout the world are closed—but opportunities remain very much alive. And not just in Outer Space. Some of the greatest opportunities gain momentum in the Inner Space of our minds before they are ready to be propelled out into action.

In the field of education, we find people using "talking typewriters" to help children learn skills such as reading. One group of children, helped by the typewriter procedure, at the end of the first grade read at the sixth-grade level—according to a prominent test.

New opportunity for children.

And adults? Plenty of opportunity for adults who go at it intelligently, rejecting the passive approach of waiting for opportunity to knock, and instead building the inner strength they need to open their eyes to opportunity, to move toward opportunity, to seize opportunity.

I mean constructive opportunity, of course, not the kind of opportunism which would enrich you while you trample all over other people en route. This kind of antisocial and inconsiderate aggression could not bolster your sense of self-respect.

Indeed, one of the great opportunities in your lifetime must be a direct attempt to build your respectful attitude toward yourself. To respect our cultural celebrities and leaders and institutions is not enough. To live well, you must respect yourself.

Living in this huge world—so heavily overpopulated that some eminent people fear the possibility of a drastic shortage of food at some future time—we are not omnipotent and must sometimes compromise or surrender.

By surrendering, we must win.

You surrender to compassion, however, not to resentment.

To courage, not to cowardice.

To your assets, not to your liabilities.

And you surrender to the opportunity within you that you create for yourself—an opportunity that will lead you to richer living and greater self-respect.

Complicated person that you are, frustrated and yet confident, negative and yet positive, failure-oriented, and yet success-oriented, you count down in the Inner Space of your mind, strengthen yourself and then launch yourself toward today's opportunities in your world.

*How is it that many individuals, who possess
only limited capabilities, manage to attract great
admiration for extraordinary results?*

Kenneth Hildebrand

LESSON 9

HOW TO MAKE THE MOST
OF YOUR ABILITIES

There is an old cattle-country axiom which states, "Success in life comes not from holding a good hand, but in playing a poor hand well."

The easiest thing to do, whenever you fail, is to put yourself down by blaming your lack of ability for your misfortunes.

The easiest thing to forget, especially when fate has been unkind to you, is that you were born to succeed, not fail.

Unfortunately, our nation has a growing number of individuals who have already sold themselves on the idea that they just don't have whatever it takes to make anything of their lives. They are already dead in spirit, aimlessly parading through a life with no purpose, no meaning.

You cannot rise above the level of your vision. The man who guides a pushcart through the alley to pick up bottles and stray bits of paper will remain between the shafts of his rickety cart as long as he believes that he has no talent for anything else.

Kenneth Hildebrand had that rare ability to make even "skid row" derelicts raise their sights and aspire to a better life. Thousands flocked to his nondenominational church, the Central Church of Chicago and his messages from the pulpit, as well as radio and television, were a beacon of hope that still lights many hearts.

From his book, *Achieving Real Happiness,* this compassionate observer of human frailties provides you with a simple plan which will enable you to take full advantage of the talents you already possess. Listen carefully . . .

A man once wrote to a person whom he admired greatly, congratulating him on his amazing abilities. The letter he received in reply contained these sentences:

> No, my friend, you are quite wrong about me. I am just an ordinary individual, without special ability in any line. In most things I am only just above the average; in some things I am under the average rather than over. This is certainly true of my physical powers. I can't run; I'm only an ordinary walker; I'm certainly not a good swimmer. I can probably ride a horse better than I can do anything else, but I am not a remarkable horseman. Neither am I a good shot. My eyesight is so poor that I have to be near my game to take any aim at all. So you can see that, as far as physical gifts are concerned, I am just an ordinary man. The same thing is true of my literary ability. I am certainly not a brilliant writer. During my lifetime I have written a good deal, but I always have to work and slave over everything I put on paper.

Who was this man of ordinary abilities who had done so much with them that he had excited the admiration of others? His name was Theodore Roosevelt. By his own judgment, he was a man of no outstanding talents—but how he used the abilities he had! This brings into focus a question which troubles many of us. What is the secret which harnesses ordinary powers to outstanding achievements? How do some individuals attract admiration for extraordinary results when actually they possess only limited talent?

Think of the word "talent" as synonymous with "ability," and several suggestions on how to make the most of our own capabilities will become evident. The first is to *take stock of our abilities*. What talents do we possess? What are our assets, our strong points? We should also take our inclinations into account. Possibly we have several talents, any one of which could develop into something useful and satisfying if we were to pursue it; our inclination helps us decide which of our assets to develop. A mother asked her little boy, "Tommy, would you rather go shopping with me this afternoon, or would you rather visit your Aunt Mary?" The little fellow answered, "Well, if I had my *druthers*, I'd druther go swimming." If we had our *druthers* of what to do with our abilities, what would we choose? A talk with a wise friend, a clergyman, a banker, a lawyer, or a vocational counselor may help. Perhaps we should take vocational guidance tests to reveal our potentials. Such consultation and analysis should aid in determining the area in which we should strive to use our abilities.

In taking stock of our abilities, we should ask ourselves if the area in which we have talent is feasible. A man who once was a member of Admiral Richard E. Byrd's Arctic expedition fell in love with the Far North. He still dreams of his experiences on that expedition. He wants to dedicate his life to polar explorations, but the ambition hardly is practical—there is a dearth of polar expeditions at present. Because he cannot fulfill his heart's desire, he is discontented and uncooperative in the work he does; frankly he makes himself a nuisance. Instead of dreaming about exploring the Arctic, would it not be more sensible to explore the needs of his neighborhood and to organize a restless young group of vandals into a boys' club, or to use his fine abilities—and he has them—in leading a Boy Scout troop? He could fire growing boys with admiration for the kind of bravery, team play, unselfishness, and integrity essential to the conquest of the polar regions—and of their own futures.

We should apply the same test to ourselves, if we are in earnest about making the most of our abilities. Is our ambition feasible? Does it lie in the range of practical possibility? If not, we are wise to turn our aspirations to other channels. We should begin by surveying the opportunities open to us. Situations which at first appear as roadblocks may later reveal themselves as walls of guidance.

On a train trip west, I was attracted to a clean-cut porter and struck up a conversation with him. He inquired about the opportunities to study pharmacy in Chicago.

"I'm a student at the University of Arizona," he said, "but it doesn't offer some of the courses I need."

"How did you decide on pharmacy as a career?" I asked him.

"I really wanted to study medicine," he explained, "but it is hard to break into the field, for the medical schools are so crowded that it is next to impossible to receive an appointment. I also thought of dentistry, but the situation is much the same. Good pharmacists are greatly needed and I believe that I can offer real service in that profession."

The young man was hitching his wagon of purpose to a practical star. He was matching his aspirations realistically with opportunity. Denied his first choice, and even his second, this did not deter him from expanding his abilities into practical and highly useful service.

A second suggestion is to *discipline our abilities for maximum usefulness*. Success demands foresight and industry. It responds to thought and care. Thorough preparation is imperative if we are to use our capabilities to the fullest. The greatest undiscovered resources in the world lie under our hats and stand in our shoes. It is our responsibility to develop them.

Someone receives a promotion, gets an important assignment, makes a major discovery, or moves into the president's office. "He was lucky," an envious person remarks. "He gets the breaks; they're always in his favor." In reality, luck or the breaks of life had little or nothing to do with it. So-called "luck" usually is found at the exact point where preparation meets opportunity. For a time, an individual may get ahead by "pull," but eventually someone with push will displace him. Success is not due to a fortuitous concourse of stars at our birth, but to a steady trail of sparks from the grindstone of hard work each day.

"Babe" Didrickson Zaharias has been called the athletic phenomenon of all time. This woman from Texas ran, jumped, rode, and played such games as basketball and baseball with superb skill. Her prowess in track and field events won five first places in the Olympic tryouts in 1932, and made her an international sensation when in the Olympic games in Los Angeles that same year she placed first in the women's eighty-meter hurdles, first in the javelin throw, and second in the high jump. Then she turned to golf. When she won the National Woman's Amateur and the British Woman's Amateur championships, certain people said, "It was inevitable. She is just a natural athlete. She is an automatic champion."

The facts, however, tell a different story about the "automatic champion." When the "Babe" took up golf she sought an exceptionally fine instructor to teach her. She studied the game. She analyzed the golf swing, dissected it, and tested each component part until she felt that she understood it thoroughly. When she went on a practice tee she would practice as much as twelve hours a day, hitting as many as one thousand balls in an afternoon. She would swing and keep swinging until her hands were so sore that she scarcely could grip a club. She would stop swinging long enough to tape her hands before picking up her club again. That is the method she used to perfect her powerful swing.

Does that sound as if she were an automatic champion? It takes preparation, training, and hard work to become a champion in any field of athletics. Later, her courageous battle against cancer, exhibiting the same high qualities of courage, perseverance, and faith, won the admiration of a nation. Ms. Zaharias subscribed to the theory that in order to make the most of one's abilities, one must prepare diligently to use them.

A definite *sense of purpose* also adds a strong motivation toward making the most of our abilities. It is doubtful that Ms. Zaharias would have worked seriously to perfect her golf game if she had not had a flaming desire to play championship golf. Nor will we cultivate and develop our capacities to their fullest until a compelling purpose inspires us to do so. We all know that purpose makes a difference; a clear picture of what we wish to accomplish and the determination to reach our goal strengthens our power to achieve it. It can make the difference between success and failure, frustration and zest for living, happiness and unhappiness. Strong lives are motivated by dynamic purposes; lesser ones exist on wishes and inclinations. The most glowing successes are but the reflections of an inner fire.

The biography of Mme. Curie, written by her daughter, depicts her long struggle to discover radium. After her husband Pierre and she had become convinced that radium existed, they struggled four long, grueling years in their shed laboratory—years filled with perplexities and bitter disappointments—in an effort to isolate radium. With a terrible patience they treated tons of pitch-blende residue kilogram by kilogram, certain that it contained radium. Experiment after experiment failed. In the film version, after the forty-eighth experiment was unsuccessful, her husband gave way to despair. "It can't be done," he cried, "it can't be done! Maybe in a hundred years it can be done, but never in our lifetime." Mme. Curie was made of sterner stuff. "If it takes a hundred years it will be a pity," she answered, "but I dare not do less than work for it so long as I have life."

Confronted by such a sense of purpose, the mysteries surrounding radium finally gave way on a night which she was to remember always as a night of magic. She had spent the earlier part of the evening with an ill child. When at last the little one slept, she said to her husband, "Suppose we go down there for a moment?" A note of supplication was in her voice—a superfluous note, for Pierre was as eager as she. Arm in arm they went through the streets to the shed. "Don't light the lamps," she said to Pierre as he unlocked the door. Then she added with a little laugh, "Do you remember the day when you said to me, 'I should like radium to be a beautiful color'?" They stepped into the room and an indescribably beautiful bluish glow lighted the darkness. Wordlessly they looked at the pale, glimmering, mysterious source of radiation—

radium, their radium, the reward of their resolution and patient labor.

Multitudes of people, drifting aimlessly to and fro without a set purpose, deny themselves such fulfillment of their capacities, and the satisfying happiness which attends it. They are not wicked; they are only shallow. They are not mean or vicious; they simply are empty—shake them and they would rattle like gourds. They lack range, depth, and conviction. Without purpose their lives ultimately wander into the morass of dissatisfaction.

As we harness our abilities to a steady purpose and undertake the long pull toward its accomplishment, rich compensations reward us. A sense of purpose simplifies life and therefore concentrates our abilities; and concentration adds power. King Edward VII of England once asked General William Booth, founder of the Salvation Army, how he could give himself with utter devotion to such an exacting—and often thankless—task. General Booth's reply is revealing:

> Some men's passion is gold.
> Some men's passion is fame.
> My passion is souls.

The concentration of his will toward serving dejected humanity gave power to his capacities.

Jane Addams, founder of Hull House in Chicago and world benefactor, discovered the purpose of her life at an early age. When only six, she glimpsed the destitution and squalor in the back streets of Freeport, Illinois. The sight impressed her so deeply that she insisted that, when she grew up, she would have a big house like the one in which she lived, only it would stand among little houses like those she had seen. The sense of compassion never deserted her. It became the focal point of her abilities, and Hull House became the big friendly house standing in the midst of little houses, fulfilling her childhood dream. But would Jane Addams ever have become Jane Addams without her sense of purpose, or would Hull House ever have been born? Without a corresponding sense of purpose, can *we* reach the levels of attainment which lie within our powers to achieve? Sustained by such a purpose, will any hardship thwart or deter us? Consult some difficult chapter in your personal experience for the answer, perhaps your struggle to gain an education. You had to make your own way financially and the going was hard. You received little help, except from your own two hands—and your will to succeed. You did without many things the other students had and there were periods when you did not think that you would be able to pull through, but somehow you did. The proud day finally arrived when, with your mortarboard on your head and your gown draped around your shoulders, you waved your sheepskin triumphantly and shouted, "I have done it!"

You would not wish to go through that trying period again, but is it not true that some of the most precious personal values you then received would not be yours if the way had been easy and the road smooth? Your talents were tempered and expanded. You learned patience and endurance—and the value of money. The sacrifices you were called to make proved worthwhile and you do not regret the hardships you endured. The lesson is clear: in whatever area we may wish to apply our abilities and to find the happiness of personal accomplishment, we must be willing to sacrifice for the expansion of our talents.

Having taken stock of our inclinations and abilities, and having prepared them for use in the light of a compelling purpose, the next step is to *put our talents to work*. In using them we develop them. Even if our abilities seem small to us, or the opportunity to use them seems insignificant, it is important to exercise them to the fullest. The third servant in the parable was condemned, not because he had used his talent for an evil purpose, but because he had failed to use it at all. That was his shortcoming.

The practical truth of this insight is demonstrated all about us. People with ordinary talents often achieve more than those with greater physical and intellectual endowments because they work harder with what they have. In the ancient story of the hare and the tortoise, the hare could run much faster than the tortoise. He had far more ability. Yet the tortoise won the race because he used his ability to the utmost. He kept plodding toward the goal, while the hare dallied along the way. "The race is not always to the swift," nor do achievement and success always accrue to those with the nimblest wits and the highest IQ's. Many individuals fail to achieve success for the same reason that Jim did not become wealthy in the gold rush days. Jim remained a ne'er-do-well in the midst of riches. A friend explained, "Jim has the gold fever, but he doesn't have the digging principle." We should not acquiesce as easily. For our own good, we should scorn the easy way and the second best; the "digging principle" is important! When we match our abilities against something hard each day, some task that seems beyond our capacity, we are exercising will, mind, and body to good purpose. As we master hard things we gain the ability to handle still more difficult assignments and fuller responsibilities. As we struggle, we grow. After Paderewski played before Queen Victoria, the sovereign exclaimed enthusiastically, "Mr. Paderewski, you are a genius!" "Ah, Your Majesty," he replied, "perhaps; but before I was a genius I was a drudge."

In putting our talents to work, *imagination* adds amazing outreach to our capacities. It opens doors of achievement and happiness which we do not anticipate and which once we would have believed to be beyond our wildest hopes of attainment. The power of imagination is one of man's greatest assets, one of the qualities which makes him unique. Think of attempting to turn a stubborn nut from a bolt with only your thumb and forefinger. Ages ago, after the discovery of the lever and the wheel, some imaginative genius fashioned an extension of the thumb and forefinger; the first wrench was born, and today specialized tools do the work of many powerful hands. Imagine trying to drive a spike with your clenched fist. Creative individuals in the distant past put their imaginations to work on the problem; first they used a convenient stone to drive a primitive peg, then devised a crude hammer. Thus man's strength was multiplied. Imagination was fascinated by fire, and the internal combustion engine captured its flame. Imagination watched steam, and the steam engine became the servant of mankind. Imagination saw mechanical fingers sorting seeds from cottom pods, dreamed of writing not done by hand that could be multiplied, envisioned mechanical means to sow and reap grain, harnessed the lightning, flung heavier-than-air machines into the air, and finally split the atom to release its power. From one step to another, imagination has led mankind to the heights of achievement. It has produced every article we use, made every discovery for the betterment of our health and comfort, built every church and institution, and sponsored the manifold complexities of modern civilization. It is the priceless ingredient of moral, sociological, and scientific advance, a better day, and a happier personal life. Imagination is creative, as industry is fully aware. The Aluminum Company of America coined a new word— "imagineering." The company explains that in imagineering "you let your imagination soar and then engineer it down to earth."

We are wise to apply the same principle in the use of our abilities. Said Marcus Aurelius, "As thy thoughts are so will thy mind be also: for the soul takes its coloring from thought." When we fail to use imagination, our lives become routine. Routine leads to a rut of complacency, and complacency is deadly to the creative expansion of our skills. Imagination looks at each situation with fresh eyes and discovers possibilities hitherto unseen. A little French girl, for instance, the daughter of a poor Parisian, had prayed for money to hire a model to pose for her; she had been born almost with a paintbrush in her hand, and painting was her consuming passion. But no francs fell in the backyard in answer to her earnest prayers. Then one day, while she was taking a walk in the marketplace, she called on her imagination to answer her problem—and there he was, standing strong and still before her, waiting to be painted! She had found her model—a farmer's horse! He would not mind posing for her, she was sure, if she did not mind painting him. In a flurry of excitement, she rushed for her easel and brushes. Today, in the Metropolitan Museum of Art in New York City, we can view a famous canvas entitled "The Horse Fair," painted by Rosa Bonheur, noted for her masterly painting of horses.

Imagination is important. So is *enthusiasm*. In the parable, the man who hid his talent in the earth lacked both. Even a superficial study of successful personalities reveals that without exception they are imbued with enthusiasm for their work and are alive with ideas for the future. They are excited about what they are doing, and they communicate the excitement to others. Their abilities take on a powerful thrust which they would lack without it.

An architect once built a model of a beautiful church which he had designed. The model was exquisite in symmetry, line, and detail, but something was missing; it was lifeless and cold. Then he placed a light inside and suddenly the inertness was gone. The little church glowed with warmth and life and beauty.

Enthusiasm does that to our abilities—it places a light inside. It makes them glow with warmth and vitality. The word itself comes from the root meaning of "god-possessed"; this makes clear both the source and the importance which the ancients attached to the quality of enthusiasm. A glance at its synonyms reveals why this should be so—eagerness, warmth, ardor, fervor, verve, vigor. Nothing kindles fire like fire; when we are aflame with enthusiasm, our powers expand and our wholeheartedness becomes contagious.

But enthusiasm, imagination, and even purpose, cannot reach satisfying objectives until they are yoked with persistent, determined effort. It follows, then, that *we must persevere in the use of our talents*.

A man overheard an aged Irishman giving some advice to a boy who was boarding a ship to seek his fortune. "Now, Michael, me boy," the old man said, "just remember the three bones and you'll get along all right." The curiosity of the bystander prompted him to ask the Irishman what he meant by the three bones. "Sure, now," replied the aged son of Erin with a twinkle in his eye, "and wouldn't it be the wishbone, the jawbone, and the backbone? It's the wishbone that keeps you going after things. It's the jawbone that helps you ask the questions that are necessary to finding them, and it's the backbone that keeps you at it until you get them!"

To find the happiness which comes through making the most of our abilities, we must persevere in using them and make them responsive to our bidding. Persistent effort often spells the difference between success and failure. As in splitting a log, in which all former ax strokes are wasted if we do not keep at it until we strike the last blow, so we waste our energies unless we demonstrate the tenacity to endure until the walls of difficulty crumble and our abilities come into their own. Certainly little of lasting worth ever has been accomplished except by those who have dared to persist in the face of frowning circumstances. Something within them was superior to the obstacles they encountered.

A final suggestion is to *fill our present place to overflowing*. Whatever position we may occupy, we can give it the benefit of our finest effort. A man may say to himself, "I am too good for this job. It is too small a position for a person of my talents. There is no opportunity here to expand my powers." In contempt, he refuses to invest his complete capacities in the meager job. Inevitably he becomes dissatisfied, restless, and unhappy. He fails his responsibility; he fails his own future opportunity; and, worst of all, he fails himself.

A successful and greatly revered businessman in a Western state says that in his early life his mother gave him a priceless gift, a vision of service. "Arthur," she told him, "it is not how much you can get from a job that is important. It is how much you can put into it that counts." The success and influence which radiate from his kindly life reveal how fully he has followed his vision. In recounting the incident, he said, "Through all the years, I have never forgotten what my mother said that day. I have tried to live by the principle of not how much, but how well."

Talent, like muscle, grows through exercise. If we fail to extend ourselves and merely go through the motions while we wait for something more fitted to our abilities to come along, we are headed for continual frustration. We may think that we have ability enough to warrant starting at the top, but almost the only chance to start at the top is in digging a hole!

Consider this fine sentence: "God has never put anyone in a place too small to grow." Wherever our place may be—on the farm, in the office, behind a counter, at a teacher's desk, in a kitchen, wearing a uniform, or caring for a child—when we fill that place to the best of our abilities, personal growth is inevitable. Three things, at least, begin to happen. We do a better job of what we are doing. We expand our talents through vigorous use. And we fit ourselves for larger responsibility and wider opportunity.

> *Many of us spend our lives searching
> for success when it is usually so close
> that we can reach out and touch it.*

Russell H. Conwell

LESSON 10

HOW TO GROW AND PROSPER IN YOUR OWN ACRE OF DIAMONDS

The lecture you are about to "hear" is one of the all-time classic pieces of success material. First delivered at a reunion of his old Civil War comrades, Russell H. Conwell went on to give the speech, *Acres of Diamonds,* more than five thousand times to enthralled audiences across the nation, earning for his efforts several million dollars with which he founded Temple University.

No one is better qualified to introduce what is to come than the man himself.

This lecture has been delivered under these circumstances: I visit a town or city, and try to arrive there early enough to see the postmaster, the barber, the keeper of the hotel, the principal of the schools, and the ministers of some of the churches, and then go into some of the factories and stores, and talk with the people, and get into sympathy with the local conditions of that town or city and see what has been their history, what opportunities they had, and what they had failed to do—and every town fails to do something—and then go to the lecture and talk to those people about the subjects which applied to their locality.

The idea—Acres of Diamonds—has continuously been precisely the same. The idea is that in this country of ours everyone has the opportunity to make more of himself in his own environment, with his own skill, with his own energy, and with his own friends!

As you can see, our faculty at the *University of Success* has no mandatory retirement age. Success, you are about to learn from an immortal, is probably right under your nose ...

When going down the Tigris and Euphrates rivers many years ago with a party of English travelers, I found myself under the direction of an old Arab guide whom we hired up at Baghdad, and I have often thought how that guide resembled our barbers in certain mental characteristics. He thought that it was not only his duty to guide us down those rivers, and do what he was paid for doing, but also to entertain us with stories curious and weird, ancient and modern, strange and familiar. Many of them I have forgotten, and I am glad I have, but there is one I shall never forget.

The old guide was leading my camel by its halter along the banks of those ancient rivers, and he told me story after story until I grew weary of his storytelling and ceased to listen. I have never been irritated with that guide when he lost his temper as I ceased listening. But I remember that he took off his Turkish cap and swung it in a circle to get my attention. I could see it through the corner of my eye, but I was determined not to look straight at him for fear he would tell another story. I did finally look, and as soon as I did he went right into another story.

Said he, "I will tell you a story now which I reserve for my particular friends." When he emphasized the words "particular friends," I listened, and I have ever been glad I did. I really feel devoutly thankful, that there are 1,674 young men who have been carried through college by this lecture who are also glad that I did listen. The old guide told me that there once lived not far from the River Indus an ancient Persian by the name of Ali Hafed. He said that Ali Hafed owned a very large farm, that he had orchards, grainfields, and gardens; that he had money at interest, and was a wealthy and contented man. He was contented because he was wealthy, and wealthy because he was contented. One day there visited that old Persian farmer one of those ancient Buddhist priests, one of the wise men of the East. He sat down by the fire and told the old farmer how this world of ours was made. He said that this world was once a mere bank of fog, and that the Almighty thrust His finger into this bank of fog, and began slowly to move

His finger around, increasing the speed until at last He whirled this bank of fog into a solid ball of fire. Then it went rolling through the universe, burning its way through other banks of fog, and condensed the moisture without, until it fell in floods of rain upon its hot surface, and cooled the outward crust. Then the internal fires bursting outward through the crust threw up the mountains and hills, the valleys, the plains and prairies of this wonderful world of ours. If this internal molten mass came bursting out and cooled very quickly it became granite; less quickly copper, less quickly silver, less quickly gold, and, after gold, diamonds were made.

Said the old priest, "A diamond is a congealed drop of sunlight." Now that is literally scientifically true, that a diamond is an actual deposit of carbon from the sun. The old priest told Ali Hafed that if he had one diamond the size of his thumb he could purchase the county, and if he had a mine of diamonds he could place his children upon thrones through the influence of their great wealth.

Ali Hafed heard all about diamonds, how much they were worth, and went to his bed that night a poor man. He had not lost anything, but he was poor because he was discontented, and discontented because he feared he was poor. He said, "I want a mine of diamonds," and he lay awake all night.

Early in the morning he sought out the priest. I know by experience that a priest is very cross when awakened early in the morning, and when he shook that old priest out of his dreams, Ali Hafed said to him:

"Will you tell me where I can find diamonds?"

"Diamonds! What do you want with diamonds?" "Why, I wish to be immensely rich." "Well, then, go along and find them. That is all you have to do; go and find them, and then you have them." "But I don't know where to go." "Well, if you will find a river that runs through white sands, between high mountains, in those white sands you will always find diamonds." "I don't believe there is any such river." "Oh yes, there are plenty of them. All you have to do is to go and find them, and then you have them." Said Ali Hafed, "I will go."

So he sold his farm, collected his money, left his family in charge of a neighbor, and away he went in search of diamonds. He began his search, very properly to my mind, at the Mountains of the Moon. Afterward he came around into Palestine, then wandered on into Europe, and at last when his money was all spent and he was in rags, wretchedness, and poverty, he stood on the shore of that bay at Barcelona, in Spain, when a great tidal wave came rolling in between the pillars of Hercules, and the poor, afflicted, suffering, dying man could not resist the awful temptation to cast himself into that incoming tide, and he sank beneath its foaming crest, never to rise in this life again.

When that old guide had told me that awfully sad story he stopped the camel I was riding on and went back to fix the baggage that was coming off another camel, and I had an opportunity to muse over his story while he was gone. I remember saying to myself, "Why did he reserve that story for his 'particular friends'?" There seemed to be no beginning, no middle, no end, nothing to it. That was the first story I had ever heard told in my life, and would be the first one I ever read, in which the hero was killed in the first chapter. I had but one chapter of that story, and the hero was dead.

When the guide came back and took up the halter of my camel, he went right ahead with the story, into the second chapter, just as though there had been no break. The man who purchased Ali Hafed's farm one day led his camel into the garden to drink, and as that camel put its nose into the shallow water of that garden brook, Ali Hafed's successor noticed a curious flash of light from the white sands of the stream. He pulled out a black stone having an eye of light reflecting all the hues of the rainbow. He took the pebble into the house and put it on the mantel which covers the central fires, and forgot all about it.

A few days later this same old priest came in to visit Ali Hafed's successor, and the moment he opened that drawing room door he saw that flash of light on the mantel, and he rushed up to it, and shouted: "Here is a diamond! Has Ali Hafed returned?" "Oh no, Ali Hafed has not returned, and that is not a diamond. That is nothing but a stone we found right out here in our own garden." "But," said the priest, "I tell you I know a diamond when I see it. I know positively that is a diamond."

Then together they rushed out into that old garden and stirred up the white sands with their fingers, and lo! there came up other more beautiful and valuable gems than the first. "Thus," said the guide to me, and, friends, it is historically true, "was discovered the diamond-mine of Golconda, the most magnificent diamond-mine in all the history of humanity, excelling the Kimberly itself. The Kohinoor, and the Orloff of the crown jewels of England and Russia, the largest on earth, came from that mine."

When that old Arab guide told me the second chapter of his story, he then took off his Turkish cap and swung it around in the air again to get my attention to the moral. Those Arab guides have morals to their stories, although they are not always moral. As he swung his hat, he said to me, "Had Ali Hafed remained at home and dug in his own cellar, or underneath his own wheatfields, or in his own garden, instead of wretchedness, starvation, and death by suicide in a strange land, he would have had "acres of diamonds." For every acre of that old farm, yes, every shovelful, afterward revealed gems which since have decorated the crowns of monarchs."

When he had added the moral to his story I saw why he reserved it for "his particular friends." But I did not tell him I could see it. It was that mean old Arab's way of going around a thing like a lawyer, to say indirectly what he did not dare say directly, that "in his private opinion there was a certain young man then traveling down the Tigris River who might better be at home in America." I did not tell him I could see that, but I told him his story reminded me of one, and I told it to him quick, and I think I will tell it to you.

I told him of a man out in California in 1847, who owned a ranch. He heard they had discovered gold in southern California, and so with a passion for gold he sold his ranch to Colonel Sutter, and away he went, never to come back. Colonel Sutter put a mill upon a stream that ran through that ranch, and one day his little girl brought some wet sand from the raceway into their home and sifted it through her fingers before the fire, and in that falling sand a visitor saw the first shining scales of real gold that were ever discovered in California. The man who had owned that ranch wanted gold, and he could have secured it for the mere taking. Indeed, thirty-eight million dollars has been taken out of a very few acres since then. About eight years ago I delivered this lecture in a city that stands on that farm, and they told me that a one-third owner for years and years had been getting one hundred and twenty dollars in gold every fifteen minutes, sleeping or waking, without taxation. You and I would enjoy an income like that—if we didn't have to pay an income tax.

But a better illustration really than that occurred here in our own Pennsylvania. If there is anything I enjoy above another on the platform, it is to get one of these German audiences in Pennsylvania before me, and fire that at them, and I enjoy it to-night. There was a man living in Pennsylvania, not unlike some Pennsylvanians you have seen, who owned a farm, and he did with that farm just what I should do with a farm if I owned one in Pennsylvania—he sold it. But before he sold it he decided to secure employment collecting coal oil for his cousin, who was in the business in Canada, where they first discovered oil on this continent. They dipped it from the running streams at that early time. So this Pennsylvania farmer wrote to his cousin asking for employment. You see, friends, this farmer was not altogether a foolish man. No, he was not. He did not leave his farm until he had something else to do. *Of all the simpletons the stars shine on I don't know of a worse one than the man who leaves one job before he has gotten another.* That has especial reference to my profession, and has no reference whatever to a man seeking a divorce. When he wrote to his cousin for employment, his cousin replied, "I cannot engage you because you know nothing about the oil business."

Well, then the old farmer said, "I will know," and with most commendable zeal (characteristic of the students of Temple University) he set himself to the study of the whole subject. He began away back at the second day of God's creation when this world was covered thick and deep with that rich vegetation which since has turned to the primitive beds of coal. He studied the subject until he found that the drainings really of those rich beds of coal furnished the coal oil that was worth pumping, and then he found how it came up with the living springs. He studied until he knew what it looked like, smelled like, tasted like, and how to refine it. Now said he in his letter to his cousin, "I understand the oil business." His cousin answered, "All right, come on."

So he sold his farm, according to the county record, for $833 (even money, "no cents"). He had scarcely gone from that place before the man who purchased the spot went out to arrange for the watering of the cattle. He found the previous owner had gone out years before and put a plank across the brook back of the barn, edgewise into the surface of the water just a few inches. The purpose of that plank at that sharp angle across the brook was to throw over to the other bank a dreadful-looking scum through which the cattle would not put their noses. But with that plank there to throw it all over to one side, the cattle would drink below, and thus that man who had gone to Canada had been himself damming back for twenty-three years a flood of coal oil which the state geologists of Pennsylvania declared to us ten years later was even then worth a hundred millions of dollars to our state, and four years ago our geologist declared the discovery to be worth to our state a thousand millions of dollars. The man who owned that territory on which the city of Titusville now stands, and those Pleasantville valleys, had studied the subject from the second day of God's creation clear down to the present time. He studied it until he knew all about it, and yet he is said to have sold the whole of it for $833, and again I say, "no sense."

As I come here tonight and look around this audience I am seeing again what through these fifty years I have continually seen—men who are making precisely that same mistake. I often wish I could see the younger people, and would that the Academy had been filled tonight with our high school scholars and our grammar school scholars, that I could have them to talk to. While I would have preferred such an audience as that, because they are most susceptible, as they have not grown up into their prejudices as we have, they have not gotten into any custom that they cannot break, they have not met with any failures as we have; and while I could perhaps do such an audience as that more good than I can do grown-up people, yet I will do the best I can with the material I have. I say to you that you have "acres of diamonds" in Philadelphia right where you now live. "Oh," but you will say, "you cannot know much about your city if you think there are any 'acres of diamonds' here."

I was greatly interested in that account in the newspaper of the young man who found that diamond in North Carolina. It was one of the purest diamonds that has ever been discovered, and it has several predecessors near the same locality. I went to a distinguished professor in mineralogy and asked him where he thought those diamonds came from. The professor secured the map of the geologic formations of our continent, and traced it. He said it went either through the underlying carboniferous strata adapted for such production, westward through Ohio and the Mississippi, or in more probability came eastward through Virginia and up the shore of the Atlantic Ocean. It is a fact that the diamonds were there, for they have been discovered and sold; and that they were carried down there during the drift period, from some northern locality. Now who can say but some person going down with his drill in Philadelphia will find some trace of a diamond-mine yet down here? Oh, friends! you cannot say that you are not over one of the greatest diamond-mines in the world, for such a diamond as that only comes from the most profitable mines that are found on earth.

But it serves simply to illustrate my thought, which I emphasize by saying if you do not have the actual diamond-mines literally you have all that they would be good for to you. Because now that the Queen of England has given the greatest compliment ever conferred upon American woman for her attire because she did not appear with any jewels at all at the late reception in England, it has almost done away with the use of diamonds anyhow. All you would care for would be the few you would wear if you wish to be modest, and the rest you would sell for money.

Now then, I say again that the opportunity to get rich, to attain unto great wealth, is here in Philadelphia now, within the reach of almost every man and woman who hears me speak tonight, and I mean just what I say. I have not come to this platform even under these circumstances to recite something to you. I have come to tell you what in God's sight I believe to be the truth, and if the years of life have been of any value to me in the attainment of common sense, I know I am right; that the men and women sitting here, who found it difficult perhaps to buy a ticket to this lecture or gathering tonight, have within their reach "acres of diamonds," opportunities to get largely wealthy. There never was a place on earth more adapted than the city of Philadelphia today, and never in the history of the world did a poor man without capital have such an opportunity to get rich quickly and honestly as he has now in our city. I say it is the truth, and I want you to accept it as such; for if you think I have come to simply recite something, then I would better not be here.

But you will say, "You cannot do anything of the kind. You cannot start without capital." Young man, let me illustrate for a moment. I must do it. It is my duty to every young man and woman, because we are all going into business very soon on the same plan. Young man, remember if you know what people need you have gotten more knowledge of a fortune than any amount of capital can give you.

There was a poor man out of work living in Hingham, Massachusetts. He lounged around the house until one day his wife told him to get out and work, and, as he lived in Massachusetts, he obeyed his wife. He went out and sat down on the shore of the bay, and whittled a soaked shingle into a wooden chain. His children that evening quarreled over it, and he whittled a second one to keep peace. While he was whittling the second one a neighbor came in and said: "Why don't you whittle toys and sell them? You could make money at that." "Oh," he said, "I would not know what to make." "Why don't you ask your own children right here in your own house what to make?" "What is the use of trying that?" said the carpenter. "My children are different from other people's children." (I used to see people like that when I taught school.) But he acted upon the hint, and the next morning when Mary came down the stairway, he asked, "What do you want for a toy?" She began to tell him she would like a doll's bed, a doll's washstand, a doll's carriage, a little doll's umbrella, and went on with a list of things that would take him a lifetime to supply. So, consulting his own children, in his own house, he took the firewood, for he had no money to buy lumber, and whittled those strong, unpainted Hingham toys that were for so many years known all over the world. That man began to make those toys for his own children, and then made copies and sold them through the boot-and-shoe store next door. He began to make a little money, and then a little more, and Mr. Lawson, in his *Frenzied Finance* says that that man is the richest man in old Massachusetts, and I think it is the truth. And that man is worth a hundred million dollars today, and has been only thirty-four years making it on that one principle—that one must judge that what his own children like at home other people's children would like in their homes, too; to judge the human heart by oneself, by one's wife or by one's children. It is the royal road to success in manufacturing. "Oh," but you say, "didn't he have any capital?" Yes, a penknife, but I don't know that he had paid for that.

I spoke thus to an audience in New Britain, Connecticut, and a woman four seats back went home and tried to take off her collar, and the collar-button stuck in the buttonhole. She threw it out and said, "I am going to get something better than that to put on collars." Her husband said: "After what Cornwell said tonight, you see there is a need of an improved collar-fastener that is easier to handle. There is a human need; there is a great fortune. Now, then, get up a collar-button and get rich." He made fun of her, and consquently made fun of me, and that is one of the saddest things which comes over me like a deep cloud of midnight sometimes— although I have worked so hard for more than half a century, yet how little I have ever really done. Notwithstanding the greatness and the handsomeness of your compliment tonight, I do not believe there is one in ten of you who is going to make a million of dollars because you are here tonight; but it is not my fault, it is yours. I say that sincerely. What is the use of my talking if people never do what I advise them to do? When her husband ridiculed her, she made up her mind she would make a better collar-button, and when a person makes up her mind "she will," and does not say anything about it, she does it. It was that New England woman who invented the snap button which you can find anywhere now. It was first a collar-button with a spring cap attached to the outer side. Any of you who wear modern waterproofs know the button that simply pushes together, and when you unbutton it you simply pull it apart. That is the button to which I refer, and which she invented. She afterward invented several other buttons, and then invested in more, and then was taken into partnership with great factories. Now that woman goes overseas every summer in her private steamship—yes, and takes her husband with her! If her husband were to die, she would have money enough left now to buy a foreign duke or count or some such title as that at the latest quotations.

Now what is my lesson in that incident? It is this: I told her then, though I did not know her, what I now say to you, "Your wealth is too near to you. You are looking right over it"; and she had to look over it because it was right under her chin.

Who are the great inventors of the world? Again this lesson comes before us. The great inventor sits next to you, or you are the person yourself. "Oh," but you will say, "I have never invented anything in my life." Neither did the great inventors until they discovered one great secret. Do you think it is a man with a head like a bushel measure or a man like a stroke of lightning? It is neither. The really great man is a plain, straightforward, everyday, common-sense man. You would not dream that he was a great inventor if you did not see something he had actually done. His neighbors do not regard him so great. You never see anything great over your back fence. You say there is no greatness among your neighbors. It is all away off somewhere else. Their greatness is ever so simple, so plain, so earnest, so practical, that the neighbors and friends never recognize it.

Greatness consists not in the holding of some future office, but really consists in doing great deeds with little means and the accomplishment of vast purposes from the private ranks of life. To be great at all one must be great here, now, in Philadelphia. He who can give to this city better streets and better sidewalks, better schools and more colleges, more happiness and more civilization, more of God, he will be great anywhere. Let every man or woman here, if you never hear me again, remember this, that if you wish to be great at all, you must begin where you are and what you are, in Philadelphia, now. He who can give to his city any blessing, he who can be a good citizen while he lives here, he who can make better homes, he who can be a blessing whether he works in the shop or sits behind the counter or keeps house, whatever be his life, he who would be great anywhere, must first be great in his own Philadelphia.

SEMESTER THREE

It is the mind that maketh good or ill,
that maketh wretch or happy, rich or poor.

Edmund Spenser

James Allen

LESSON 11

HOW TO TRANSFORM YOUR THOUGHTS INTO REALITY

Already, with two important semesters under your belt, you have a much greater understanding of why you are the way you are and, more important, you are beginning to realize that you need not be a superman or wonder woman in order to accomplish great things with your life.

Now, with your groundwork in place and the awareness of your potential so multiplied, are you ready to take that first step forward?

Not quite. Not until you digest one of the oldest principles of success—*you are literally what you think and your character is the complete sum of all your thoughts!* So, what you are thinking now, and tomorrow, and next month, is what you will eventually become. This gentle warning has resounded through the ages but none ever delivered it better than a little-known essayist from the small village of Ilfracombe on the Devon coast of England. James Allen's small masterpiece, *As a Man Thinketh,* from which this lesson is taken, has been constantly in print for almost a hundred years and he is undoubtedly one of the most quoted writers in all of history.

What is it that you truly seek from life? Think long on this. "Man is made or unmade by himself; in the armory of thought he forges the weapons by which he destroys himself; he also fashions the tools by which he builds for himself heavenly mansions of joy and strength and peace."

Success, love, happiness, contentment, wealth ... if these are the things you want, you are about to discover how their roots

107

all grow from seeds of thought, seeds that only you can plant now
that you understand this great truth and the control you have over
your own destiny . . .

All that a man achieves and all that he fails to achieve is the
direct result of his own thoughts. In a justly ordered universe,
where loss of equipoise would mean total destruction, individual
responsibility must be absolute. A man's weakness and strength,
purity and impurity, are his own, and not another man's; they are
brought about by himself, and not by another; and they can only
be altered by himself, never by another. His condition is also his
own, and not another man's. His suffering and his happiness are
evolved from within. As he thinks, so he is; as he continues to
think, so he remains.

A strong man cannot help a weaker unless that weaker is
willing to be helped, and even then the weak man must become
strong of himself; he must, by his own efforts, develop the strength
which he admires in another. None but himself can alter his
condition.

It has been usual for men to think and to say, "Many men
are slaves because one is an oppressor; let us hate the oppressor."
Now, however, there is among an increasing few a tendency to
reverse this judgment, and to say, "One man is an oppressor
because many are slaves; let us despise the slaves." The truth is
that oppressor and slave are cooperators in ignorance, and, while
seeming to afflict each other, are in reality afflicting themselves. A
perfect Knowledge perceives the action of law in the weakness of
the oppressed and the misapplied power of the oppressor; a perfect Love, seeing the suffering which both states entail, condemns
neither; a perfect Compassion embraces both oppressor and
oppressed.

He who has conquered weakness, and has put away all
selfish thoughts, belongs neither to oppressor nor oppressed. He is
free.

A man can only rise, conquer, and achieve by lifting up his
thoughts. He can only remain weak, and abject, and miserable by
refusing to lift up his thoughts.

Before a man can achieve anything, even in worldly things,
he must lift his thoughts above slavish animal indulgence. He may

not, in order to succeed, give up *all* animality and selfishness, by any means; but a portion of it must, at least, be sacrificed. A man whose first thought is bestial indulgence could neither think clearly nor plan methodically; he could not find and develop his latent resources, and would fail in any undertaking. Not having commenced only to control his thoughts, he is not in a position to control affairs and to adopt serious responsibilities. He is not fit to act independently and stand alone. But he is limited only by the thoughts which he chooses.

There can be no progress, no achievement without sacrifice, and a man's worldly success will be in the measure that he sacrifices his confused animal thoughts, and fixes his mind on the development of his plans, and the strengthening of his resolution and self-reliance. And the higher he lifts his thoughts, the more upright and righteous he becomes, the greater will be his success, the more blessed and enduring will be his achievements.

The universe does not favor the greedy, the dishonest, the vicious, although on the mere surface it may sometimes appear to do so; it helps the honest, the magnanimous, the virtuous. All the great Teachers of the ages have declared this in varying forms, and to prove and know it a man has but to persist in making himself more and more virtuous by lifting up his thoughts.

Intellectual achievements are the result of thought consecrated to the search for knowledge, or for the beautiful and true in life and nature. Such achievements may be sometimes connected with vanity and ambition, but they are not the outcome of those characteristics; they are the natural outgrowth of long and arduous effort, and of pure and unselfish thoughts.

Spiritual achievements are the consummation of holy aspirations. He who lives constantly in the conception of noble and lofty thoughts, who dwells upon all that is pure and unselfish, will, as surely as the sun reaches its zenith and the moon its full, become wise and noble in character, and rise into a position of influence and blessedness.

Achievement, of whatever kind, is the crown of effort, the diadem of thought. By the aid of self-control, resolution, purity, righteousness, and well-directed thought, a man ascends; by the aid of animality, indolence, impurity, corruption, and confusion of thought, a man descends.

A man may rise to high success in the world, and even to lofty altitudes in the spiritual realm, and again descend into weakness and wretchedness by allowing arrogant, selfish, and corrupt thoughts to take possession of him.

Victories attained by right thoughts can only be maintained

by watchfulness. Many give way when success is assured, and rapidly fall back into failure.

All achievements, whether in the business, intellectual, or spiritual world, are the result of definitely directed thought, are governed by the same law and are of the same method; the only difference lies in *the object of attainment*.

He who would accomplish little must sacrifice little; he who would achieve much must sacrifice much; he who would attain highly must sacrifice greatly.

VISIONS AND IDEALS

The dreamers are the saviors of the world. As the visible world is sustained by the invisible, so man, through all their trials and sins and sordid vocations, are nourished by the beautiful visions of their solitary dreamers. Humanity cannot forget its dreamers; it cannot let their ideals fade and die; it lives in them; it knows them as the *realities* which it shall one day see and know.

Composer, sculptor, painter, poet, prophet, sage, these are the makers of the afterworld, the architects of heaven. The world is beautiful because they have lived; without them, laboring humanity would perish.

He who cherishes a beautiful vision, a lofty ideal in his heart, will one day realize it. Columbus cherished a vision of another world, and he discovered it; Copernicus fostered the vision of a multiplicity of worlds and a wider universe, and he revealed it; Buddha beheld the vision of a spiritual world of stainless beauty and perfect peace, and he entered into it.

Cherish your visions; cherish your ideals; cherish the music that stirs in your heart, the beauty that forms in your mind, the loveliness that drapes your purest thoughts, for out of them will grow all delightful conditions, all heavenly environment; of these, if you but remain true to them, your world will at last be built.

To desire is to obtain; to aspire is to achieve. Shall man's basest desires receive the fullest measure of gratification, and his purest aspirations starve for lack of sustenance? Such is not the Law: such a condition of things can never obtain: "Ask and receive."

Dream lofty dreams, and as you dream, so shall you become. Your Vision is the promise of what you shall one day be; your Ideal is the prophecy of what you shall at last unveil.

The greatest achievement was at first and for a time a dream. The oak sleeps in the acorn; the bird waits in the egg; and in the highest vision of the soul a waking angel stirs. Dreams are the seedlings of realities.

Your circumstances may be uncongenial, but they shall not long remain so if you but perceive an Ideal and strive to reach it. You cannot travel *within* and stand still *without*. Here is a youth hard pressed by poverty and labor; confined long hours in an unhealthy workshop; unschooled, and lacking all the arts of refinement. But he dreams of better things; he thinks of intelligence, of refinement, of grace and beauty. He conceives of, mentally builds up, an ideal condition of life; the vision of a wider liberty and a larger scope takes possession of him; unrest urges him to action, and he utilizes all his spare time and means, small though they are, to the development of his latent powers and resources. Very soon so altered has his mind become that the workshop can no longer hold him. It has become so out of harmony with his mentality that it falls out of his life as a garment is cast aside, and, with the growth of opportunities which fit the scope of his expanding powers, he passes out of it forever.

Years later we see this youth as a full-grown man. We find him a master of certain forces of the mind which he wields with worldwide influence and almost unequalled power. In his hands he holds the cords of gigantic responsibilities; he speaks, and lo! lives are changed; men and women hang upon his words and remold their characters, and, sunlike, he becomes the fixed and luminous center around which innumerable destinies resolve. He has realized the Vision of his youth. He has become one with his Ideal.

And you, too, youthful reader, will realise the Vision (not the idle wish) of your heart, be it base or beautiful, or a mixture of both, for you will always gravitate toward that which you, secretly, most love. Into your hands will be placed the exact results of your own thoughts; you will receive that which you earn; no more, no less. Whatever your present environment may be, you will fall, remain, or rise with your thoughts, your Vision, your Ideal. You will become as small as your controlling desire; as great as your dominant aspiration: in the beautiful words of Stanton Kirkham Davis,

You may be keeping accounts, and presently you shall walk out of the door that for so long has seemed to you the barrier of your ideals, and shall find yourself before an audience— the pen still behind your ear, the ink stains on your fingers— and then and there shall pour out the torrent of your inspiration. You may be driving sheep, and you shall wander to the city—bucolic and openmouthed; shall wander under the intrepid guidance of the spirit into the studio of the master, and after a time he shall say, "I have nothing more to teach you." And now you have become the master, who did so recently dream of great things while driving sheep. You shall lay down the saw and the plane to take upon yourself the regeneration of the world.

The thoughtless, the ignorant, and the indolent, seeing only the apparent effects of things and not the things themselves, talk of luck, of fortune, and chance. Seeing a man grow rich, they say, "How lucky he is!" Observing another become intellectual, they exclaim, "How highly favored he is!" And noting the saintly character and wide influence of another, they remark, "How chance aids him at every turn!" They do not see the trials and failures and struggles which these men have voluntarily encountered in order to gain their experience; have no knowledge of the sacrifices they have made, of the undaunted efforts they have put forth, of the faith they have exercised, that they might overcome the apparently insurmountable, and realize the Vision of their heart. They do not know the darkness and the heartaches; they only see the light and joy, and call it "luck"; do not see the long and arduous journey, but only behold the pleasant goal, and call it "good fortune"; do not understand the process, but only perceive the result, and call it "chance."

In all human affairs there are *efforts*, and there are *results*, and the strength of the effort is the measure of the result. Chance is not. "Gifts," powers, material, intellectual, and spiritual possessions are the fruits of effort; they are thoughts completed, objects accomplished, visions realized.

The Vision that you glorify in your mind, the Ideal that you enthrone in your heart—this you will build your life by, this you will become.

*You possess a potent force
that you either use, or misuse,
hundreds of times every day.*

J. Martin Kohe

LESSON 12

HOW TO USE YOUR GREATEST POWER TO CHANGE YOUR LIFE

Now you know that every action you take has its origin as a thought, and that the sum of all your actions produces the person that you are.

Do you accept James Allen's concept, which was also that of Buddha, Socrates, Mohammed, and scores of other wise men?

If you do, can you explain the great mystery of why we are not all happy, healthy, and wealthy? One person could, and did, in a challenging book, *Your Greatest Power.* J. Martin Kohe was a publisher and distributor of inspirational self-help books during the first half of this century and among his publications were Napoleon Hill's two classics, *The Laws of Success,* and *Think and Grow Rich,* both of which you will enjoy in later lessons.

Those who fail, those who wallow in self-pity, those who always complain—according to Mr. Kohe—do so because they fail to use the greatest power they possess, or they misuse it with disastrous results that brings grief to themselves and to those whose lives they touch.

Since you, and only you, are in charge of *your* mind, you also have full reign over this great power, and by using it wisely you cannot help but become a better person, in your business and your personal life.

The odds are great that you will find yourself returning to this lesson, again and again, in the months to come, just to be reminded of a simple law of life that we all should know, but many unfortunately do not . . .

You are the possessor of a great and wonderful power. This power, when properly applied, will bring confidence instead of timidity, calmness instead of confusion, poise instead of restlessness, and peace of mind in place of heartache.

Millions of people are complaining about their lot, disgusted with life . . . and the way things are going, not realizing that there is a power which they possess which will permit them to take a new lease on life. Once you recognize this power and begin to use it, you can change your entire life and make it the way you would like to have it. A life that was filled with sorrow can be a life filled with joy. Failure can be turned into success. Where poverty once gripped an individual's life, it can be changed to prosperity. Timidity can be turned into confidence. A life of disappointment can become a life of interesting experiences and pleasant associations. Fear can be changed to freedom.

Too many times, as life goes on, a person may have had a number of reverses; he may have run into a series of difficulties; he may even have had a number of various troubles to contend with. Before long he adopts the attitude that life is difficult, that life is a battle, that the cards are stacked against him . . . so what's the use . . . "you can't win." Then this same individual settles back and is convinced that no matter what you do is "no good." Beaten in his own desire to win in life, he finally turns to his children, hoping that with them it will be different. Sometimes, this is a way out, and sometimes the children fall into the same way of life as the parent. Many times the individual comes to the conclusion that there is only one way out, and he finally comes to the end of life through his own hand . . . suicide.

Yet, all this time, the individual fails to discover this great power that will change his life. He doesn't recognize it . . . he doesn't even know it exists . . . he sees millions of others struggling the way he is and decides that THIS IS LIFE.

Raimundo DeOvies tells a story that, when the great library of Alexandria was burned, one book was saved. But it was not a valuable book; and so a poor man, who could read a little, bought it for a few coppers. It was not very interesting; yet there was a most interesting thing in it! It was a thin strip of vellum on which was written the secret of the "Touchstone."

The touchstone was a small pebble that could turn any common metal into pure gold. The writing explained that it was on the shores of the Black Sea, lying among thousands and thousands of other pebbles which looked exactly like it. But the secret was this. The real stone would feel warm, while ordinary pebbles are cold. So the man sold his few belongings, bought some simple supplies, camped on the seashore, and began testing pebbles. This was his plan.

He knew that if he picked up ordinary pebbles and threw them down again because they were cold, he might pick up the same pebble hundreds of times. So, when he felt one that was cold, he threw it into the sea. He spent a whole day doing this and there were none of them the touchstone. Then he spent a week, a month, a year, three years; but he did not find the touchstone. Yet he went on and on this way. Pick up a pebble. It's cold. Throw it into the sea. And so on and on.

But one morning he picked up a pebble and it was *warm* . . . he threw it into the sea. He had formed the "habit" of throwing them into the sea. He had gotten so into the habit of throwing them into the sea, that when the ONE HE WANTED CAME ALONG . . . HE STILL THREW IT AWAY.

Oh! How many times have we contacted this GREAT POWER and did not recognize it? How many times have we had THIS GREAT POWER right in our hands and we threw it away, because we did not recognize it? How often have we seen it before our very eyes? How many times have we seen THIS GREAT POWER demonstrated right before us? Yet, we did not see it with all its possibilities, with all its wonderworking effects. That is the reason we have devoted this entire treatise to THIS GREAT POWER . . . THE GREATEST POWER THAT MAN POSSESSES!

Before we tell you what this GREAT POWER is, we want you to know about an incident that took place in Africa. There was an explorer who went into the wilds of Africa. He took a number of trinkets along with him for the natives. Among some of the things that he took with him were two full-size mirrors. He placed these two mirrors against two different trees, and then sat down to talk to some of his men about the exploration. Then the explorer noticed that a savage approached the mirror with a spear in his hand. As he looked into the mirror, he saw his reflection. He began to jab his opponent in the mirror as though it were a real savage, going through all the motions of killing him. Of course, he broke the mirror into bits. In the meantime, the explorer walked over to the savage and asked him why he smashed the mirror. The native replied, "He go kill me. I kill him first." The explorer explained to the savage that that was not the purpose of the mirror, and then led the savage over to the second mirror. He explained to him. "Look, the mirror is an object whereby you may see if your hair is combed straight, to see if the paint on your face is proper, to see how chesty you are, and see how muscular you are." The savage replied, "Oh! me no know."

So it is with so many millions of people. They go through life fighting it. They expect a battle at every turn and that is the way it turns out. They expect to have enemies, and they certainly do. They expect to have one difficulty after another, and that is exactly the way it happens. "If it isn't one thing, it's another . . . there is always something" . . . and that is the way it has been and will continue to be for millions of people who fail to recognize this GREAT POWER. This GREAT POWER that could completely change the world remains as hidden as the diamonds from the farmer who had them in his own backyard. Millions of people will continue to live plain, ordinary, miserable lives because this GREAT POWER escapes them and they never have been able to catch up with it. YOU CAN'T FIGHT LIFE. You have tried it. Millions have tried it and have failed. Then what is the answer? THE ANSWER IS THAT WE MUST UNDERSTAND LIFE . . . IF WE WISH TO MAKE THE MOST OF IT.

The amazing part about this power is that anyone and everyone can use it. It doesn't require any special training or education. It isn't a power that requires any special aptitudes to make it work successfully. It isn't a power that anyone has any special claims to, nor does it require wealth or prestige to make it work. It is a power that everyone is given at birth, whether he be rich or poor, successful or unsuccessful, whether he be born on the right side of the tracks or not. The sooner we recognize this power, the quicker we get on the main road and stay there. The more of us who will get on the main road and stay there, the more hope will spring in the hearts of others to follow this healthy pattern of life.

Millions of people fail to realize that when they go into a shoe store, they may choose to buy a pair of black shoes or they may choose to buy a pair of brown shoes; that when they go into a clothing store, they choose to buy a light garment or they choose to buy a dark garment; that when they turn on the radio they may choose to tune in one station or they may choose to tune in another station; that when they go into an ice-cream parlor, they may choose to buy a chocolate sundae or a pineapple soda; that when they go to the movies, they may choose to go to a neighborhood movie or they may choose to go to a downtown movie. Yes, it is true, if you CHOOSE, when you go on a vacation, to go to the seashore instead of going to the mountains, that YOU MADE THIS CHOICE. When you buy a car YOU CHOOSE to buy a car of one particular make, or YOU CHOOSE to buy a car of another manufacturer. In other words, THE GREATEST POWER THAT A PERSON POSSESSES IS

THE POWER TO CHOOSE.

Yes, you have this power, regardless of your religious beliefs. You choose the shoes, the car, the radio program, the picture show, the vacation, the mate. You have this power. There was nothing outside of yourself to force you to make the decision that you did. You did it, because you made this choice. You made this choice because YOU WANTED IT SO. If the choice was bad, then, of course, we want something or someone to blame. So, some people will say, "It was God's Will." But was it? You are probably familiar with the old saying "God helps those who help themselves." Regardless of what we believe regarding God, God does give each and every man and woman the right TO HELP HIMSELF . . . OR IN OTHER WORDS, *THE RIGHT TO CHOOSE*.

If we choose to eat so much that we make ourselves sick, who is to blame? If we choose to drive our cars so fast that we cannot control them, who is to blame? If we choose to allow ourselves to have nasty, disagreeable personalities, who is to blame? If we try to become the "richest man in the cemetery" and make ourselves invalids, who is to blame? If we have failed to learn how to live, whom shall we blame? God? Oh, no! GOD LOVES YOU. He doesn't hurt anybody. We hurt ourselves through the bad use of this GREAT POWER that God gave us . . . THE POWER TO CHOOSE.

*You are an extremely valuable, worthwhile,
significant person even though your present
circumstances may have you feeling otherwise.*

James W. Newman

LESSON 13

HOW TO RAISE YOUR SELF-ESTEEM
AND DEVELOP SELF-CONFIDENCE

"The only event in the entire world you can control is what you are thinking and feeling at the present instant—but that is enough! That's all you *need* to be able to control."

Those words are from the pen of James W. Newman, whose PACE (Personal and Company Effectiveness) Seminars have already had a profound and positive effect on hundreds of thousands of success-minded men and women of all ages, from many nations.

In his best-selling book, *Release Your Brakes!* from which this lesson is taken, this multitalented member of our faculty employs an analogy we all can understand:

Have you ever driven your automobile with the brakes on? I suppose that most of us who have driven for any length of time have had that experience. I can remember times when I have arrived at my destination, reached down to pull on the parking brake, and found that it had been on all the time that I had been driving. What a ridiculous way to drive a car!

Yet, without realizing it—or intending to do so—you are moving through life with your brakes partly set. The horsepower is there, but the vast areas of potential are blocked, bottled up, restricted from effective application.

What do you think of yourself? Do you like the person you think you are? As you can see, we're still dealing with your mind, and your thoughts.

If your self-esteem, the image of how you see yourself, is on the low side of the scale, then you are probably driving with your brakes on and that's not allowed on this campus ...

How do you feel about your worthiness and importance as a human being? That feeling—your level of self-esteem—is one of the most fundamental and vital attitude structures in your "REALITY" system. High self-esteem is an almost universal common denominator of excellence—a releasing mechanism that allows your potential to flow easily and freely.

You have developed a pattern of "truth" about your value as a part of your self-image, and you tend to behave in a manner that is consistent with that attitude. Your self-esteem began to develop in the early years of your life. When you were very small you got a lot of messages and signals from parents and other experts about what kind of person you were. Some of those signals were very positive, loving, encouraging, and reinforcing. *"I love you." "You're a great kid!" "I'm glad you're a part of our family."*

Some of the messages from those very important people in your childhood may not have been so positive. *"Pick up your feet, clumsy!" "What did you do a stupid thing like that for?"*

But, here's an important point. It was not just what *kind* of messages you received, but what you *did* with those messages that counted. Look at that very carefully. It was not what those other people, those "experts," those authority figures *said* to you that counted, nearly so much as what you were *thinking and feeling within yourself* about what you were perceiving. That is what built your level of self-esteem. Your own unique personal feeling of worthiness was started in those early years with your own programming process; you have been building and revising it ever since with your conscious-level thoughts and feelings about yourself. Your present level of self-esteem is the cumulative result of the positive and negative rocks which your thoughts and feelings have deposited on that scale since you were born.

Self-esteem is a matter of degree. You don't either have it or not have it. You are somewhere on a scale ranging from the very negative to the very positive—from low to high self-esteem. The person who excels, the high performance person, tends to function most of the time toward the upper end of the scale—most of the time feels a very real, honest, positive sense of personal worth and value.

The person at the low end of the scale is convinced that he is worthless, insignificant, unlikable. He is unsure of his abilities, eager to stay close to home—to do things that are familiar and easy. He "knows" there isn't much chance that he will do anything very useful, is uncomfortable when given a compliment or praise, feels little control over his future, and is sure things will get worse in the future. Unfortunately, there are a great many people in this world who live with that kind of self-image—who genuinely, honestly, deeply *feel* that way about themselves. Negative as it may be, it's "the way things are" for a lot of people. It's easy enough to see how that kind of "REALITY" applies the brakes to a person's effectiveness.

As you reflect on how it must feel to have such a low level of self-esteem, think about the kinds of messages or signals that a person might receive from his environment, from other significant human beings, that might stimulate the thoughts and feelings at a conscious level which cumulatively would develop into that sort of self-image profile—the kinds of self-talk or inner thought processes which would build such a negative "REALITY" about one's self.

Now let's turn to a more positive self-esteem level. How does a person at the high end of this scale deeply, honestly feel down inside about the self? Valuable. Important. Worthy of respect and consideration. Able to influence others. The high self-esteem person enjoys new and challenging tasks and expects things to go well in the future. That's a little more refreshing and, I hope, a little easier for you to identify with.

Note that self-esteem is not quite the same as self-confidence. You may have a great deal of confidence in yourself in a particular area, or with respect to a particular activity, even though your overall level of self-esteem is rather low. On the other hand, a person can have a very high self-esteem level and still lack confidence in specific departments such as public speaking or painting pictures. *Self-confidence* is more narrowly focused on a particular skill or type of situation. *Self-esteem* is a deeper feeling that you have about yourself, about your value as a person.

If you have a solid base of self-esteem, it is much more likely that you will develop confidence in your ability to handle various skills and circumstances.

Right now, you are somewhere on the scale of zero to one hundred—negative to positive—self-esteem. Ask yourself for a moment whether it might be profitable, worthwhile, desirable to move up that scale—to move in the direction of a more accurate, more valid, more honest appraisal of the real worth, value, significance that you do have. If you can accept the possibility that you may genuinely *be* a very worthy, valuable human being, then might it not be valuable to take some deliberate action steps to move in the direction of greater self-acceptance—a more honest feeling of self-worth?

Here are some ways to do that—some simple techniques or methods that you can put into action right away that will take you in that direction.

The first is simply a practical application of Constructive Imagination. Build a positive affirmation about your worthiness and include it in your list of images that you are reinforcing every day. Define exactly what self-esteem means to *you;* then translate it into an affirmation. An example is, "I like and respect myself. I am a worthy, valuable person." As you work with that affirmation, let yourself experience—in your imagination—how it feels to be in a real situation, *knowing* that you are worthwhile, valuable, and significant. It might be a staff meeting, a party, an outing with your family, or a sales interview. Project yourself into that event and let the *feeling* of self-esteem flow through your system.

You can re-experience an event in which you felt very good about yourself, reinforcing that positive experience. Or think of a situation in which you felt badly about the way you handled things and relive it in your imagination on a more positive level. Handle the entire scene well, and let *yourself* feel good about *you.* Feel the warm, joyful glow of pride and satisfaction.

Another way to move up the self-esteem scale is to decide that you are going to spend a little more time dwelling on your successes—the things you feel *good* about having done—and less time wallowing in errors and failures. When you do a good job, feel good about it! Not only does that increase the probability that you will repeat that excellent performance, but it also helps you to feel better about yourself as a person. When things go badly (they will still do that), avoid the temptation to wallow in the error or failure. There's a world of difference between *having failed* and *being a failure*—a lot of difference between *having done something badly* and *being bad!*

There is a pair of very useful words which can serve as an "antiwallowing" device if you want to use them. Nothing magical about them, but they can very easily help you to shift gears from berating yourself and wallowing in the error to a more positive kind of programming.

"NEXT TIME"

When something goes badly, recognize what has happened—acknowledge the error—and then shift into the thought about how you will handle that kind of situation should it ever happen again. I am not suggesting at all that it is desirable or useful to *ignore* your errors or failures. Certainly you will occasionally stub your toe or do something that just doesn't work out very well. There will be times when you will not close the sale or you will not make the part exactly according to specifications. You may say something to one of your children (or to your mate) that you realize later wasn't really what you wanted to say, or the way that you wanted to say it. When that happens, you have a choice. You can wallow in the error, feeling bad with, "Oh boy, am I stupid!" or "I always do things like that, what's the matter with me?" diminishing your self-esteem level. Or, you can *use* the error to do a better job in the future. Instead of wallowing in "how awful it was," or "how dumb I was," or "how clumsy I was," look at that particular situation and think, "Well, that didn't work out very well; next time here's how I'll handle it differently." **Pre-program the system** so that should that same kind of event come up again you are ready to handle it in a more productive, more effective manner.

When you are tempted to hang a negative label on yourself, there is another useful phrase which can help you to remind yourself of the fact that you are constantly changing.

"UP UNTIL NOW . . ."

Instead of, "I just can't make speeches!" it will be more accurate and more helpful to change to, "Up until now, it hasn't been easy for me to speak to groups." You are constantly changing, and there is no reason at all why the way that you have done things in the past will be the way that you will do them in the future.

Allowing your thoughts and feelings about yourself to move in a positive direction is particularly important the last few minutes at night, just before you go to sleep.

I think it is very likely—and very tragic—that hundreds of thousands, perhaps millions of people lie in bed for thirty minutes or an hour each night thinking, dwelling on, re-experiencing all of the things they have done wrong all day—thus virtually guaranteeing that they are going to do them all over again.

Just before you fall asleep is a very special time to be sure that you are directing your thoughts toward the things that you feel good about having done, or the activities that you are looking forward to in the future.

Here's another way in which it is possible for you to reinforce, develop, enhance your personal level of self-esteem. You can build your own feelings of worth, value, and significance by reinforcing and strengthening the self-esteem of the epi-organisms of which you are a part. Think about your family, the department in which you work or some other group to which you belong. Each member of the group has some feelings about the value or significance of that epi-organism, and when you put all of those attitudes together, you have a group attitude—"How we feel about us."

Your family has a self-esteem level. Mom has some feelings about the family, Dad has some, Judy, Mary, Johnny—each member of the family has some feelings about "our family." If you are very fortunate, you are part of a family with a high self-esteem level, where the prevailing attitude is, "What a terrific place to be!" or "I'm proud and happy that I'm a part of this family. I feel sorry for people who are not a part of a family like this one. We love each other, we do things together, and express ourselves to each other. What a great family!" Whatever potential exists within *that* family is likely to be flowing easily and naturally.

Unfortunately, all too frequently, we find families in which the prevailing attitude is: "How do you get out of this outfit?" That certainly says something about the self-esteem level of that group personality, and whatever potential exists within that group is probably locked up tightly. The brakes are on!

Look at this as it applies to a company. You may be part of a company—or other organization—in which the prevailing attitude is: "What a great place this is to work—I really like being here! I'm working with terrific people. We're doing important things and we're doing them well."

Your group's self-esteem level is somewhere on the scale from low to high.

If it is in the lower range of the scale, maybe it would be to your advantage to get busy and do what you can to move it up. Consider that carefully. Can you see that it will be to your personal profit and benefit to help the group feel better about itself? There are at least two important ways in which it will be to your self-interest. First, you will find it much easier to achieve your own goals if the groups within which you are living and working are functioning effectively. Second, when you know that you are a part of a winning team, you feel better about yourself and that helps to release your own abilities.

How much value will it be to the tackle on the football team to go into the huddle between plays and say to his teammates, "Boy, we are a bunch of clods!"? If you have ever played on any kind of athletic team, you know how dramatically productive it is for someone on the squad to "talk it up." It is contagious; before you know it everyone is more energetic, better coordinated, and expecting to win the game. That surge of positive self-talk within the team and the resulting feelings *do* increase the chances of victory.

Because the athletic world in our culture is so visible, it is easy to see a process like this at work in a team of professional athletes. What happens when a player is traded to the top team in a league? Whether it is in baseball, hockey, basketball, or soccer, when that player puts on the uniform of the championship team, his performance improves. Just knowing that he is good enough to have been traded to the top team causes him to walk taller, play better. The new uniform doesn't change his potential—it stimulates a thought and feeling sequence which releases his brakes!

You can see this same phenomenon with certain branches of the armed services, too. Some units "know" that they are the finest—and they *act* that way when they are in combat. In every industry there are companies which have that same atmosphere of high self-esteem, and it is no coincidence that they are leading the way and attracting the best people from their competitors.

Take a very close look at this idea—again from your own selfish viewpoint. See if you could profit by spending a little more time reinforcing the positive feelings about your group. Look at the application to your family, your bowling team, your company, your department, your service club, trade association, church or synagogue, community, and your country. Anything that you can do, say, express in any way that will reinforce the good feeling within that group about the group will help the group to function better, achieve its goals more easily, and help *you* to get where you want to go a lot faster.

How long has it been since you sat at the dinner table and said to your family, "I'm really proud to be a part of this family. We are really terrific!" Don't say it unless you feel that way about the family, but if you do feel it, why not express it? It may feel a little uncomfortable the first time. That goes back to some childhood programming about not expressing your emotions, but go ahead and release that brake. When you have a positive feeling about your group, *say it!* You will enjoy the results.

When the group does something badly, use NEXT TIME to avoid wallowing in the error and reinforcing it. When others in the group slip into the trap of "That's like us, we're always goofing things up!" step in, gently, with a question: "What could we do to handle situations like this better in the future?" Help the group to find a way to change the procedures which led to the difficulty so that it is less likely to happen again.

Nations have self-esteem levels, too, and they are constantly changing, just like those of individuals. A look back through the pages of history will disclose some dramatic examples of the ebb and flow of self-esteem within various nations, and the relationship between how a country felt about itself and its ability to use whatever potential it possessed. Great Britain, Russia, Germany, Israel, Japan, Mexico—as you think of each country can you see how the national self-esteem level has changed, and how that has affected progress, productivity, and the effectiveness of the citizens of the country?

How valuable is it to our country—and to you as a citizen of the country—to talk about and reinforce all of the things we have done wrong? Might it not be more useful to dwell on the incredible successes of our nation and feel good about them? In those areas where we have failed, what can we do to correct the system so that if we ever encounter a similar situation again we will be more likely to handle it well?

Now let's look at how you can help other people to reinforce *their* feelings of self-esteem. This may be the most exciting and productive way of building your own feelings of value and worth. One of the interesting peculiarities of this basic releasing mechanism is that the more you give away to other people, the more you get! The more you reinforce, enhance, undergird the self-esteem of the other people in your world, the better *you* like *you*. The reverse is also true, and perhaps even more obvious. Anything I do to cause you to dislike yourself creates an uneasy feeling within me about myself.

So, one of the ways that you can build your own personal self-esteem level is by helping others to build and reinforce theirs. And, there is an extra bonus benefit to this process. By providing other people with the opportunity to enhance the positive feelings they have about themselves, you are enriching your environment.

Pause for a moment and think about the dozen most important people in your world—the people you live with, work with, have frequent contact with on a social level. Who are the twelve most important, significant other human beings in your world?

They might include a mate, your children, people with whom you work closely in your professional or vocational activity, close friends, or neighbors. Think about those people for a moment and ask yourself this question, "What would it mean to me if those individuals, in the next month, really, honestly, deeply liked themselves better?" What would that mean to you? Would it be useful, to your advantage—or would it be harmful, unpleasant? Would it be a plus or a minus if those people with whom you interact every day, people with whom you have daily contact, were to move up that self-esteem scale and really like themselves better?

I feel certain that as you think about this idea you will see that life is a lot easier when you are dealing with people who have a high level of self-esteem. Instead of working (or living) with people who are defensive, withdrawn, inclined to "shift the blame," you have a more open, honest, trusting relationship with mutually set goals and more direct communication. Much more exciting, positive things happen when people who have an abundance of self-esteem are working together. Try this. Set yourself a project in the next month. Pick out specific people with whom you have regular, frequent contact, and decide that you are going to do whatever you can to help those individuals to genuinely, honestly feel better about themselves.

How do you do that? By spending more time and effort putting those people up, and less time and effort putting them down.

An exercise that you may want to test came from one of our *PACE* Youth Conferences. One of the most important—and exciting—programs which my organization offers is a Conference for teenagers in which we explore the entire *PACE* framework as it applies to young people. In the summer of 1968, one of the participants in a *PACE* Youth program created this exercise and called it "The No Put-down Game." The way to play it is simply to time yourself and see how long you can go without putting anyone down. Can you go for fifteen minutes? An hour? It may not be as easy as it seems.

The rules prohibit putting anyone down, out loud, including yourself, even in jest. The "joking" put-down is outlawed because it usually has a sharp barb attached to it. It is certainly possible to tease someone in a warm, loving way, but to rule out the possibility that the teasing, joking put-down is just a clever way of sneaking in a little dig, avoid it as you play this game. Moreover, this is an individual, personal, private project. Do not tell anyone else what you are doing; just time yourself and see how long you can go. You are only working on *yourself*! Calling another person's attention to the fact that he has just put someone down is a put-down, even if you were the one being attacked.

When you find out how long you can go without any put-downs, then see if you can break your record. See if you can go for a longer period next time.

At the same time, develop the habit of putting other people *up* instead of down. See what happens if instead of undermining other people, you reinforce their good feelings about themselves. Be alert to the positive feelings that you have about another person. Be aware of what is going on inside of you and when you feel a sense of admiration or regard or warmth for another person, go ahead and express it. You will be delighted with the results. As you spend a little more time putting people up and less time putting them down, you will not only be enhancing your environment, but you will find yourself liking you better, too. You will be building *your* feelings of self-esteem as you develop the ability to reinforce the positive qualities of others.

In your dealings with other human beings, you always accomplish a great deal more by praising the qualities that you admire than you can ever accomplish by criticizing those that you condemn. I'm sure you have noticed that. It can be very tempting sometimes to criticize the behavior or attitudes of other people when they are doing something "wrong"—which means they are not doing it the way that you would do it. But it is much more productive to reinforce the behavior—or qualities—that you admire.

Imagine a husband and wife sitting in a restaurant. One of them says to the other, "You're not really going to eat that piece of banana cream pie, are you?" The question (and the tone of voice that goes with it) has a reinforcing effect, but probably not in the direction the person who asked it had in mind! Calling attention to behavior you do not admire and would like to see changed often has just the reverse effect. It might be better to wait until the other person passes up dessert to comment on that in a positive manner. "I know how much you like desserts, honey, and I really admire your decision to not have any."

If you are in a management role, or if you are a parent, you will occasionally encounter situations in which someone under your supervision has done something badly. Your child crawled up on the counter, reached for a cookie, and broke the cookie jar. Something needs to be said, but what the child does *not* need is to have someone tell him, "You broke the cookie jar!" He knows that. He's already aware of the fact that the cookie jar is broken, and he probably feels bad about it. Now there are a lot of little pieces of ceramic mixed in with the cookies and they don't taste as good. So, he's upset enough with himself and with the situation without having someone help him to feel worse about what he's done.

What he needs is some help in how to handle this kind of project differently—better—NEXT TIME. He needs some loving, coaching guidance about how to get cookies without breaking cookie jars. It might be more productive to say, "Next time, get a taller chair," or "Next time, call me and I'll get the cookie for you." Sometimes a question can be valuable. "That didn't work out so well, did it? How could you handle that differently the next time you want a cookie?"

A sales manager might say to one of the sales people, "When the telephone rang in the middle of your presentation, you lost your momentum and never quite got back on track. Next time a phone call breaks your stride, how can you handle it better? What can you do to get back on track and close the sale?" In many cases it will be desirable to give your opinion about something which might work well next time. Above all, be sure to discuss the *activity* or the *behavior*, not the *person*. The coaching kind of helpfulness on the part of a manager or parent is more likely to be in the category of a "next time" message and an expression of opinion, rather than advice.

Before we leave self-esteem, there is one other puzzle it will be valuable to examine. What about the person who has so much self-esteem that you can't stand him? I suspect that if you really think about that person, the one who is always bragging and boasting about past accomplishments, you will probably find that you are not dealing with someone who has an overabundance of self-esteem. Chances are that a person who blows his horn all the time is pretty near to the lower end of the self-esteem scale.

Here is someone whose "REALITY" structure is saying, "I know that I am worthless; and if anybody else ever really knew me, they wouldn't like me either. So, I can't let that happen." He presents a facade self, a false front. Talking constantly about something that he has done well, he tries desperately to convince others that he may have some value—and at the same time, he is trying to convince himself! Of course, the transparent facade evokes a flood of messages from other people that they don't admire the fraudulence, the falseness; and so he tries harder and harder to be a likable person and to pretend that he is more worthwhile than he really believes that he is.

If you have someone in your world who is trying to compensate for low self-esteem with bragging and conceit, your natural inclination may be to get out your needle and see if you can pop his balloon. When someone is blowing his horn all the time there seems to be an almost automatic urge to whittle him down to size. But the reverse approach is much more productive. It may not be easy, but if you think it through you will find that it is much more profitable. If you will devote some time and effort to reinforcing that person's inner feeling of value and significance, you will find that the bragging diminishes.

That may be just the opposite of your initial impulse, but try it. When you run across someone who seems to be trying very hard to impress everyone, look for something that the person does that you feel good about. Find something that you can genuinely, honestly, sincerely compliment. Not flattery, but something about that person—his taste in shoes, the idea he presented at the staff meeting—that you admire, and express that positive feeling to the person. Express your admiration instead of reinforcing the low self-esteem by reacting negatively to his bragging. Remember that how you feel as you do this is what really counts. Set aside the external behavior of that person for a moment and acknowledge the true worth and value that is there if he will only let it out.

Another possible indication that a person may be at the lower end of the self-esteem scale is a negative reaction to compliments. That is not a universally dependable symptom, but it can often provide an interesting clue that a person's self-esteem is sagging. When you admire a person's clothing, saying, "That's certainly an attractive jacket you are wearing," the response of, "Oh, this old thing?" may tell you something about how he feels about himself—especially if the jacket is obviously brand-new. When a person is uncomfortable about a compliment, what is probably happening in his mental system is, "I know I have terrible taste, and here is someone telling me that my jacket is attractive." The conflict between what he is perceiving and his "REALITY" is uncomfortable.

Sometimes people don't wait for the compliment to run themselves down. "I'm sorry that I look so awful today," or, "I'm sorry the house is such a mess." You might not have noticed if they hadn't brought it up!

So, one possible signal which can tell you something about a person's self-esteem is his response to a compliment. If you say to a person with very *high* self-esteem, "You really did a fantastic job on that project, Shirley," what will her response be? Probably a simple, "Thank you." Or perhaps, "Thank you. I appreciate your saying that. I feel pretty good about it myself." Praise is more acceptable to the person with a solid sense of personal worth, because it is consistent with what he knows and feels about himself.

*Your life need not be a succession of
twenty-four hour vacuums, nor must you live
in an emotional dungeon any longer.*

Dr. Maxwell Maltz

LESSON 14

HOW TO WIN YOUR WAR AGAINST NEGATIVE FEELINGS

Maxwell Maltz is one of a very small group of experts who will make a second appearance in *The University of Success*. This semester, on the power of your thoughts, would not be complete without him.

For many years, as one of the world's most renown plastic surgeons, Dr. Maltz had studied the personality changes that took place in his patients after he had removed their scars or deformities through plastic surgery. Many who had lost their self-respect and pride because of what they considered their ugliness, immediately developed a good image of themselves, after surgery, and became happy, confident human beings. But, many others still felt as inferior, dejected, and hostile as they had been *before* their operations!

"The change in their physical image," according to Dr. Maltz, "meant nothing to them, so weak was their concept of themselves as people—so weak was their self-image."

Out of his observations came several popular books, among them *Creative Living for Today,* from which this lesson is taken so that you will understand how to tackle your life situations healthfully, without allowing prejudice against yourself to eat its way into your mind. Dr. Maltz considered this to be possibly the most valuable book he had ever written.

He writes, "Deeply ingrained negative attitudes permeate our culture, and every day, people you know may try to submerge you in them. You must not allow yourself to be railroaded into adopting stereotyped, humiliating attitudes toward yourself."

131

Your thoughts, your concepts, your images, are your most precious assets. Listen to an expert as he teaches you how to protect them ...

Your self-image will sustain you in creative living if you learn to declare war on your negative feelings—and win the war in the battlefield of your mind.

Your mind is a battlefield, never doubt this, and if you win, you will experience peace of mind during your fulfilling days.

Your infantry, crawling slowly through the underbrush seeking contact with the enemy, creeping through the darkness behind his lines to discover his positions, is your awareness of the supreme importance of your thinking and of your mental imaging.

Your air force, equipped with the latest-model jets and tactical striking force, is your adoption of an active philosophy, your setting of goals, your use of your success mechanism. The buildup of your air power is your work to strengthen your self-image, your picture of yourself, your concept of your own worth.

Your navy cannot transport your troops to victory, however, until it has located your great enemy—your failure mechanism. Before you can go forward in this war, you must discover this mechanism of self-defeat and root it out of your mind.

Does this comparison of your thinking with war make you smile? It shouldn't. It shouldn't at all. In our troubled world, so many people's minds are full of misery. To scoop this misery out, to expose the cancerous thoughts to the light, then to crush these morbid ideas and replace them with happy concepts and images— this often requires a war. A very vital war. One, with apologies to Woodrow Wilson, "to make your mind safe for happiness."

Many years ago Edward Bulwer-Lytton said that "The pen is mightier than the sword," and this saying is now almost everyone's cultural heritage.

Today, with the strident advances made in the knowledge of the human mind during the last one hundred years, we can say that *a person's thoughts, his images, are mightier than guns*.

So let us declare war on our negative feelings, on our failure mechanism. But let us resolve that our basic aim is destruction only of negativism—after that, peace and happiness.

Then goals. Goals and full living.
Years of creative living.
Without fear.

OVERCOMING FALSE BELIEFS

No goal is more vital than to dehypnotize yourself from the false beliefs which paralyze your success mechanism.

You, reading this, are a man or a woman—not a god.

What goals are meaningful, what can you do with yourself if your beliefs pull you down into failure? What can you do but sink into the nonactivity of depression, renouncing all goals, blotting sunshine out of your life, moping dejectedly in a dark room while others go out into the world and live?

In creative living you must dehypnotize yourself from your false, negative beliefs about yourself.

The word "dehypnotize" is not too strong because so many people have beliefs which are unshakable, which must be jarred out of them, which only a forceful countersuggestion can uproot. Their beliefs, so often absurd, cement inferiority complexes formed of unfortunate early experiences and ridiculous misinformation.

The results are sad.

- Do you believe that your life will be empty because you are an inferior person who has never done anything worthwhile and never will?
- Do you believe that you should suffer to atone for the mistakes you've made?
- Do you believe that life has no meaning for you because a loved one has passed away?
- Do you believe that the only way to live in an atomic age is to spend every day worrying about a nuclear holocaust?

If you think along these or similar lines, you are harboring false beliefs. Granted that you've known tragedy and that you have your faults, you are still hypnotizing yourself with false, negative ideas. Worse, you are torturing yourself with them. You are crucifying yourself; even your worst enemy might be kinder.

In my sixty-five plus years of tenure in this funny world, I have learned some of the most amazing things. One is that people who are completely objective in appraising political trends or medical conditions or stock market movements or mechanical gadgets—*or other people*—are often totally blind to the irrationality of their false beliefs about themselves. Not only that; considerate of others, they can be ruthlessly vindictive toward themselves.

I have operated on dozens and dozens of people to improve deficient features only to find that, after surgery, they replaced this real physical fault in their minds with a nonsensical belief which continued their unswerving fixation on their inferiority. Their negative beliefs varied; their movement toward failure was the same kind of mechanism.

But *your* negative, false belief about *yourself* is true, isn't it? Steve's is laughable and Betty's is idiotic, but yours is true?

Is this what you think?

Then let me tell you a story.

VICTORY OVER THE "AFRICAN BUG"

Many years ago, shortly after I opened my office to start practicing as a plastic surgeon, a tall black came to see me. Over six feet four inches tall, he towered above me; he complained about his lip.

I examined him (I'll call him Mr. R.). His underlip protruded somewhat, but I could find nothing wrong with it and I told him this.

Mr. R. said that it was not his idea, but his girl friend's. She had told him that she was ashamed to be seen with him in public because of the protuberance of his lip.

I found him a sweet, dignified giant of a man and thought to myself that a woman in love would never be so critical of such a man.

When I told him this, he still wanted me to perform an operation on his lip. Thinking that an outrageous fee would influence him to forget about a lip operation, I said that it would cost twelve hundred dollars.

Mr. R. said he couldn't afford such a fee and bid me good-bye, thanking me, and bowing in a most courtly manner.

But the next morning he was back, a little black bag in his hand. He dumped its contents on a table. Bills poured out, hundreds and hundreds of bills. Twelve hundred dollars worth of bills—his life savings. He offered them to me most graciously to pay me for operating on his lip.

I was shocked, a little sad too, because I didn't want to deprive him of what was for him a huge sum of money. I told him that I had asked him an exorbitant fee so that he'd give up the idea of a lip operation that he didn't need.

But when he said that he wanted plastic surgery and would go to another doctor if I wouldn't accept him as a patient, I agreed to operate—for a smaller fee and on condition that he tell his "lady love" my fee was twelve hundred dollars.

The operation was simple enough. Under local anesthesia, I cut the superfluous tissue from inside the lip, approximated the rims of the wound with extremely fine silk, and bandaged the lip outside for support. Within half an hour, I was finished. The patient returned a few times to be treated and have the bandages changed; the last one was removed a week later. All the surgery was done inside the lip; there was no visible scar.

Mr. R. was happy with his lip. He crushed my hand in his great grip and thanked me in his hearty, polite tones. Then he strode from my office, a commanding figure.

A few weeks later he was back, but I could hardly recognize him. His body seemed to have shrunk; his hands had lost their strength; his voice was squeaky. I asked him what had happened.

"The bug, sir—the bug!"

"What bug?"

"The African bug, sir," he said. "It's got me, and it's killing me."

He told me his woes. After the bandages on his lip had been removed, he went to see his woman. She had remarked on his new lip and asked him how much it had cost. When he told her "twelve hundred dollars," as I had asked, her whole manner toward him changed. Furious, she accused him of cheating her of the twelve hundred dollars that should have been hers and told him she'd never really loved him. She cursed him and told him that he would die from this curse.

Deeply troubled, R. had gone to his room and lain there for four days. Then he thought of the curse. He was an educated man, had received good schooling; curses and magic were for the ignorant. Still, this woman had held him under her spell from the time he had met her. He figured that if she could put him under a spell when she didn't hate him, then perhaps she could bring on his death with her curse.

Then, running his tongue around, he discovered the horrible thing inside his mouth.

Shortly after this, his landlady, concerned that he was just lying in his room, not eating, brought him a visitor, a "doctor." R. had told him about the terrible thing in his mouth and the "doctor," examining it, cried out as he removed his finger from the thing in R.'s mouth. "It's killing you," he said. "The slimy African bug stuck inside your mouth because of the curse that is on you!"

The tall man, breathing fearfully, covered his face with his hands.

"It is really in your mouth?" I asked him.

"Yes sir." He told me about how the "doctor" tried to help him drive the "African bug" away with liquids, pastes, and potions—but the curse was too strong. Nothing could destroy the "African bug." All he could think of was the "African bug." Fear of the "African bug" kept him awake at night. "It burned inside my lip—"

"Your lip?"

"Yes sir. Inside my mouth."

"You didn't say your *lip* before."

I examined it "That it?"

He nodded.

"Should I get rid of it?"

"Please sir."

Filling a syringe with Novocain, I injected it in his lip. After the Novocain had taken effect, I removed the "African bug" with the knife and forceps. It took a second.

I showed Mr. R. the "African bug" on a piece of gauze; it was no bigger than a grain of rice.

"Is that the bug, sir?" He looked disbelieving.

"It's just a bit of scar tissue which formed on your lip where I removed the stitches after the operation."

"Then there was no African bug?"

I smiled.

Mr. R. stood up. He seemed to have regained his full height in that instant; a rich smile spread over his face and his voice boomed out again as he thanked me in his usual gravely courteous way, bowing as he left.

There was a happy ending to this story; it arrived in the mail. R., enclosing a snapshot of his childhood sweetheart whom he had married, sent me his regards and in a postscript laughed at "African bugs." In the picture he was a smiling, handsome giant of thirty—his true age—with a lovely girl beside him.

WHAT IS YOUR AFRICAN BUG?

This story points a fascinating moral. Here is this fine young man, tall and strong, courtly and dignified—unsophisticated, perhaps, but intelligent—yet a ridiculous belief had almost destroyed him.

His fear of the "African bug" is so ridiculous that you may laugh and ask, "How can this possibly apply to me?"

But we all have our "African bugs."

Have you spent your last fifteen years worrying about some

catastrophe that has never happened? Then you have an "African bug."

Do you constantly criticize yourself for talking too much or not talking enough or talking incoherently? Is your self-blame so severe that your conversation has become contrived and dead? Then you have an "African bug."

Are you so worried about money that nothing else matters to you? Do you watch your savings account like a Silas Marner, suffering acute indigestion every time you must make a withdrawal, worrying over every dollar that is wasted? Then you have an "African bug."

All these "African bugs" must be brought to light and exposed for what they are—negative beliefs that pull us down from our true level as human beings, offensive obsessions that disfigure our self-images, that destroy our aspirations for the happiness that is our reasonable expectation.

As in the case of Mr. R., they have a hypnotic effect which must be canceled out. They cause failure. We must wage a relentless war to exterminate them.

OVERCOMING THE FAILURE MECHANISM

Indeed, we must war against all aspects of the "failure mechanism," which is what I call the system of self-reinforcing negative symptoms which can disrupt an unaware individual's positive instincts.

For, just as certain positive predispositions can accelerate the happy functioning of a person's success mechanism, so can negative forces build up with the speed of a rolling stone going downhill, producing chains of negative feedback within the individual which can lead only to defeat.

I like to spell out the components of the failure mechanism since I feel that this aids people in remembering them. *Frustration, Aggressiveness, Insecurity, Loneliness, Uncertainty, Resentment, Emptiness*—(F-A-I-L-U-R-E)—these are the elements of the failure mechanism.

These are the enemy; its weapons of destructiveness are horrifying. Let us consider them one by one so that we may penetrate through camouflage to their effect on the human being.

1. *Frustration*. We feel frustration when we fail to achieve important goals or to satisfy basic desires. Everyone feels frustrated now and then because of our imperfect natures and the complex nature of the world; it is chronic frustration which is a

symptom of failure. When an individual finds himself caught in a
pattern of repeated frustrations, he should ask himself why. Are
his goals too perfectionist? Does he block his aims with his own
self-criticism? Does he regress to his feelings as an infant when
frustration plus crying resulted in satisfaction? Frustrated rage
does not get results; for infants, it may, but not for adults. A
morbid concentration on one's grievances with life will only make
one's problems more severe. Far better to focus on one's successes,
to gain confidence from seeing oneself winning out. Then one can
forge ahead in life.

2. *Aggressiveness*. Frustration produces aggressiveness (misdirected). There is nothing wrong with aggressiveness, properly
channeled; to reach our goals we must at times be aggressive. But
misdirected aggressiveness is a surefire symptom of failure,
following on the heels of frustration, contributing to a vicious cycle
of defeat. It is usually linked up with the setting of inappropriate
goals which the individual cannot achieve. This leads to frustrated
rage which the person discharges wildly, in all directions, like a
mad dog gone beserk or fireworks sputtering into the night. Innocent parties become targets to a person trapped in the frustration-
aggression cycle; he may snap at his wife for no reason, bawl out
his children, insult his friends, antagonize his coworkers. Furthermore, his rage will increase as his relations with people deteri-
orate, causing still more frustration and more blind lashing out.
Where does this dreadful cycle end? The answer lies not in the
elimination of aggression, but in properly channeling it toward the
achievement of goals that will bring satisfaction, reducing the
unbearable buildup of frustration. The frustrated-aggressive person must see that he can act to reach successes for himself.

3. *Insecurity*. This is another unpleasant feeling; it is based
on a feeling of inner inadequacy. When you feel that you do not
meet your challenges properly, you feel insecure. Often, however,
it is not our inner resources that are lacking; the trouble lies in our
setting of perfectionist standards. The insecure person is frequently
quite competent but, living with impossible expectations, he tends
to criticize himself constantly. His feelings of insecurity cause him
to trip himself up so that he falls pathetically short of his true
potentials.

4. *Loneliness*. We are all lonely now and then, but I refer
here to the extreme feeling of being separated from other people,
from yourself, and from life; this is an important symptom of
failure. Indeed, it is one of the leading failure areas of modern
civilization; the commonness of loneliness is enough to fill one's

heart with unending sorrow. To know that God's creatures can be so estranged, this is very sad.

5. *Uncertainty*. This failure-type symptom is characterized by indecisiveness. The uncertain person believes that if he does not make a decision, he is safe! He is safe from the criticisms he might receive if he took the chance and was proved wrong—safe from the consequences of a decision he made that backfired. This type of person must see himself as perfect; therefore, he cannot afford to be wrong. When a decision is necessary, he looks upon it as a life-or-death decision. If he makes the wrong choice, he will destroy his idealized picture of himself. Therefore, he may dawdle over a trivial decision for long periods of time, wasting his precious hours worrying. When he finally does make up his mind, his decision will be subject to distortions—and he will very likely blunder. The uncertain person cannot live fully because he is afraid to take the plunge and get his feet wet.

6. *Resentment*. This is the excuse-making reaction of the failure-type personality to his status in life. Unable to bear the pain of his failures, he seeks out scapegoats to take the sting out of his own self-blame. Everywhere he finds evidence that life is short-changing him and feels resentment; he does not realize that he may be shortchanging himself. But his resentment does not make failure easier to accept; on the contrary, a vicious cycle is set up which involves more frustration and misdirected aggression. Always full of grievances, the resentful person antagonizes other people and thus sets into motion a chain reaction of hatreds. Others dislike his dishonesty, reject his hostility, feel contempt for his self-pity. Chronic resentment leads to self-pity because the resentful person feels he is a victim of injustice. Haven't people blocked his aspirations? Hasn't bad luck entered into the conspiracy to keep him down? The more he pities himself, the more inferior he feels and the more he comes to hate himself and to resent other people—and the world. He does not realize that his inner resentment is a breeding ground for failure. Only when he sees that he is an actor in life, that he is responsible for setting his goals and channeling his aggression to achieve them, can he break this cycle of failure. Only when he can feel respect for himself, form a realistic image of himself, can he break the habit of resentful thinking which is such a basic component of the failure mechanism.

7. *Emptiness*. Do you know people who are "successful," yet who seem frustrated, resentful, uncertain, insecure, lonely, and misdirectedly aggressive? Then they have achieved success without tools in their hands! Don't be too sure that their "success" is

real. For many people gain all the outward signs of success and then feel emptiness because all along the failure mechanism has enmeshed them, and they have really lacked the capacity for creative living. They have made money, but don't know what to do with it. Life is boring to them. They travel here and there, but nowhere can they escape their feeling of emptiness. They feel empty in New York or Paris; they would feel empty on Mars. They have given up on creative goal-striving; they avoid work, shun responsibility. When they wake up in the morning and see the sun, they do not see their opportunities for enjoying the day— instead they worry about what they can do to pass the time. Emptiness is symptomatic of a weak self-image. Having achieved "success," the empty person feels he is a criminal because he thinks he has stolen something that he does not deserve. Thus he feels guilty and turns his victories into failures as he repudiates his creative faculties. His sense of emptiness symbolizes the total operation of his always present failure mechanism.

These are the elements of the failure mechanism; these are the enemy. I have spelled them out for you so that you can remember them easily.

Now, what can you do about them?

How can you win your one great war?

RISING ABOVE FAILURE

To win the war against your enemy—your failure mechanism— you must first be able to pierce the disguises behind which it hides. Plausible rationalizations and seemingly logical thinking may obscure its functioning. Do not fool yourself, or you will lose this wonderful fight for your survival as a contented human being.

You must fire all your emotional artillery at your false beliefs about yourself until you have leveled them to the ground. You must redirect your frustrated aggression and resentment and find ways to surmount your feelings of loneliness and emptiness.

At the same time, let me once again make one point clear: *the act of failing is not a part of the failure mechanism.* The act of failing in some action or project simply means that you are human.

May I assure you of this: if you've never failed at anything, it's a certainty that you never really tried anything.

Or, in the words of the Roman philosopher Seneca, "If thou art a man, admire those who attempt great things, even though they fail."

Was Thomas Edison a failure? Of course not. The thought is absurd. Yet dozens of failures preceded most of his brilliant creations. Edison learned from his failures and built his successes on them.

Discovery is born in error; there are no creations without unsuccessful experiments.

This sums up one of the chief lessons that I have learned from life: that blunders, errors in judgment and in application, are unavoidable unless you retreat from life into a state of apathy—and, even then, in your inertia you'll make mistakes. *The secret of successful living is to rise above your failures to your good moments.* This is the key concept, to forget your errors, to stop grieving over them, to have compassion for your own human fallibility. Then, unburdened with guilt, you can step out determinedly into the world, seeing yourself at your best, formulating your goals, and bringing out into the game of life your success instincts.

This principle is especially applicable when you try new things. For, when you experiment, you are bound to make mistakes. Never deny your mistakes; admit them freely. But learn to minimize these mistakes, to be as tolerant toward yourself as you would be toward a friend, or you must throttle your experimentation.

Then you can rise to your true potential as a human being and make each year the enriching vindication of your individuality that it should be.

- Every day examine the negative beliefs which pull you down.
- Do you feel that you are stupid?
- Are you obsessed with the feeling that you are ugly?
- Or do you destroy yourself with the allegation that you are weak?
- Unmasculine?
- Unfeminine?
- Undeserving of anything good?

These are a few choice areas for self-torture.

I don't know what negative beliefs you use to undermine yourself; you must ferret them out for yourself.

Your exercise is this: let's think about these self-destroying thoughts and see if we can do something about them (even if you're positive that you're just no good) because I assure you that your thinking is irrational.

Irrational thinking has run beserk down through history. We have had medicine men, alchemists, gold rushes, haunted houses, expeditions after a "fountain of youth"—not to speak of the brutal wars that have bloodied the pages of history books. For many years there were outrageous beliefs about women thought to be "witches."

"Witches" were burned in Europe: Joan of Arc was executed as a "witch," and in the United States we had the shameful episode in Salem, in which a number of "witches" were put to death.

Yet, sad to say, many of us today treat ourselves as if we were "witches."

In examining your accusations against yourself, let's see if you are not being unfair.

If you castigate yourself as "stupid," on what do you base this charge? Granted that you've been unwise, perhaps many times, have you *never* been wise? Have you never been shrewd? Have you never been intelligent? Then your self-criticism is basically self-mutilation. What it comes down to is that you feel you have no rights; you believe in shortchanging yourself.

Examine the "African bugs" which plague you. There might be a grain of reality to them—just as there was a bit of scar tissue in Mr. R.'s mouth. But are these the devastating indictments that you build them into? No, this is irrational thinking.

People are people. The strong are weak, and the weak are strong.

- Some low-to-medium IQ people have rare common sense.
- Some homely looking women are devoted friends—and can look beautiful.
- Some people with physical handicaps are most compassionate.
- Some emotionally unstable people are extremely brilliant.

Psychologists have found that many adult stutterers will talk fluently when they are talking to children.

Some criminals can become responsible members of society if someone will give them a helping hand.

These are grays; there are no blacks-and-whites. But what do you do to yourself with your negative beliefs? You make yourself all evil, all thumbs, all negating.

Everyone knows defeat at times. Joe Louis was for years heavyweight champion; in his prime he was almost invincible, a symbol of power.

Yet, when he first tried boxing, Louis was bumbling, awkward. Unknown amateurs beat him time and again. In one amateur bout he was knocked down nine times in one fight.

Now that you've examined your negative beliefs about yourself and are in the process of reducing them to reasonable proportions, let's see if you can't discard them. If you can't, at least maintain them at reasonable dimensions so that you can live with them.

Go to the next step now, and repicture a success, one that you're really proud of.

Fill your mind with it, see it, smell it, feel it, grab hold of this success picture, and hold it in your mind.

When the critical thoughts counterattack, kick them out and come back, once again, with the good self-image—in technicolor.

To live creatively, you must win this war in your mind. Don't give up! Keep fighting, and chances are you will win.

Say to yourself: "I shall concentrate on the confidence of my past successes, not on my past failures. I deserve the good things in life. I am the captain of my ship, and I shall steer my mind to a productive goal."

YOUR PACEMAKER

Let your self-image be the pacemaker of your heart, your mind, and your soul. Each day reactivate your successful instincts until the success habit becomes part of you, until it hypnotizes you—for, after all, habit is a form of self-hypnosis.

Work hard to banish negative beliefs, to exterminate the seeds of loneliness. Work hard; it is not easy. But you can do it.

War is hellish and if your mind is deeply entrenched in negative concepts, you will have to struggle fiercely to win your battle. But it is a battle worth winning.

So that you can live creatively—with joy.

So that you can laugh and sing and walk the streets proudly in broad daylight.

Let your strengthened self-image inspire you to move forward into a more vital way of life.

Belief, belief in yourself, that is the best pacemaker of all.

Dr. Marcus Bach

LESSON 15

HOW TO BENEFIT FROM
THE ART OF EXPECTATION

Are there special traits or habits or personality ingredients common to all successful people? Man has been seeking common denominators in all achievers for centuries but they are not as obvious as one would expect. You have only to read a series of profiles of famous individuals to realize how different each is from the other, how varied are their methods of operation, how unlike are their work habits, even their personal lives.

Still, there is one practice that many of those who accomplish great things will admit they have indulged in, especially during their leaner years. They were able to picture themselves, vividly, having already attained their goals and they retained that image in their minds constantly, assuring themselves again and again that they *knew* they would succeed.

The mind is a mysterious area of which we still know too little. Most who have admitted to this "picturization" process can offer no explanation as to how it works, except that they *know* it does. As a man thinketh?

Dr. Marcus Bach has been a student of the mind for many years. He is an expert in the field of contemporary religious trends, an author of seventeen books, a lecturer, and an authority in the area of international and interreligious relations. Travel with him now, in this excerpt from his book *The Power of Perception,* on an unique journey of exploration, that is certain to provide you with a whole new perception of your life, and your future . . .

When I think of the unscientific, homespun upbringing I had, I marvel that I turned out as well as I did. No Dr. Spock, no Montessori school, no psychological guidance, no character measurements, no Rorschach Test; none of these figured in my coming of age, not even a Roentgen kymograph which charts the art of sucking, swallowing, and breathing. Yet I never got into any serious scrapes, was never hauled before a judge or jury, never, so far as I know, disgraced my parents or myself overly much. On the contrary, as long as I am singing these *a cappella* praises, let me mention that I was Exhibit A when it came to filling a niche worthy of our family hall of fame, such as it is.

I was twelve when, after I had done exceptionally well in a music competition, my mother complimented me and added, "I am especially proud of you because you were one child I really didn't want."

Such an admission nowadays would send both mother and child into nine months of analytical sessions and possibly a series of shock treatments. I considered my mater's statement an exciting compliment. Here I was, uninvited but making good! Here I stood, an accident of birth, but apparently in divine order! It was wonderful. I remember how my mother laughed and embraced me and how I felt uniquely special whenever I reflected that I was an unwanted wanted child.

I often think of this when I am counseling with students. Some tell me with great concern that they were adopted and hadn't been advised of it or that they learned they were illegitimate or that they have feelings of unwantedness. Others complain there is a gap between their parents and themselves, that their dads don't understand them, they don't understand their dads, there's a gulf they can't bridge, they can't communicate; and constantly there is the commonplace complaint that, "I don't know what to do with my life and there is no one at home to counsel me."

I try to remember whether my dad ever counseled me, and I can't. I cannot recall a time that my father and I ever sat down for a man-to-man talk. The facts of life were never discussed. Sex was never mentioned. I would be hard put to explain where I learned what I learned about what every young man should know. As for a career, I was on my own with no parental strings attached. In everything, with the possible exception of religion, I was a free traveler on an open road. But I was lucky. My father impressed just one indelible phrase on me, words that stuck like a brand mark on a maverick. He simply said, "All I expect of you, my boy, is that you do something worthwhile with your life."

My mother, who by no means agreed with everything my father said and who never actually counseled me with any long-range view, did concur in this paternal directive, "All we expect of you is that you do something worthwhile with your life."

Whether it was the way it was said or the calculated timing when it was said, or if there was a certain receptivity on my part while it was said, I have never figured out. I only know that an expectation was born in me and that it sensitized me to life, has kept me sensitized, and serves, as far as I know, as a solid basis for feeling the commonly unfelt. I am disposed by nature to great expectations. Even the Scripture saying, "To whom much has been given, much is expected," has affected my disposition. Much was given to me, not in the way of counsel and advice and admonitions, but in the way of camaraderie. But even that was never overly intimate. It was comfortable, a comfortable feeling challenging me with a goal: it was expected that I do something worthwhile with my life.

There were certain unwritten precepts in our household which were rarely discussed and only infrequently broken. Everyone simply expected everyone in the household to abide by them. For instance, there was the wine decanter. This lovely crystal piece with its rose-colored contents was a natural fixture on the dining room buffet. None of us four children ever thought about taking a sip out of it, though I cannot remember that we were ever warned not to. So, too, my father regularly enjoyed his Thursday nights in the town tavern over a game of German *Skat*. My mother frowned on this, especially since the local priest was one of the players. She was more afraid of Catholic contamination than she was of Schlitz. Yet none of us boys ever gave cards or beer or the tavern a serious thought. We were expected to know that things acceptable for Dad might not be good for us. Nor were we surprised when later on in life my father gave up *Skat* and my mother began to fraternize with the Catholics. There was nothing righteous about it either way.

FISHING WITH FATHER

I remember during the deep-feeling years of my boyhood, I went fishing with my father one Sunday morning despite the objections of my church-devoted mother. Most youngsters today would take such an outing as a lark, but for me it was a fateful decision.

Sunday morning was structured on the expectation that everyone would unquestioningly go to Sunday school and church. But on this particular Sabbath the fishing season was scheduled to open at the crack of dawn. Now actually my father was a fairly dedicated churchman, but after a hard week at the store the Sunday out-of-doors called a good deal louder and more appealingly than the old church bell, especially when the Wisconsin earth was breaking forth with spring.

My mother contended we could go fishing before the service or afterward, though that would be sinful enough, but my father, a well-versed Waltonian, explained that by some divine quirk the crappies bit best from ten to twelve, exactly the hours for Sunday School and church.

Why my mother did not say, "Well, you go but leave the boy here," I will never know, unless there was a strange kind of unspoken love and wisdom behind it all. At any rate, it meant that she would have to face *Herr Pastor* as well as the horror of several aunts who already had me slated for the ministry at the age of ten.

So we took the devil by the horns and pedaled our bikes the four miles to Lodi's Mill, where a willow-sheltered pond provided a popular crappie and sunfish habitat. Cane poles strapped to our bicycles betrayed to churchgoing cars where we were headed. Minnow bait in canvas buckets strapped to our handlebars, sandwiches and pop in our bike baskets, we skimmed over the black-topped highway with a song in our hearts, and not necessarily a church song either.

Great expectations.

Great expectations made me want to do things well whether riding the bike or thinking great thoughts, and every detail of that Sunday adventure stands out brave and clear, actually more clear than brave because the road to Lodi's Mill near Sauk City, where we lived, led past the town cemetery, and as I glimpsed the jagged rows of headstones my thoughts were anything but courageous. My uncle's preachments had impressed upon me the fact that these gruesome, weather-scarred markers were God's trump card.

We might escape His wrath, even as we were escaping the morning services, but He would get us in the end. It did not matter whether a person was Protestant or Catholic, or whether the cemeteries were strictly segregated between the two faiths as they were in my hometown: man's mortal end was there for all to see, no matter which of the iron gates the coal-black hearse drove through.

But suddenly a sense of victory surged through me. I was with my father. We were side by side on man-sized bikes, riding together as if we had found a knowledge bigger than death and dying. A flash of secret wisdom told me I knew things that even my preacher-uncle did not know, knew them because I felt them on this beautiful spring morning. God liked fishing. Jesus liked fishermen. God liked this Sunday-morning world. He liked the green and growing pine trees better than He did the stained old marble stones. The mounds of tended grass, the lifeless slabs, the rusted iron crosses in these weeping acres were not the true world at all. "Don't let them fool you!" an inner voice was saying to me. "Don't let these man-made markers which the workmen have set in hard concrete so that they can't be pushed over on Halloween get mixed up with God. Consider the trees and the sumac! And what do you see when you look at the roses making beautiful the cemetery's white picket fence?"

God's world was life and freedom. God's world was the open road and the farmyard and the young corn coming up in clean cultivated fields. God's world was the man-sized bike and the legs that made the wheels go round. God's world was Dad and I and Lodi's Mill. God's world included people going to church or going fishing, just as long as they really loved the Lord.

In the all-encompassing bigness of that world I saw my mother, too, as part of God's great and wonderful plan. I saw her dressed in her Sunday finest, hat properly on her head, white gloves drawn up to her elbows, her patent-leather purse dangling from her arm, her Peloubet Sunday-school notes folded neatly into her white Bible. God's world. It was big enough to take in Uncle *Pfarrer* with his black *mütze* and his stern, unsmiling face, and his long black pulpit coat, the tail of which once got caught in the pulpit door. Thank you, God, for your sense of humor! And thank you for the silent beauty of Lodi's Mill where we laid our bikes in the deep grass and stalked our way silently to the water's unruffled edge.

I matured that morning more than I had in many a year. It dawned on me that there is something a person wants more than happiness for himself and something he wishes for more than even a mess of fish: an awareness of God's good and God's approachableness, an expectation of rightness and freedom in His presence, and a sensitive response to all life everywhere.

Nowadays I talk of fishing for marlin at Mazatlán and of the salmon run in the Frazer. I sing the praises of steelheads and the kokanee which I have sought in many waters, but memory carries no deeper feeling than the Sunday morning at Lodi's Mill. A sensitivity was born that day, and it was signed and sealed when my father and I came home and proudly dumped our colorful catch into the kitchen sink.

"Well," said my mother with an exaggerated sigh of marvel and concern, "what is a person to say?"

"Say it was good fishing," said my father.

"But on a Sunday," my mother lamented, "and during church time at that."

With a wink at me my father remarked, "We have enough to take a mess to *Onkel Pfarrer*."

My mother threw up her hands. "I should say not!" she exclaimed. "It is better for everyone to think you didn't catch any at all."

But she was already tying on her apron and calling for the fish knife as if the mill pond, for just a moment in the rush of time, might have been the Sea of Galilee.

A MIRACLE WE CAN ALL PERFORM

I am disposed by nature to great expectations. I believe in them, anticipate them, invite them, and therefore usually find them verified in the experience of others who, as I, bring them to life by first feeling them *in* life.

I thought of this recently in Toronto, Canada, when I visited Avery Cooke, who was observing his centennial birthday. There he was, walking like a man of sixty, enthusiastically showing a group of visitors his rose garden. I asked him the inevitable question, "To what do you attribute your long life and your wonderful health?"

"Well, I'll tell you," he said, "I just never expected anything else. I expected I'd live to see a hundred. I expected to be well. I expected to be just what I am, so there is no miracle about it at all."

No miracle excepting the miracle of great expectations, a miracle that we can all perform if we put our minds to it. Expectation is a feeling. It generates the qualities needed for the attainment of the goal, qualities that get into the subconscious and chart a pattern. Theoreticians say, "Think great, visualize greatness, hope greatly, and be grateful." My father said, "All I expect of you is that you do something worthwhile with your life."

He had enough of an assignment doing something with his life, and that may be why he turned me over to myself. He let it be known that the one person whom I could do something with was *me*. I could best take up the challenge of my life. I could most clearly see the unseen within myself and hear the unheard and feel the commonly unfelt. I and I alone could expect some hint of divinity in my life and try to live up to it. Only I could keep turning back the layers of doubt and guilt, the masks and the make-believe, the aims and aspirations until I came down to the real *me,* and there would always be moments in which I would be called upon to prove the person I professed and hoped to be.

It was said that when the ship *Lakonia* went down near the Madeiras there was a man among the lifeboat survivors dressed in a neat suit, a tweed topcoat over his arm, and carrying a briefcase. He refused help when he climbed aboard the rescue ship *Salta* and calmly aided other survivors as they came aboard. An officer on the *Salta* congratulated him on his composure and asked for an explanation. The man replied, "I'm an Englishman, sir. It is expected of me."

THE STUFF WISHES ARE MADE OF

Expectation is a servant of the will, the will is the result of a wish, and a wish is spun from the power of spirit. This is far from explaining the entire nature of it, nor does it answer the question why some individuals seem more spiritually or psychically motivated than others. Some people do respond more readily to a deep-feeling level, perhaps because they sense the reward of it, desire the joy of it, feel the challenge of it, or anticipate the karmic good of it.

Some say, "I expect nothing out of life one way or the other." Yet even this is quite an expectation! It is like the Oriental who says, "I desire only desirelessness." Expectation presupposes faith. It is faith plus, faith felt, faith fortified.

Even when expectation is hidden behind a negativism, it makes things happen. Had I not been introduced to Iowa farmers I might never have understood this, but during my years in the Midwest I got to know them and admire them. They are a special breed. They will never let you see their deeper selves. They hide their emotions. They shy away from admitting their true love for nature or the land. After you have lived with them for any length of time, you will want to revise your whole concept of the power of positive thinking, for they are as negative about success as a fox would have you believe it is negative about chickens.

Spring, according to the farmers' customary complaint, comes too early or too late. The ground at planting time is too wet or too dry. The corn grows too slow or too fast. The market is too unsteady or too fixed. Harvest time comes too soon or not soon enough. Yet rarely, if ever, does the Iowa farmer fail to have a bumper crop and never in my extended sojourn in the Hawkeye State did he ever have a bad year. On the contrary, heaven opens its windows on him as if he had a magic combination. He now produces one hundred seventy-five bushels of corn per acre where once he got less than ninety. He will never let you in on it, but he is playing a game, a game of great expectations behind a make-believe of discontent through which, if you look closely, you will see him smile. He doesn't even want nature or the land to know how great his faith in their ability actually is. Don't say it, he warns, think it. Don't talk about it, feel it.

Mask your expectations. Do not let even the fates catch on to the greatness and depths of your desires. How deeply did my father's expectation for me actually go? How great was his concern; how strong was his wish? Wisely, shrewdly, he never let me know. He sowed the seed just deeply enough at just the right time and evidently he knew the nature of the planting.

I have great expectations for getting good mail. Sometimes this gets to be a phobia. I get good letters, life-changing letters because I expect them, but if I ever dropped my game of make-believe that mail doesn't really matter, I would lose my magic touch.

It is a subtle and, at times, a difficult game. Take, for example, the old adage that "expectation is greater than realization." This is generally true and we ought by rights hold it as a basic truth at a deep level of feeling. Failing to do this, we must keep relearning the same lesson over and over again. Expect greatly, but expect, too, that expectation is usually greater than realization.

THE ART OF PLANNING

It is an extremely fine art, this matter of planning without planning too hard, of visualizing without creating a rigid dream, of programming without setting up such a tight agenda that the spirit of spontaneity has no room in which to move. All of which eventually brings one around to the conclusion that life taken in stride is fully as rich and rewarding as life planned by design.

Recently we invited a friend up to our guest house, *The Crow's Nest,* tucked away on a wooded hill with a wonderful view of lake and mountains and with a feeling of quietude so rare that a robin immediately appropriated one of the logs below the over-hang and confidently hatched out its chirping brood. My wife and I were excited about the prospect of having everything shipshape for our first guest, a bachelor friend of long standing who, we were sure, was precisely the one to initiate and bless this house.

We thought we knew his likes and dislikes—no noise, a shelf of good books, colorful draperies, good lighting, no guests, plenty of hot water, and so on. We fell more and more in love with *The Crow's Nest* as we readied it with great expectations.

Like Nicodemus, our friend came at night, which, I have now discovered, is the worst possible time for a guest to come straight from a bustling city to a mountain retreat. The contrast is too great, the night too awesome, the silence too deep, even though a hi-fi is calming the air with subdued welcoming music.

The lake, lovely in the daytime or when the moon is bright, lay ink-black and eerie along the shadowy shoreline, making strange murmuring sighs as the restless water lapped against the lonely crags. We thought *The Crow's Nest* looked intriguing with its mellow lights and soft decor, but I felt our guest's vibrations when I told him he would be "absolutely alone," and that the soft whisper of the wind would "lull him to sleep." All of which apparently was the very worst welcome we could possibly have accorded him. He was not used to being absolutely alone. He did not want the wind to lull him to sleep. I realized this when he asked pointed questions about the locks on the doors and about the distance from the guest house to the main cabin. I knew when he spotted a diffident spider in the bathtub that he was unused to the Canadian out-of-doors and, when he asked with a start, "What's that?" as the mother robin took a night flight past the window screen, I knew that our high hope for a housewarming was growing cold.

At six in the morning there was a banging at our cabin door. My friend stood there, haggard and abashed, oblivious of the beauty of sunrise over the lake and deaf to the entrancing warble of a loon out on the open waters.

"Dammit!" he said. "I had a miserable night!"

Over a pot of coffee he recounted his complaints, the list of which caused me to hang my head in shame. The new hot-water heater had gurgled and regurgitated all night long, setting up banshee sounds that curdled his blood. The toilet stuck and he had to remove the top and adjust the plunger, always a messy job. There were peculiar tappings on the roof—I had neglected to tell him that a tree squirrel occasionally used it as a shortcut from tree to tree. The lock on the door didn't lock, and another spider had crawled up through the bathtub drain. Moaning with exhaustion, he wondered if he might flop down in the big cabin and get some rest, which is what he did, and which was what he might have done from the start had we not had such high expectations that *The Crow's Nest* was outfitted exactly for him. He stayed only two days and the robins never even got to know his name.

Then I think of the unexpected, unprepared, unannounced visitors who have come down the lane and who, even though we sometimes shuddered to think how their visit would pan out, brought the informal warmth and joy that only spontaneity can bring. No preparations were made; no rooms were cleaned in advance; no program was worked out; no illusions were built up one way or another. Everything turned out to be in order because we had not had time to tamper with destiny's plans.

Evidently there is a divine current of some kind ready to carry us through certain phases of life, and the more we realize this and give ourselves over to it, the better off we are. Yet who has the courage to believe it, the daring to expect it, the wisdom to understand it, or the prudence to conform to it?

A reluctant swimmer who has come close to drowning can hardly be impressed with the confident assurance that "the water is your friend!" Even drownproofing seems to him merely an insidious technique to help him drown all the faster. Sometimes, though, it is possible by an act of grace or by some recognition of the deeper self to get the feeling of the friendliness for the mystic stream. For it is a feeling, the art of feeling the commonly unfelt.

Truly successful people always hold great expectations even though, like the Iowa farmer, they may hedge a bit. Brave men, though fearful, are never afraid of fear. Healthy persons have no time for sickness, and to the pure of heart things are not as impure as they seem.

We catch on to the truth and technique of expectation in those rare moments when we are stirred by an awareness of a guidance seemingly higher and greater than our own, when for a little while we are taken over by a force and an intelligence above and beyond those commonly felt. Confident and free, filled with wonder and ready acceptance, we permit ourselves to be taken over by our unquestioning self. How can we repeat these experiences? One way is to expect their repetition and to feel ourselves worthy of having them happen again.

REASONS FOR FAILURE

My father tried to impress it upon me that people patronized the business places that gave evident of affluence and success. I disagreed. I wanted to trade at the places which were having a hard time of it. I felt for them. But gradually I learned that my feeling was misplaced and that in identifying myself with them I was thinking failure instead of success and that my attitude was more patronizing than sincere. I also eventually tired of their complaining, their contention that they were not getting the breaks, that people were against them, and that they were probably born under an unlucky star. But there are reasons for failure and success beyond the zodiac, and the art of expectation on the proper level is the key.

There is a significant saying in the Book of Job, "The thing that I have feared has come upon me," and I have seen the truth of this demonstrated many times. Among a group of travelers whom I took to the Orient was a man who complained bitterly when the stewardess neglected to serve him his coffee. "She passed me by," he reported. "She served everyone around me and left me sitting here. But that always happens to me. I fully expect it." Sure enough, on the return flight with an entirely new crew, the stewardess not only forgot to bring his coffee, she forgot to serve him his meal. Fiery mad, he pressed the call button. "I'm so sorry," said the stewardess. "I can't imagine how I overlooked you." "They all do it to me!" he told her. They all did. And Job was right.

While house-hunting in southern California we were shown a place which a woman was renting temporarily. She said, "I wanted to buy a place in a certain section in Santa Barbara but was told there wasn't adequate fire protection. I live in deathly fear of fires. So I didn't buy. I came down to L.A. and bought a house in a canyon. Two months after I moved in I was burned out. You know, I think I carried that fire with me."

Wise old Job. But what did Job do about it? What can anyone do about it when he expects the worst and by his expectation invites the worst to happen?

We can do what Job did. We can learn that if we have a propensity for fear, we have an even greater propensity for faith. If we think we are slated for failure, it may be because we know we are meant for success. Our negative expectations are our positive determinations gone astray, but they are not *gone*. We come back to the formula: expectation is a matter of feeling, feeling is a servant of the will, the will is the result of a wish, and a wish is spun from the power of spirit.

Just how this works, or by what kind of a psychological test this can be measured, I do not know. My father never told me. In fact, the only thing he ever said was, "All I expect of you is that you do something worthwhile with your life."

SEMESTER
FOUR

We first make our habits,
and then our habits make us.

John Dryden

Drs. Tom Rusk & Randy Read

LESSON 16

HOW TO FIND THE COURAGE
TO TAKE RISKS

Now you're ready to move forward!

Now you know that it's your choice, and yours alone, as to what you will do with the rest of your life.

Perhaps you have even been convinced, after three very personal semesters, that whatever you think you will eventually become . . . and you do have all that potential, don't you?

So now what's holding you back? Afraid to take a chance?

Have you ever heard of "the Jonah complex"? You probably have it if you're living in your own little comfort zone, performing unchallenging tasks where no one will ever hassle you, taking no risks, facing few problems, never concerned about growth or testing your potential. This is living? Hopefully, it's hurting you, deep down inside.

Why?

"People don't change when they feel good. They change when they're fed up. When things are going all right, we all tend to do pretty much what we've been doing. Pain pushes us to those crucial turning points—. We hurt, then finally choose. It's that adverb, *finally*. Enough is enough!"

Those are the conclusions of two young and distinguished West Coast doctors, Tom Rusk and Randy Read, whose long list of credentials includes their positions as adjunct professors of psychology and law, respectively, at the University of San Diego.

This lesson, from their bold and honest book, *I Want to Change, But I Don't Know How,* may be just the medicine you need to cure you of ever hiding in your comfort zone again . . .

All too often we humans indulge in the cowardice of being too "careful," selling out for a promise of security. And we get cheated. You've seen it. The futility of using one's job as a way to hide. "I am a lawyer" (doctor, manager, and so forth) as if to say "I am a lawyer and nothing else." Or the futility of seeking meaning through a spouse's accomplishments—the "doctor's wife syndrome" (seen also in the spouses of politicians, business executives, ministers, lawyers, entertainers . . . indeed in any wife or husband who avoids challenges beyond the daily routine or who believes that vicariously enjoying a spouse's success is enough to make their life more meaningful. Pathetic!)

It's futile to live for some future time when things will be different, believing that as soon as "I'm older," "richer," "more educated," (or in a more sophisticated vein: "when I finish my therapy") then all will be well . . . dream on, for these are but futile delusions.

And it's futile to live in some past phase of your life when: "I was younger," "stronger," "my spouse was living," or before: "my marriage," "my divorce," "my surgery," "my heart attack," "I lost my job," "the children were born" . . . more hopeless deadends.

Charles Dickens depicts the tragic figure of Lady Havisham, sitting in her bedroom in full bridal regalia decades after her rejection by the would-be groom. Her monumental cowardice keeps her afraid to face her life as it is. If we want, we too can have dreams and cobwebs, fantasies about what was or might be. Thomas Wolfe made the same point in *You Can't Go Home Again*. An old vaudeville joke says the same thing in yet another way: "Your money or your life" demands the robber. "Take my life, I'm saving my money for my old age" the overcautious hero replies.

Incredibly, many people continue their old life-styles, their habits even if they feel miserable, lonely, bored, inadequate, or abused. Why? Of course . . . because habit is an easy place to hide. How many women marry several alcoholics sequentially, insisting they "never suspected."

A man spends his whole life working 60 to 100 hours a week, trying to get rich. Why? Because he watched his father slave his life away, never enjoying himself, dying while working, and he doesn't want this to happen to him!

Others attempt to live cautiously in the safety of established patterns. They do not feel fulfilled, yet they have found a formula not of success (whatever that is), but of avoiding failure. This is the living death—when security becomes the overwhelming consideration. Man does not live by security alone. (And, of course, neither does woman.)

Life has inevitable risk. Each next breath is a chance. Heart attacks, auto accidents, tax assessment, business problems—every conceivable kind of bad news waits to spring upon us without warning. So it's hard for us humans to play the gamble of life. It's a difficult balance. At times we might put too much on the next spin of the wheel, and at other times we feel so hurt and cheated that we want to stop playing forever. But the goal, in a sense, is to find a style of playing the game of life that keeps our hand in without burning us out.

When we reach beyond the safety and familiarity of our habits and behave in any way differently than our routines, we experience some tension. It may be mild, a slight tightness in the chest, or more pronounced, a rapid heart rate, nausea, diarrhea, fainting, or even panic. If we think about the possible consequences of a new change too long, the rats of fear come out of our mental basements and may overwhelm us. Anything new can be scary. The risk-taking in life is very much like investing money— the potential returns reflect in part the degree of risk. The higher the stakes, the more frightening the game.

And the clock keeps on ticking. Time accelerates with age, of course; nothing can be done about that. Yet, two minutes in a roller coaster is far more intense than eight hours of boring meetings. Variety prolongs time. Change wakes us up. Share time with different people, in different places, doing different things, and we can experience a week in just one day. Times of high emotional intensity, as in passionate lovemaking, can last far longer and fulfill far more than the same physical acts without the passion. Perceived time is an elastic commodity that depends on our age (uncontrollable) and on how we consume it (controllable). The intensity dial is in our grasp. We are given time, how much we make of it is up to us.

Human beings do need some stress. We were "designed" by evolution to survive in the stress of food chain competition. A certain amount of pressure is necessary for our health. Of course, too much stress, like too much sound, is bad. But no stress, like total silence, makes us unbalanced.

Many people try to insure themselves against every possible

danger. They want to never hurt, never be scared, never be lonely. So they adopt a formula of life where they live for material goods, feel as little as possible and hide behind old habits. Yet that hunger for "natural" stresses remains. Gradually they fill the gap with "internally manufactured" stress—worries and fears.

Of course they don't say to themselves "I'm going to adopt a life-style which will minimize my chance-taking, even though I'm aware it will give me an empty and boring life." They just grow up that way. But you *can* say to yourself "How much chance-taking is right for me? What kinds of stresses will help me on my path?" Some may find physical stress helpful—sports, exercise, or even fasting. For others the answer may be skydiving, motorcycle racing, or passionate interpersonal relationships. For still others, it will be retreat to a monastery and a courageous journey through the turbulence within. Each of us has a job in life: to fulfill our own needs, find what stresses and risks fit us best.

BOREDOM IS THE LEGACY OF FEAR

Risk taking is a major part of the "cure" so don't hope that somehow you'll be able to avoid it. Chronic capitulation to fear only insures mediocrity. The life-style we are advocating is one where you ask yourself for each new thing you try, "What's the risk and what's the possible payoff?" It's an attitude where you expect chance-taking to be part of what you're doing on this planet. Not necessarily crazy risks—if we get too extreme in our chance-taking, we don't hang around long enough to learn anything new. But careful, measured increases in risk seem to be the best way to go. For example, when you're learning how to ride a bicycle, you wouldn't start out in heavy automobile traffic. Instead, you'd pick a street where if you do fall down, at least you won't get run over.

So explore and experiment. Look for that balance between taking suicidal chances on one hand, and running from risking on the other. Some days will feel right for risks; others will feel better if you play it safe. Experiment to find out what's best for that moment. Since anything new will always be stressful, judge yourself by your efforts. No matter what you try, there's somebody else who probably does it better. The point is to find those things that let you feel exhilarated and alive. The point is to learn to season life's banquet with those redolent spices of stress and risk.

COURAGE AS LOSING YOURSELF

Perhaps the ultimate experiences in any life are those that transcend day-to-day existence. The sweet, rare times when involvement in an activity leads to a fulfillment beyond our wildest dreams. People in the arts and the devoutly religious base their lives on this "high" but anybody can get it. You can have it with someone you love or even someone you hate. It can come from cooking or woodworking or just walking.

It's an experience that's like being lifted up, swept away, forgetting worries and self-consciousness. It's been called merging, flowing, satori, and countless other names. Like love, however, it's one of those things that if never experienced is hard to believe. Any human endeavor from checking out groceries to tuning an engine can be performed in this creative state or reduced to a perfunctory routine.

One of the things we've often seen are people sitting around waiting for "it" to happen, as though they'll suddenly get some kind of badge of membership they can show to other people, as if to say "See, I rate; I've got *it* too." But, like anything else done primarily for the benefit of the audience, it's a performance that's bound to flop. If you are standing on a hilltop looking out over the countryside and suddenly have that experience of flowing and being part of it all, but then try to condense that experience into a tourist snapshot for the folks back home, you'll lose it in an instant. It can't be canned. You can experience it but you can't sell it.

And in a sense that's the greatest risk of all. You can't possess it. You can't "prove" it. You can only be it. You can let yourself go in what you do, or you can hold back. You can strive to immerse yourself, to take that risk of losing your identity in what you're doing. Or, you can stiffly straight-arm your life to keep it at a safe distance. You can try to reduce everything into "explainable" experiences. You can label and classify all that you see in a desperate attempt to stay in control. Or you can stop strutting and fretting and let go.

Fundamental to this process is the issue of losing control. There is a paradox in it that goes something like this: "The highest form of control is when one surrenders all control." It's like you never really own anything unless you can give it away. When we're trying to learn something, if we struggle to stay in control, we learn slowly if at all. When we're learning to ride a bicycle, if we keep struggling for control, stiffly directing our arms and legs with commandments on how to behave, we'll fall down more frequently. Instead, we can surrender our myth of being in charge, surrender our identity, and become part of the bicycle.

We learn best by losing ourselves. If we can be strong enough to just forget about who we are for a moment instead of taking ourselves so damn seriously, if we forget about what we think, what we believe, what we want—take the risk of forgetting ourselves—we learn with the grace of a blossoming flower. It takes the highest courage to use this self-surrender in any activity we undertake. But the rewards are equally high. We gain a peace, that sense of rightness, and most importantly, our full powers to create and grow.

This is the advanced course of "acting as if." Instead of pretending that one can ride a bicycle, one gives oneself to the act. Rather than trying, one just lets go. Most teaching presupposes that technical mastery is not the means but the end. But technical skill has no life of its own; it merely makes us free to surrender completely. Unless you have this experience of letting go; unless there is some area in your life where you have struggled through the technical mastery enough to give you that ability to flow, you'll never believe that such things happen.

If you want to play handball, for example, there are some technical skills that are useful to learn. But ultimately "your game" is the creative way in which you string together these basic elements. If you see them only as separate and isolated elements, you'll never have an exciting game. You'll just be another robot trying to imitate somebody else.

What kind of life do you want? How courageous will you be? The choice is yours.

Creativity is a fascinating topic. Throughout recorded history people have studied the very creative to find out their secrets. These gifted people themselves have at times reflected upon their own experiences and attempted to find some sort of "formula." But there is none. Creativity isn't a "step-by-step" process.

More than any other group in present-day American society, athletes seem to be conscious of how creativity is learned. "Concentration" is the phrase most often used to describe that state which is the essential prerequisite for peak performance. A "good game" can often be differentiated from a "bad game" by the degree of concentration. And what this state of concentration seems to be is a suspension of doubt and self-consciousness, a way of clearing the mind of all the distracting rubble and trash.

Some Oriental philosophies have made this state of mind their primary focus. Indeed, the concept of acting without self-conscious thought was probably first crystalized by the Samurai swordsmen of medieval Japan. Using some of the philosophical concepts of their time, they determined that the best way to beat one's adversary in a duel was to fight without the delay of thinking. Polished technical skill was a prerequisite, but the actual moves were dictated by feeling rather than thought. By refining their intuitive sense through the constant discipline of practice duels they were able to develop a state of mind that minimized the clutter of such thoughts as "oh, no, is he going to try to attack me from the left or the right?" Instead, poised and balanced, the Samurai could respond, as if he were at one with his opponent, as if he "knew" each moment what would happen next.

"The body learns instead of the mind." In other words, when you are learning something it's worth it to turn off, unplug, or tune out the mind for a little while. You can't tell the mind to shut up because then it just talks back to you, but you can quietly note what it's telling you, then switch to another channel for awhile. Like the Samurai, Zen archers of the Orient gained their discipline, not by focusing on the target, but by striving for the feeling of "rightness" in the shot. If the shot was "right," hitting the target comes naturally. Bull's-eyes on tiny targets in darkened rooms are part of what Zen archers do, but not for the sake of hitting targets. Their purpose is a form of meditation, a quest for that feeling of "rightness."

So, if you want to learn something new, concentrate on getting that "right" feeling that is true to yourself. Take the risk of letting go the precious little control you've struggled to gain, letting go enough to immerse yourself in what you are doing.

Then do it.

Sure, natural or genetic endowment, study and practice and even luck all play important parts in creativity, but ultimately what is necessary is this giving of one's self over to what one does. We like to think of it as a sort of *"two-phase process"*: first, you immerse yourself in your *creative action*, let go and do it. Second, *critically review*. You mentally stand back a little, take a little distance and weigh the results. "Did it get me closer to where I want to be?" Like a painter before the canvas, first there is the brush stroke that occurs in this trancelike state, and then a step back to gain a new perspective and gaze upon the outcome. These two phases flow into each other, but in a sense represent separate states of mind—*creative action* and *critical reviewing*.

Now, the point of all this is that many people become preoccupied with achieving a particular result such as fame, fortune, approval from others, or even something as evanescent as happiness. But if you get locked into outcomes you'll never be able to let yourself go long enough to experience intensely. After you give it a good try, *then* think and review. But don't try to review while you're trying to create. Edit after you invent. If your awareness is focused on the outcome, you can't allow yourself to let go.

Ultimately it comes down to what kind of value system you want—"all that counts is winning," or "to try is to succeed." The creative state requires forgetting about winning and focusing on trying. Anyway, playing just to win is a dead end. In the big scheme of existence, what game ever matters all that much? What could ever be worth the brutal cut-throat craziness of forcing ourselves to play only to win? All we humans really want is to feel good, to feel right, to find peace; we just get tricked by our myth that winning brings all those things automatically.

One of the most common reasons why people don't take control of themselves and don't accept responsibility for everything they do is fear of failure, fear of being a "loser." Only by giving yourself credit for *every effort* can you ever find the courage to immerse yourself in creative action.

If we live by the principle that to try is to succeed, that to give our best effort is what it's all about, we gain a mastery and peace. With that attitude we slip more easily into cycles of creating and reviewing. Good results are only a fringe benefit which may come and go, but what we do with ourselves is always in our control.

A farmer for fifteen years has managed to produce a good living for himself and his family. He never asked for a handout or special treatment. To him, welfare is an obscenity. Independence, hard work, "As ye sow, so shall ye reap" are his guiding principles.

One year, despite his fine efforts, a freak storm wipes out his entire crop. His reserves are inadequate to meet his financial obligations. Reluctantly he goes on welfare and accepts disaster aid. Both are "handouts." He feels a failure. Do you agree?

We hope not. If you agree then we understand why you fear change, risk, and experimentation. Fear of failure must paralyze you. Letting your self-respect depend on results makes you a slave to every whim of chance. Break free. If you're going to love yourself, love yourself no matter what. Actually what we are saying is not all that new: "It's not whether you win, it's how you play the game." But that noble tradition has been dying a slow death. Coach Vince Lombardi often said: "Winning isn't everything but trying to is." Yet didn't you think he said "Winning is everything"?

This common misquote shows a tragic truth about our social values. Lombardi was a great teacher and leader, but once again, people hear what they want to hear.

Be a strong coach for yourself. Encourage your own efforts. If you set a goal, but don't reach it, you have a choice.

You could put yourself down:

"I *knew* I couldn't. Maybe some people can change but I can't. My childhood screwed me up so bad, I just keep making the same mistakes over and over again. I'll *never* get it together."

Or you can cheer yourself on:

"I tried magnificently. I'm proud of me. I was truly immersed in the effort. I failed in my attempt; I accept that; I accept the pain. But I remain proud and love myself for my courage."

What is success? Who measures your value, you or your audience? Whom are you trying to impress? Your parents, living or dead, your spouse, your neighbors, or that mythical vague "they" out there you learned to dress up for on Sundays and holidays so as not to embarrass your family?

The myth, the cruel hoax perpetrated by our schools, by the media, by our churches or synagogues, suggest success as a place, a status, a thing, a level to be attained. Choose a career, work at it until you achieve "success." Then others will respect you and you will be happy . . . ridiculous!

Few experiences are more resonantly hollow than to be hailed as successful, only to feel undeserving of the admiring hoard. You need only look at the catalog of superstar entertainers whose lives prematurely ended in an agony of self-destruction. You play first, last and ultimately to an audience of *one*. Disappoint that one and you are bankrupt.

Cowardice stems from clutching desperately for a success we feel we don't deserve. Learn to lose yourself in your efforts. Learn to let go and you will have gained true courage.

Have the guts to face the light. Strive for as much courage as you can. That doesn't mean work yourself to the bone. Play is a vital need too. But don't wait for neat formulas, guaranteed tricks to solve your problems. Have the courage to live a life where some days will be hard and some easy no matter how clever you are. Let go with love and energy will fill you. Success is courageously living each moment as fully as possible. Success means the courage to flow, struggle, change, grow, and all the other contradictions of the human condition. Success means being true to you.

Charles "Tremendous" Jones

LESSON 17

HOW TO BECOME
A SELF-MOTIVATOR

Let's imagine that you have come to this classroom early. You need some time alone to reflect on what you have just learned about values and courage and being true to yourself.

A huge bear of a man walks into the room, glances up at the blackboard and prints, in large white letters, Charles "Tremendous" Jones. Is this your next professor? Do professors have names like *that?*

Well, this one does, and his powerful lectures and seminars, delivered before more enthusiastic audiences than he cares to remember, have motivated thousands to become positive and more productive individuals.

He turns and notices you, sitting here alone. He smiles, walks down to your desk, and extends his hand, introducing himself in a hoarse voice. If you were an old friend he wouldn't be shaking your hand but giving you a bone-crushing hug instead.

"How are you doing?" he asks.

"I'm catching on," you reply.

He nods and smiles. "Do me and yourself a favor during this lesson. If you are to profit as others have, don't remember what I say here. The value of this lecture, from my book, *Life Is Tremendous!* is for you to remember what you *think* as a result of what I say. My number-one objective is to stir up your thought processes and help you frame your own best thoughts with words so that you can harness and use them. Is that a deal?"

You nod. He returns to the blackboard, faces you again, and shouts, "And *please* don't take things so seriously. Success can be

169

fun! Life can be fun! Life is tremendous! Maybe, if I'm lucky, I'll even have you smiling, once or twice ..."

Today we're surrounded by motivators—people and things strive to motivate people to buy a product, pay for advice, or enlist in a cause. Motivation classes are crammed and motivation books are best-sellers. Motivation is big business!

But look closely at these motivators—some reach the point where they can motivate anybody into doing anything and success is running out their ears, yet they are miserable because they forgot to learn how to motivate themselves!

Which would you rather be—a miserable, successful motivator, or a happy, motivated flop? I would rather be a happy, motivated flop. If I am learning to be motivated, I'll eventually become a successful motivator of others, and be happy doing it. The motivator who can motivate everybody but himself may win the world but he'll never enjoy it.

How well I remember my great desire as a young salesman to become a master motivator. I couldn't wait to finish my training so I could use my dynamic motivational skills. The sales presentations were powerful; in fact they were so powerful that I felt I had to temper them or the prospect might die of a heart attack before I asked him to buy. I knew no one could resist the logic, the benefits, the security, the peace of mind—there hardly seemed a problem in the world that my presentation couldn't solve!

I recall how I expected the prospect to snatch the pen from my hand to sign on the dotted line . . . but he never did. Right in the hottest part of the sizzle, my prospect would yawn or interrupt with some scintillating statement like, "I'm insurance-poor," or "I have five thousand dollars with double *identity*!"

My heart would hit the floor. I'd sink so low I'd have to reach up to touch bottom. You never saw a more discouraged young salesman than I was. I soon began to be learning my problem wasn't how to motivate people—my problem was how to keep them from demotivating me!

Sometimes I would become so discouraged, there was nothing to do but go cry on the boss' shoulder, only to find he was more discouraged than I was! The prospects were discouraging me, the boss was discouraging me, friends were discouraging me, and I thought at times even my wife was discouraging me.

Sometimes a fellow at a seminar will come up and murmur: "Do you know why I'm not a success? I have a miserable wife."

I enjoy giving these fellows the shock treatment: "Do you really have a miserable wife? Well, you don't know how lucky you are. The best asset a man can have is a *miserable wife!* What if my wife had been sympathetic when I went home and told her how miserable things were and she said, 'Oh, my sweet little daddy, you stay home here with mommy and I'll take care of you'? We would have consoled each other among our furniture on the sidewalk!"

If you have a miserable wife, you'll keep working or she'll remind you what an idiot you were to take such a job in the first place. But don't despair if you don't have a miserable wife; you can probably make the grade without this asset.

I'm kidding, but I want to make it clear that there are no barriers you can't overcome if you are learning to be motivated. I believe with all my heart that everything that touches your life is to make you a more deeply motivated person—who in turn can motivate others to higher goals.

Some people ask what is my secret of being motivated. Well, I didn't find it—it found me. One of my achievements during my first five years in selling was five years of consecutive weekly production. This means that I never missed one week in selling a policy. This sounds impressive, but it's not the whole truth.

The whole truth is that I believed in goals and so I made a vow that I would sell a policy every week *or buy one*. Let me tell you, after I bought twenty-two policies I began to get motivated! Little did I realize that a simple vow would have the greatest influence on my work the rest of my life. For out of that vow and what it cost me to keep it, I began to learn *involvement and commitment*.

Some people get involved with their work but are not committed. Others are committed but don't get deeply involved. The two go together, and I'm convinced that there is no way to learn to be a motivated person without being totally involved and committed to whatever you are engaged in!

The greatest motivations I've had have come from my own heart and home. Someone else's experience or story can never motivate you as deeply as your own.

I used to tell a prospect who said he was insurance-poor that he was actually insurance-rich. But I discovered something far more effective through a little episode at home. This experience allowed me to agree wholeheartedly with an insurance-poor prospect, but gave me additional motivation to pass on to him.

My son Jere, six years old at the time, came in from the yard one day yelling at the top of his lungs for his mother. Naturally, this distracted me from my work in my office (really our living room—we had moved the furniture into the hallway). Jere upped his yell several decibels, and I thought, "I can't wait to get successful so I can move to a plush office downtown where I can fail in style."

Finally Jere gave up, and just then Gloria came up from the basement where she had been running the washer. She said, "What did you want, Jere?" He replied, "Nothing; just wanted to know where you were."

I've told that story thousands of times because it shows why I pay the premiums on those twenty-two policies. I may never leave my six children an empire, a block of real estate, or a huge stock portfolio, but I'm going to leave them a priceless gift: a fulltime mother. Because of my life insurance all six could come yelling for their mother knowing she was somewhere around the house, even though she didn't answer.

Another time I was sitting in the rocker reading the paper when eight-year-old Pam slipped her little blond head under my arm and wiggled onto my lap. I kept reading and then she said those few words that have helped me sell millions of dollars in life insurance. Looking at me with big, sad eyes, she said, "Daddy, if you won't ever leave me, I won't ever leave you."

I couldn't understand what prompted those words, but I immediately thought: "Well, dearest, I would never leave you, but if the Lord should rule otherwise at least I'll never leave you *without*."

Years ago I learned there were two kinds of dads, the *see*-kind and the *have*-kind. The see-kind says, "I want my family to have everything I can give them as long as I'm here to see it." The have-kind says, "I want them to have it whether I'm here to see it or not."

That is what happened to me as a result of commitment and involvement.

You say, "I'm not in the insurance field," or "I don't have a selling career." Listen, the principles we are talking about are the same for a student, wife, office worker, salesman, or whatever you are. The great things in your life will be greater if you are capitalizing on them to help you *be motivated*. Remember, you are building a life, not an empire. One of my best friends got mixed up on this very thing and lost almost everything of value.

I've heard men say, "I put my business first," and other men say, "I put my family first." A few say, "I put my church or synagogue first." (The truth is they probably put themselves first.) But I've found that my best lessons for business come from my family and church. And the best lessons for my family come from my business and church. And the best lessons for church come from my family and business.

Another son, Jeff, gave me some of the best motivation training of my life. When he was six, I asked Jeff what he wanted to do with his life. Now get this, six years old, and he still had no idea what he wanted to do with his life!

When I was six, I knew what I wanted to be. One day I wanted to be a fighter pilot, the next day I wanted to be a French Foreign Legionnaire. I wanted to be a boxer. I wanted to be a police officer. I always wanted to be something. Not my Jeff; still drifting.

So I said, "Jeff, we're going to have a little project. Here's a *Boys' Life*—you pick out a job. You're going to do something, partner." The next day he had it all worked out: he was joining the Junior Executive Sales Club of America. He filled out the coupon and sent it in.

I find that kids are dying to get on with the show! They want to do something. They're not getting much direction from anybody—except in the wrong way.

Two weeks later when I came home, Jeff greeted me at the door, "Look, Dad." And here was the biggest box of greeting cards I'd ever seen. I opened it up. There was a badge, credentials, and a notice that said, "Send in the money in thirty days." Jeff said, "What do I do now?" I said, "Well you have to learn the sales talk first."

Every night I would come home and Jeff would say, "Well, Dad, am I ready?" I'd say, "Have you got the sales talk down?" He'd say, "No." I said, "You're not going out there ad-libbing if you're going to represent me. I want you to know what you are going to say."

Two weeks later, Jeff finally told me: "I don't like that sales talk." "Well, write one yourself," I said.

Next morning at the breakfast table, there was a little piece of paper that said, "Good morning, Mrs. Smith, I'm Jeffrey John Jones. I represent the Sales Club of America." That's all! Two weeks had gone by and in two more weeks I had to send in the money! That night I came home and I told Jeff, "Get out the tape recorder; we're going to make up a talk. We're going to work until you have a sales talk."

We started rehearsing; the talk was like this: "Good morning, Mrs. Smith, I'm Jeffrey John Jones of the Junior Executive

Sales Club of America. Would you look at these greeting cards, please? You'll notice they carry the Good Housekeeping Seal of Approval, and are an exceptionally good value at only one dollar and twenty-five cents per box. Would you like one or two boxes (smile) pleeeeze?"

We rehearsed and rehearsed, and as we used the tape recorder to play back, I could see the tiger begin to develop in Jeff. Finally he said, "Am I ready yet?" I said, "No, you're not ready yet. You know how it goes here, but you don't know how it is in the field. You go out into the hall, and I'll be your prospect. Take two boxes with you, knock on the door, and I'll show you what to expect when you get out in the field."

Bursting with excitement and confidence, Jeff leaped into the hall to show me his power. He thought he was really ready. He knocked on the door. I threw open the door with a scowl and a roar: "What do you mean busting in on my lunch!" The Junior Executive Salesman sank slowly to the floor in a state of shock.

I got him up and we started over. I let him get through the second line, and I shot him down, the third line and I shot him down. His mother downstairs thought I was killing her baby! But I was getting her baby ready for a little living! You know who's "killing their baby" today? The parent who is raising his kid to think the world is going to give him a hug and a kiss every time he turns around. I was getting this boy of mine ready for reality!

Finally Jeff had his talk down pat and he made it through. "Well," he said, "are we ready?" I said, "You're ready. Here's how we start. Go down St. John's Road with two boxes. Wear a coat and a tie. As soon as you get ten no's, make a beeline for the house." (I knew that more than ten no's would ruin him.) "And as soon as two people say yes, make a beeline for the house." (I knew that more than two yesses might ruin him, too—I've seen prosperity kill about as many salesmen as failure has. He went out and sold those cards like hot cakes!)

Then one day he disobeyed me. On an unbelievably hot July day Jeff came in after taking nineteen straight no's. He was beaten, drenched with perspiration, and he slumped on the sofa. He said, "If they want any cards from me from now on, they'll have to come and get 'em!"

I said, "Now wait a minute, Jeff. You've just had a hard day, pardner." "Oh, Dad," he said, "all the other kids have found out what I'm doing and they're selling cards too."

I said, "I *know* somebody out there wants to buy." (Somebody *had* to be buying; I could never use that many greeting cards.) I said, "You need somebody to go along with you. You've got to get yourself a helper. Take your sister Candy along. Pay her ten cents to carry the boxes, and she'll give you moral support."

Did they get out there and encourage each other like I thought? No. They got out there and both started griping, and they *both quit!* (That was a good reminder for me: if you get discouraged, don't cry on a friend's shoulder. A friend will give you sympathy, and you're already giving yourself twice as much sympathy as you need. You'd better get back into the swing of things and *work* all the harder.)

Now I had all these cards on my hands, plus two quitters. I had to come up with something. "Jeff, on Saturday I'm going out with you myself." Then I called up one of my assistants and said, "Jack, on Saturday we're coming over to Green Lane Farms, and Jeff's in a slump. If I don't get him out of this slump soon, I'll have to buy these cards myself. I'll let him out two houses from your house. I want him to get two no's and then have a yes waiting at your house."

And so we got over to Green Lane Farms on Saturday. The first house said yes instead of no, and the second house said yes. You should have seen Jeff's face as he ran back to the car with a one thousand percent batting average! He was motivated!

Last year I lent Jeff twenty-four dollars to finance a home-cleaning product. He took thirty-eight no's on a hot August day, but he didn't quit. He is learning that if you stay motivated you don't mind the no's, and he knows there is a "Green-Lane-Farm" experience ahead if you keep going.

One of the greatest stories I've heard that shows the difference between outward and inward motivation is told by Bob Richards, the former pole-vault champion. A college boy on the football team was a number-one goof-off, a goldbricker. He liked to hear the cheers, but not to charge the line. He liked to wear the suit, but not to practice. He didn't like to put out.

One day the players were doing fifty laps and this showpiece was doing his usual five. The coach came over and said, "Hey, kid, here's a telegram for you."

The kid says, "Read it for me, coach." He was so lazy he didn't even like to read.

Coach opened it up and read: "Dear son, your father's dead. Come home immediately." The coach swallowed hard. He said, "Take the rest of the week off." He didn't care if he took the rest of the year off.

Well, funny thing, game time came on Friday and here comes the team rushing out on the field, and lo and behold, the last kid out was the goof-off. No sooner did the gun sound than the kid was saying, "Coach, can I play today? Can I play?"

The coach thought, "Kid, you're not playing today. This is homecoming. This is the big game. We need every real guy we have, and you're not one of them."

Everytime the coach turned around, the kid badgered him: "Coach, please let me play. Coach, I've got to play."

The first quarter ended with the score lopsided against ol' alma mater. At halftime the coach braced them in the locker room with a fight talk. "All right, men, get out there and hit 'em. This is a long way from being over. Win this one for the old coacheroo!"

The team rushed out and began tripping over their own feet again. The coach, mumbling to himself, began writing out his resignation. And up came this kid. "Coach, coach, let me play, please!" The coach looked up at the scoreboard. "All right," he said, "get in there, kid. You can't hurt nothin' now."

No sooner did the kid hit the field than his team began to explode. He ran, passed, blocked, tackled like a star. The electricity leaped to the team. The score began to even up. In the closing seconds of the game this kid intercepted a pass and ran all the way for the winning touchdown!

Whooooo! The stands broke loose. Pandemonium. People hoisted the hero onto their shoulders. Such cheering you never heard. Finally the excitement subsided and the coach got over to the kid and said, "I never saw anything like that. What in the world happened to you out there?"

He said, "Coach, you know my dad died last week."

"Yes," he said, "I read you the telegram."

"Well, Coach," he said, "my dad was blind. And today was the first day he ever saw me play!"

Wouldn't it be great if life were a game? Wouldn't it be wonderful if the field of life had cheering sections on each side, and when we reached the impossible situation and didn't know how to go on and no one understood us and we're about ready to fold and say those terrible words, "I quit," wouldn't it be wonderful if the stands would come alive and they'd yell, "Charlie, boy, keep on going; we're with you!" I'd say, "Whooooo! That's all I needed." Boy, I'd go down the field to another touchdown!

But life isn't a game, is it? It's a battlefield. Instead of players and spectators, we're all soldiers, including some goldbrickers and some AWOL's! But we're all in the struggle, whether we know it or not. And the person who knows how to be motivated doesn't need any cheering section. He has motivation built in. He's not looking for a crutch that might break, a bonus that will be taxed away; he's learning motivation from within.

Without goals, and plans to reach
them, you are like a ship that has
set sail with no destination.

Dr. Fitzhugh Dodson

LESSON 18

HOW TO PROGRAM
YOURSELF FOR SUCCESS

Stand on any busy downtown street corner and spend ten minutes watching humanity pass before you. How many, out of each hundred, would you guess have specific goals in their life which they are pursuing with all their vigor?

If you were a betting person you could probably wager considerable sums of money that *none*—out of any hundred who passed— had any goals that extended beyond that particular day!

Setting goals, you would learn from these individuals, if you had the courage to ask, is "something that the 'company bosses' do when they are planning next year's budget. Setting goals is what football coaches and baseball managers often do. Setting goals is what presidents and governors and fund raisers always talk about since they're involved with large operations. But how can we think about setting goals for ourselves when our paychecks aren't even large enough to cover our bills?

Perhaps those paychecks are not large enough to pay their bills, and maybe never will be, *because they have no goals,* no concrete plans on how to improve their life, no ideas on how to raise their income, improve their talents, expand their knowledge, or increase their value to society! Regretfully, most of them are skippers of ships heading nowhere!

Dr. Fitzhugh Dodson became internationally known through his two classics on child raising, *How to Parent,* and *How to Father.* Unlike many goal-setting systems, which can be complicated, he, from his book, *The You That Could Be,* shares with you a simple and commonsense plan for fulfillment that can help you to begin planning the life you deserve ...

I want to talk about your goals and plans and how you can program yourself for success. Your Potential Self thrives on well-made goals that reflect what is important to you.

A goal is an objective you want to achieve. A plan is a specific way of reaching that goal. Both goals and plans are *ideas in your mind*.

Look around you. Everything you see in the world around you (unless it is a part of nature) began as an idea in somebody's mind. The suit or dress you are wearing. The car you drive. The music you listen to.

The words you are reading began as an idea in my mind. Then the idea became a goal, and I created a plan to achieve it. The typewriter I wrote it on was originally the idea of an eighteenth-century Englishman named Henry Mill. It has been continuously developed and refined by a series of other people since and represents an achieved goal for each of them. Everything you wear, everything in your house or apartment, even the building itself had to be thought of before it could exist. And then the design, manufacturing, and marketing of it became goals for someone. Even your toothbrush began as an idea, with a specific plan to achieve it.

All tangible objects began as goals, plans, or ideas in the minds of people. This is a revolutionary concept, once you really allow it to grasp you, for it brings home the importance of the world of thought. Unfortunately, many Americans tend to downgrade the world of thought. When we call a person an intellectual, it is not always meant as a compliment. We respect the people who are characterized as "doers," forgetting that every "doer" is first a thinker. Looking at things in this incomplete manner prevents us from seeing clearly that *the world is changed by goals and plans conceived in the minds of men and women*.

It is really incredible when you realize that our school system consistently neglects to teach students how to set their own goals and make realistic plans to achieve them. Did you ever hear of a course like that in high school? In college? I never have.

Frequently our schools even neglect to call attention to the fact that such vital activities exist. The thought of setting goals and making plans just "escapes the mind" of many people. And yet, few things are more important to a person in achieving success in all fields of life than learning how to do it. This idea should really exist as a way of life and should be passed on from parents to their children.

I sometimes mention goals and plans to people and ask them what it brings to mind. Most people say: "Oh, success in the business world, in science, or something like that." They usually don't mention the nonprofessional, personal world, such as their marriage.

I think of a former patient of mine, Arthur, a forty-three-year-old man who owned his business and came to me because of increasing "attacks of nerves," as he put it, in his work. He had just opened his second men's clothing store. Business was doing well financially, but his problems with the manager of his newly opened store were increasing. The manager had been a most satisfactory employee until he assumed his new position. Now suddenly he wanted to change many of the concepts that had brought success to Arthur in the first place. Having always prided himself on his business judgment, Arthur was now losing confidence in himself. Was he falling behind the times? At forty-three, was he becoming an old fogy?

As he discussed his business problems, Arthur kept mentioning his wife, Marie. They had been married for twenty years and had two teenage children. He often remarked how supportive and helpful his wife had been in the beginning when he had to struggle to establish his business. Although he hadn't come to me for marriage counseling, we started discussing his relationship with Marie. I pointed out that the closeness he had enjoyed during their early marriage seemed to have been replaced by a dull flatness. I suggested we also work on some goals and plans for his marriage. He said, "I'm amazed, Doc! I never thought about setting goals for my marriage like I do for my business!" He mentioned somewhat sheepishly that before he was married he used to "romance" his wife, as he put it, but it had been years since they had done anything spontaneous or romantic.

After considerable discussion, we decided to start with a few simple plans to implement his newfound goals of putting some romance back into the marriage. I suggested starting with the easiest plans to achieve. He decided to buy a supply of "love message" cards for his wife and mail her one from time to time. He told me they had dutifully celebrated their anniversary on June sixteenth every year. So as an additional plan I suggested they celebrate an "anniversary" on the sixteenth of every month. Finally, I suggested he take her out to dinner more often, just the two of them, without the kids.

Some of you may be thinking, "Well, there's very little spontaneity in those plans. Aren't those the sort of things he should think of on his own?" Sure they are. But the answer is that if I had left it up to him, he might never have thought of them spontaneously! This way, once he got started on this program, his wife was so pleased that she began to cook special dishes he liked and do other little thoughtful things the way she had done early in their marriage. He told me happily, "We're beginning to live with a kind of 'zing' I'd forgotten about." Incidentally, as his marriage relationship began to change, he was also making a great deal of progress in his business relationships. Creativity in one area often helps in another.

That most people have no goals or plans is unfortunate but not surprising, since the whole concept is a neglected area in our culture. Many people just exist from day to day, week to week, year to year. Others have goals but they are so vague or passive they are virtually worthless. Often I refer to these as "money goals." They want a new Porsche, a trip to Europe, or a mink coat. Fine. Who doesn't? But to achieve such goals you need the money to pay for them. On this point, the person is usually quite vague and has no plan about how to get such a sum of money.

There are some people who "kind of" have goals but they are still in their unconscious mind, vague, and undefined. These people have never taken the time to sit down and pinpoint the specific objectives of their lives.

Still other people have goals that are impossible to obtain. One of my former patients, Bruce, had as his goal an early retirement at age thirty-five. Since he was unable to do this, it had ruined his whole thirty-fifth birthday celebration. Obviously, this was an unrealistic goal, in spite of the fact that this bright young man was highly successful in the business world. How many people are able to retire by the age of thirty-five? And on what? And why? In Bruce's case he had no particular notion of what he wanted to do after retirement. Retirement was his whole goal, rather than it being somehow related to the rest of his life. If he had actually retired at thirty-five, he would have discovered it to be an empty achievement. This man's goal was not only unrealistic; it was incomplete.

Now I want to teach you how to develop meaningful goals, how to define them clearly, and how to create definite plans for reaching them.

First, there is the area of your work. You may have many goals in mind here, including "money goals," such as travel, a new house, a new car, or college for your children. The place you are most likely to achieve these money goals is in your world of work.

There is the area of your marriage. Setting goals in this area may head off divorce in the future, or deepen an already satisfactory relationship.

There is the area of children. Most parents have relatively few goals and plans for their children. Like fire fighters, they rush around putting out daily fires and are too busy to set long-term goals and plans. These parents are missing a great deal in their emotional relationships with their children by not thinking about the future direction the children may take.

If you are not married, then you may be concerned to set goals and plans so that you can find and marry someone with whom you can achieve a happy and lasting relationship. As someone has commented: "Most people put more time and care into choosing a new car than into choosing the right person to spend the rest of their life with."

Finally, there is the whole area of friends. How superficial most relationships are with "friends" in today's culture. You may want to set some goals and plans here.

Did mentioning these areas stimulate anything in your mind? Do you already have some goals in mind, or did you get a new idea or two? Obviously, this is worth putting some thoughtful time into. Consider these things as you go about the routine tasks of the day—think about your work and its rewards; the quality of your home life, of your marriage, of your relationships with your children, or your friends. Think about your children's future. Think about your own day-to-day existence. Be imaginative as you consider these aspects of your life and how you could change or augment them. Let your creative mind be fanciful; think up far-out ideas. Rediscover your dreams.

At some point in this process, perhaps in a day or somewhat longer, you will be ready for specific planning. This is the most important step—taking specific action on your thoughts.

Find half an hour when you will be free of all distractions. Use it to make a list of the previous goals you have thought of plus any new ones that occur to you. Include the most outrageous goals you can imagine. Don't worry about whether your ideas are realistic or unrealistic at this point; just write them down. After you have noted all your goals, go over the list carefully and pick out the five which are the most important to you. You may find this a very exciting process.

Your next step is to determine how to reach each of these five goals. Here's where most people go astray because they start out with a plan that is much too ambitious. When it can't be achieved right away, they get discouraged and give up. These are the people who have not learned the lesson of the teaching machine.

Even though many of you have heard the phrase "teaching machine," you may not be familiar with the manner in which it works or the psychological principles on which it is based. (The "brother" of the teaching machine, the programmed book, is a teaching machine in book form, based on exactly the same principles.) The teaching machine or programmed book is planned so that the learner starts out answering very easy questions. He cannot go on to the next question until he has successfully answered the previous one. Finally, at the end of the program or book, the learner is answering very hard questions. The teaching machine or programmed book is constructed so that the student will be successful right from the beginning.

Let the teaching machine be your model. First you write down your goal; your second job is to break your goal into a series of steps, beginning with steps which are absurdly easy. For example, I had a former patient, Max, forty-six years old, who was really out of shape physically. One of his goals was to get back into good physical shape. When I asked him how he planned to do this, Max named a gym—the most expensive in the area—and told me he was going to sign up for its full physical fitness program. He planned to swim twenty laps in the club's pool each morning on his way to work and stop by on the way home each evening to work out on their machines. I immediately realized that this was too elaborate a program and that he would last only a few weeks and then quit.

I suggested we use the teaching machine approach instead. He liked the idea of jogging, so we agreed he should begin by jogging around his house and yard a mere three minutes a day. He wanted to do sit-ups to improve his stomach muscles. We decided he begin by doing only *one* sit-up a day for the first week. Starting with this very easy program, of course, he was successful. Little by little, over a period of five months, he worked up to jogging half an hour and doing fifty sit-ups each morning.

When you are designing a step-by-step plan to achieve your goal, whatever it is, think of my patient and his physical fitness program. Make your first steps to your goal absurdly easy so that you are sure to succeed. Then gradually increase them. Don't rush.

Thinking of Max and his physical fitness program brings to

mind Janet, another former patient. Janet had been reducing off and on for years. She must have gained, lost, and regained the same twenty-five pounds at least a dozen times. What she really wanted to do was to lose weight and make sure it stayed off. When we discussed her goal, she realized that in the past she had lost a lot of weight quickly on a crash diet, but then regained it just as quickly.

Janet had been doing a lot of reading about weight control, and she realized she would have a better chance of keeping the weight off if she lost it more slowly. After some discussion, she decided to try to lose half a pound a week. Since it takes 3,500 calories less than your normal diet to lose a pound a week, Janet needed to eat only 250 calories less each day in order to lose half a pound a week. This was not an impossible task. And to make it easier, she set up a reward system for herself. Since she was paid every two weeks at her job, she marked on her calendar the weight she expected to be on each payday for the next six months. (That is, one pound lighter than she had been the previous pay period.) If she *was* a pound lighter, she bought herself an inexpensive present (as long as it wasn't food!). Rewarding herself for accomplishing her goal at each stage proved to be the added incentive she needed. For the first time in her life she not only lost the weight, but she did not gain it back again.

Another example explores an entirely different area of human relationships. A thirty-two-year-old woman patient, Ellen, was overwhelmed by feelings of isolation after her divorce. Her goal was to get back into the world of social relationships, but she was terribly afraid of being rejected. I suggested a plan in several steps. First, she was to apply for membership in Parents Without Partners, but she was *not* to go to any of the activities the first month. In fact, she was instructed not even to read the monthly newsletter, listing the various activities. The second month she was to read the newsletter but not to attend any activities. The third month she was to participate in one discussion group only. The fourth month she was to go to two discussion groups. Finally, the fifth month she was to attend a dance. It worked. With each succeeding month and each succeeding step she built up the courage to try the next step of the plan.

Some of these early steps may sound so slow that they don't make sense, and you may feel "nothing is happening." Wrong! Something *is* happening, but it isn't particularly obvious. What is taking place is that your Potential Self is getting into gear for the eventual achievement of your goal. Often your goal is something you would have accomplished already, if some repressive mechanism inside you had not interfered. In addition to guaranteeing success at each step by going slowly at first, you are allowing your sincere desire for the goal to start directing your actions.

Some people, in working toward a goal, find themselves seized by inertia when it comes time for action. If this should happen to you, despite the small graduated steps, then it is time to reexamine your goal. Consider how important it actually is and then either discard the goal (and replace it with a more suitable one) or continue the steps with a renewed sense of the value of achieving it.

When you have chosen your first five goals, be sure to give your unconscious mind a chance to help plan the steps to make them work. With both your conscious and unconscious mind working on the problem, you will be making the best use of your creative mental resources.

My suggestion on how you can best accomplish the planning stage is to write, in brief form on three-by-five cards, the five goals and any steps to achieve them. Tape one of these cards to your mirror where you can see it every day. Put the second one in your pocket or purse. This way you will be thinking daily, both consciously and unconsciously, of these five goals and the steps by which you can achieve them. I do not mean for you to fret and stew, pressuring yourself to come up immediately with the "right way" to achieve them. Just think about them consciously from time to time as you go about your normal routine. At the same time, your unconscious will be doing its work. Your unconscious will usually contribute its part at some unexpected time, such as when you are eating lunch or playing tennis. When this happens, jot down the idea as soon as you can.

For the most part, I am talking about practical, attainable goals. If you happen to choose a long-range endeavor, such as becoming a doctor, you will need to break it down into many, many steps leading to it.

It is important, of course, to be realistic about goals. If you are fifty years old, it is not very realistic to decide to become a doctor. If you are twenty-two it may be. First determine that you have the intellectual equipment and emotional stamina for the job. Get a professional evaluation of this before committing yourself to the goal.

Some goals may be realistic when you set them, but life changes. Do not delude yourself into thinking that everything is standing still while you are moving toward your goals. Your goal may be to improve your marriage relationship, but while you are working toward this, your wife starts action for divorce. Your goal may be to become president of your company. But a new scientific discovery suddenly creates the possibility of a new manufacturing division within your company structure. You realize that your real rewards lie in directing that new division rather than the entire firm. It is important that you not think of either your goals or your plans to achieve them as unalterable and carved in white marble. Goals are made to be shifted and plans are made to be changed. You have not "failed" if you shift a goal or change a plan, whether the choice was yours or not.

A goal is an ideal, then, and something entirely outside of your control may force you to lower your sights. Realistically speaking, you may be able to achieve only 25 percent of the goal you originally set. But remember, if you had not set it, you would not have achieved even that 25 percent.

For example, you may have the goal of getting your children to take a more active part in doing chores around the house. You construct a set of plans to involve them in these activities. But after considerable effort on your part and theirs, they are still doing only about 50 percent of the chores you would like. It looks as if things are not going to improve any further, no matter what you try. Then it may be wise for you to accept the 50 percent as the most they are able to do and congratulate them and yourself for the improvements they have made.

Some goals are ideals you will want to continue striving for in spite of difficulties. But when a goal no longer seems realistic, it is best to turn your attention to other goals. A goal should never be used as a perfectionistic standard that forces you to call yourself a "failure" if you do not achieve it 100 percent.

Remember the concept of a baseball player's batting average. A player who bats .300 is considered an excellent hitter. That means he gets three hits out of every ten trips to the plate. Try to allow yourself the same kind of margin with your goals and plans. Don't demand that you bat 1.000 with your goals. Perfection, after all, is not very "human."

If you do the things outlined here, I can practically guarantee you will be more successful in your life than most people. You will have defined your goals clearly, five at a time. You may not achieve all of every goal, but you will achieve at least part of each.

Be sure to use the model of the teaching machine in programming your plans to achieve your goals. Always begin with ridiculously easy plans at first. This not only helps to start you off, but also to begin it successfully. It is likely you will continue to be successful as you advance from easier plans to harder ones.

Above all, be flexible. Do not hesitate to change either a goal or the plan leading up to it at any time. Do not let your goals run you. You run your goals. After all, you are not trying to add pressures and burdens to your life; you are adding focus.

But be careful not to let yourself slip into the situation where your goals concern only your business or making money. Think of your marriage, your children, and your friends as important areas in which to improve your life.

I have suggested you start by choosing five goals, which is a reasonable number to focus on. Obviously you are not going to keep those same five goals forever. One of two things will happen. As you reach a goal, you will cross it off your list and replace it with a new one; or you will realize that a particular goal is no longer desirable or realistic, and you will adjust or replace it. And so you will go through your life, achieving, adjusting, or discarding goals and replacing them with new ones. In contrast to most people, who let their lives just "go along," your life will always be focused on specific goals with specific plans for achieving them. You will be "on the move" in all important areas of your life with a steady, consistent pace. You will be improving your situation and increasing your happiness.

LESSON 19

HOW TO BECOME ENTHUSIASTIC
AND STAY THAT WAY

Chances are that if you were asked to define a "quitter" you would probably say that he or she is a person who gives up too easily.

Have you ever wondered why some individuals hang on against all odds until they turn certain defeat into victory while others abandon the race, sometimes in sight of the finish line?

Is bravery—the guts to endure, to get up off the canvas, to stick to something until it is completed—an inherited trait? No!

Then what's the big difference between the person who perseveres and the person who quits?

Enthusiasm!

If you think back on your life you will agree that whenever you lost your enthusiasm for any activity you also lost your desire to keep working at it—and when that happened it was eventually pushed aside. You didn't call it quitting, but that's what it was. In many minor matters your quitting didn't really matter so much, but in your major life functions such as marriage or career, the results are often disastrous.

Is there a danger that you might even lose your enthusiasm to work as hard as necessary to change your life for the better? Yes! You can lose your enthusiasm for *anything* unless you know how to keep those flames of ambition constantly burning inside you.

W. Clement Stone, beginning as a newsboy on the sidewalks of Chicago, built the largest insurance company of its kind in the world once he learned, and applied, the secret of generating enthusiasm within and maintaining it until he accomplished goal after goal. From the pages of his magazine, *Success Unlimited,* he shows you how, providing you are perceptive enough to spot his secret ...

As a houseguest on many occasions, Father John O'Brien, research professor of theology at Notre Dame University, and I, spent many delightful hours exchanging ideas. I recall a discussion on enthusiasm in which I stated: *"Enthusiasm is one of the most important factors necessary for success in selling."*

"Yes," he responded *"the first ingredient which I believe is absolutely necessary for a successful, efficient, and competent salesman or individual is enthusiasm."*

"What is your meaning of enthusiasm?" I asked. He replied:

"I think you would be interested in knowing what the etymology—the derivation of this word, which is so widely used, really is. It comes from two Greek words and they let you look into the root of this word—into its basic, fundamental, original meaning. The first is *'Theos,'* which means God. The other two words are *'En-Tae.'* So that in the early usage of this term among the ancient Greeks, it literally meant *'God within you'* . . . the Divine Being who is the author and the source of all goodness and beauty and truth, honesty and love. God is in the heart of the individual who is possessed by a vision . . . who burns with ardor . . . who is determined to make a dream come true. God is there. God is kindling the fire. It is being kindled by God himself." He hesitated with an expression of deep thought and continued:

"On one occasion, Knute Rockne was visiting at the hospital bedside of one of the most gifted and brilliant players whoever walked upon the striped field of Notre Dame Stadium. He had all the evidence of a fatal illness. His name was George Gibb. He was nicknamed 'The Gipper.' He's a legend for us. *The Gipper* brings inspiration and joy—hope—courage to every player who wears the uniform of Notre Dame. George Gibb is the only man of whom it has been said that he never allowed a pass to be completed by an opponent in his territory.

"After a brief talk in which Rockne knelt at his bedside and prayed to Almighty God to give George the courage and the strength to face the greatest event of his life—his departure, George Gibb looked up at him and said, 'Rock, it's tough to go now.' This was toward the latter part of the football season.

" 'It's tough to go now, but someday,' he said, 'when the going is tough and the breaks are beating our players, tell them to go in and win one more for The Gipper. I don't know where I'll be but I do know this—that I shall know of its occurrence.'

"About five years later, when Notre Dame was playing its favorite adversary back in those days, thirty years ago—the Army, Knute Rockne had one of the weakest teams that he ever coached at Notre Dame. The score at the end of the first half was 21 to 7 in favor of the Army. When the players trooped off the field into the locker room at intermission between the halves, Rockne told them the story of *The Gipper* with all the sincerity and emotion he knew how to express.

"And he said, 'Boys, I know that the conditions are fulfilled which would justify me in telling you the story of *The Gipper*. I've never told it to you before. But the time has come. I know that the going has been tough today . . . unfortunate breaks have been beating you down . . . you feel licked . . . but you must now regain the pride that has forever graced the player that wore the honored colors of Notre Dame . . . *The Gipper*.' He told the story of George Gibb's last words to him and then in a commanding voice said, '*Let's go out there with enthusiasm and . . . win one more for The Gipper*.'

"The players were emotionalized. They rushed from the locker room. They played as men transformed . . . they hit . . . they ran . . . they passed . . . they blocked . . . they transcended their known abilities. Rockne later said, 'I have never seen a team of such mediocre talent play with such courage . . . vigor . . . zeal and . . . enthusiasm.'

"And when the shadows settled upon that field that dark day in November the score: Army—West Point 21 . . . Notre Dame 28.

"If you walk into the locker rooms where the athletes dress, you will find on a bronze tablet those words: '*When the going gets tough and the breaks are beating our boys, go in there and win one more for The Gipper*.' It is that spirit which I think year after year has taken players of rather mediocre ability . . . transformed them . . . given them a courage and . . . an enthusiasm without which no battle of any importance can be won.' "

DEVELOP ENTHUSIASM AT WILL

Whoever you may be: executive, lawyer, doctor, teacher, sales manager, superintendent, foreman, athletic coach, priest, or rabbi, you will have many struggles and battles of importance in influencing others . . . achieving your desirable goals and . . . eliminating your undesirable habits.

You will win or lose depending upon your willingness to pay the price to regularly engage in thinking and planning time and . . . to use your mind power to develop a truly positive mental attitude and eliminate the negative.

"No battle of any importance can be won without enthusiasm," said Father O'Brien. "But how do you develop enthusiasm?" you may ask. Here's my response:

- "To become enthusiastic for achieving a desirable goal, keep your mind on your goal day after day. The more worthy and desirable your objective . . . the more dedicated and enthusiastic you will become.

- "Understand and act on Professor William James's statement: 'The emotions are not always immediately subject to reason but *they are always immediately subject to action.'*

- "Illustration: Say you are called upon to make a speech before a few thousand persons and you are not experienced in public speaking. You will be timid and afraid. To get up on the platform to speak, you can use the self-motivators that appeal to reason such as: *Success is achieved by those who try,* and *Where there is nothing to lose by trying and a great deal to gain if successful by all means try.* Then use the self-starter: *DO IT NOW* and immediately get into action. Walk up to the podium. When you get there, you may be under the emotion of fear. To neutralize this fear: Talk *loudly . . . rapidly . . . emphasize important words . . . hesitate where there is a period, comma, or other punctuation in the written word . . . keep a smile in your voice and . . . then use modulation.* When the butterflies stop flying in your stomach, you can talk just as enthusiastically in the conversational tone. It works 100 times out of 100.

- "Professor James pointed out a universal truth: *that feelings . . . moods and . . . emotions will follow action.* If you want to be enthusiastic . . . *act enthusiastically.*

LESSON 20

HOW TO ELIMINATE
YOUR BAD HABITS

Rare is the wise man who has not had a definite opinion about habits.

John Dryden said, "We first make our habits, and then our habits make us." Horace Mann wrote, "Habit is a cable. We weave a thread of it every day, and at last we cannot break it." And Samuel Johnson exclaimed, "The chains of habit are generally too small to be felt until they are too strong to be broken."

If this classroom is packed beyond its capacity it is because you have all gathered here for the same purpose—to hear America's first authentic genius, Benjamin Franklin, describe to you in his own characteristic style exactly how he broke the chains of his own bad habits, habits that would have prevented him from ever reaching the stature that he finally attained.

During your lifetime you have accumulated thousands of habits. Most of them are good ones. Some are even necessary for your survival. For example, you probably drive an automobile one or more times each day. Soon after your first driving lesson, the countless actions necessary to pilot your vehicle became habits. If you always had to stop and think before you engaged in every step necessary to drive, you would probably become a highway fatality in short order.

Along with all those good habits, however, you *know* you also have some that are harmful and if you were pressed you could probably compile a fairly complete list of them. You might even admit, if you happen to be feeling sorry for yourself, that you realize

191

they are holding you back but you just don't know what to do about them.

That won't be your excuse any longer, after Mr. Franklin in this excerpt from *The Autobiography of Benjamin Franklin,* has had a talk with you ...

Though I seldom attended any public worship, I had still an opinion of its propriety and of its utility when rightly conducted, and I regularly paid my annual subscription for the support of the only Presbyterian minister or meeting we had in Philadelphia. He used to visit me sometimes as a friend and admonish me to attend his administrations, and I was now and then prevailed on to do so, once for five Sundays successively. Had he been in my opinion a good preacher, perhaps I might have continued, notwithstanding the occasion I had for the Sunday's leisure in my course of study; but his discourses were chiefly either polemic arguments, or explications of the peculiar doctrines of our sect, and were all to me very dry, uninteresting, and unedifying, since not a single moral principle was inculcated or enforced, their aim seeming to be rather to make us Presbyterians than good citizens.

At length he took for his text that verse of the fourth chapter of Philippians, "Finally, brethren, whatsoever things are true, honest, just, pure, lovely, or of good report, if there be any virtue, or any praise, think on these things." And I imagined, in a sermon on such a text, we could not miss of having some morality. But he confined himself to five points only, as meant by the apostle, namely: 1. Keeping holy the Sabbath day 2. Being diligent in reading the holy Scriptures 3. Attending duly the public worship 4. Partaking of the Sacrament 5. Paying a due respect to God's ministers. These might be all good things; but, as they were not the kind of good things that I expected from the text; I despaired of ever meeting with them from any other, was disgusted, and attended his preaching no more. I had some years before composed a little Liturgy or form of prayer for my own private use (namely, in 1728) entitled, *Articles of Belief and Acts of Religion.* I returned to the use of this and went no more to the public assemblies. My conduct might be blameable, but I leave it without attempting further to excuse it, my present purpose being to relate facts and not to make apologies for them.

"THE BOLD AND ARDUOUS PROJECT OF ARRIVING AT MORAL PERFECTION . . ."

It was about this time I conceived the bold and arduous project of arriving at moral perfection. I wished to live without committing any fault at any time; I would conquer all that either natural inclination, custom, or company might lead me into. As I knew, or thought I knew, what was right and wrong, I did not see why I might not always do the one and avoid the other. But I soon found I had undertaken a task of more difficulty than I had imagined. While my care was employed in guarding against one fault, I was often surprised by another; habit took the advantage of inattention; inclination was sometimes too strong for reason. I concluded, at length, that the mere speculative conviction that it was our interest to be completely virtuous was not sufficient to prevent our slipping; and that the contrary habits must be broken and good ones acquired and established before we can have any dependence on a steady, uniform rectitude of conduct. For this purpose I therefore contrived the following method.

In the various enumerations of the moral virtues I had met with in my reading I found the catalog more or less numerous, as different writers included more or fewer ideas under the same name. Temperance, for example, was by some confined to eating and drinking, while by others it was extended to mean the moderating of every other pleasure, appetite, inclination, or passion, bodily or mental, even to our avarice and ambition. I proposed to myself, for the sake of clearness, to use rather more names with fewer ideas annexed to each than a few names with more ideas; and I concluded under thirteen names of virtues all that at that time occurred to me as necessary or desirable and annexed to each a short precept which fully expressed the extent I gave to its meaning.

These names of virtues with their precepts were:

1. TEMPERANCE. Eat not to dullness; drink not to elevation.

2. SILENCE. Speak not but what may benefit others or yourself; avoid trifling conversation.

3. ORDER. Let all your things have their places; let each part of your business have its time.

4. RESOLUTION. Resolve to perform what you ought; perform without fail what you resolve.

5. FRUGALITY. Make no expense but to do good to others or yourself; that is, waste nothing.

6. INDUSTRY. Lose no time; be always employed in something useful; cut off all unnecessary actions.

7. SINCERITY. Use no hurtful deceit; think innocently and justly, and, if you speak, speak accordingly.

8. JUSTICE. Wrong none by doing injuries or omitting the benefits that are your duty.

9. MODERATION. Avoid extremes; forbear resenting injuries so much as you think they deserve.

10. CLEANLINESS. Tolerate no uncleanliness in body, clothes, or habitation.

11. TRANQUILITY. Be not disturbed at trifles, or at accidents common or unavoidable.

12. CHASTITY. Rarely use venery but for health or offspring, never to dullness, weakness, or the injury of your own or another's peace or reputation.

13. HUMILITY. Imitate Jesus and Socrates.

My intention being to acquire the *habitude* of all these virtues, I judged it would be well not to distract my attention by attempting the whole at once, but to fix it on one of them at a time; and, when I should be master of that, then to proceed to another, and so on, till I should have gone through the thirteen; and, as the previous acquisition of some might facilitate the acquisition of certain others, I arranged them with that view as they stand above. Temperance first, as it tends to procure that coolness and clearness of head which is so necessary where constant vigilance was to be kept up and guard maintained against the unremitting attraction of ancient habits and the force of perpetual temptations. This being acquired and established, Silence would be more easy; and my desire being to gain knowledge at the same time that I improved in virtue, and considering that in conversation it was obtained rather by the use of the ears than of the tongue, and therefore wishing to break a habit I was getting into of prattling, punning, and joking which only made me acceptable to trifling company, I gave Silence the second place. This and the next, Order, I expected would allow me more time for attending to my project and my studies. Resolution, once become habitual, would keep me firm in my endeavors to obtain all the subsequent virtues; Frugality and Industry freeing me from my remaining debt, and producing affluence and independence, would make more easy the practice of Sincerity and Justice, and so forth. Conceiving then that agreeably to the advice of Pythagoras in his Golden Verses daily examination would be necessary, I contrived the following method for conducting that examination.

I made a little book in which I allotted a page for each of the virtues. I ruled each page with red ink so as to have seven columns, one for each day of the week, marking each column with a letter for the day. I crossed these columns with thirteen red lines, marking the beginning of each line with the first letter of one of the virtues, on which line and in its proper column I might mark by a little black spot, every fault I found upon examination to have been committed respecting that virtue upon that day.

I determined to give a week's strict attention to each of the virtues successively. Thus in the first week my great guard was to avoid even the least offense against Temperance, leaving the other virtues to their ordinary chance, only marking every evening the faults of the day. Thus, if in the first week I could keep my first line, marked *T*, clear of spots, I supposed the habit of that virtue so much strengthened and its opposite weakened that I might venture extending my attention to include the next, and for the following week keep both lines clear of spots. Proceeding thus to the last, I could go through a course complete in thirteen weeks and four courses in a year. And like him who, having a garden to weed, does not attempt to eradicate all the bad herbs at once, which would exceed his reach and his strength, but works on one of the beds at a time, and, having accomplished the first, proceeds to a second, so I should have, I hoped, the encouraging pleasure of seeing on my pages the progress I made in virtue by clearing successively my lines of their spots till in the end by a number of courses I should be happy in viewing a clean book after a thirteen-weeks' daily examination.

I entered upon the execution of this plan for self-examination and continued it with occasional intermissions for some time. I was surprised to find myself so much fuller of faults than I had imagined; but I had the satisfaction of seeing them diminish. To avoid the trouble of renewing now and then my little book, which, by scraping out the marks on the paper of old faults to make room for new ones in a new course, became full of holes, I transferred my tables and precepts to the ivory leaves of a memorandum book on which the lines were drawn with red ink that made a durable stain, and on those lines I marked my faults with a black lead pencil, which marks I could easily wipe out with a wet sponge. After awhile I went through one course only in a year, and afterward only one in several years, till at length I omitted them entirely, being employed in voyages and business abroad with a multiplicity of affairs that interfered; but I always carried my little book with me.

My list of virtues contained at first but twelve; but a Quaker friend having kindly informed me that I was generally thought proud; that my pride showed itself frequently in conversation; that I was not content with being in the right when discussing any point, but was overbearing, and rather insolent, of which he convinced me by mentioning several instances; I determined endeavoring to cure myself, if I could, of this vice or folly among the rest, and I added Humility to my list, giving an extensive meaning to the word.

I cannot boast of much success in acquiring the *reality* of this virtue, but I had a good deal with regard to the *appearance* of it. I made it a rule to forbear all direct contradiction to the sentiments of others and all positive assertion of my own. I even forbade myself, agreeably to the old laws of our Junto, the use of every word or expression in the language that indicated a fixed opinion, such as "certainly," "undoubtedly," and so forth, and I adopted, instead of them, "I conceive," "I apprehend," or "I imagine" a thing to be so or so; or it "so appears to me at present." When another asserted something that I thought an error, I denied myself the pleasure of contradicting him abruptly and of showing immediately some absurdity in his proposition; and in answering I began by observing that in certain cases or circumstances his opinion would be right, but in the present case there *appeared* or *seemed* to me some difference, and so forth. I soon found the advantage of this change in my manner; the conversations I engaged in went on more pleasantly. The modest way in which I proposed my opinions procured them a readier reception and less contradiction; I had less mortification when I was found to be in the wrong, and I more easily prevailed with others to give up their mistakes and join with me when I happened to be in the right.

And this mode, which I at first put on with some violence to natural inclination, became at length so easy, and so habitual to me that perhaps for these fifty years past no one has ever heard a dogmatical expression escape me. And to this habit (after my character of integrity) I think it principally owing that I had early so much weight with my fellow-citizens when I proposed new institutions or alterations in the old and so much influence in public councils when I became a member; for I was but a bad speaker, never eloquent, subject to much hesitation in my choice of words, hardly correct in language, and yet I generally carried my points.

SEMESTER
FIVE

Dost thou love life?
Then do not squander time, for that
is the stuff life is made of.

Benjamin Franklin

*Procrastination is one of the most
common and deadliest of diseases and its toll
on success and happiness is heavy.*

Dr. Wayne W. Dyer

LESSON 21

HOW TO STOP
PUTTING THINGS OFF

"Never put off till tomorrow, that which you can do today."

All of us have lived with Benjamin Franklin's wise admonition since our early youth. It is a favorite utterance of all parents. We heard it from ours and now we repeat it to our own children. And yet, although we acknowledge the great truth in that axiom we usually conduct our lives as if its words were transposed to read, "Never do today, that which you can put off till tomorrow."

Unfortunately there is no tomorrow. It can only be found in the calendars of fools. Tomorrow, for them, is the day when they will begin their journey toward success and riches; tomorrow is the day they will reform, work harder, change their habits, repair broken friendships, repay old debts, apply for a better job.

But tomorrow never comes and countless lives that held so much promise are wasted in procrastination. As Stephen Leacock wrote, long ago, "The child says, 'When I'm a big boy' but what is that? The big boy says, 'When I grow up' and then, grown up, he says, 'When I get married.' But to be married, what is that, after all? The thought changes to 'When I'm able to retire.' And when retirement comes, he looks back over the landscape traversed; a cold wind seems to sweep over it; somehow he has missed it all, and it is gone."

Success and procrastination are absolutely incompatible. In order to succeed you must, and you can, cure yourself of putting things off and best-selling author, Dr. Wayne W. Dyer, will teach you how from his book, *Your Erroneous Zones.*

Profit from this lesson, not tomorrow but *now ...*

201

Are you a procrastinator? If you're like most people, the answer to that is yes. But chances are that you'd rather not live with all that anxiety that accompanies putting things off as a way of life. You may find yourself postponing many tasks that you want to accomplish, and yet for some reason you just keep suspending action. This procrastination business is a mighty tiresome facet of life. If you've got a bad case, hardly a day goes by that you don't say, "I know I should be doing it, but I'll get around to it later." Your "putting it off" erroneous zone is difficult to blame on outside forces. It's all yours—both the putting off and the discomfort you endure as a result of it.

Procrastination is the closest there is to a universal erroneous zone. Very few people can honestly say that they are not procrastinators, despite the fact that it is unhealthy in the long run. As in all erroneous zones, there is nothing unhealthy about the behavior itself. Putting it off, in fact, doesn't even exist. You simply do, and those things you don't do, in reality, are just undone, rather than postponed. It is only the accompanying emotional reaction and immobilization that represent neurotic behavior. If you feel that you put things off, and like it, with no attending guilt, anxiety or upset, then by all means hang on to it. However, for most people procrastination is really an escape from living present moments as fully as possible.

HOPING, WISHING, AND MAYBE

Three neurotic phrases of the procrastinator make up the support system for maintaining putting-it-off behavior.

- "I hope things will work out."
- "I wish things were better."
- "Maybe it'll be OK."

There you have the deferrer's delight. As long as you say maybe, or hope, or wish, you can use these as a rationale for not doing anything now. All wishing and hoping are a waste of time—the folly of fairyland residents. No amount of either ever got anything accomplished. They are merely convenient escape clauses from rolling up your sleeves and taking on the tasks that you've decided are important enough to be on your list of life activities.

You can do anything that you set your mind to accomplish. You are strong, capable, and not the least bit brittle. But by putting things off for a future moment, you are giving in to escapism, self-doubt, and most significantly, self-delusion. Your putting-it-off zone is a movement away from being strong in your now, and toward the direction of hoping that things will improve in the future.

INERTIA AS A STRATEGY FOR LIVING

Here is a sentence that can keep you inert, in your present moments: "I'll wait, and it'll get better." For some this becomes a way of life—they are always putting it off for a day that can never arrive.

Mark, a recent client of mine, came to me complaining about his unhappy marriage. Mark was in his fifties and had been married for almost thirty years. As we began to talk about his marriage, it became clear that Mark's complaints were long-standing. "It's never been any good, even from the beginning," he said at one point. I asked Mark what had made him hold on for all these years of misery. "I kept hoping things would get better," he confessed. Almost thirty years of hope and Mark and his wife were still miserable.

As we talked more about Mark's life and marriage, he admitted to a history of impotence that went back at least a decade. Had he ever sought help for this problem, I asked. No, he had merely avoided sex more and more and hoped that the problem would go away on its own. "I was sure things would get better," Mark echoed his original comment.

Mark and his marriage were a classic case of inertia. He avoided his problems and justified his avoidance by saying, "If I wait and do nothing, maybe it'll work itself out." But Mark learned that things never work themselves out. They remain precisely as they are. At best, things change, but they don't get better. Things themselves (circumstances, situations, events, people) will not improve alone. If your life is better, it is because you have done something constructive to make it better.

Let's take a closer look at this procrastination behavior and how to eliminate it with some rather simple resolutions. This is one zone that you can clean up without a lot of hard "mental work," since it is one that you alone have created for yourself, without any of the cultural reinforcement that is the hallmark of so many other erroneous zones.

HOW PROCRASTINATION WORKS

Donald Marquis called procrastination "the art of keeping up with yesterday." To this I would add, "and avoiding today." This is how it works. You know there are certain things you want to do, not because others have so dictated, but because they are your deliberate choices. However, many of them never get done, despite your telling yourself that they will. Resolving to do something in the future which you could do now is an acceptable substitute for doing it, and permits you to delude yourself that you are really not compromising yourself by not doing what you have set out to do. It's a handy system that works something like this. "I know I must do that, but I'm really afraid that I might not do it well, or I won't like doing it. So, I'll tell myself that I'll do it in the future, then I don't have to admit to myself that I'm not going to do it. And it is easier to accept myself this way." This is the sort of convenient if fallacious reasoning that can be brought into play when you are faced with having to do something which is unpleasant or difficult.

If you are a person who lives one way and says you are going to live another way in the future, those proclamations are empty. You are simply a person who is always adjourning and never getting things done.

There are, of course, degrees of procrastination. It is possible to put things off up to a point, and then complete a task just prior to the deadline. Here again is a common form of self-delusion. If you allow yourself an absolute minimum amount of time to get your work done, then you can justify sloppy results or less than top-notch performance by saying to yourself, "I just didn't have enough time." But you have plenty of time. You know that busy people get things done. But if you spend your time complaining about how much you have to do (procrastination), then you'll have no present-moment time for doing it.

I once had a colleague who was a procrastination specialist. He was always busy chasing down deals and talking about how much he had to do. When he talked, others got tired just imagining the pace of his life. But a close look would reveal that my colleague actually did very little. He had a zillion projects going in his mind and never got down to work on any of them. I imagine that each night before dozing off, he deluded himself with a promise that tomorrow he would get that job finished. How else could he go off to sleep with his self-delusional system intact? He may have known that he would not, but so long as he swore that he would, his present moments were safe.

You are not necessarily what you say. Behavior is a much better barometer of what you are than words. What you do in your present moments is the only indicator of what you are as a person. Emerson wrote,

> Do not say things. What you are stands over you the while, and thunders so that I cannot hear what you say to the contrary.

Next time as you say you'll get it done, but know that you won't, keep those words in mind. They are the antidote to procrastination.

CRITICS AND DOERS

Putting it off as a way of life is one technique that you can use to avoid doing. A nondoer is very often a critic, that is, someone who sits back and watches doers, and then waxes philosophically about how the doers are doing. It is easy to be a critic, but being a doer requires effort, risk, and change.

The Critic

Our culture is full of critics. We even pay to hear them.

As you observe yourself and the people around you, take note of how much social intercourse is devoted to criticism. Why? Because it is just plain easier to talk about how someone else has performed than to be the performer. Take note of real champions, those who have sustained a high level of excellence over a period of time. The Henry Aarons, the Johnny Carsons, the Bobby Fishers, the Katharine Hepburns, the Joe Louises, and people of that ilk. Doers at the highest levels. Champions in every way. Do they sit around poking serious criticism at others? The real doers of the world have no time for criticizing others. They're too busy doing. They work. They help others who are not as talented, rather than serve as their critics.

Constructive criticism can be useful. But if you've chosen the role of an observer rather than a doer, you are not growing. Moreover, you may be using your criticism to absolve yourself of the responsibility for your own ineffectiveness by projecting it onto those who are really making an effort. You can learn to ignore the faultfinders and self-appointed critics. Your first strategy will be to recognize these same behaviors in yourself, and resolve to eliminate them entirely, so that you can be a doer rather than a procrastinating critic.

BOREDOM:
A SPIN-OFF OF PROCRASTINATION

Life is never boring but some people choose to be bored. The concept of boredom entails an inability to use up present moments in a personally fulfilling way. Boredom is a choice; something you visit upon yourself, and it is another of those self-defeating items that you can eliminate from your life. When you procrastinate, you use your present moments doing nothing, as an alternative to doing anything. Doing nothing leads to boredom. The tendency is to blame boredom on the environment. "This town is really dull" or "What a boring speaker." The particular town or speaker is never dull; it is you experiencing the boredom, and you can eliminate it by doing something else with your mind or energy at that moment.

Samuel Butler said, "The man who lets himself be bored is even more contemptible than the bore." By doing what you choose, now, or using your mind in creative new ways now, you can insure that you'll never again choose boredom for yourself. The choice, as always, is yours.

SOME TYPICAL PROCRASTINATING BEHAVIOR

Here are some areas where procrastination is a much easier choice than action.

• Staying in a job in which you find yourself stuck and unable to grow.

• Hanging onto a relationship that has gone sour. Staying married (or unmarried) and merely hoping that it will get better.

• Refusing to work on relationship difficulties such as sex, shyness, or phobias. Simply waiting for them to improve, instead of trying to do something constructive about them.

• Not tackling addictions such as alcoholism, drugs, pills, or smoking. Saying, "I'll quit when I'm ready," but knowing that you are putting it off because you doubt that you can.

• Putting off arduous or menial tasks such as cleaning, repairing, sewing, lawn work, painting, and the like—providing you really care about whether or not they get done. If you wait long enough, maybe it will get done by itself.

• Avoiding a confrontation with others, such as an authority figure, a friend, a lover, a salesperson, or a serviceman. By waiting, you end up not having to do it, although the confrontation might have improved the relationship or the service.

• Being afraid to change locations geographically. You stay in the same place for a lifetime.

• Putting off spending a day or an hour with your children which you might enjoy because you have too much work or are bogged down in serious matters. Similarly, not going out for an evening to dinner, or to the theater or a sports event with your loved ones and using your "I'm busy" line to postpone it forever.

• Deciding to start your diet tomorrow or next week. It's easier to put-it-off than to take-it-off, so you say, "I'll get to it tomorrow," which of course will never arrive.

• Using sleep or tiredness as a reason for putting it off. Did you ever notice how tired you get when you are close to actually doing something uncomfortable or difficult? A little fatigue is a terrific deferring device.

• Getting sick when you are faced with a disquieting or troublesome task. How could you possibly do it now, when you feel so terrible? Like exhaustion above, it's an excellent technique for procrastinating.

• The "I don't have time to do it" ruse, in which you justify not doing something because of your busy schedule, which always has room for those things that you really want to do.

• Constantly looking forward to a vacation or that dream-trip. Next year we'll find Nirvana.

• Being a critic and using your criticism of others to camouflage your own refusal to do.

• Refusing to get a physical checkup when you suspect some dysfunction. By putting it off you don't have to deal with the reality of possible illness.

• Being afraid to make a move toward someone you're fond of. It's what you want, but you'd rather wait it out and hope that things work out.

• Being bored at any time in your life. This is merely a way of putting off something and using the boring event as a reason for not doing something more exciting.

• Planning but never putting in action a regular exercise program. "I'll get started on that right away . . . next week."

• Living your entire life for your children and always putting off your own happiness. How can we afford a vacation when we have the kids' education to worry about?

REASONS FOR CONTINUING TO PUT IT OFF

The rationale for putting it off is composed of one part self-delusion and two parts escape. Here are the most important rewards for hanging on to procrastination.

• Most obviously, putting it off allows you to escape from unpleasant activities. There may be things you're afraid to do or things part of you wants to do and part of you doesn't. Remember, nothing is black or white.

• You can feel comfortable with your self-delusional system. Lying to yourself keeps you from having to admit that you are not a "doer" in this particular present moment.

• You can stay exactly as you are forever, as long as you keep putting it off. Thus you eliminate change and all the risks that go with it.

• By being bored you have someone or something else to blame for your unhappy state; thus you shift responsibility away from yourself and onto the boring activity.

• By being a critic you can feel important at the expense of others. It is a way of using others' performance as stepping-stones for elevating yourself in your own mind. More self-delusion.

• By waiting for things to get better you can blame the world for your unhappiness—things just never seem to break for you. A great strategy for doing nothing.

• You can avoid ever having to fail by avoiding all activities which involve some risk. In this way you never have to come face-to-face with your self-doubt.

• Wishing for things to happen—Santa Claus fantasies—allows you to return to a safe and protected childhood.

• You can win sympathy from others and feel sorry for yourself for the anxiety that you live with as a result of not doing what you'd like to have done.

• You are able to justify a sloppy or less than acceptable performance on anything if you put it off long enough, and then just allow a minimal time segment for getting it done. "But I just didn't have time."

• By putting it off, you might be able to get someone else to do it for you. Thus, procrastination becomes a means of manipulating others.

• Putting it off enables you to delude yourself into believing that you are something other than what you really are.

• By avoiding a task you can escape success. If you don't

succeed you avoid having to feel good about yourself and accepting all of the continuing responsibility that goes with success.

Now that you have some insight into why you procrastinate, you can begin to do something about eliminating this self-destructive erroneous zone.

SOME TECHNIQUES FOR OUSTING THIS POSTPONING BEHAVIOR

• Make a decision to live five minutes at a time. Instead of thinking of tasks in long-range terms, think about now and try to use up a five-minute period doing what you want, refusing to put off anything that would bring about satisfaction.

• Sit down and get started on something you've been postponing. Begin a letter or a book. You'll find that much of your putting it off is unnecessary since you'll very likely find the job enjoyable, once you give up the procrastination. Simply beginning will help you to eliminate anxiety about the whole project.

• Ask yourself, "What is the worst thing that could happen to me if I did what I'm putting off right now?" The answer is usually so insignificant that it may jar you into action. Assess your fear and you'll have no reason to hang on to it.

• Give yourself a designated time slot (say Wednesday from 10:00 to 10:15 P.M.) which you will devote exclusively to the task you've been putting off. You'll discover that the fifteen minutes of devoted effort are often sufficient to see you over the hump of procrastination.

• Think of yourself as too significant to live with anxiety about the things you have to do. So, the next time you know you are uncomfortable with postponement anxiety, remember that people who love themselves don't hurt themselves that way.

• Look carefully at your now. Decide what you are avoiding in your current moments and begin to tackle the fear of living effectively. Procrastination is substituting the now with anxiety about a future event. If the event becomes the now, the anxiety, by definition, must go.

• Quit smoking . . . now! Begin your diet . . . this moment! Give up booze . . . this second. Do one push-up as your beginning exercise project. That's how you tackle problems . . . with action now! Do it! The only thing holding you back is you, and the neurotic choices you've made because you don't believe you're as strong as you really are. How simple . . . just do it!

• Start using your mind creatively in what were previously

boring circumstances. At a meeting, change the dull tempo with a pertinent question, or make your mind go off in exciting ways such as writing a poem, or memorizing twenty-five numbers backward, just for the sheer drill of memory training. Decide to never be bored again.

• When someone begins to criticize you, ask this question, "Do you think I need a critic now?" Or when you find yourself being a critic, ask the person in your company if he wants to hear your criticism, and if so, why? This will help you to move from the critic to the doer column.

• Look hard at your life. Are you doing what you'd choose to be doing if you knew you had six months to live? If not, you'd better begin doing it because, relatively speaking, that's all you have. Given the eternity of time, thirty years or six months make no difference. Your total lifetime is a mere speck. Delaying anything makes no sense.

• Be courageous about undertaking an activity that you've been avoiding. One act of courage can eliminate all that fear. Stop telling yourself that you must perform well. Remind yourself that doing it is far more important.

• Decide not to be tired until the moment before you get into bed. Don't allow yourself to use fatigue or illness as an escape or to put off doing anything. You may find that when you take away the reason for the illness or exhaustion—that is, avoidance of a task—physical problems "magically" disappear.

• Eliminate the words "hope," "wish," and "maybe" from your vocabulary. They are the tools of putting it off. If you see these words creeping in, substitute new sentences. Change

"I hope things will work out," to "I will make it happen."
"I wish things were better," to "I am going to do the following things to ensure that I feel better."
"Maybe it will be OK," to "I will make it OK."

• Keep a journal of your own complaining or critical behavior. By writing these actions down, you'll accomplish two things. You'll see how your critical behavior surfaces in your life—the frequency, patterns, events, and people that are related to your being a critic. You'll also stop yourself from criticizing because it will be such a pain to have to write in the journal.

• If you are putting something off which involves others (a move, a sex problem, a new job), have a conference with all involved and ask their opinions. Be courageous about talking of your own fears, and see if you are delaying for reasons that are only in your head. By enlisting the aid of a confidant to help you with your procrastination, you'll have made it a joint effort. Soon you'll dissipate much of the anxiousness that goes along with procrastination by sharing that as well.

• Write a contract with your loved ones in which you will deliver the goods you want to but which you may have been postponing. Have each party keep a copy of the contract, and build in penalties for defaulting. Whether it's a ball game, dinner out, vacation, or theater visit, you'll find this strategy helpful and personally rewarding, since you'll be participating in events that you also find enjoyable.

If you want the world to change, don't complain about it. Do something. Rather than using up your present moments with all kinds of immobilizing anxiety over what you are putting off, take charge of this nasty erroneous zone and live now! Be a doer, not a wisher, hoper, or critic.

*You possess as much of this precious commodity
as the richest person in the world and
yet you may not realize how wealthy you are.*

Arnold Bennett & Arthur Brisbane

LESSON 22

HOW TO CHERISH AND USE
THE MAGIC OF TIME

If you kept a careful diary of all your activities for any seven-day period you would probably be shocked and shamefaced at the number of hours you fritter away each week doing little or nothing.

This is an unusual lesson since not one, but two, distinguished individuals will make brief appearances before you with but one purpose—to help you appreciate that mysterious gift we all receive called *time.*

Arnold Bennett was a prolific English novelist, best known for his masterful work, *The Old Wives Tale.* Since he wrote nearly half a million words a year during the height of his career, his friends were always inquiring as to the secret of his incredible production. In response, he finally wrote a small book, *How to Live On Twenty-Four Hours a Day,* which has been treasured by millions for more than seventy years and is still in print. His portion of this lesson is from that book.

Following Mr. Bennett is another man of letters, Arthur Brisbane, with a powerful suggestion that could be worth a fortune to you. Mr. Brisbane, an American editor and columnist, managed to earn an incredible income from his enterprises, exceeding more than a million dollars a year even during the depths of the Great Depression, primarily because he knew how to make the greatest possible use of what he called his "odd moments."

First read Mr. Bennett, followed by Mr. Brisbane's lesson from the book, *Elbert Hubbard's Scrapbook,* but proceed with this warning. Do not let the brevity of either lecture lull you into taking its words lightly. Chances are you may find yourself recalling their wisdom often, in the years to come . . .

"Yes, he's one of those men who don't know how to manage. Good situation. Regular income. Quite enough for luxuries as well as needs. Not really extravagant. And yet the fellow's always in difficulties. Somehow he gets nothing out of his money. Excellent flat—half empty! Always looks as if he'd had the pawnbrokers in. New suit—old hat! Magnificent necktie—baggy trousers! Asks you to dinner: cut glass—bad mutton, or Turkish coffee—cracked cup! He can't understand it. Explanation simply is that he fritters his income away. Wish I had the half of it! I'd show him—"

So we have most of us criticized, at one time or another, in our superior way.

We are nearly all chancellors of the exchequer: it is the pride of the moment. Newspapers are full of articles explaining how to live on such-and-such a sum, and how these articles provoke a correspondence whose violence proves the interest they excite. Recently, in a daily organ, a battle raged round the question whether a woman can exist nicely in the country on £85 a year. I have seen an essay, "How to live on eight shillings a week." But I have never seen an essay, "How to live on twenty-four hours a day." Yet it has been said that time is money. That proverb understates the case. Time is a great deal more than money—usually. But though you have the wealth of a cloakroom attendant at the Carlton Hotel, you cannot buy yourself a minute more time than I have, or the cat by the fire has.

Philosophers have explained space. They have not explained time. It is the inexplicable raw material of everything. With it, all is possible; without it, nothing. The supply of time is truly a daily miracle, an affair genuinely astonishing when one examines it. You wake up in the morning, and lo! your purse is magically filled with twenty-four hours of the unmanufactured tissue of the universe of your life! It is yours. It is the most precious of possessions. A highly singular commodity, showered upon you in a manner as singular as the commodity itself!

For remark! No one can take it from you. It is unstealable. And no one receives either more or less than you receive.

Talk about an ideal democracy! In the realm of time there is no aristocracy of wealth, and no aristocracy of intellect. Genius is never rewarded by even an extra hour a day. And there is no punishment. Waste your infinitely precious commodity as much as you will, and the supply will never be withheld from you. No mysterious power will say:—"This man is a fool, if not a knave. He does not deserve time; he shall be cut off at the meter." It is more certain than bonds, and payment of income is not affected by Sundays. Moreover, you cannot draw on the future. Impossible to get into debt! You can only waste the passing moment. You cannot waste tomorrow; it is kept for you. You cannot waste the next hour; it is kept for you.

I said the affair was a miracle. Is it not?

You have to live on this twenty-four hours of daily time. Out of it you have to spin health, pleasure, money, content, respect, and the evolution of your immortal soul. Its right use, its most effective use, is a matter of the highest urgency and of the most thrilling actuality. All depends on that. Your happiness—the elusive prize that you are all clutching for, my friends!—depends on that. Strange that the newspapers, so enterprising and up-to-date as they are, are not full of "How to live on a given income of time," instead of "How to live on a given income of money"! Money is far commoner than time. When one reflects, one perceives that money is just about the commonest thing there is. It encumbers the earth in gross heaps.

If one can't contrive to live on a certain income of money, one earns a little more—or steals it, or advertises for it. One doesn't necessarily muddle one's life because one can't manage on a thousand pounds a year; one braces the muscles and makes it guineas, and balances the budget. But if one cannot arrange that an income of twenty-four hours a day shall exactly cover all proper items of expenditure, one does muddle one's life definitely. The supply of time, though gloriously regular, is cruelly restricted.

Which of us lives on twenty-four hours a day? And when I say "lives," I do not mean exists, nor "muddles through." Which of us is free from that uneasy feeling that the "great spending departments" of his daily life are not managed as they ought to be? Which of us is quite sure that his fine suit is not surmounted by a shameful hat, or that in attending to the crockery he has forgotten the quality of the food? Which of us is not saying to himself— which of us has not been saying to himself all his life: "I shall alter that when I have a little more time"?

We never shall have any more time. We have, and we have always had, all the time there is.

*　　*　　*

In these days, much of the profit and sometimes the whole of success depend upon utilizing the odds and ends, the so-called "by-products."

The by-product is something apart from the main article manufactured, and yet something that has an actual value of its own. For instance, in the manufacture of gas there are many by-products; these are obtained from the coal as the latter is made into lighting-gas. And these by-products, including the coke from the coal, actually suffice to pay the cost of the gas.

All kinds of big businesses have their by-products, their little odds and ends that pay well. In Mr. Armour's enormous meat-factory, for instance, there are endless by-products, from the pig-tails which are dried and sold as a delicacy, to the hair of animals made into a powerful, valuable kind of rope.

If Mr. Armour neglected making the hair rope, or selling the pigtails, it would make a big difference in his dividends. The point for the reader is this: the individual man does not manufacture, as a rule. But we are, all of us, dealers in time.

Time is the one thing we possess. Our success depends upon the use of our time, and its by-product, the odd moment.

Each of us has a regular day's work that he does in a routine, more or less mechanical, way. He does his clerking, his writing, his typewriting, or whatever it may be, so many hours per day. And that ends it.

But what about the by-product, the odd moments? Do you know that the men that have made great successes in this world are the men who have used wisely those odd moments? Thomas A. Edison, for instance, was hammering away at a telegraph-key when he was telegraph-operator on a small salary. He didn't neglect the by-product, the odd moments. He thought, and planned, and tried between messages. And he worked out, as a by-product of his telegraph job, all the inventions that have given him millions, and given to the inhabitants of the world thousands of millions worth of dollars in new ideas.

Benjamin Franklin in his story of his life shows an endless number of such efforts along the lines using the odd moments. In a hundred different ways he managed to make the extra hours useful and productive.

What a man does in his odd moments is not only apt to bring him profit; it is apt also to increase his mental activity. The mind craves a change, and it often does well the unusual thing, out of the routine.

"Letting well enough alone" is a foolish motto in the life of a man who wants to get ahead. In the first place, nothing is "well enough," if you can do better. No matter how well you are doing, do better. There is an old Spanish proverb which says, "Enjoy the little you have while the fool is hunting for more."

The energetic American ought to turn this proverb upside down and make it read, "While the fool is enjoying the little he has, I will hunt for more."

The way to hunt for more is to utilize your odd moments.

Every minute that you save by making it useful, more profitable, is so much added to your life and its possibilities. Every minute lost is a neglected by-product—once gone, you will never get it back.

Think of the odd quarter of an hour in the morning before breakfast, the odd half hour after breakfast; remember the chance to read, or figure, or think with concentration on your own career, that comes now and again in the day. All of these opportunities are the by-products of your daily existence.

Use them, and you may find what many of the greatest concerns have found, that the real profit is in the utilization of the by-products.

Among the aimless, unsuccessful or worthless, you often hear talk about "killing time." The man who is always killing time is really killing his own chances in life; while the man who is destined to success is the man who makes time live by making it useful.

*Can there possibly be a system for
handling your job in such a manner that
you would never have to suffer the
ordeal of seeing work pile up on you?*

Alan Lakein

LESSON 23

HOW TO MAKE THE MOST
OF YOUR PRIORITIES

Time-management. The teaching of that subject has virtually become a growth industry. Everywhere you look, seminars are being conducted to instruct you on the finer aspects of survival through better control of your time. Most of them have adopted and refined, a brilliant technique for saving time that has been used profitably for more than half a century.

When Charles Schwab was chairman of Bethlehem Steel, he was presented by Ivy Lee, a business consultant, with a simple plan that Mr. Lee guaranteed him would greatly increase the work productivity of every executive in Mr. Schwab's employ.

All you need to do, advised Mr. Lee, is take a pad of paper, this evening, and list the most urgent projects which confront you. Then, study the list and number them, assigning number one to the most important job, number two to the next most vital, and so on down the list. Beginning tomorrow, tackle number one and stay on it until it is finished before you move on to number two. Work on down the list. When the day is through, prepare a new list, again assigning top priority to the most important task still undone and so on down the list. Do this every day and after you discover how well it works, share it with your people.

Several weeks later, Ivy Lee received a check for twenty-five thousand dollars.

219

Alan Lakein has counseled corporations and their executives in the management of time for many years, numbering among his clients The Bank of America and IBM, as well as many celebrities in the field of entertainment. From his popular book, *How to Get Control of Your Time and Your Life,* he will demonstrate how to clear your path to success by working exactly as some of America's top executives do . . .

The main secret of getting more done every day took me several months of research to discover. When I first started delving into better time use, I asked successful people what the secret of their success was. I recall an early discussion with a vice-president of Standard Oil Company of California who said, "Oh, I just keep a 'To Do' list." I passed over that quickly, little suspecting at the time the importance of what he said.

I happened to travel the next day to a large city to give a time-management seminar. While I was there I had lunch with a businessman who practically owned the town. He was chairman of the gas and light company, president of five manufacturing companies, and had his hand in a dozen other enterprises. By all standards he was a business success. I asked him the same question of how he managed to get more done and he said, "Oh, that's easy—I keep a To Do List." But this was a list with a difference. He told me he considered it a game.

The first thing in the morning, he would come in and lay out his list of what he wanted to accomplish that day. In the evening he would check to see how many of the items he had written down in the morning still remained undone and then give himself a score. His goal was to have a "no miss" day in which every single item was crossed off.

He played the To Do List game much as you cover the squares on a bingo card, getting items on his list done during the day as opportunities presented themselves— talking to someone on the phone, bringing up points at a meeting, exploring a creative project in the evening with his wife. He made sure to get started on the top-priority items right away. Toward the end of the day he initiated whatever calls, actions, or letters were necessary to finish up his "bingo card" for a perfect score.

Again and again when I talked to successful businessmen and government administrators, the To Do List came up. So during one of my seminars I asked how many people had heard of keeping a priority list of things to do. Virtually everyone had. Then I asked how many people conscientiously made up a list of things to do *every* day, arranged the items in priority order, and crossed off each task as it was completed. I discovered that very few people keep a list of things to do every day, although most people occasionally make a To Do List when they are particularly busy, have a lot of things they want to remember to do, or have some particularly tight deadline.

ONLY A DAILY LIST WILL DO

People at the top and people at the bottom both know about To Do Lists, but one difference between them is that the people at the top use a To Do List every single day to make better use of their time; people at the bottom know about this tool but don't use it effectively. One of the real secrets of getting more done is to make a To Do List every day, keep it visible, and use it as a guide to action as you go through the day.

Because the To Do List is such a fundamental time-planning tool, let's take a closer look at it. The basics of the list itself are simple: head a piece of paper "To Do," then list those items on which you want to work; cross off items as they are completed and add others as they occur to you; rewrite the list at the end of the day or when it becomes hard to read.

One of the secrets to success is to write all your "To Do" items on a master list or lists to be kept together, rather than jotting down items on miscellaneous scraps of paper. You may want to keep your list in your appointment book. One executive keeps a special pad on his desk reserved for his To Do List. I know one woman who never buys a dress without a pocket in it so she can keep her To Do List always with her.

Another homemaker was forever losing the lists she made. She spent more time looking for yesterday's list than she spent making today's. To help her get control of her time, I had her put all her lists in a notebook. She had the added benefit of being able to cull undone A's from previous lists.

Some people try to keep To Do Lists in their heads but in my experience this is rarely as effective. Why clutter your mind with things that can be written down? It's much better to leave your mind free for creative pursuits.

WHAT BELONGS ON THE LIST

Are you going to write down everything you have to do, including routine activities? Are you only going to write down exceptional events? Are you going to put down everything you *might* do today, or only whatever you decided you *will* do today? There are many alternatives, and different people have different solutions. I recommend that you not list routine items but do list everything that has high priority today and might not get done without special attention.

Don't forget to put the A-activities for your long-term goals on your To Do List. Although it may appear strange to see "begin learning French" or "find new friends" in the same list with "bring home a quart of milk" or "buy birthday card," you want to do them in the same day. If you use your To Do List as a guide when deciding what to work on next, then you need the long-term projects represented, too, so you won't forget them at decision time and consequently not do them.

Before you even consider doing anything yourself, look over the list and see how many tasks you can delegate. Not just to your subordinates or the babysitter, but to those at your level and even higher, who do a job more quickly and easily, or who could suggest shortcuts you'd overlook.

Depending on your responsibilities, you might, if you try hard enough, get all the items on your To Do List completed by the end of each day. If so, by all means try. But probably you can predict in advance that there is no way to do them all. When there are too many things to do, conscious choice as to what (and what not) to do is better than letting the decision be determined by chance.

I cannot emphasize strongly enough: you must *set priorities*. Some people do as many items as possible on their lists. They get a very high percentage of tasks done, but their effectiveness is low because the tasks they've done are mostly of C-priority. Others like to start at the top of the list and go right down it, again with little regard to what's important. The best way is to take your list and label each item according to *ABC* priority, delegate as much as you can, and then polish off the list accordingly.

One person I know color-codes the entries, using black for normal entries and red for top-priority items. For people who have trouble living with priorities, I have found that it's helpful to use one piece of paper for the A's and B's and another page for the more numerous C's. The A and B paper is kept on top of the C list, and every time you raise the *A* and *B* list to do a *C*, you're aware that you're not making the best use of your time.

Items on the To Do List may be arranged in several forms. One form is functional: to see, to telephone, to follow up, to think about, to decide, to dictate. Or you can group activities based on the similarity of the work content (everything about water pollution), the same location (several customers in one neighborhood), or the same person (several topics needing the boss's opinion). You can have a single item on your To Do List represent a group (processing the papers in your in-box, doing errands).

DON'T WORRY ABOUT COMPLETING YOUR LIST

Now go down your list, doing all the *A*'s before the *B*'s and the *B*'s before the *C*'s. Some days you may get all the items on your list done, but more likely there will not be time to do them all. If you are doing them in *ABC* order you may not even finish all the *A*'s sometimes. On other days you will do the *A*'s and *B*'s, and on the other days *A*'s, *B*'s, and some *C*'s. One rarely reaches the bottom of a To Do List. It's not completing the list that counts, but making the best use of your time. If you find yourself with only *B*'s and *C*'s left, take a fresh look at possible activities and add to your list items such as revising your filing system for greater accessibility, finishing *War and Peace*, picking out a birthday present for your aunt—all *A*'s that were in the back of your mind but didn't make it to the original list. With a little extra time, today they can be started.

Many office workers, homemakers, and professional people have come to my seminars because they felt the need to "get organized." Most report a couple of months later that they feel much more organized simply because they regularly list and set priorities. For example, a newly appointed head nurse used the listing/setting priorities approach for her home life after she had found how well it worked at the hospital. Good time use is as important off the job as on it. You don't want to turn your off-work time into a worklike situation, but you can relax even more if those things you have to do are organized with the aid of a To Do List, then gotten out of the way quickly.

If little things mean a lot, a list of things to do in priority order means a great deal because it provides you with the security of knowing that nothing is missing; an affirmation of all your important activities; a motivation to cross off items you don't need to do; and a reservoir from which you can select activities to be done next.

By doing more A's and fewer C's, the hierarchy of your accomplishments will change. You can break up your old A's into new A's and B's, downgrading your old B's to C's and dropping most of the old C's off your list entirely.

HOW TO DO MORE THINGS THAT MATTER

For instance, a year ago attending Parents' Day at your daughter's school would have been rated A. But now you're involved in a part-time fashion-design business, and your daughter understands how busy you are and how much satisfaction you derive from your business, so you won't go to Parents' Day unless it's a slow time in your business. Last year you attended to every detail of the annual inventory yourself. Happily, while you were doing it, you recorded the necessary steps so that this year, with that reference guide in hand, last year's A (figuring out what to do) becomes this year's C: following a routine. Now you are able to delegate the annual inventory to the new stock boy and use your time to merchandise your products better.

The salesman who continually upgrades his customers finds that last year's A—the $100-unit customer—is this year's C. Now his A-customer is a $500-unit account; his B is a $250-unit account. He upgraded his business this way by conscientiously going after the A-accounts. He spent more and more of his time with those who bought over $100, so gradually he was able to consider anyone below $100 to be a C. To encourage this continual upgrading, he went through his customer files each week and threw away at least one low dollar prospect or customer. In my experience, most salesmen could benefit substantially by arbitrarily weeding out 20 percent of their customers in terms of present and potential volume.

Learning a musical instrument is much the same. When you first play the piano your A is to practice easy pieces. Once you become proficient, it would be a C to continue playing them. So you practice more and more difficult pieces. When you are learning a difficult piece, the A is to play it slowly but accurately and the C to play it fast with what would likely be many mistakes. As you become more proficient in playing a passage, the A becomes playing the passage at its correct tempo.

In learning and applying time use skills, it may be an A to watch how to spend every five minutes for an hour so that you become much more aware of time use. Once you become automatically aware of time use, it is a *C* even to think about time passing unless you want to sharpen up that skill again.

The good time user has a constant stream of *A*'s going through the pipeline and is not hung up on which *A* to do or how to do it or trying to be a perfectionist about a particular *A*. Rather, he does a number of *A*-tasks daily and remembers that as soon as he has identified the best use of his time, the time to do it is now.

Michael LeBoeuf

LESSON 24

HOW TO GET
YOURSELF ORGANIZED

William Faulkner once lamented that the saddest thing in life is that the only thing we can do for eight hours a day, day after day, is work. We can't eat for eight hours a day, or drink for eight hours a day, or make love for eight hours a day. All that we can do for that long a period, he said, is work, which is the reason man makes himself and everybody else so miserable and unhappy.

Researcher and consultant, Michael LeBoeuf, conducts invaluable seminars teaching people how to make the most of their time and their effort so that even their working hours can be free of crisis and unhappiness.

In his brilliant book, *Working Smart,* from which this lesson is taken, he asks, "What does work mean to you? Do you think of it as an activity that takes more from you than it gives you? Do you think of the distinction between play and work as that between pleasure and pain? Do you live to work? Do you work to live? Regardless of your answers one thing is certain: Work is here to stay."

If you have decided to use Alan Lakein's To Do List technique, from your last lesson, you have already made a major move toward removing much of the chaos and hassle that comes with every job.

Unfortunately, although you may have the greatest To Do List in the world each morning, you just might never get around to crossing even that first item off your list if you're disorganized.

And having little to show for your efforts, at the end of a hard day, produces frustration, exhaustion, and worse.

Not to worry. Mr. LeBoeuf is about to show you how to get your act together, an important step on that yellow brick road to success . . .

In one of his films, W. C. Fields plays an executive whose desk top is a morass of clutter. In one scene he returns to his desk to find that an efficiency expert has organized, rearranged, and streamlined it. The desk top is now a picture of neatness and efficiency, but Fields is frustrated. He can't find anything! So he vigorously throws the neat stacks of paper up in the air, tossing them in the way a gourmet would a salad. Then he backs off, surveys the desk top with satisfaction, deftly reaches into the pileup and pulls out the desired document.

To fully appreciate the satire of that scene we should place it in historical perspective. At the time Fields was in his glory, efficiency exerts were preaching the gospel of organization. One of the cardinal sins of inefficency was to have a desk that had anything on top of it other than the immediate work at hand. A clear desk was heralded as the badge of efficiency and productivity.

Today we are less sure of this. Certainly a life of organization is usually a great deal more effective than one of chaos. Most of us could enhance our effectiveness with more organization. However, hard and fast rules are not the order of the day when it comes to organizing. This is what W. C. Fields was trying to tell us in the film. We all must organize to suit our own personality and the task at hand.

As you plan your life, resist the temptation of becoming overly organized—it's an effectiveness killer. I had a friend in college who flunked out after one semester. The main reason was that he spent all his study time reading various books on how to study and never got around to studying. The same problem can arise as you try to work smarter. Remember, these ideas are merely means to an end and that end is to increase your lifetime effectiveness. Running around with a stopwatch and keeping a totally clear desk isn't going to accomplish what you want in life.

Nevertheless, there are some good guidelines for organizing your life and your thoughts. If you practice these guidelines as guidelines rather than as hard and fast rules, you will find they will aid you in getting the most from your time and effort. With that thought in mind, let's look at a few of them.

GET THE PROPER TOOLS
· TO DO THE JOB

Thomas Carlyle once remarked, "Man is a tool-using animal . . . without tools he is nothing, with tools he is all." Those are words worth remembering. How many times have you labored at an unsuccessful activity only to find out that having a particular tool could have saved you a great deal of time, energy, and frustration? This type of experience is usually most apparent to us when we are trying to repair the family car or something around the house. This is because we tend to think of tools as tangible instruments, as many of them are. However, to make the most of this guideline we have to use the word "tool" in a much broader context.

A tool is anything you use to help you achieve your goals. No matter what your goals or what activities you pursue, all of them involve tools. If you are an accountant your tools include the obvious pencils, papers, and calculators, as well as your CPA certificate and your practical knowledge. If you work in an office, the office itself with its desk, chair, and floor space is a tool.

Other examples of less obvious tools are automobiles, statistical tables, newspapers, foreign languages, and interviewing techniques. The list is endless.

Before setting out to perform a task or achieve a goal stop and ask yourself, "What are the necessary tools to complete the task successfully, and do I have them?" If you don't have the proper tools, first consider getting someone else to do the job. Your time, energy, and expenses may be greatly reduced by employing someone else. However, if it's something only you can do, make an effort to first equip yourself with the best tools available. The difference between wise men and fools is often found in their choice of tools.

ORGANIZE YOUR WORKSPACE

Consider the environment in which you will be performing the task. Organizing your workspace is largely a personal matter that depends on your own tastes and the job to be done. However, there are several basic factors to keep in mind:

1. *Location*. If you are fortunate enough to choose your workspace, choose one that is conducive to performing the task. If the job requires concentration, look for a quiet, private place. On the other hand, if you are opening your own business, choose a well-traveled location where potential customers have easy access to your establishment.

2. *Space*. After you have chosen the proper work location, measure how much space you have to work with. Most of us usually find we have less than we want. It helps to know what space is available before furnishing it with the necessary tools.

3. *Easy access to the tools you use frequently*. It helps here to make a list of the tools you use and rank them in order of how often you use them. Then you will have a guide to arranging them for easiest access.

Refrain from cluttering your workspace with nonessential items. The moosehead you had mounted after your last hunting trip to Canada may well be a sight worth seeing, but if it distracts you, you should place it somewhere else. Besides, it may occupy space where a more useful tool such as a memo board could be put.

4. *Comfort*. Some people don't believe that workspaces should be designed for comfort. They are generally people who play the hard-work tape or the work-is-inherently-unpleasant tape. The fact is that discomfort is a distraction that serves only to hinder productivity. Why make things more difficult than they have to be? Life is already filled with a more than ample supply of discomforts, distractions, and frustrations.

A comfortable workspace generally has the proper seating, ventilation, and lighting. If you work sitting down for long periods, choose a firm, comfortable chair that gives good back support. Try to find one comfortable enough that you won't have to get up every ten minutes, but not so comfortable that you will fall asleep in it. To avoid eyestrain use indirect, uniform lighting.

Adequate ventilation will help prevent unnecessary fatigue from stuffiness in the work environment. Which temperature range you work best in is a personal matter. However, be sure to locate your place in the workspace out of a draft.

MASTER THE ART
OF DESKMANSHIP

A great many of us perform some or all of our work at a desk. As I mentioned earlier, a desk is a tool—and it is one of the most abused and misused of tools. So before delving into the application of this tool and how to get the most from it, we ought to consider what a desk is not.

Specifically, a desk is *not:*

1. *A place to conduct a paper drive.* Judging from the many cluttered desk tops I've seen, I'm convinced that paper recyclers would fare better if they raided desk tops in office buildings rather than collecting old newspapers from the local shopping center.

2. *A storage depot for food, clothing, umbrellas, and other nonjob sundries.* I once moved into an office only to find I was sharing a desk with a colony of ants. It seems that my predecessor had willed me a large open bag of candy in the top right-hand drawer, but the clever little devils had beaten me to it.

3. *A place to stack items you want to remember.* A German executive once remarked to Alec Mackenzie that desk tops get stacked because we put things there we don't want to forget. The problem is that it works. Every time we look up, we see all these things we don't want to forget and our mind wanders, breaking our train of thought. With time, the stacks grow higher and we forget what's in each one. So we waste large amounts of time retrieving lost items and thinking about all those things we don't want to forget. Merrill Douglass, a time-management consultant, tells of keeping a close time log on one executive who had a stacked desk. The log revealed that he spent two and a half hours per day looking for information on the top of his desk!

4. *A status symbol or place to display awards, trophies, and the like.* This mistaken use of desks causes us only to make desks larger than they have to be. With more surface area we have more room for clutter and somehow more clutter magically appears to fill up any available space.

Now that we have discussed what a desk is not, let's look at what a desk is. It's a tool that expedites the receiving and processing of information and should be utilized with those objectives in mind.

You may have a desk and not need one. Lawrence Appley, former president of the American Management Association, remarked that most desks only bury decisions. Some executives have thrown out their desks and declared their effectiveness has increased. They have replaced the standard office desk and chair with a lounge chair, clipboard, small writing table on casters, and file cabinets. Advocates of the deskless office report an improvement in face-to-face communication and an atmosphere of greater freedom. They no longer feel chained to a desk. Consider the possibility that you may not need a desk and, if you can get rid of it, try working without it and see what happens.

How to Reorganize Your Desk for Effectiveness

Assuming you do need your desk, you may want to embark on a reorganization project. If you decide to reorganize your desk, block out several hours in your schedule when you won't be interrupted. Desk reorganization is a good Saturday morning project and can be accomplished by the following procedure:

1. Get a large trash can.

2. Take everything off the top of the desk and empty all drawers. Discard every item that is no longer of any use.

3. Make a list of all the remaining items that were in or on your desk and rank them in order of importance. When you consider each item ask yourself "What's the worst thing that will happen if I throw this away?" If the answer isn't very bad, throw away the item and leave it off the list.

4. Critically view all the nondiscarded items and put only the most essential ones in your desk. Articles that you don't need immediate access to should be stored somewhere else, such as in a file cabinet or bookcase.

5. Make a filing system in the deep drawers, with files well labeled and organized for quick and easy access. Periodically review all of your desk files and keep only the current essential ones in your desk. Over ninety percent of all files over one year old are never referred to.

6. To use the input-output principle for processing information, get two large stacking file baskets—one to store incoming work and one for storing work you have processed and are ready to send on. Pending items of low priority or needing later attention may be filed in the desk drawer, as long as the drawers are regularly monitored.

Guidelines for Working at a Desk

If you have gone to the trouble of reorganizing your desk, you have taken a giant step toward making your desk a more effective tool. Some find it helpful to repeat desk reorganization every six months. The following guidelines are designed to increase your desk-work effectiveness by reducing the amount of clutter.

1. Have only one project at a time on top of your desk—it should be your top priority for the moment.

2. Keep items off your desk until you are ready for them. Store them in file cabinets or drawers, but get them out of sight.

3. Don't allow yourself to be sidetracked by other tasks because they are easier or more appealing. You should work on the top-priority item and keep at it until it is completed.

4. When you complete a task, put it in the out basket and send it on its way. Then check your priorities and move on to the next item.

5. If you have one, a secretary can help by keeping your desk clear and seeing that the day's top-priority item is waiting on your desk at the beginning of each day.

As I pointed out earlier, these are merely guidelines and they may not be suitable for you. Making a fetish out of a clean desk isn't going to get the job done, and for some it becomes just another detractor from effectively doing the job. Choose a style suitable for you and the work to be done, but be honest with yourself. Few of us do our best work with a heavily cluttered and disorganized desk.

IMPROVE YOUR ABILITY
TO CONCENTRATE

Concentration in any form is an amazing phenomenon. As a six-year-old, I was spellbound when one of my friends ignited a piece of paper by focusing the sun's rays on the paper through a magnifying glass. Our own time and energy are much like the sun's rays. To the degree that we concentrate our efforts we will succeed in getting what we want out of life. The ability to concentrate has enabled many men of modest capabilities to reach heights of success that have often eluded geniuses.

Think with a Pencil in Your Hand

When you write down your ideas you automatically focus your full attention on them. Few if any of us can write one thought and think another at the same time. Thus a pencil and paper make excellent concentration tools.

Whenever you need to concentrate, make it a habit to think with a pencil in your hand. As ideas come to you, jot them down. As you write down ideas, you will automatically be thinking them through and clarifying them in your mind. Soon you will have a list of thoughts to consider. You will be much more likely to see which ideas are irrational, erroneous, or in conflict with each other if you can view them all at once.

Reserve Your Work Place Exclusively for Work

We are all creatures of habit, and most of our behavior involves little or no thought. We learn to associate certain behavior with a given environment. If we don't take pains to develop good habits in the work environment, all sorts of unproductive ones can develop and rob us of our time and energy.

One way to improve your ability to concentrate is to reserve your work place only for working. For example, if you work behind a desk in an office, don't do anything at your desk unrelated to work. If a visitor drops in, get up and move away from the desk. If you allow yourself to socialize behind the desk you will come to associate that location as more than a work location. When you take a break, move away from where you work. Sit in another chair or go to another room. If you develop the habit of choosing a certain spot to work, you will find yourself getting down to business much more rapidly and automatically when it's time to work.

Slow Down and Stop Constructively

One of the keys to the art of staying with a task is in knowing how and when to back off. Blind perseverance is for fools. It involves working harder rather than smarter.

When you find yourself mentally blocked from solving problems, make a tactical retreat from your work. Pushing ahead will only lead to confusion and frustration. Perhaps you need to get more input about the task or need more time to digest and integrate information.

When you have to quit working, there are several things you can do to make your work more enjoyable and productive when you start back:

1. Try to end your work on a high note. If you quit at a point of satisfaction, you will tend to think of the work as gratifying and be more eager to return to it.

2. Try to stop at a point of accomplishment.

3. If you quit at a point where you are stalled, write down the problem and try to clarify what's blocking your progress.

4. Have a logical starting point at which to resume. This will reduce your start-up time when you return to the task.

IMPROVE YOUR FOLLOW-THROUGH

Knowing when to stop is a good tactical maneuver, but it doesn't get the job done. Somewhere along the line you must tackle the task and follow through to completion. Here are some ideas that you will find helpful in successfully finishing what you start.

1. Get interested in your work. Interest and motivation go together like Siamese twins. Get more information. The more you know about something the greater the odds you will become absorbed in it.

2. Try to imagine the satisfaction that will come from seeing the task achieved. Think of how much better you'll look after you've shed those twenty pounds, or how much better you'll feel when you quit smoking. Think of the better job you will have and the happier life you'll lead when you finally get that degree or that promotion.

3. Challenge yourself with deadlines for completion.

4. Try to shield yourself from interruptions and distractions.

5. Take part in a joint effort with someone else who is dependable. When you make a commitment to do something with someone else, you are more likely to do the job than if you tackle it alone. When I was in graduate school we would study in groups or pairs to reinforce our commitment to learn. We called it "cooperate and graduate." The important thing is that each person be dependable. If both parties are committed, each can set the pace for the other.

IMPROVE YOUR MEMORY

One of our greatest time- and energy-saving tools is our memory. Without a memory all of our learning would be useless. We would have to respond to every situation as if we had never experienced it. We use our memories to learn to walk, talk, absorb facts, solve problems, drive cars, read, and do numerous other things. The uses and capacity of the human memory are a miracle. You can store more bits of information in your two-pound brain than in today's most advanced computers.

Unfortunately, storing information is one thing and retrieving it is another. This is where the computer is our superior. However, most of us can improve our ability to store and retrieve information if we understand how our memory works and apply some simple concepts of memory improvement.

Your memory is not a thing; it's a test of skills. It can't be seen, felt, examined, or weighed. Memory skills are generally divided into three stages:

1. *Remembering*. Leaving the information to be stored.
2. *Recording*. Storing the material in the brain until needed.
3. *Retrieving*. Getting the material out when needed. This final stage is the cause of our greatest problems. How many times have you said to yourself, "It's on the tip of my tongue?"

We can do little or nothing to improve our retrieval ability per se. However, our ability to retrieve is somewhat dependent on how we record information, and we can improve our memory by modifying our methods of recording. Briefly, here are some guidelines to aid you in making the most of your memory:

1. Commit things to memory when you are rested. If you try to memorize when you are fatigued, you will most likely find it frustrating.

2. Break down lists into smaller, manageable units and subcategories before trying to memorize them. If you have to learn the capital cities of 20 nations, break them up into 5 groups of 4, or 6 groups of 3, and 1 group of 2.

3. Repeat the material to yourself several times. Writing the material also helps.

4. Space your learning into several periods. Begin each new period by reviewing what you have previously memorized to keep it firmly planted in your memory.

5. Relate material you are learning to familiar ideas, persons, symbols, and other things that are already firmly planted in your memory. For example, you can probably recall roughly what the map of Italy looks like, because it's shaped like a boot. Can you do the same for Yugoslavia?

6. Arrange ideas to be learned into a formula system or code word to aid your recall. For example, advertising teachers use the code word AIDA, for "arouse Attention, create Interest, stimulate Desire, and move to Action." Another example is the five-step study method called SQ3R which stands for Survey, Question, Read, Recite, Review.

7. Use spare moments, such as waiting time, for memorizing. Carry note cards in your pocket for quick and easy referral.

I used those seven guidelines to overcome my two greatest memory challenges. In order to get my Ph.D. degree I had to pass exams in translating two foreign languages (French and German) into English. I had had no previous exposure to German and the French I knew was limited to spelling my name and reading New Orleans street signs. Nevertheless, I passed both of those tests six weeks after starting from scratch. I started out by buying the appropriate vocabulary cards (a thousand of them) and a set of graded readers. Each day I read for one hour in the reader and learned thirty new words from the vocabulary cards. Before learning new words I would review the words previously learned to reinforce my recall. At the end of five weeks I had learned all one thousand words and my reading and translating proficiency was well underway. The last week was reserved for polishing and reviewing. I passed both exams with flying colors.

If you use some of the modern memory aids, known as mnemonics, you will be able to amaze yourself and others with memory feats. With proper training almost anyone can learn to look through a shuffled deck of cards and remember them in order, meet fifty people and instantly recall their names, or recall over one hundred phone numbers. If you want more information on memory improvement, there are several good books on the subject, including Dr. Kenneth Higbee's *Your Memory*.

DEAL WITH TRIVIA IN BATCHES

All of us are plagued with a number of necessary minor tasks that must be done in the near future. Examples of these are paying bills, running errands, shopping, housework, yard work, minor repairs, correspondence, reading and making telephone calls. Attacking these tasks in a random fashion is one sure way to work more and accomplish less.

One way to keep trivia from hindering your effectiveness is to organize the tasks into batches and handle a batch at a time. Try to run several errands at one time. Go to the grocery, bank, car wash, and filling station in one trip. Do several household chores in sequence, or combine several if possible. Save up your bills and pay them all at a certain time each month. Try to make telephone calls and write letters in batches. Trivia sessions are an effective method of preventing the minor things in your life from hindering your accomplishment of major goals.

PROBLEM-SOLVING STRATEGY

As you realize by now, planning and goal setting are basically a process of decision making, and decision making is problem solving. Organizing your approach to a problem puts you halfway toward solving it. The following general guidelines will help you achieve a basic readiness to meet and penetrate all roadblocks to success.

Don't Needlessly Complicate Your Problems

We live in an age of technological sophistication with trips to the moon, electronic brains, and nuclear power. Complexity is the norm. As a result, we have come to expect complexity in all facets of life. There appears to be an unwritten rule in our society that nothing has the right to be simple anymore. All too often when given the choice between a simple and complex solution to a problem, many of us opt for the latter. The story of using five men to change a light bulb (one to hold the bulb and four to turn the man on the ladder) makes us chuckle. But like most good humor it carries an underlying message containing some truth. As you try to solve a problem, look first for a simple satisfactory solution. It may save you a great deal of time.

Approach the Problem Creatively

Often our problem-solving ability is hindered by being locked into a particular way of viewing the problem. Many of us have heard the story of the truck being stuck in an underpass. A team of engineers was called out to decide how to dislodge the truck. True to their profession, they took an engineering approach to solving the problem and began making a series of complex stress calculations. A small boy standing by asked one of the engineers, "Hey mister, why don't you let the air out of the tires?" Immediately the problem was solved.

The more ways we allow ourself to view a problem, the better the odds of our finding a satisfactory solution.

Alex F. Osborne, advertising genius, has a checklist for new ideas to stimulate your creative abilities. You may find the checklist helpful, as I have, when confronted with problem solving:

Could we . . .
1. Modify?
———————— what to add
———————— more time, greater frequency
———————— stronger, higher, longer, thicker
———————— duplicate, multiply, exaggerate
2. Minimize?
———————— what to subtract
———————— smaller, condense
———————— omit, streamline, split up
———————— lower, shorten, lighten

3. Substitute?
——————— other process, ingredient, material
——————— other place, other approach or form of approach
4. Rearrange?
——————— interchange components
——————— other sequence, schedule, pattern, layout
——————— other person
5. Reverse?
——————— transpose positive and negative
——————— try opposite, turn backward or upside down
——————— reverse roles
6. Combine?
——————— uses, purposes, ideas, approaches
7. Put to Other Uses?
——————— new ways to use
——————— other uses if modified
——————— what else is like this?

William James once said, "Genius means little more than the faculty of perceiving in an unhabitual way." Whether you choose to use Osborne's checklist, brainstorm, or whatever, it generally helps to try and see things from a different perspective.

Distinguish Between Urgency and Importance

When Dwight Eisenhower became President he tried to arrange his administration so that only urgent and important matters were called to his attention. Everything else was to be delegated to lower echelons. However, he discovered that urgency and importance seldom appear together. This concept also applies to our lives. Important things are seldom urgent and urgent things are seldom important. The urgency of fixing a flat tire when you are late for an appointment is much greater than remembering to pay your auto insurance premium, but its importance is, in most cases, relatively small.

Unfortunately, many of us spend our lives fighting fires under the tyranny of the urgent. The result is that we ignore the less urgent but more important things in life. It's a great effectiveness killer.

When you are faced with a number of problems to solve, ask yourself which are the important ones and make them your first priority. If you allow yourself to be governed by the tyranny of the urgent, your life will be one crisis after another. You'll be very active and may even be the busiest beaver around. However, someday you may wake up to find you've been building your dam on an empty lake.

Try to Anticipate Potential Crises

Doctors tell us that the best medicine is preventive medicine. You don't have to concern yourself with curing an illness if you don't have it. Thus, you take precautionary measures designed to maintain your health, such as getting enough rest, proper diet, exercise, vaccines, and so on.

General problem-solving operates in much the same way. If you anticipate crises and take steps to prevent or deal with them, you will be wisely investing your time. Things seldom evolve to the crisis level without some warning. A little foresight and preventive maintenance can insure that you spend your time achieving your goals rather than reacting to crises.

Put Your Subconscious to Work

Some of our greatest problem-solving ability lies somewhere beneath our level of awareness. Often we have trouble coming up with solutions to problems simply because we are pressing ourselves too hard for an answer. The anxiety and tension we create by agonizing for a solution cripple our creative abilities, as well as needlessly wasting time.

Some years ago, when I first entered graduate school, I agonized over what I would choose to write my doctoral thesis on. Although I wouldn't need to decide for at least two years, the thought of a thesis topic plagued me because I had never done one before. The idea of additional coursework and examinations was of no worry. I had been through all that before and felt confident of capable performance.

The more I pressed myself for a topic, the more anxious I became, and my thesis topic ideas remained nil. One day I mentioned this to one of my professors and he suggested that I simply forget about it and concentrate on the work at hand. "Turn the problem over to your subconscious," he said, "and let it work for you. When you get ready to tackle that thesis, your subconscious will have a topic for you. Most important decisions are usually made at the subconscious level."

I took his advice and it really worked. Six months before I was ready to tackle the thesis a topic idea came to me. The value of subconscious decision making was one of the greatest lessons I learned in graduate school.

*When you truly understand this lesson
you will be as close as you can possibly get
to a single universal law of success.*

Dr. Napoleon Hill

LESSON 25

HOW TO USE THE LAW
OF INCREASING RETURNS

Napoleon Hill was an incredible man. Against great odds and pressures he devoted more than twenty-five years of his life to interviewing and researching the careers of achievers. His goal? To isolate and define the reasons why so many fail and so few succeed.

Hundreds of thousands of success books have appeared in the past five decades and yet the vast majority of them all have roots that can be traced back to the findings of Dr. Hill. Undoubtedly, his all-time best-seller, *Think and Grow Rich,* has affected more lives in this century than any other book except the Bible.

Think and Grow Rich, however, was only a condensed version of an earlier work of Hill, in sixteen languages, entitled *The Laws of Success.* It was such a monumental work that it contained priceless testimonials from Thomas Edison, Cyrus Curtis, William Howard Taft, Woodrow Wilson, William Wrigley, Jr., John Wanamaker, George Eastman, and F. W. Woolworth!

Your lesson has been taken from the original book and its subject, according to Dr. Hill, will, of itself, practically insure success to anyone who will practice it in all they do. He wrote, "You may not like the work in which you are now engaged. There are two ways of getting out of that work. One way is to take but little interest in what you are doing, aiming merely to do enough with which to 'get by.' Very soon you will find a way out, because the demand for your services will cease."

But there is another and better way for you to "get out of that work you don't like" and the greatest success writer of them all is about to explain how ...

241

When a man is engaged in work that he loves it is no hardship for him to do more work and better work than that for which he is paid, and for this very reason every man owes it to himself to do his best to find the sort of work he likes best.

I have a perfect right to offer this advice to the students of this philosophy for the reason that I have followed it, myself, without reason to regret having done so.

This seems to be an appropriate place to inject a little personal history concerning both the author and the Law of Success philosophy, the purpose of which is to show that labor performed in a spirit of love for the sake of the labor, itself, never has been and never will be lost.

This entire lesson is devoted to the offering of evidence that it really pays to render more service and better service than one is paid to render. What an empty and useless effort this would be if the author had not, himself, practiced this rule long enough to be able to say just how it works out.

For over a quarter of a century I have been engaged in the labor of love out of which this philosophy has been developed, and I am perfectly sincere when I repeat that I have been amply paid for my labors, by the pleasure I have had as I went along, even if I received nothing more.

My labors on this philosophy made it necessary, many years ago, for me to choose between immediate monetary returns, which I might have enjoyed by directing my efforts along purely commercial lines, and remuneration that comes in later years, and which is represented by both the usual financial standards and other forms of pay which can be measured only in terms of accumulated knowledge that enables one to enjoy the world about him more keenly.

The man who engages in work that he loves best does not always have the support, in his choice, of his closest friends and relatives.

Combating negative suggestions from friends and relatives has required an alarming proportion of my energies, during the years that I have been engaged in research work for the purpose of gathering, organizing, classifying, and testing the material which has gone into my writings and courses.

These personal references are made solely for the purpose of showing the students of this philosophy that seldom, if ever, can one hope to engage in the work one loves best without meeting with obstacles of some nature. Generally, the chief obstacles in the way of one engaging in the sort of work one loves best is that it may not be the work which brings the greatest remuneration at the start.

To offset this disadvantage, however, the one who engages in the sort of work he loves is generally rewarded with two very decided benefits, namely; first, he usually finds in such work the greatest of all rewards, HAPPINESS, which is priceless, and secondly, his actual reward in money, when averaged over a lifetime of effort, is generally much greater, for the reason that labor which is performed in a spirit of love is usually greater in quantity and finer in quality than that which is performed solely for money.

Please keep in mind that during all these years of research I was not only applying the law covered by this lesson, by DOING MORE THAN PAID FOR, but, I was going much further than this by doing work for which I did not, at the time I was doing it, hope ever to receive pay.

Thus, out of years of chaos, adversity, and opposition this philosophy was finally completed and reduced to manuscripts, ready for publication.

There are more than a score of sound reasons why you should develop the habit of performing more service and *better service* than that for which you are paid, despite the fact that a large majority of the people are not rendering such service.

There are two reasons, however, for rendering such service, which transcend, in importance, all the others; namely,

First: By establishing a reputation as being a person who always renders more service and better service than that for which you are paid, you will benefit by comparison with those around you who do not render such service, and the contrast will be so noticeable that *there will be keen competition for your services, no matter what your lifework may be*.

It would be an insult to your intelligence to offer proof of the soundness of this statement, because it is obviously sound. Whether you are preaching sermons, practicing law, writing books, teaching school, or digging ditches, you will become more valuable and you will be able to command greater pay the minute you gain recognition as a person who does more than that for which he is paid.

Second: By far the most important reason why you should render more service than that for which you are paid; a reason that is basic and fundamental in nature; may be described in this way:

suppose that you wished to develop a strong right arm, and suppose that you tried to do so by tying the arm to your side with a rope, thus taking it out of use and giving it a long rest. Would disuse bring strength, or would it bring atrophy and weakness, resulting, finally, in your being compelled to have the arm removed?

You know that if you wished a strong right arm you could develop such an arm *only by giving it the hardest sort of use*. Take a look at the arm of a blacksmith if you wish to know how an arm may be made strong. Out of resistance comes strength. The strongest oak tree of the forest is not the one that is protected from the storm and hidden from the sun, but it is the one that stands in the open, where it is compelled to struggle for its existence against the winds and rains and the scorching sun.

It is through the operation of one of Nature's unvarying laws that struggle and resistance develop strength, and the purpose of this lesson is to show you how to harness this law and so use it that it will aid you in your struggle for success. By performing more service and better service than that for which you are paid, you not only exercise your service-rendering qualities, and thereby develop skill and ability of an extraordinary sort, but you build reputation that is valuable. If you form the habit of rendering such service you will become so adept in your work that you can *command* greater remuneration than those who do not perform such service. You will eventually develop sufficient strength to enable you to remove yourself from any undesirable station in life, and no one can or will desire to stop you.

If you are an employee you can make yourself so valuable, through this habit of performing more service than that for which you are paid, that you can practically set your own wages and no sensible employer will try to stop you. If your employer should be so unfortunate as to try to withhold from you the compensation to which you are entitled, this will not long remain as a handicap because other employers will discover this unusual quality and offer you employment.

The very fact that most people are rendering as little service as they can possibly get by with serves as an advantage to all who are rendering more service than that for which they are paid, because it enables all who do this to profit by comparison. You can "get by" if you render as little service as possible, but that is all you will get; and when work is slack and retrenchment sets in, you will be one of the first to be dismissed.

For more than twenty-five years I have carefully studied men with the object of ascertaining why some achieve noteworthy success while others with just as much ability do not get ahead; and it seems significant that every person whom I have observed applying this principle of rendering more service than that for which he was paid, was holding a better position and receiving more pay than those who merely performed sufficient service to "get by" with.

Personally I never received a promotion in my life that I could not trace directly to recognition that I had gained by rendering more service and better service than that for which I was paid.

I am stressing the importance of making this principle a habit as a means of enabling an employee to promote himself to a higher position, with greater pay, for the reason that this will be studied by thousands of young men and young women who work for others. However, the principle applies to the employer or to the professional man or woman just the same as to the employee.

Observance of this principle brings a twofold reward. First, it brings the reward of greater material gain than that enjoyed by those who do not observe it; and, second, it brings that reward of happiness and satisfaction which come only to those who render such service. If you receive no pay except that which comes in your pay envelope, you are underpaid, no matter how much money that envelope contains.

We will now analyze the law upon which this entire lesson is founded, namely—

THE LAW OF
INCREASING RETURNS!

Let us begin our analysis by showing how Nature employs this law in behalf of the tillers of the soil. The farmer carefully prepares the ground, then sows his wheat and waits while the Law of Increasing Returns brings back the seed he has sown, *plus a manyfold increase.*

But for this Law of Increasing Returns, man would perish, because he could not make the soil produce sufficient food for his existence. There would be no advantage to be gained by sowing a field of wheat if the harvest yield did not return more than was sown.

With this vital "tip" from Nature, which we may gather from the wheat fields, let us proceed to appropriate this Law of Increasing Returns and learn how to apply it to the service we render, to the end that *it may yield returns in excess of and out of proportion to the effort put forth.*

First of all, let us emphasize the fact that there is no trickery or chicanery connected with this Law, although quite a few seem not to have learned this great truth, judging by the number who spend all of their efforts either trying to get something for nothing, or something for less than its true value.

It is to no such end that we recommend the use of the Law of Increasing Returns, for no such end is possible, within the broad meaning of the word *success*.

Another remarkable and noteworthy feature of the Law of Increasing Returns is the fact that it may be used by those who purchase service with as great returns as it can be by those who render service, for proof of which we have but to study the effects of Henry Ford's famous Five-Dollar-a-day minimum wage scale which he inaugurated some years ago.

Those who are familiar with the facts say that Mr. Ford was not playing the part of a philanthropist when he inaugurated this minimum wage scale; but, to the contrary, he was merely taking advantage of a sound business principle which has probably yielded him greater returns, in both dollars and goodwill, than any other single policy ever inaugurated at the Ford plant.

By paying more wages than the average, he received more service and better service than the average!

At a single stroke, through the inauguration of that minimum wage policy, Ford attracted the best labor on the market and placed a premium upon the privilege of working in his plant.

I have no authentic figures at hand bearing on the subject, but I have sound reason to conjecture that for every five dollars Ford spent, under this policy, he received at least seven dollars and fifty cents' worth of service. I have, also, sound reason to believe that this policy enabled Ford to reduce the cost of supervision, because employment in his plant became so desirable that no worker would care to run the risk of losing his position by "soldiering" on the job or rendering poor service.

Where other employers were forced to depend upon costly supervision in order to get the service to which they were entitled, and for which they were paying, Ford got the same or better service by the less expensive method of placing a premium upon employment in his plant.

Marshall Field was probably the leading merchant of his time, and the great Field store, in Chicago, stands today as a monument to his ability to apply the Law of Increasing Returns.

A customer purchased an expensive lace waist at the Field store, but did not wear it. Two years later she gave it to her niece as a wedding present. The niece quietly returned the waist to the Field store and exchanged it for other merchandise, despite the fact that it had been out for more than two years and was then out of style.

Not only did the Field store take back the waist, but, what is of more importance it did so *without argument!*

Of course there was no obligation, moral or legal, on the part of the store to accept the return of the waist at that late date, which makes the transaction all the more significant.

The waist was originally priced at fifty dollars, and of course it had to be thrown on the bargain counter and sold for whatever it would bring, but the keen student of human nature will understand that the Field store not only did not lose anything on the waist, but it actually profited by the transaction to an extent that cannot be measured in mere dollars.

The woman who returned the waist knew that she was not entitled to a rebate; therefore, when the store gave her that to which she was not entitled the transaction won her as a permanent customer. But the effect of the transaction did not end here; it only began; for this woman spread the news of the "fair treatment" she had received at the Field store, far and near. It was the talk of the women of her set for many days, and the Field store received more advertising from the transaction than it could have purchased in any other way with ten times the value of the waist.

The success of the Field store was built largely upon Marshall Field's understanding of the Law of Increasing Returns, which prompted him to adopt, as a part of his business policy, the slogan, "The customer is always right."

When you do only that for which you are paid, there is nothing out of the ordinary to *attract favorable comment* about the transaction; but, when you willingly do more than that for which you are paid, your action attracts the favorable attention of all who are affected by the transaction, and goes another step toward establishing a reputation that will eventually set the Law of Increasing Returns to work in your behalf, for this reputation will create a demand for your services, far and wide.

Carol Downes went to work for W. C. Durant, the automobile manufacturer, in a minor position. He is now Mr. Durant's right-hand man, and the president of one of his automobile distributing companies. He promoted himself into this profitable position solely through the aid of the Law of Increasing Returns, which he put into operation by rendering more service and better service than that for which he was paid.

In a recent visit with Mr. Downes I asked him to tell me how he managed to gain promotion so rapidly. In a few brief sentences he told the whole story.

"When I first went to work with Mr. Durant," said he, "I noticed that he always remained at the office long after all the others had gone home for the day, and I made it my business to stay there, also. No one asked me to stay, but I thought someone should be there to give Mr. Durant any assistance he might need. Often he would look around for someone to bring him a letter file, or render some other trivial service, and *always he found me there ready to serve him*. He got into the habit of calling on me; that is about all there is to the story."

"He got into the habit of calling on me!"

Read that sentence again, for it is full of meaning of the richest sort.

Why did Mr. Durant get into the habit of calling on Mr. Downes? Because *Mr. Downes made it his business to be on hand where he would be seen*. He deliberately placed himself in Mr. Durant's way in order that he might render service that would place the Law of Increasing Returns back of him.

Was he told to do this? *No!*

Was he paid to do it? *Yes!* He was paid by the opportunity it offered for him to bring himself to the attention of the man who had it within his power to promote him.

We are now approaching the most important part of this lesson, because this is an appropriate place at which to suggest that *you* have the same opportunity to make use of the Law of Increasing Returns that Mr. Downes had, and you can go about the application of the Law in exactly the same way that he did, *by being on hand and ready to volunteer your services in the performance of work which others may shirk because they are not paid to do it*.

Stop! Don't say it—don't even think it—if you have the slightest intention of springing that old timeworn phrase entitled, "But *my employer is different*."

Of course he is different. All men are different in most respects, but they are very much alike in this—they are somewhat *selfish;* in fact they are selfish enough not to want a man such as Carol Downes to cast his lot with their competitor, and this very selfishness may be made to serve you as an asset and not as a liability *if*—

You have the good judgment to make yourself so useful that the person to whom you sell your services cannot get along without you.

One of the most advantageous promotions I ever received came about through an incident which seemed so insignificant that it appeared to be unimportant. One Saturday afternoon, a lawyer, whose office was on the same floor as that of my employer, came in and asked if I knew where he could get a stenographer to do some work which he was compelled to finish that day.

I told him that all of our stenographers had gone to the ball game, and that I would have been gone had he called five minutes later, but that I would be very glad to stay and do his work as I could go to a ball game any day and his work had to be done then.

I did the work for him, and when he asked how much he owed me I replied, "Oh, about a thousand dollars, as long as it is you; if it were for anyone else, I wouldn't charge anything." He smiled, and thanked me.

Little did I think, when I made that remark, that he would ever pay me a thousand dollars for that afternoon's work, but *he did!* Six months later, after I had entirely forgotten the incident, he called on me again, and asked how much salary I was receiving. When I told him he informed me that he was ready to pay me that thousand dollars which I had laughingly said I would charge him for the work I had performed for him and he *did pay it* by giving me a position at a thousand dollars a year increase in salary.

Unconsciously, I had put the Law of Increasing Returns to work in my behalf that afternoon, by giving up the ball game and rendering a service which was obviously rendered out of a desire to be helpful and not for the sake of a monetary consideration.

It was not my duty to give up my Saturday afternoon, but—
It was my privilege!

Furthermore, it was a profitable privilege, because it yielded me a thousand dollars in cash and a much more responsible position than the one I had formerly occupied.

It was Carol Downes' *duty* to be on hand until the usual quitting time, but it was his *privilege* to remain at his post after the other workers had gone, and that privilege properly exercised brought him greater responsibilities and a salary that yields him more in a year than he would have made in a lifetime in the position he occupied before he exercised the privilege.

I have been thinking for more than twenty-five years of this *privilege* of performing more service and better service than that for which we are paid, and my thoughts have led me to the conclusion that a single hour devoted each day to rendering service for which we are not paid, can be made to yield bigger returns than we received from the entire remainder of the day during which we are merely performing our *duty.*

(We are still in the neighborhood of the *most important part* of this lesson, therefore, *think* and assimilate as you pass over these pages.)

The Law of Increasing Returns is no invention of mine, nor do I lay claim to the discovery of the principle of rendering more service and better service than paid for, as a means of utilizing this Law. I merely appropriated them, after many years of careful observation of those forces which enter into the attainment of success, just as *you will appropriate them* after you understand their significance.

You might begin this appropriation process now by trying an experiment which may easily open your eyes and place back of your efforts powers that you did not know you possessed.

Let me caution you, however, not to attempt this experiment in the same spirit in which a certain woman experimented with that biblical passage which says something to the effect that *if you have faith the size of a grain of mustard, and say to yonder mountain be removed to some other place, it will be removed*. This woman lived near a high mountain that she could see from her front door; therefore, as she retired that night she commanded the mountain to remove itself to some other place.

Next morning she jumped out of bed, rushed to the door and looked out, but lo! the mountain was still there. Then she said:

"Just as I had expected! I knew it would be there."

I am going to ask you to approach this experiment with full *faith* that it will mark one of the most important turning points of your entire life. I am going to ask you to make the object of this experiment the removal of a mountain that is standing where *your temple of success should stand*, but where it never can stand until you have removed the mountain.

You may never have noticed the mountain to which I refer, but it is standing there in your way just the same, unless you have already discovered and removed it.

"And what is this mountain?" you ask!

It is the feeling that you have been cheated unless you receive material pay for all the service you render.

That feeling may be unconsciously expressing itself and destroying the very foundation of your *temple of success* in scores of ways that you have not observed.

In the very lowly bred type of humanity, this feeling usually seeks outward expression in terms something like this:

"I am not paid to do this and I'll be blankety-blankety-blank if I'll do it!"

You know the type to which reference is made; you have met

with it many times, but you have never found a single person of this type who was successful, and you *never will.*

Success must be *attracted* through understanding and application of laws which are as immutable as is the law of gravitation. It cannot be driven into the corner and captured as one would capture a wild steer. For this reason you are requested to enter into the following experiment with the object of familiarizing yourself with one of the most important of these laws; namely, the Law of Increasing Returns.

The experiment:

During the next six months make it your business to render useful service to at least one person every day, for which you *neither expect nor accept monetary pay.*

Go at this experiment with *faith* that it will uncover for your use one of the most powerful laws that enter into the achievement of enduring success, and *you will not be disappointed.*

The rendering of this service may take on any one of more than a score of forms. For example, it may be rendered personally to one or more specific persons; or it may be rendered to your employer, in the nature of work that you perform after hours.

Again, it may be rendered to entire strangers whom you never expect to see again. It matters not to whom you render this service so long as you render it with willingness, and solely for the purpose of benefiting others.

If you carry out this experiment in the proper attitude of mind, you will discover that which all others who have become familiar with the law upon which it is based have discovered; namely, that—

You can no more render service without receiving compensation than you can withhold the rendering of it without suffering the loss of reward.

"Cause and effect, means and ends, seed and fruit, cannot be severed," says Emerson; "for the effect already blooms in the cause, the end preexists in the means, the fruit in the seed."

"If you serve an ungrateful master, serve him the more. Put God in your debt. Every stroke shall be repaid. The longer the payment is withholden, the better for you; for compound interest on compound interest is the rate and usage of this exchequer."

"The law of Nature is, Do the thing and you shall have the power; but they who do not the thing have not the power."

Men suffer all their life long, under the foolish superstition that they can be cheated. But it is as impossible for a man to be cheated by anyone but himself, as for a thing to be, and not to be, at the same time. There is a third silent party to all our bargains. The nature and soul of things takes on itself the guaranty of fulfillment of every contract, so that *honest service cannot come to loss.*

Before you begin the experiment that you have been requested to undertake, read Emerson's essay, "Compensation," for it will go a very long way toward helping you to understand *why* you are making the experiment.

Perhaps you have read "Compensation" before. Read it again! One of the strange phenomena that you will observe about this essay may be found in the fact that every time you read it you will discover new truths that you did not notice during previous readings.

We go through two important periods in this life; one is that period during which we are gathering, classifying, and organizing knowledge, and the other is that period during which we are struggling for recognition. We must first learn something, which requires more effort than most of us are willing to put into the job; but, after we have learned much that can be of useful service to others, we are still confronted with the problem of convincing them that we can serve them.

One of the most important reasons why we should always be not only ready but *willing* to render service, is the fact that every time we do so, we gain thereby another opportunity to prove to someone that we have ability; we go just one more step toward gaining the necessary recognition that we must all have.

Instead of saying to the world, "Show me the color of your money and I will show you what I can do," reverse the rule and say, "Let me show you the color of my service so that I may take a look at the color of your money if you like my service."

Life is but a short span of years at best. Like a candle we are lighted, flicker for a moment, and then *go out!* If we were placed here for the purpose of laying up treasures for use in a life that lies beyond the dark shadow of Death, may it not be possible that we can best collect these treasures by rendering all the service we can, to all the people we can, in a loving spirit of kindness and sympathy?

I hope you agree with this philosophy.

Here this lesson must end, but it is by no means *completed.* Where I lay down the chain of thought it is now *your duty* to take it up and develop it, in your own way, and to your own benefit.

By the very nature of the subject of this lesson it can never be finished, for it leads into the heart of all human activities. Its purpose is to cause you to take the fundamentals upon which it is based and use them as a stimulus that will cause your mind to unfold, thereby releasing the latent forces that are yours.

This lesson is not for the purpose of teaching you, but it is intended as a means of causing you to teach yourself one of the great truths of life. It is intended as a source of education, drawing out, developing from within, those forces of mind which are available for your use.

When you deliver the best service of which you are capable, striving each time to excel all your previous efforts, you are making use of the highest form of education. Therefore, when you render more service and better service than that for which you are paid, you, more than anyone else, are profiting by the effort.

It is only through the delivery of such service that mastery in your chosen field of endeavor can be attained. For this reason you should make it a part of your *definite chief aim* to endeavor to surpass all previous records in all that you do. Let this become a part of your daily habits, and follow it with the same regularity with which you eat your meals.

Make it your business to render more service and better service than that for which you are paid, and lo! before you realize what has happened, you will find that THE WORLD IS WILLINGLY PAYING YOU FOR MORE THAN YOU DO!

Compound interest upon compound interest is the rate that you will be paid for such service. Just how this pyramiding of gains takes place is left entirely to you to determine.

Now, what are you going to do with that which you have learned from this lesson? and when? and how? and why? This can be of no value to you unless it moves you to adopt and use the knowledge it has brought you.

Knowledge becomes POWER only through organization and USE! Do not forget this.

You can never become a Leader without doing more than you are paid for, and you cannot become successful without developing leadership in your chosen occupation.

SEMESTER SIX

Wealth is not of necessity a curse,
nor poverty a blessing.

R. D. Hitchcock

*The acquisition of money has always been
a simple matter to those who can practice a
little discipline and follow a few rules.*

P. T. Barnum

LESSON 26

HOW TO BECOME A
MONEY-GETTER

Phineas Taylor Barnum was undoubtedly the greatest showman that America has ever seen. If he had not existed, Horatio Alger would have probably invented him as a hero for one of his "rags to riches" epics.

From a truly humble beginning as a grocery clerk, and with only a grammar school education, P. T. Barnum eventually built the largest circus combine in the world which he billed as "The Greatest Show on Earth."

Barnum had very definite ideas on success and how to attain it and he included his practical advice, all of it still valid today, in his autobiography, *The Life of P. T. Barnum, Written by Himself.* Invariably when he was invited to deliver a speech he would refer to the "rules of success" from his book and as his lecture increased in popularity he began calling it "The Art of Money-Getting." P. T. was wise enough to understand, from his own experiences as promoter and politician, that there was one subject of which the public never tired—money.

This lesson is taken from his "money" speech. Although it was addressed primarily to America's youth, with the purpose of teaching them how to pursue wealth with integrity and character, you are certain to discover, whatever your age may be, much that will help you think clearly about where you are going and *how* you want to get there.

When this full semester has been completed you will understand the basic principles of accumulating money, even though you realize, by now, that money alone carries with it no guarantee of happiness. You will have also learned much more, especially the powerful truth that principles of success never change—as the most colorful member of our faculty is about to remind you . . .

In the United States, where we have more land than people, it is not at all difficult for persons in good health to make money. In this comparatively new field there are so many avenues of success open, so many vocations which are not crowded, that any person of either sex who is willing, at least for the time being, to engage in any respectable occupation that offers, may find lucrative employment.

Those who really desire to attain an independence, have only to set their minds upon it, and adopt the proper means, as they do in regard to any other object which they wish to accomplish, and the thing is easily done. But however easy it may be found to make money, I have no doubt many of my hearers will agree it is the most difficult thing in the world to keep it.

The road to wealth is, as Benjamin Franklin truly says, "as plain as the road to mill." It consists in expending less than we earn; that seems to be a very simple problem. Mr. Micawber, one of those happy creations of the genial Dickens, puts the case in a strong light when he says that to have an income of twenty pounds, per annum, and spend twenty pounds and sixpence, is to be the most miserable of men; whereas, to have an income of only twenty pounds, and spend but nineteen pounds and sixpence, is to be the happiest of mortals. Many of my hearers may say, "We understand this; this is economy, and we know economy is wealth; we know we can't eat our cake and keep it also." Yet I beg to say that perhaps more cases of failure arise from mistakes on this point than almost any other. The fact is, many people think they understand economy when they really do not.

True economy consists in always making the income exceed the outgo. Wear the old clothes a little longer if necessary; dispense with the new pair of gloves; mend the old dress; live on plainer food if need be; so that under all circumstances, unless some unforeseen accident occurs, there will be a margin in favor of the income. A penny here, and a dollar there, placed at interest, goes on accumulating, and in this way the desired result is attained. It requires some training, perhaps, to accomplish this economy, but when once used to it, you will find there is more satisfaction in rational saving, than in irrational spending. Here is a recipe which I recommend; I have found it to work an excellent cure for extravagance and especially for mistaken economy: When you find that you have no surplus at the end of the year, and yet have a good income, I advise you to take a few sheets of paper and form them into a book and mark down every item of expenditure. Post it every day or week in two columns, one headed "necessaries" or even "comforts," and the other headed "luxuries," and you will find that the latter column will be double, treble, and frequently ten times greater than the former. The real comforts of life cost but a small portion of what most of us can earn. Dr. Franklin says, "It is the eyes of others and not our own eyes which ruin us. If all the world were blind except myself I should not care for fine clothes or furniture." It is the fear of what Mrs. Grundy may say that keeps the noses of many worthy families to the grindstone. In America many persons like to repeat "We are all free and equal," but it is a great mistake in more senses than one.

That we are born "free and equal" is a glorious truth in one sense, yet we are not all born equally rich, and we never shall be. One may say, "There is a man who has an income of fifty thousand dollars per annum, while I have but one thousand dollars; I knew that fellow when he was poor like myself; now he is rich and thinks he is better than I am; I will show him that I am as good as he is; I will go and buy a horse and buggy—no, I cannot do that but I will go and hire one and ride this afternoon on the same road that he does, and thus prove to him that I am as good as he is."

My friend, you need not take that trouble, you can easily prove that you are as good as he is; you have only to behave as well as he does, but you cannot make anybody believe that you are as rich as he is. Besides, if you put on these "airs," and waste your time and spend your money, your poor wife will be obliged to scrub her fingers off at home, and buy her tea two ounces at a time, and everything else in proportion, in order that you may keep up "appearances," and after all, deceive nobody.

Men and women accustomed to gratify every whim and caprice, will find it hard, at first, to cut down their various unnecessary expenses, and will feel it a great self-denial to live in a smaller house than they have been accustomed to, with less expensive furniture, less company, less costly clothing, fewer servants, a less number of balls, parties, theater-goings, carriage-ridings, pleasure excursions, cigar-smokings, liquor-drinkings, and other extravagances; but, after all, if they will try the plan of laying by a "nest egg," or in other words, a small sum of money, at interest or judiciously invested in land, they will be surprised at the pleasure to be derived from constantly adding to their little "pile," as well as from all the economical habits which are engendered by this course.

The old suit of clothes, and the old bonnet and dress, will answer for another season; the Croton or spring water will taste better than champagne; a cold bath and a brisk walk will prove more exhilarating than a ride in the finest coach; a social chat, an evening's reading in the family circle, or an hour's play of "hunt the slipper" and "blind man's buff," will be far more pleasant than a fifty- or a five-hundred-dollar party, when the reflection on the difference in cost is indulged in by those who begin to know the pleasures of saving. Thousands of men are kept poor, and tens of thousands are made so after they have acquired quite sufficient to support them well through life, in consequence of laying their plans of living on too broad a platform. Some families expend twenty thousand dollars per annum, and some much more, and would scarcely know how to live on less, while others secure more solid enjoyment frequently on a twentieth part of that amount. Prosperity is a more severe ordeal than adversity, especially sudden prosperity. "Easy come, easy go," is an old and true proverb. A spirit of pride and vanity, when permitted to have full sway, is the undying cankerworm which gnaws the very vitals of a man's worldly possessions, let them be small or great, hundreds or millions. Many persons, as they begin to prosper, immediately expand their ideas and commence expending for luxuries, until in a short time their expenses swallow up their income, and they become ruined in their ridiculous attempts to keep up appearances, and make a "sensation."

I know a gentleman of fortune who says, that when he first began to prosper, his wife would have a new and elegant sofa. "That sofa," he says, "cost me thirty thousand dollars!" When the sofa reached the house, it was found necessary to get chairs to match; then sideboards, carpets, and tables "to correspond" with them, and so on through the entire stock of furniture; when at last it was found that the house itself was quite too small and old-fashioned for the furniture, and a new one was built to correspond with the new purchases; "thus," added my friend, "summing up an outlay of thirty thousand dollars caused by that single sofa, and saddling on me, in the shape of servants, equipage, and the necessary expenses attendant upon keeping up a fine 'establishment,' a yearly outlay of eleven thousand dollars, and a tight pinch at that; whereas, ten years ago, we lived with much more real comfort, because with much less care, on as many hundreds. The truth is," he continued, "that sofa would have brought me to inevitable bankruptcy, had not a most unexampled tide of prosperity kept me above it, and had I not checked the natural desire to 'cut a dash.' "

AVOID DEBT

Young men starting in life should avoid running into debt. There is scarcely anything that drags a person down like debt. It is a slavish position to get in, yet we find many a young man hardly out of his "teens" running in debt. He meets a chum and says, "Look at this; I have got trusted for a new suit of clothes." He seems to look upon the clothes as so much given to him. Well, it frequently is so, but, if he succeeds in paying and then gets trusted again, he is adopting a habit which will keep him in poverty through life. Debt robs a man of his self-respect, and makes him almost despise himself. Grunting and groaning and working for what he has eaten up or worn out, and now when he is called upon to pay up, he has nothing to show for his money: this is properly termed "working for a dead horse." I do not speak of merchants buying and selling on credit, or of those who buy on credit in order to turn the purchase to a profit. The old Quaker said to his farmer son, "John, never get trusted; but if thee gets trusted for anything, let it be for manure, because that will help thee pay it back again."

Mr. Beecher advised young men to get in debt if they could to a small amount in the purchase of land in the country districts. "If a young man," he says, "will only get in debt for some land and then get married, these two things will keep him straight, or nothing will." This may be safe to a limited extent, but getting in debt for what you eat and drink and wear is to be avoided. Some families have a foolish habit of getting credit at the stores, and thus frequently purchase many things which might have been dispensed with.

Money is in some respects like fire—it is a very excellent servant but a terrible master. When you have it mastering you, when interest is constantly piling up against you, it will keep you down in the worst kind of slavery. But let money work for you, and you have the most devoted servant in the world. It is no "eye-servant." There is nothing animate or inanimate that will work so faithfully as money when placed at interest, well secured. It works night and day, and in wet or dry weather.

Do not let it work against you; if you do, there is no chance for success in life so far as money is concerned. John Randolph, the eccentric Virginian, once exclaimed in Congress, "Mr. Speaker, I have discovered the philosopher's stone: pay as you go." This is indeed nearer to the philosopher's stone than any alchemist has ever yet arrived.

WHATEVER YOU DO, DO WITH ALL YOUR MIGHT

Work at it, if necessary, early and late, in season and out of season, not leaving a stone unturned, and never deferring for a single hour that which can be done just as well *now*. The old proverb is full of truth and meaning, "Whatever is worth doing at all, is worth doing well." Many a man acquires a fortune by doing his business thoroughly, while his neighbor remains poor for life because he only half does it. Ambition, energy, industry, perseverance, are indispensable requisites for success in business.

Fortune always favors the brave, and never helps a man who does not help himself. It won't do to spend your time like Mr. Micawber, in waiting for something to "turn up." To such men one of two things usually "turns up": the poorhouse or the jail; for idleness breeds bad habits, and clothes a man in rags. The poor spendthrift vagabond said to a rich man:

"I have discovered there is money enough in the world for all of us, if it was equally divided; this must be done, and we shall all be happy together."

"But," was the response, "if everybody was like you, it would be spent in two months, and what would you do then?"

"Oh! divide again; keep dividing, of course!"

I was recently reading in a London paper an account of a like philosophic pauper who was kicked out of a cheap boardinghouse because he could not pay his bill, but he had a roll of papers sticking out of his coat pocket, which, upon examination, proved to be his plan for paying off the national debt of England without the aid of a penny. People have got to do as Cromwell said: "not only trust in Providence, but keep the powder dry." Do your part of the work, or you cannot succeed. Mohammed one night, while encamping in the desert, overheard one of his fatigued followers remark: "I will loose my camel, and trust it to God." "No, no, not so," said the prophet, "tie thy camel, and trust it to God!" Do all you can for yourselves, and then trust in Providence, or luck, or whatever you please to call it, for the rest.

DON'T GET ABOVE YOUR BUSINESS

Young men after they get through their business training, or apprenticeship, instead of pursuing their avocation and rising in their business, will often lie about doing nothing. They say, "I have learned my business, but I am not going to be a hireling; what is the object of learning my trade or profession, unless I establish myself?"

"Have you capital to start with?"

"No, but I am going to have it."

"How are you going to get it?"

"I will tell you confidentially; I have a wealthy old aunt, and she will die pretty soon; but if she does not, I expect to find some rich old man who will lend me a few thousand to give me a start. If I only get the money to start with, I will do well."

There is no greater mistake than when a young man believes he will succeed with borrowed money. Why? Because every man's experience coincides with that of Mr. John Jacob Astor, who said it was more difficult for him to accumulate his first thousand dollars, than all the succeeding millions that made up his colossal fortune. Money is good for nothing unless you know the value of it by experience. Give a boy twenty thousand dollars and put him in business and the chances are that he will lose every dollar of it before he is a year older. Like buying a ticket in the lottery, and drawing a prize, it is "easy come, easy go." He does not know the value of it; nothing is worth anything, unless it costs effort. Without self-denial and economy, patience and perseverance, and commencing with capital which you have not earned, you are not sure to succeed in accumulating. Young men instead of "waiting for dead men's shoes" should be up and doing, for there is no class of persons who are so unaccommodating in regard to dying as these rich old people, and it is fortunate for the expectant heirs that it is so. Nine out of ten of the rich men of our country today, started out in life as poor boys, with determined wills, industry, perseverance, economy, and good habits. They went on gradually, made their own money and saved it; and this is the best way to acquire a fortune. Stephen Girard started life as a poor cabin boy; now he pays taxes on a million and a half dollars of income per year. John Jacob Astor was a poor farmer boy, and died worth twenty million. Cornelius Vanderbilt began life rowing a boat from Staten Island to New York; now he presents our government with a steamship worth a million dollars, and he is worth fifty million.

DO NOT SCATTER YOUR POWERS

Engage in one kind of business only, and stick to it faithfully until you succeed, or until your experience shows that you should abandon it. A constant hammering on one nail will generally drive it home at last, so that it can be clinched. When a man's undivided attention is centered on one object, his mind will constantly be suggesting improvements of value, which would escape him if his brain was occupied by a dozen different subjects at once. Many a fortune has slipped through a man's fingers because he was engaging in too many occupations at a time. There is good sense in the old caution against having too many irons in the fire at once.

BEWARE OF "OUTSIDE OPERATIONS"

We sometimes see men who have obtained fortunes, suddenly become poor. In many cases this arises from intemperance, and often from gaming and other bad habits. Frequently it occurs because a man has been engaged in "outside operations" of some sort. When he gets rich in his legitimate business, he is told of a grand speculation where he can make a score of thousands. He is constantly flattered by his friends, who tell him that he is born lucky, that everything he touches turns into gold. Now if he forgets that his economical habits, his rectitude of conduct, and a personal attention to a business which he understood, caused his success in life, he will listen to the siren voices. He says:

"I will put in twenty thousand dollars. I have been lucky, and my good luck will soon bring me back sixty thousand dollars."

A few days elapse and it is discovered he must put in ten thousand dollars more; soon after he is told it is all right, but certain matters not foreseen require an advance of twenty thousand dollars more, which will bring him a rich harvest; but before the time comes around to realize, the bubble bursts, he loses all he is possessed of, and then he learns what he ought to have known at the first, that however successful a man may be in his own business, if he turns from that and engages in a business which he doesn't understand he is like Samson when shorn of his locks— his strength has departed, and he becomes like other men.

If a man has plenty of money, he ought to invest something in everything that appears to promise success and that will probably benefit mankind; but let the sums thus invested be moderate in amount, and never let a man foolishly jeopardize a fortune that he has earned in a legitimate way, by investing it in things in which he has had no experience.

DON'T BLAB

Some men have a foolish habit of telling their business secrets. If they make money they like to tell their neighbors how it was done. Nothing is gained by this, and ofttimes much is lost. Say nothing about your profits, your hopes, your expectations, your intentions. And this should apply to letters as well as to conversation. Goethe made Mephistopheles say: "Never write a letter nor destroy one." Businessmen must write letters, but they should be careful what they put in them. If you are losing money, be specially cautious and not tell of it, or you will lose your reputation.

PRESERVE YOUR INTEGRITY

It is more precious than diamonds or rubies. The old miser said to his sons: "Get money; get it honestly, if you can, but get money." This advice was not only atrociously wicked, but it was the very essence of stupidity. It was as much as to say, "If you find it difficult to obtain money honestly, you can easily get it dishonestly. Get it in that way." Poor fool, not to know that the most difficult thing in life is to make money dishonestly; not to know that our prisons are full of men who attempted to follow this advice; not to understand that no man can be dishonest without soon being found out, and that when his lack of principle is discovered, nearly every avenue to success is closed against him forever. The public very properly shun all whose integrity is doubted. No matter how polite and pleasant and accommodating a man may be, none of us dare to deal with him if we suspect "false weights and measures." Strict honesty not only lies at the foundation of all success in life financially, but in every other respect. Uncompromising integrity of character is invaluable. It secures to its possessor a peace and joy which cannot be attained without it—which no amount of money, or houses and lands can purchase. A man who is known to be strictly honest, may be ever so poor, but he has the purses of all the community at his disposal;—for all know that if he promises to return what he borrows, he will never disappoint them. As a mere matter of selfishness, therefore, if a man had no higher motive for being honest, all will find that the maxim of Dr. Franklin can never fail to be true, that "honesty is the best policy."

To get rich, is not always equivalent to being successful. "There are many rich poor men," while there are many others, honest and devout men and women, who have never possessed so much money as some rich persons squander in a week, but who are nevertheless really richer and happier than any man can ever be while he is a transgressor of the higher laws of his being.

The inordinate love of money, no doubt, may be and is "the root of all evil," but money itself, when properly used, is not only a "handy thing to have in the house," but affords the gratification of blessing our race by enabling its possessor to enlarge the scope of human happiness and human influence. The desire for wealth is nearly universal, and none can say it is not laudable, provided the possessor of it accepts its responsibilities, and uses it as a friend to humanity.

The history of money-getting, which is commerce, is a history of civilization, and wherever trade has flourished most, there, too, have art and science produced the noblest fruits. In fact, as a general thing, money-getters are the benefactors of our race. To them, in a great measure, are we indebted for our institutions of learning and of art, our academies, colleges, and religious institutions. It is no argument against the desire for, or the possession of wealth, to say that there are sometimes misers who hoard money only for the sake of hoarding, and who have no higher aspiration than to grasp everything which comes within their reach. As we have sometimes hypocrites in religion, and demagogues in politics, so there are occasionally misers among money-getters. These, however, are only exceptions to the general rule. But when, in this country, we find such a nuisance and stumbling block as a miser, we remember with gratitude that in America we have no laws of primogeniture, and that in the due course of nature the time will come when the hoarded dust will be scattered for the benefit of humanity. To all men and women, therefore, do I conscientiously say, make money honestly, and not otherwise, for Shakespeare has truly said, "He that wants money, means, and content, is without three good friends."

Dr. Napoleon Hill

LESSON 27

HOW TO TURN
YOUR DESIRES INTO GOLD

When Andrew Carnegie, founder of the iron and steel industry in the United States, was at the height of his power he was interviewed by an earnest young man from a national business magazine. During that interview, Carnegie slyly dropped hints of a mysterious master power he used; a magic law of the mind—a little-known psychological principle which could accomplish great wonders.

Napoleon Hill listened eagerly as Carnegie suggested that upon that single principle he could build the philosophy of all personal success, whether it be measured in terms of money, power, position, prestige, influence, or fame.

What was Carnegie's secret? Napoleon Hill eventually published it in a book that became the all-time best-selling book in the entire world on the subject of success, *Think and Grow Rich!* This lesson, from that classic, deals with the application of Carnegie's magic formula as it pertains to riches although it will help you to achieve any goal providing your desire is strong enough.

Andrew Carnegie was convinced that much of what is taught in schools is of no value in helping the individual to earn a living or accumulate wealth. He sincerely felt that if his formula could be taught in public schools and colleges it would revolutionize the entire educational system. Unfortunately, his hope has never been realized but we are proud to include his secret in *The University of Success*. Will it work for you? Only you can answer that. Remember, there are no limitations to your mind except those you acknowledge . . .

267

When Edwin C. Barnes climbed down from the freight train in East Orange, N.J., more than fifty years ago he may have resembled a tramp, but his *thoughts* were those of a king!

As he made his way from the railroad tracks to Thomas A. Edison's office, his mind was at work. He saw himself *standing in Edison's presence*. He heard himself asking Mr. Edison for an opportunity to carry out the one consuming obsession of his life, a burning desire to become the business associate of the great inventor.

Barnes's desire was not a *hope!* It was not a *wish!* It was a keen desire, which transcended everything else. It was definite.

A few years later Edwin C. Barnes again stood before Edison in the same office where he first met the inventor. This time his desire had been translated into reality. *He was in business with Edison.* The dominating dream of his life had become a reality.

Barnes succeeded because he chose a definite goal and placed all his energy, all his will power, all his effort, everything, back of that goal.

NO WAY TO RETREAT

Five years passed before the chance he had been seeking made its appearance. To everyone except himself he appeared only another cog in the Edison business wheel, but in his own mind he was the partner of Edison every minute of the time, from the very day that he first went to work there.

It is a remarkable illustration of the power of a definite desire. Barnes won his goal because he wanted to be a business associate of Mr. Edison more than he wanted anything else. He created a plan by which to attain that purpose. But he burned all bridges behind him. He stood by his desire until it became the dominating obsession of his life—and—finally, a fact.

When he went to East Orange he did not say to himself, "I will try to induce Edison to give me a job of some sort." He said, "I will see Edison, and put him on notice that I have come to go into business with him."

He did not say, "I will keep my eyes open for another opportunity, in case I fail to get what I want in the Edison organization." He said, "There is but *one* thing in this world that I am determined to have, and that is a business association with Thomas A. Edison. I will burn all bridges behind me, and stake my entire future on my ability to get what I want."

He left himself no possible way of retreat. He had to win or perish!

That is all there is to the Barnes story of success!

HE BURNED HIS BOATS

A long while ago, a great warrior faced a situation which made it necessary for him to make a decision which insured his success on the battlefield. He was about to send his armies against a powerful foe, whose men outnumbered his own. He loaded his soldiers into boats, sailed to the enemy's country, unloaded soldiers and equipment, then gave the order to burn the ships that had carried them. Addressing his men before the first battle, he said, "You see the boats going up in smoke. That means that we cannot leave these shores alive unless we win! We now have no choice—*we win—or we perish!*"

They won.

Every person who wins in any undertaking must be willing to burn his ships and cut all sources of retreat. Only by so doing can one be sure of maintaining that state of mind known as a burning desire to win, essential to success.

The morning after the great Chicago fire, a group of merchants stood on State Street, looking at the smoking remains of what had been their stores. They went into a conference to decide if they would try to rebuild, or leave Chicago and start over in a more promising section of the country. They reached a decision— all except one—to leave Chicago.

The merchant who decided to stay and rebuild pointed a finger at the remains of his store and said, "Gentlemen, on that very spot I will build the world's greatest store, no matter how many times it may burn down."

That was almost a century ago. The store was built. It stands there today, a towering monument to the power of that state of mind known as a burning desire. The easy thing for Marshall Field to have done would have been exactly what his fellow merchants did. When the going was hard and the future looked dismal, they pulled up and went where the going seemed easier.

Mark well this difference between Marshall Field and the other merchants, because it is the same difference which distinguishes practically all who succeed from those who fail.

Every human being who reaches the age of understanding of

the purpose of money wishes for it. *Wishing* will not bring riches. But *desiring* riches with a state of mind that becomes an obsession, then planning definite ways and means to acquire riches, and backing those plans with persistence which *does not recognize failure*, will bring riches.

SIX STEPS THAT TURN DESIRES INTO GOLD

The method by which *desire* for riches can be transmuted into its financial equivalent consists of the following six definite, practical steps:

1. Fix in your mind the *exact* amount of money you desire. It is not sufficient merely to say "I want plenty of money." Be definite as to the amount.
2. Determine exactly what you intend to *give* in return for the money you desire. (There is no such reality as "something for nothing.")
3. Establish a definite date when you intend to *possess* the money you desire.
4. Create a definite plan for carrying out your desire, and begin *at once*, whether you are ready or not, to put this plan into *action*.
5. Write out a clear, concise statement of the amount of money you intend to acquire, name the time limit for its acquisition, state what you intend to give in return for the money, and describe clearly the plan through which you intend to accumulate it.
6. Read your written statement aloud twice daily, once just before retiring at night, and once after arising in the morning. As you read—see and feel and believe yourself already in possession of the money.

It is important that you follow the instructions described in these six steps. It is especially important that you observe, and follow the instructions in the sixth paragraph. You may complain that it is impossible for you to "see yourself in possession of money" before you actually have it. Here is where a *burning desire* will come to your aid. If you truly *desire* money so keenly that your desire is an obsession, you will have no difficulty in convincing yourself that you will acquire it. The object is to want money, and to become so determined to have it that you *convince* yourself you will have it.

PRINCIPLES WORTH $100,000,000

To the uninitiated, who have not been schooled in the working principles of the human mind, these instructions may appear impractical. It may be helpful, to all who fail to recognize the soundness of the six steps, to know that the information they convey was received from Andrew Carnegie, who began as an ordinary laborer in the steel mills, but managed, despite his humble beginning, to make these principles yield him a fortune of considerably more than one hundred million dollars.

It may be of further help to know that the six steps here recommended were carefully scrutinized by Thomas A. Edison, who placed his stamp of approval upon them as being, not only the steps essential for the accumulation of money, but for the attainment of any goal.

The steps call for no "hard labor." They call for no sacrifice. They do not require one to become ridiculous, or credulous. To apply them calls for no great amount of education. But the successful application of these six steps does call for sufficient *imagination* to enable one to see and to understand that accumulation of money cannot be left to chance, good fortune, and luck. One must realize that all who have accumulated great fortunes first did a certain amount of dreaming, hoping, wishing, desiring, and planning *before* they acquired money.

You may as well know, right here, that you can never have riches in great quantities *unless* you can work yourself into a white heat of *desire* for money, and actually *believe* you will possess it.

GREAT DREAMS CAN TURN INTO RICHES

We who are in this race for riches should be encouraged to know that this changed world in which we live is demanding new ideas, new ways of doing things, new leaders, new inventions, new methods of teaching, new methods of marketing, new books, new literature, new features for television, new ideas for moving pictures. Back of all this demand for new and better things, there is one quality which one must possess to win, and that is *definiteness of purpose*, the knowledge of what one wants, and a burning *desire* to possess it.

We who desire to accumulate riches should remember the real leaders of the world always have been men who harnessed and put into practical use the intangible, unseen forces of unborn opportunity, and have converted those forces (or impulses of thought) into skyscrapers, cities, factories, airplanes, automobiles, and every form of convenience that makes life more pleasant.

In planning to acquire your share of the riches, let no one influence you to scorn the dreamer. To win the big stakes in this changed world you must catch the spirit of the great pioneers of the past, whose dreams have given to civilization all that it has of value, the spirit which serves as the lifeblood of our own country— your opportunity and mine, to develop and market our talents.

If the thing you wish to do is right and *you believe in it,* go ahead and do it! Put your dream across, and never mind what "they" say if you meet with temporary defeat, for "they," perhaps, do not know that every failure brings with it the seed of an equivalent success.

The Wright brothers dreamed of a machine that would fly through the air. Now one may see evidence all over the world that they dreamed soundly.

Marconi dreamed of a system for harnessing the intangible forces of the ether. Evidence that he did not dream in vain may be found in every radio and television set in the world. It may interest you to know that Marconi's "friends" had him taken into custody and examined in a psychopathic hospital when he announced he had discovered a principle through which he could send messages through the air without the aid of wires or other direct physical means of communication. The dreamers of today fare better.

The world is filled with an abundance of opportunity which the dreamers of the past never knew.

THEY PUT DESIRE BEHIND THEIR DREAMS

A burning desire to be and to do is the starting point from which the dreamer must take off. Dreams are not born of indifference, laziness, or lack of ambition.

Remember that almost all who succeed in life get off to a bad start, and pass through many heartbreaking struggles before they "arrive." The turning point in the lives of those who succeed usually comes at the moment of some crisis, through which they are introduced to their "other selves."

John Bunyan wrote *Pilgrim's Progress,* which is among the finest of all English books, after he had been confined in prison and sorely punished because of his views on the subject of religion.

O. Henry discovered the genius which slept within his brain after he had met with great misfortune and was confined in a prison cell in Columbus, Ohio. Being forced, through misfortune, to become acquainted with his "other self" and to use his imagination, he discovered himself to be a great author instead of a miserable criminal and outcast.

Charles Dickens began by pasting labels on blacking pots. The tragedy of his first love penetrated the depths of his soul and converted him into one of the world's truly great authors. That tragedy produced first *David Copperfield,* then a succession of other works that made this a richer and better world for all who read his books.

Helen Keller became deaf, dumb, and blind shortly after birth. Despite her greatest misfortune, she has written her name indelibly in the pages of the history of the great. Her entire life has served as evidence that *no one is ever defeated until defeat has been accepted as a reality.*

Robert Burns was an illiterate country lad. He was cursed by poverty, and grew up to be a drunkard in the bargain. The world was made better for his having lived because he clothed beautiful thoughts in poetry, and thereby plucked a thorn and planted a rose in its place.

Beethoven was deaf; Milton was blind; but their names will last as long as time endures because they dreamed and translated their dreams into organized thought.

There is a difference between wishing for a thing and being ready to receive it. No one is *ready* for a thing until he *believes* he can acquire it. The state of mind must be *belief,* not mere hope or wish. Open-mindedness is essential for belief. Closed minds do not inspire faith, courage, or belief.

Remember, no more effort is required to aim high in life, to demand abundance and prosperity, than is required to accept misery and poverty. A great poet has correctly stated this universal truth through these lines:

> I bargained with Life for a penny,
>   And Life would pay no more,
> However I begged at evening
>   When I counted my scanty store.
>
> For Life is a just employer,
>   He gives you what you ask,
> But once you have set the wages,
>   Why, you must bear the task.
>
> I worked for a menial's hire,
>   Only to learn, dismayed,
> That any wage I had asked of Life,
>   Life would have willingly paid.

DESIRE PERFORMS THE "IMPOSSIBLE"

As a fitting climax, I wish to introduce one of the most unusual persons I have ever known. I first saw him a few minutes after he was born. He came into the world without any physical sign of ears, and the doctor admitted, when pressed for an opinion on the case, that the child might be deaf and mute for life.

I challenged the doctor's opinion. I had the right to do so; I was the child's father. I too reached a decision and rendered an opinion, but I expressed the opinion silently, in the secrecy of my own heart.

In my own mind I knew that my son would hear and speak. How? I was sure there must be a way, and I knew I would find it. I thought of the words of the immortal Emerson, "The whole course of things goes to teach us faith. We need only obey. There is guidance for each of us, and by lowly listening, we shall hear *the right word*."

The right word? *Desire!* More than anything else, I desired that my son should not be a deaf mute. From that desire I never receded, not for a second.

What could I do about it? Somehow I would find a way to transplant into that child's mind my own burning desire for ways and means of conveying sound to his brain without the aid of ears.

As soon as the child was old enough to cooperate I would fill his mind so completely with a burning desire to hear that nature would, by methods of her own, translate it into physical reality.

All this thinking took place in my own mind, but I spoke of it to no one. Every day I renewed the pledge I had made to myself that my son should not be a deaf mute.

As he grew older and began to take notice of things around him, we observed that he had a slight degree of hearing. When he reached the age when children usually begin talking he made no attempt to speak, but we could tell by his actions that he could hear certain sounds slightly. That was all I wanted to know! I was convinced that if he could hear, even slightly, he might develop still greater hearing capacity. Then something happened which gave me hope. It came from an entirely unexpected source.

WE FIND A WAY

We bought a phonograph. When the child heard the music for the first time he went into ecstasies, and promptly appropriated the machine. On one occasion he played a record over and over for almost two hours, standing in front of the phonograph *with his teeth clamped on the edge of the case.* The significance of this self-formed habit of his did not become clear to us until years afterward, for we had not heard of the principle of "bone conduction" of sound at that time.

Shortly after he appropriated the phonograph, I discovered that he could hear me quite clearly when I spoke with my lips touching his mastoid bone, at the base of the skull.

Having determined that he could hear the sound of my voice plainly, I began immediately to transfer to his mind the desire to hear and speak. I soon discovered that the child enjoyed bedtime stories, so I went to work creating stories designed to develop in him self-reliance, imagination, and a *keen desire to hear and to be normal.*

There was one story in particular, which I emphasized by giving it some new and dramatic coloring each time it was told. It was designed to plant in his mind the thought that his affliction was not a liability, but an asset of great value. Despite the fact that all the philosophy I had examined clearly indicated that every adversity brings with it the seed of an equivalent advantage, I must confess that I had not the slightest idea *how* this affliction could ever become an asset.

NOTHING COULD STOP HIM

As I analyze the experience in retrospect, I can see now that my son's *faith in me* had much to do with the astounding results. He did not question anything I told him. I sold him the idea that he had a distinct *advantage* over his older brother, and that this advantage would reflect itself in many ways. For example, the teachers in school would observe that he had no ears and, because of this, they would show him special attention and treat him with extraordinary kindness. They always did. I sold him the idea too that when he became old enough to sell newspapers (his older brother had already become a newspaper merchant) he would have a big advantage over his brother, for the reason that people would pay him extra money for his wares, because they could see that he was a bright, industrious boy, despite the fact he had no ears.

When he was about seven he showed the first evidence that our method of "programming" his mind was bearing fruit. For several months he begged for the privilege of selling newspapers, but his mother would not give the project her consent.

Finally he took matters in his own hands. One afternoon, when he was left at home with the servants, he climbed through the kitchen window, shinnied to the ground, and set out on his own. He borrowed six cents in capital from the neighborhood shoemaker, invested it in papers, sold out, reinvested, and kept repeating until late in the evening. After balancing his accounts and paying back the six cents he had borrowed from his banker, he had a net profit of forty-two cents. When we got home that night we found him in bed asleep, with the money tightly clenched in his hand.

His mother opened his hand, removed the coins, and cried. Of all things! Crying over her son's first victory seemed so inappropriate. My reaction was the reverse. I laughed heartily, for I knew that my endeavor to plant in the child's mind an attitude of faith in himself had been successful.

His mother saw, in his first business venture, a little deaf boy who had gone out in the streets and risked his life to earn money. I saw a brave, ambitious, self-reliant little businessman whose stock in himself had been increased a hundred percent because he had gone into business on his own initiative, and had won. The transaction pleased me, because I knew that he had given evidence of resourcefulness that would go with him all through life.

A BREAKTHROUGH IN HEARING

The little deaf boy went through the grades, high school, and college without being able to hear his teachers, except when they shouted loudly at close range. He did not go to a school for the deaf. We would not permit him to learn the sign language. We were determined that he should live a normal life and associate with normal children, and we stood by that decision although it cost us many heated debates with school officials.

While he was in high school he tried an electrical hearing aid, but it was of no value to him.

During his last week in college, something happened which marked the most important turning point of his life. Through what seemed to be mere chance, he came into possession of another electrical hearing device, which was sent to him on trial. He was slow about testing it, due to his disappointment with a similar device. Finally he picked up the instrument and more or less carelessly placed it on his head, hooked up the battery, and lo! as if by a stroke of magic his lifelong desire for normal hearing became a reality! For the first time in his life he heard practically as well as any person with normal hearing.

Overjoyed because of the changed world which had been brought to him through his hearing device, he rushed to the telephone, called his mother, and heard her voice perfectly. The next day he plainly heard the voices of his professors in class for the first time in his life! For the first time in his life he could converse freely with other people, without the necessity of their having to speak loudly. Truly, he had come into possession of a changed world.

Desire had commenced to pay dividends, but the victory was not yet complete. The boy still had to find a definite and practical way to convert his handicap into an *equivalent asset*.

THE "DEAF" BOY HELPS OTHERS

Hardly realizing the significance of what had already been accomplished, but intoxicated with the joy of his newly discovered world of sound, he wrote a letter to the manufacturer of the hearing aid enthusiastically describing his experience. Something in his letter caused the company to invite him to New York. When he arrived he was escorted through the factory, and while talking with the chief engineer, telling him about his changed world, a hunch, an idea, or an inspiration—call it what you wish—flashed into his mind. It was *this impulse of thought* which converted his affliction into an asset, destined to pay dividends in both money and happiness to thousands for all time to come.

The sum and substance of that impulse of thought was this: it occurred to him that he might be of help to the millions of deafened people who go through life without the benefit of hearing devices if he could find a way to tell them the story of his changed world.

For an entire month he carried on an intensive research, during which he analyzed the entire marketing system of the manufacturer of the hearing device, and created ways and means of communicating with the hard of hearing all over the world for the purpose of sharing with them his newly discovered changed world. When this was done, he put in writing a two-year plan based upon his findings. When he presented the plan to the company, he was instantly given a position for the purpose of carrying out his ambition.

Little did he dream, when he went to work, that he was destined to bring hope and practical relief to thousands of deafened people who, without his help, would have been doomed forever to deafness.

There is no doubt in my mind that Blair would have been a deaf mute all his life if his mother and I had not managed to shape his mind as we did.

When I planted in his mind the desire to hear and talk, and live as a normal person, there went with that impulse some strange influence which caused nature to become bridge builder, and span the gulf of silence between his brain and the outer world.

Truly, a burning desire has devious ways of transmuting itself into its physical equivalent. Blair desired normal hearing; now he has it! He was born with a handicap which might easily have sent one with a less defined desire to the street with a bundle of pencils and a tin cup.

The little "white lie" I planted in his mind when he was a child, by leading him to believe his affliction would become a great asset, has justified itself. Verily there is nothing, right or wrong, which belief, plus burning desire, cannot make real. These qualities are free to everyone.

DESIRE WORKS MAGIC FOR A SINGER

One short paragraph in a news dispatch concerning Mme. Ernestine Schumann-Heink gives the clue to this unusual woman's stupendous success as a singer. I quote the paragraph, because the clue it contains is none other than desire.

> Early in her career, Mme. Schumann-Heink visited the director of the Vienna Court Opera, to have him test her voice. But he did not test it. After taking one look at the awkward and poorly dressed girl, he exclaimed, none too gently, "With such a face, and with no personality at all, how can you ever expect to succeed in opera? My good child, give up the idea. Buy a sewing machine, and go to work. *You can never be a singer.*"

Never is a long time! The director of the Vienna Court Opera knew much about the technique of singing. He knew little about the power of desire when it assumes the proportion of an obsession. If he had known more of that power, he would not have made the mistake of condemning genius without giving it an opportunity.

Several years ago, one of my business associates became ill. He became worse as time went on, and finally was taken to the hospital for an operation. The doctor warned me that there was little if any chance of my ever seeing him alive again. But that was the doctor's opinion. It was not the opinion of the patient. Just before he was wheeled away, he whispered feebly, "Do not be disturbed, Chief, I will be out of here in a few days." The attending nurse looked at me with pity. But the patient did come through safely. After it was all over, his physician said, "Nothing but his own desire to live saved him. He never would have pulled through if he had not refused to accept the possibility of death."

I believe in the power of desire backed by faith because I have seen this power lift men from lowly beginnings to places of power and wealth; I have seen it rob the grave of its victims; I have seen it serve as the medium by which men staged a comeback after having been defeated in a hundred different ways; I have seen it provide my own son with a normal, happy, successful life, despite Nature's having sent him into the world without ears.

Through some strange and powerful principle of "mental chemistry" which she has never divulged, Nature wraps up in the impulse of strong desire, "that something" which recognizes no such word as "impossible," and accepts no such reality as failure.

*It is true that money cannot buy happiness
but it does make it possible for you
to enjoy the best that the world has to offer.*

George S. Clason

LESSON 28

HOW TO BUILD
YOUR FINANCIAL NEST EGG

Settle back and relax. You are about to learn, in an unique way, the most effective method for accumulating wealth that has ever been devised. Keep that pen or pencil in hand, however, because there is much you will want to remember from your encounter with *The Richest Man in Babylon.*

For many years George S. Clason was the creator of short stories which he called "Babylonian parables." In them he described the success secrets of the ancients and how they handled their finances. These stories were printed, at first, in small booklets which were distributed free to their clients by banks, insurance companies, and investment houses. Eventually they became so popular that Mr. Clason published a collection of his favorite pieces in a book titled *The Richest Man in Babylon,* named after his most famous parable. The book has been acclaimed as the greatest of all inspirational works on the subject of thrift and financial planning.

Mr. Clason's premise was that money is governed today by the same laws which controlled it when prosperous individuals thronged the streets of Babylon, six thousand years ago. "Babylon," he claimed, "became the wealthiest city of the ancient world because its citizens were the richest people of their time. They appreciated the value of money. They practiced sound financial principles in acquiring money, keeping money and making their money earn more money. They provided for themselves what we all desire ... incomes for the future."

This lesson is the complete text of Mr. Clason's most famous story, *The Richest Man in Babylon*. It can point you to a way of life that may have seemed beyond your reach ...

In old Babylon there once lived a certain very rich man named Arkad. Far and wide he was famed for his great wealth. Also was he famed for his liberality. He was generous in his charities. He was generous with his family. He was liberal in his own expenses. But nevertheless each year his wealth increased more rapidly than he spent it.

And there were certain friends of younger days who came to him and said: "You, Arkad, are more fortunate than we. You have become the richest man in all Babylon while we struggle for existence. You can wear the finest garments and you can enjoy the rarest foods, while we must be content if we can clothe our families in raiment that is presentable and feed them as best we can.

"Yes, once we were equal. We studied under the same master. We played in the same games. And in neither the studies nor the games did you outshine us. And in the years since, you have been no more an honorable citizen than we.

"Nor have you worked harder or more faithfully, insofar as we can judge. Why, then, should a fickle fate single you out to enjoy all the good things of life and ignore us who are equally deserving?"

Thereupon Arkad remonstrated with them, saying, "If you have not acquired more than a bare existence in the years since we were youths, it is because you either have failed to learn the laws that govern the building of wealth, or else you do not observe them.

" 'Fickle Fate' is a vicious goddess who brings no permanent good to anyone. On the contrary, she brings ruin to almost every man upon whom she showers unearned gold. She makes wanton spenders, who soon dissipate all they receive and are left beset by overwhelming appetites and desires they have not the ability to gratify. Yet others whom she favors become misers and hoard their wealth, fearing to spend what they have, knowing they do not possess the ability to replace it. They further are beset by fear of robbers and doom themselves to lives of emptiness and secret misery.

"Others there probably are, who can take unearned gold and add to it and continue to be happy and contented citizens. But so few are they, I know of them but by hearsay. Think you of the men who have inherited sudden wealth, and see if these things are not so."

His friends admitted that of the men they knew who had inherited wealth these words were true, and they besought him to explain to them how he had become possessed of so much property, so he continued:

"In my youth I looked about me and saw all the good things there were to bring happiness and contentment. And I realized that wealth increased the potency of all these.

"Wealth is a power. With wealth many things are possible.

- "One may ornament the home with the richest of furnishings.
- "One may sail the distant seas.
- "One may feast on the delicacies of far lands.
- "One may buy the ornaments of the gold worker and the stone polisher.
- "One may even build mighty temples for the Gods.
- "One may do all these things and many others in which there is delight for the senses and gratification for the soul.

"And, when I realized all this, I declared to myself that I would claim my share of the good things of life. I would not be one of those who stand afar off, enviously watching others enjoy. I would not be content to clothe myself in the cheapest raiment that looked respectable. I would not be satisfied with the lot of a poor man. On the contrary, I would make myself a guest at this banquet of good things.

"Being, as you know, the son of a humble merchant, one of a large family with no hope of an inheritance, and not being endowed, as you have so frankly said, with superior powers or wisdom, I decided that if I was to achieve what I desired, time and study would be required.

"As for time, all men have it in abundance. You, each of you, have let slip by sufficient time to have made yourselves wealthy. Yet, you admit, you have nothing to show except your good families, of which you can be justly proud.

"As for study, did not our wise teacher teach us that learning was of two kinds: the one kind being the things we learned and knew, and the other being in the training that taught us how to find out what we did not know?

"Therefore did I decide to find out how one might accumulate wealth, and when I had found out, to make this my task and do it well. For, is it not wise that we should enjoy while we dwell in the brightness of the sunshine, for sorrows enough shall descend upon us when we depart for the darkness of the world of spirit?

"I found employment as a scribe in the hall of records, and long hours each day I labored upon the clay tablets. Week after week, and month after month, I labored, yet for my earnings I had nought to show. Food and clothing and penance to the gods, and other things of which I could remember not what, absorbed all my earnings. But my determination did not leave me.

"And one day Algamish, the money lender, came to the house of the city master and ordered a copy of the Ninth Law, and he said to me, 'I must have this in two days, and if the task is done by that time, two coppers will I give to thee.'

"So I labored hard, but the law was long, and when Algamish returned the task was unfinished. He was angry, and had I been his slave he would have beaten me. But knowing the city master would not permit him to injure me, I was unafraid, so I said to him, 'Algamish, you are a very rich man. Tell me how I may also become rich, and all night I will carve upon the clay, and when the sun rises it shall be completed.'

"He smiled at me and replied, 'You are a forward knave, but we will call it a bargain.'

"All that night I carved, though my back pained and the smell of the wick made my head ache until my eyes could hardly see. But when he returned at sunup, the tablets were complete.

" 'Now,' I said, 'tell me what you promised.'

" 'You have fulfilled your part of our bargain, my son,' he said to me kindly, 'and I am ready to fulfill mine. I will tell you these things you wish to know because I am becoming an old man, and an old tongue loves to wag. And when youth comes to age for advice he receives the wisdom of years. But too often does youth think that age knows only the wisdom of days that are gone, and therefore profits not. But remember this, the sun that shines today is the sun that shone when thy father was born, and will still be shining when thy last grandchild shall pass into the darkness.

" 'The thoughts of youth,' he continued, 'are bright lights that shine forth like the meteors that oft make brilliant the sky, but the wisdom of age is like the fixed stars that shine so unchanged that the sailor may depend upon them to steer his course.

" 'Mark you well my words, for if you do not you will fail to grasp the truth that I will tell you, and you will think that your night's work has been in vain.'

"Then he looked at me shrewdly from under his shaggy brows and said in a low, forceful tone, 'I found the road to wealth when I decided that *a part of all I earned was mine to keep.* And so will you.'

"Then he continued to look at me with a glance that I could feel pierce me but said no more.

" 'Is that all?' I asked.

" 'That was sufficient to change the heart of a sheepherder into the heart of a moneylender,' he replied.

" 'But *all* I earn is mine to keep, is it not?' I demanded.

" 'Far from it,' he replied. 'Do you not pay the garment-maker? Do you not pay the sandal-maker? Do you not pay for the things you eat? Can you live in Babylon without spending? What have you to show for your earnings of the past month? What for the past year? Fool! You pay to everyone but yourself. Dullard, you labor for others. As well be a slave and work for what your master gives you to eat and wear. If you did keep for yourself one tenth of all you earn, how much would you have in ten years?'

"My knowledge of the numbers did not forsake me, and I answered, 'As much as I earn in one year.'

" 'You speak but half the truth,' he retorted. 'Every gold piece you save is a slave to work for you. Every copper it earns is its child that also can earn for you. If you would become wealthy, then what you save must earn, and its children must earn, that all may help to give to you the abundance you crave.

" 'You think I cheat you for your long night's work,' he continued, 'but I am paying you a thousand times over if you have the intelligence to grasp the truth I offer you.

" 'A part of all you earn is yours to keep. It should be not less than a tenth no matter how little you earn. It can be as much more as you can afford. Pay yourself first. Do not buy from the clothes-maker and the sandal-maker more than you can pay out of the rest and still have enough for food and charity and penance to the gods.

" 'Wealth, like a tree, grows from a tiny seed. The first copper you save is the seed from which your tree of wealth shall grow. The sooner you plant that seed the sooner shall the tree grow. And the more faithfully you nourish and water that tree with consistent savings, the sooner may you bask in contentment beneath its shade.'

"So saying, he took his tablets and went away.

"I thought much about what he had said to me, and it seemed reasonable. So I decided that I would try it. Each time I

was paid I took one from each ten pieces of copper and hid it away.
And strange as it may seem, I was no shorter of funds than before.
I noticed little difference as I managed to get along without it. But
often I was tempted, as my hoard began to grow, to spend if for
some of the good things the merchants displayed, brought by
camels and ships from the land of the Phoenicians. But I wisely
refrained.

"A twelfth month after Algamish had gone he again returned
and said to me, 'Son, have you paid to yourself not less than one
tenth of all you have earned for the past year?'

"I answered proudly, 'Yes, master, I have.'

" 'That is good,' he answered beaming upon me, 'and what
have you done with it?'

" 'I have given it to Azmur, the brickmaker, who told me he
was traveling over the far seas and in Tyre he would buy for me
the rare jewels of the Phoenicians. When he returns we shall sell
these at high prices and divide the earnings.'

" 'Every fool must learn,' he growled, 'but why trust the
knowledge of a brickmaker about jewels? Would you go to the
breadmaker to inquire about the stars? No, by my tunic, you
would go to the astrologer, if you had power to think. Your savings
are gone, youth; you have jerked your wealth-tree up by the roots.
But plant another. Try again. And next time if you would have
advice about jewels, go to the jewel merchant. If you would know
the truth about sheep, go to the herdsman. Advice is one thing
that is freely given away, but watch that you take only what is
worth having. He who takes advice about his savings from one who
is inexperienced in such matters, shall pay with his savings for
proving the falsity of their opinions.' Saying this, he went away.

"And it was as he said. For the Phoenicians are scoundrels
and sold to Azmur worthless bits of glass that looked like gems.
But as Algamish had bid me, I again saved each tenth copper, for I
now had formed the habit and it was no longer difficult.

"Again, twelve months later, Algamish came to the room of
the scribes and addressed me. 'What progress have you made
since last I saw you?'

" 'I have paid myself faithfully,' I replied, 'and my savings I
have entrusted to Agger the shieldmaker, to buy bronze, and each
fourth month he does pay me the rental.'

" 'That is good. And what do you do with the rental?'

" 'I do have a great feast with honey and fine wine and spiced
cake. Also I have bought me a scarlet tunic. And some day I shall
buy me a young ass upon which to ride.'

"To which Algamish laughed, 'You do eat the children of

your savings. Then how do you expect them to work for you? And how can they have children who will also work for you? First get thee an army of golden slaves and then many a rich banquet may you enjoy without regret.' So saying he again went away.

"Nor did I again see him for two years, when he once more returned and his face was full of deep lines and his eyes drooped, for he was becoming a very old man. And he said to me, 'Arkad, hast thou yet achieved the wealth thou dreamed of?'

"And I answered, 'Not yet all that I desire, but some I have and it earns more, and its earnings earn more.'

" 'And do you still take the advice of brickmakers?'

" 'About brickmaking they give good advice,' I retorted.

" 'Arkad,' he continued, 'you have learned your lessons well. You first learned to live upon less than you could earn. Next you learned to seek advice from those who were competent through their own experiences to give it. And, lastly, you have learned to make gold work for you.

" 'You have taught yourself how to acquire money, how to keep it, and how to use it. Therefore, you are competent for a responsible position. I am becoming an old man. My sons think only of spending and give no thought to earning. My interests are great and I fear too much for me to look after. If you will go to Nippur and look after my lands there, I shall make you my partner and you shall share in my estate.'

"So I went to Nippur and took charge of his holdings, which were large. And because I was full of ambition and because I had mastered the three laws of successfully handling wealth, I was enabled to increase greatly the value of his properties. So I prospered much, and when the spirit of Algamish departed for the sphere of darkness, I did share in his estate as he had arranged under the law."

So spake Arkad, and when he had finished his tale, one of his friends said, "You were indeed fortunate that Algamish made of you an heir."

"Fortunate only in that I had the desire to prosper before I first met him. For four years did I not prove my definiteness of purpose by keeping one tenth of all I earned? Would you call a fisherman lucky who for years so studied the habits of the fish that with each changing wind he could cast his nets about them? Opportunity is a haughty goddess who wastes no time with those who are unprepared."

"You had strong will power to keep on after you lost your first year's savings. You are unusual in that way," spoke up another.

"Will power!" retorted Arkad. "What nonsense. Do you think

will power gives a man the strength to lift a burden the camel cannot carry, or to draw a load the oxen cannot budge? Will power is but the unflinching purpose to carry a task you set for yourself to fulfillment. If I set for myself a task, be it ever so trifling, I shall see it through. How else shall I have confidence in myself to do important things? Should I say to myself, 'For a hundred days as I walk across the bridge into the city, I will pick from the road a pebble and cast it into the stream,' I would do it. If on the seventh day I passed by without remembering, I would not say to myself, 'Tomorrow I will cast two pebbles which will do as well.' Instead, I would retrace my steps and cast the pebble. Nor on the twentieth day would I say to myself, 'Arkad, this is useless. What does it avail you to cast a pebble every day? Throw in a handful and be done with it.' No, I would not say that nor do it. When I set a task for myself, I complete it. Therefore, I am careful not to start difficult and impractical tasks, because I love leisure."

And then another friend spoke up and said, "If what you tell is true, and it does seem as you have said, reasonable, then being so simple, if all men did it, there would not be enough wealth to go around."

"Wealth grows wherever men exert energy," Arkad replied. "If a rich man builds him a new palace, is the gold he pays out gone? No, the brickmaker has part of it and the laborer has part of it, and the artist has part of it. And everyone who labors upon the house has part of it. Yet when the palace is completed, is it not worth all it cost? And is the ground upon which it stands not worth more because it is there? And is the ground that adjoins it not worth more because it is there? Wealth grows in magic ways. No man can prophesy the limit of it. Have not the Phoenicians built great cities on barren coasts with the wealth that comes from their ships of commerce on the seas?"

"What then do you advise us to do that we also may become rich?" asked still another of his friends. "The years have passed and we are no longer young men and we have nothing put by."

"I advise that you take the wisdom of Algamish and say to yourselves, 'A part of all I earn is mine to keep.' Say it in the morning when you first arise. Say it at noon. Say it at night. Say it each hour of every day. Say it to yourself until the words stand out like letters of fire across the sky.

"Impress yourself with the idea. Fill yourself with the thought. Then take whatever portion seems wise. Let it be not less than one tenth and lay it by. Arrange your other expenditures to do this if necessary. But lay by that portion first. Soon you will realize what a rich feeling it is to own a treasure upon which you alone have claim. As it grows it will stimulate you. A new joy of life will thrill you. Greater efforts will come to you to earn more. For of your increased earnings, will not the same percentage be also yours to keep?

"Then learn to make your treasure work for you. Make it your slave. Make its children and its children's children work for you.

"Insure an income for thy future. Look thou at the aged and forget not that in the days to come thou also will be numbered among them. Therefore invest thy treasure with greatest caution that it be not lost. Usurious rates of return are deceitful sirens that sing but to lure the unwary upon the rocks of loss and remorse.

"Provide also that thy family may not want should the Gods call thee to their realms. For such protection it is always possible to make provision with small payments at regular intervals. Therefore the provident man delays not in expectation of a large sum becoming available for such a wise purpose.

"Counsel with wise men. Seek the advice of men whose daily work is handling money. Let them save you from such an error as I myself made in entrusting my money to the judgment of Azmur, the brickmaker. A small return and a safe one is far more desirable than risk.

"Enjoy life while you are here. Do not overstrain or try to save too much, If one tenth of all you earn is as much as you can comfortably keep, be content to keep this portion. Live otherwise according to your income and let not yourself get niggardly and afraid to spend. Life is good and life is rich with things worthwhile and things to enjoy."

His friends thanked him and went away. Some were silent because they had no imagination and could not understand. Some were sarcastic because they thought that one so rich should divide with old friends not so fortunate. But some had in their eyes a new light. They realized that Algamish had come back each time to the room of the scribes because he was watching a man work his way out of darkness into light. When that man had found the light, a place awaited him. No one could fill that place until he had for himself worked out his own understanding, until he was ready for opportunity.

These latter were the ones, who, in the following years, frequently revisited Arkad, who received them gladly. He counseled with them and gave them freely of his wisdom as men of broad experience are always glad to do. And he assisted them in so investing their savings that it would bring in a good interest with safety and would neither be lost nor entangled in investments that paid no dividends.

The turning point in these men's lives came upon that day when they realized the truth that had come from Algamish to Arkad and from Arkad to them.

A PART OF ALL YOU EARN
IS YOURS TO KEEP

*Three short rules that can help you to
become as great as you want to be.*

Cavett Robert

LESSON 29

HOW TO ATTRACT SUCCESS

In the past twenty-eight lessons you have already been supplied with more in-depth information on self-achievement than the average individual receives in a lifetime.

But these lessons are only rungs on your newly built ladder of success. You, and only you, can accomplish each step upward, through patience, desire, courage, and hard work.

Listen to America's supreme motivational speaker, Cavett Robert:

We've heard the expression "climbing the ladder of success" so often that its significance is lost in its simplicity. We know that a ladder is nothing but a tool—just an instrument to use in order to arrive at some destination. Likewise, a job is just a tool to be used in arriving at our goals in life. Let's consider the reason that a ladder is so symbolic.

First, a ladder is designed for vertical and not horizontal use. It is to be used only for an upward climb. Also, a ladder cannot be climbed except by using one rung at a time. Just as people do not explode into success but grow into it, a ladder offers only a progressive means of travel. We use each rung as a foundation to reach greater heights. If we try to skip a rung, disaster is imminent.

Perhaps the most important similarity between one's job and a ladder is that it requires *effort* to climb in either case. Not all people are willing to make the sacrifice in effort to reach the top of the ladder but I can't conceive of anyone having so little ambition that he or she doesn't want to go up far enough to escape the congestion at the bottom.

From his widely read book, *Success With People Through Human Engineering and Motivation,* Mr. Robert will teach you what you need to do in order to handle yourself with pride on your new ladder . . .

Back in 1935 I had a privilege I shall always cherish.

I was invited to a luncheon as a guest. To my amazement and delight Will Rogers was the speaker. This was one of the last speeches Will Rogers ever made because a few weeks later he and Wiley Post started their flight around the world. We all know the tragic death they met in Alaska.

Now Mr. Rogers did not have the scholarly flavor or the academic taste that one might expect from some of the economic prognosticators of his day. But in a few words he gave some of the most profound advice I have ever heard.

I've read many books on success. I've heard dozens upon dozens of records on this same subject. But I don't believe there is a surer formula or a more certain blueprint leading to success, if followed conscientiously, than this one.

"If you want to be successful," he said, "it's just this simple.
"Know what you are doing.
"Love what you are doing.
"And believe in what you are doing.
"Yes," he said, "it's just that simple."
Now let's look into this advice a little more closely.

KNOW WHAT YOU ARE DOING

First, know what you are doing. There is no substitute for knowledge.

In our approach to knowledge we must realize that preparation is a constant process with no ending. It must be forever moving, never static. School is never out for the person who really wants to succeed. There is no saturation point. All economic research centers agree that because of the rapidly changing phases of our economy, the average person in any line of endeavor today, regardless of his particular field, must be retrained at least four times during his lifetime. Think of this:

What was not only right, but even plausible yesterday, is questionable today and might even be wrong tomorrow. It is somewhat disenchanting, I know, to find that just as we learn one role in life we are suddenly called upon to play an entirely new part, unrehearsed, as the drama of life must go on either with us, or without us.

Knowledge is accumulating so fast and methods of doing things improving so rapidly that a person today must run to stand still.

Up to 1900 it was said that the accumulation of knowledge doubled every century. At the end of World War II, knowledge doubled every twenty-five years. Today all research centers tell us that the volume of knowledge in existence doubles every five years. Where does that leave the person today who thinks he can stand still and survive?

TRUE SUCCESS IS A JOURNEY, NOT A DESTINATION

The constant demands of readjustment offer a challenge today that never existed before. No longer is preparation something that can be put in a drawer and forgotten about. Success itself has taken on a new definition. It might even be termed today as the constant and continuing preparation of ourselves to meet the constant and continuing changes of our economic system. Yes, success today is a journey, and not a destination.

Furthermore, in making this trip the important thing is that we must be constantly moving forward—yes, the progressive realization of a predetermined goal. And our growth should never end. Any person who selects a goal in life which can be fully achieved, has already defined his own limitations. When we cease to grow, we begin to die.

HORIZONS OF CHANGE

One of the confusing mysteries to a child who travels along any road is that he cannot ever catch up with the horizon. None of us today can ever catch up with the horizons of change. We can only move in their direction. I am sure it is a blessing that our reach does exceed our grasp. If our ambitions in life can be fully reached, then we have not hitched our wagon to a star. We would do a great injustice to anyone if we painted the journey as being a path of roses. It is a pilgrim's road, full of obstacles and sacrifices. The only promise we can make is that if a person is willing to brave the hazards of the road, he will grow strong in the journey and keep pace with changing times.

I am sure you agree with me that regardless of how well qualified a person may be to meet the rigors of life today, if he is lulled into a sense of false security in feeling that he needs no additional preparation for the future, that his journey can ever be ended, soon he will find that he is lost in the frustrations of medieval thinking.

We have heard it said many times that there is nothing in life as powerful as an idea whose time has arrived—knowledge that is timely. If ideas are to be current and if knowledge is to be up to date, they must be forever moving, never static.

And so, first and foremost, we must embrace the principle that in order to be knowledgeable in these changing times we must pursue a constant program of self-improvement, a never-ending journey into new fields of knowledge and learning.

A DAY OF SPECIALIZATION

Because of the rapidly accumulating volume of knowledge today, it is becoming increasingly important to specialize in some business, industry, or profession. There is no escape. This, of course, doesn't mean that an individual should not be well informed in the broad fundamentals and generalities. But it does mean that in addition to this he should to some extent be particularly knowledgeable in some aspect of his endeavors.

A rather frustrated individual the other day said, "Since we must know more and more about less and less, I guess this also means we must know less and less about more and more, which also means, pretty soon we are going to know everything about nothing and nothing about everything."

JUST HOW SPECIALIZED ARE WE?

Two fellows were talking the other day and one said, "Do you know, things are getting so specialized today that the National Biscuit Company even has a vice-president in charge of fig newtons."

The other said, "I don't believe it."

"I'll bet you," said the first.

So they put up the money and then proceeded to call the National Biscuit Company.

One said, "I want to speak to the vice-president in charge of fig newtons."

The answer came back, "Packaged or loose?"

The president of one of the largest rubber companies was recently making a speech. After he finished, the chairman opened the meeting for questions. A young man in the front row said, "Would it be too personal if I asked you how you got to be president of this big company?"

"Not at all," was the president's reply, "I was working in a filling station and not making much progress. One day I read that if a person wanted to get ahead he must know all there was to know about his particular product.

"So, on one of my vacations I went back to the home office and watched them make rubber tires. I'd watch them put in the nylon cords. On one vacation I went to Africa to watch them plant the rubber trees and even extract the base of crude rubber.

"So that when I talked about my product, I didn't say, 'this is what I'm told,' or 'this is what I read,' or 'this is what I think.' No, I said, 'this is what I know. I was there. I watched them put those nylon cords in to make the finest tire ever made, to protect your family against blowouts. I watched them extract that crude rubber to make the finest tire in the world.' "

He then continued, "There is no force in the world that has a greater impact than the statement of a knowledgeable person fortified by confidence and experience."

A man who knows, and knows he knows, can speak with authority that has no comparison. The world makes way for a man who knows what he's doing.

ONLY ONE WEALTH ON THIS EARTH

Lincoln once said, "The older I get the more I realize that there is but one wealth, one security, on this earth and that is found in the ability of a person to perform a task well." But he didn't stop there. He went on to say, "And first and foremost this ability must start with knowledge."

A superficial knowledge is not enough. It must be a knowledge capable of analyzing a situation quickly and making an immediate decision.

A quarterback in the closing moments of an important game called the wrong signal. A pass was intercepted and the game and conference championship were lost. That was on a Saturday. By Tuesday afternoon he had courage enough to venture out and be seen. He had to go out and get a haircut.

The barber, after a long silence, said, "I've been studying and thinking about that play you called last Saturday ever since you called it, and you know, if I had been in your shoes I don't believe I would have called it."

The quarterback without changing expression said, "No, and if I'd had until Tuesday afternoon to think about it, I wouldn't have either."

In this modern competitive and fast moving economy of today we often don't have time to think things over and give the careful consideration to each situation which we would desire.

But still, I repeat, a superficial knowledge is not enough. Furthermore, a person who tries to substitute "gimmicks and gadgets and gizmos" for knowledge usually finds that it all boomerangs on him—he meets himself coming around the corner.

Such an attempt reminds one of the head hunter who bought himself a new boomerang. Then he spent the rest of life trying to throw the old one away.

I feel very sorry for anyone who thinks it's possible to substitute pull or personality or any other quality for fundamental knowledge.

Yes, let's remember the sound advice of Will Rogers. If we are to be successful we must first know what we are doing.

LOVE WHAT YOU ARE DOING

But knowledge, important as it is, is not enough to insure success in our complex society today. We have often heard it said, "A merely well-informed man is the most useless bore on earth."

What was Will Rogers' next statement?

Not only know what you are doing, but love what you are doing.

What are we working for? Do we love our work or are we working for money alone? If it's for money alone we are underpaid, regardless of what we are making—furthermore, that's all we shall be working for as long as we live.

Everybody loves to do business with an optimist. We can only be an optimist if we love what we are doing.

Nothing takes a greater toll on us than to be around a pessimist—a person always finding fault and criticizing others. We've all seen the type. He has mental B.O. He's a one man grievance committee, always in session. He criticizes everyone and everything. You ask him how is business and he says, "Well, I made a sale Monday. I didn't sell anything Tuesday. Wednesday the deal I made Monday fell through—so, I guess Tuesday was really my best day."

I was recently in Boston attending a convention. I was kicked out of the hotel after two days. I thought I had a three-day reservation.

As the elevator came down it stopped at the seventh floor, but nothing happened. I was irritated and in a hurry to catch an early plane and said, "Come on in."

Nothing happened.

Again I said firmly, "Come in; let's get the show on the road."

Still nothing happened.

Finally, in a loud voice, I said, "Come on in—let's go. I'll be left."

At that moment a fine looking man with a white cane, completely blind, stepped in cautiously feeling his way along.

I felt awful. I had to say something, so I cleared my throat and said, "How are you today?"

He smiled and said, "Grateful, my friend, grateful."

I couldn't say a thing—I was choked up. Any impatience or worry I had, simply shriveled into nothingness.

Here was a man blessing the darkness while I was cursing the light. I couldn't have cared less whether I caught that plane. I found myself that night in my prayers asking that some day I might see as well as that person.

Actually, each morning when we wake up if we don't find our names listed in the obituary column we should be so grateful that we are happy all day.

We can say something nice about every person or subject involved in a conversation. If not, we can at least remain silent. Nothing is *all* wrong.

Someone said that even the Black Hole of Calcutta was easy to heat.

Down in Mississippi we would say that Prohibition was horrible but that it was better than no whiskey at all.

I heard a man's name brought up the other day and someone lowered his voice and said, "Why, that fellow's a confirmed alcoholic."

The other person present said, "Well, at least, he ain't no quitter."

Let's follow Will Rogers's advice; let's constantly seek a little larger slice out of life, a few more acres of the Garden of Eden. Let's look for the happier things of existence. The great Will

Rogers had the reputation of never criticizing. Why? Because he never met a man he didn't like.

BELIEVE IN WHAT YOU ARE DOING

Yes, Will Rogers said, "Know what you are doing—love what you are doing."

But he didn't stop there. He went further and said, "Believe in what you are doing."

I heard of a man who telephoned his friend and said, "Jake, I'm having a little informal birthday party tomorrow night and I want you to come to it. Come just as you are; don't stand on any ceremony. Just come right on up to the door and ring the door bell with your elbow and come right in."

The fellow said, "Well, that's all fine and good, but why my elbow?"

His friend said, "Jake, maybe you didn't understand. It's my birthday. You are not coming empty-handed, are you?"

Above all else I don't want you to be empty-handed. If you feel amused at a few anecdotes, if you are emotionally stirred or even mentally stimulated, that's not enough.

THE ULTIMATE IN HUMAN PERSUASION

In order that you will not be empty-handed I shall give you in the next few sentences the greatest principle of human persuasion that exists. There is nothing which is even a close second. If there is anything that is worth remembering it is this:

People are persuaded more by the depth of your conviction than by the height of your logic—more by your own enthusiasm than any proof you can offer.

If I could describe the art of persuasion in one sentence it would be this and I know I would be right: persuasion is converting people—no, not to our way of thinking but to our way of feeling and believing. And if a person's belief is sincere enough and deep enough he is a walking climate of positive acceptance. He has an obsession that cannot be denied.

The most persuasive person in the world is the man who has a fanatical belief in an idea, a product, or a service. The one common denominator of all great men in history is that they believed in what they were doing. If we could choose but one lantern to guide our footsteps over the perilous quicksands of the future it should be the guiding light of dedication.

It has been said that words are the fingers that mold the mind of man. Words, however, can be refused. But a positive attitude that springs from a sincere belief cannot.

YOU MUST FIRST BELIEVE IN
THE IDEA YOURSELF

I've heard people say in effect, "Do you believe in clairvoyance, telepathy, or psychoprediction? It's a strange thing, I knew that person was going to accept my idea the moment I walked in. Do you think I could have received thought transference?"

The answer is too obvious to need elaboration. The person presenting the idea had already made the big sale. He had bought the idea himself so completely that he was practically hypnotic in his persuasive powers.

On the other hand, I have heard a person say, "I can't explain it but I knew that fellow was not going to accept my idea even before I opened my mouth."

Of course he wasn't. The person presenting the idea didn't believe in it and he radiated this lack of belief. He was simply admitting that he had no enthusiasm for the idea and consequently he couldn't project any enthusiasm.

Yes, I repeat, the world is a looking glass and gives back to every person a reflection of his own thoughts, beliefs, and enthusiasm.

I have a picture at home that a friend painted for me. It's a picture of an old tramp sitting on a park bench. He has holes in his shoes, his knees are out, and he needs a shave. His hair looks as though it had been combed with an eggbeater and he's chewing a straw. A Rolls Royce goes by driven by a chauffeur, carrying a man in a tall silk hat.

The tramp looks at it lazily and philosophically says, "There, except for me, go I."

DON'T CHAIN YOURSELF TO MEDIOCRITY

The only chains and shackles that prevent any of us from realizing our life's dreams are those we ourselves forge in the fires of doubt and hammer out on the anvil of lack of belief in what we say or do.

Will Rogers, bless his great heart, said:

KNOW WHAT YOU ARE DOING
LOVE WHAT YOU ARE DOING
BELIEVE IN WHAT YOU ARE DOING

Where can we find any directional compass in life better than this?

I know of no qualities that can be a better formula to follow—a safer directional compass—than these three great directives of Will Rogers. Study them carefully and have faith in their guiding quality. They can lead only to success.

*The quality of your work, in the long run,
is the deciding factor on how much
your services are valued by the world.*

Orison Swett Marden

LESSON 30

HOW TO INCREASE YOUR VALUE

Charles Kettering of General Motors fame said,

I tell my people that I don't want any fellow who has a job working for me; what I want is a fellow whom a job has. And I want the job to get a hold on this young man so hard that no matter where he is, the job has got him for keeps. I want that job to have him in its clutches when he goes to bed at night and in the morning I want that job to be sitting at the foot of the bed telling him, "It's time to get up and go to work!" And when a job gets a fellow that way, he's *sure to amount to something.*

Unfortunately, Mr. Kettering's ideal employee is becoming more and more of a rarity in any company, large and small. Quality of any sort is now such a precious commodity that we are willing to pay exorbitant amounts for an automobile that has been assembled properly, a camera that doesn't jam, even a wallet that won't fall apart. This applies as well to personal services. A first-class attorney, salesman, doctor, or mechanic—anyone who still takes pride in his work—is worth his or her weight in gold.

Orison Swett Marden was America's first popular writer on the subject of success. His classic, *Pushing to the Front,* swept across the nation before the turn of the century, was published in several languages, and even became a best-seller in Japan.

There is a special quality in the older writings on success that one does not find very often today. Perhaps those writers of another era wrote with greater intensity which, combined with the antiquity of their grammar, lends an almost biblical flavor to their work.

In any event, it is hoped that Mr. Marden's extraordinary power with words, in this lesson from *Pushing to the Front,* will cause you to think twice the next time you may be tempted to deliver less than your best . . .

Years ago a relief lifeboat at New London sprung a leak, and while being repaired a hammer was found in the bottom that had been left there by the builders thirteen years before. From the constant motion of the boat the hammer had worn through the planking, clear down to the plating.

Not long since, it was discovered that a girl had served *twenty years* for a twenty months' sentence, in a southern prison, because of the mistake of a court clerk who wrote "years" instead of "months" in the record of the prisoner's sentence.

The history of the human race is full of the most horrible tragedies caused by carelessness and the inexcusable blunders of those who never formed the habit of accuracy, of thoroughness, of doing things to a finish.

Multitudes of people have lost an eye, a leg, or an arm, or are otherwise maimed, because dishonest workmen wrought deception into the articles they manufactured, slighted their work, covered up defects and weak places with paint and varnish.

How many have lost their lives because of dishonest work, carelessness, criminal blundering in railroad construction? Think of the tragedies caused by lies packed in car-wheels, locomotives, steamboat boilers, and engines; lies in defective rails, ties, or switches; lies in dishonest labor put into manufactured material by workmen who said it was good enough for the meager wages they got! Because people were not conscientious in their work there were flaws in the steel, which caused the rail or pillar to snap, the locomotive or other machinery to break. The steel shaft broke in mid-ocean, and the lives of a thousand passengers were jeopardized because of somebody's carelessness.

Even before they are completed, buildings often fall and bury the workmen under their ruins, because somebody was careless, dishonest—either employer or employee—and worked lies, deceptions, into the building.

The majority of railroad wrecks, of disasters on land and sea, which cause so much misery and cost so many lives, are the result of carelessness, thoughtlessness, or half-done, blotched, blundering work. They are the evil fruit of the low ideals of slovenly, careless, indifferent workers.

Everywhere over this broad earth we see the tragic results of botched work. Wooden legs, armless sleeves, numberless graves, fatherless and motherless homes everywhere speak of somebody's carelessness, somebody's blunders, somebody's habit of inaccuracy. The worst crimes are not punishable by law. Carelessness, slipshodness, lack of thoroughness, are crimes against self, against humanity, that often do more harm than the crimes that make the perpetrator an outcast from society. Where a tiny flaw or the slightest defect may cost a precious life, carelessness is as much a crime as deliberate criminality.

If everybody put his conscience into his work, did it to a complete finish, it would not only reduce the loss of human life, the mangling and maiming of men and women, to a fraction of what it is at present, but it would also give us a higher quality of manhood and womanhood.

Most people think too much of quantity, and too little of quality in their work. They try to do too much, and do not do it well. They do not realize that the education, the comfort, the satisfaction, the general improvement, and bracing up of the whole man that comes from doing one thing absolutely right, from putting the trademark of one's character on it, far outweighs the value that attaches to the doing of a thousand botched or slipshod jobs.

We are so constituted that the quality which we put into our lifework affects everything else in our lives, and tends to bring our whole conduct to the same level. The entire person takes on the characteristics of one's usual way of doing things. The habit of precision and accuracy strengthens the mentality, improves the whole character.

On the contrary, doing things in a loose-jointed, slipshod, careless manner deteriorates the whole mentality, demoralizes the mental processes, and pulls down the whole life.

Every half-done or slovenly job that goes out of your hands leaves its trace of demoralization behind. After slighting your work, after doing a poor job, you are not quite the same man you were before. You are not so likely to try to keep up the standard of your work, not so likely to regard your word as sacred as before.

The mental and moral effect of half doing, or carelessly doing things; its power to drag down, to demoralize, can hardly be estimated because the processes are so gradual, so subtle. No one can respect himself who habitually botches his work, and when self-respect drops, confidence goes with it; and when confidence and self-respect have gone, excellence is impossible.

It is astonishing how completely a slovenly habit will gradually, insidiously fasten itself upon the individual and so change his whole mental attitude as to thwart absolutely his life-purpose, even when he may think he is doing his best to carry it out.

I know a man who was extremely ambitious to do something very distinctive and who had the ability to do it. When he started on his career he was very exact and painstaking. He demanded the best of himself—would not accept his second-best in anything. The thought of slighting his work was painful to him, but his mental processes have so deteriorated, and he has become so demoralized by the habit which, after awhile, grew upon him, of accepting his second-best, that he now slights his work without a protest, seemingly without being conscious of it. He is today doing quite ordinary things, without apparent mortification or sense of humiliation, and the tragedy of it all is, *he does not know why he has failed!*

One's ambition and ideals need constant watching and cultivation in order to keep up to the standards. Many people are so constituted that their ambition wanes and their ideals drop when they are alone, or with careless, indifferent people. They require the constant assistance, suggestion, prodding, or example of others to keep them up to standard.

How quickly a youth of high ideals, who has been well trained in thoroughness, often deteriorates when he leaves home and goes to work for an employer with inferior ideals and slipshod methods!

The introduction of inferiority into our work is like introducing subtle poison into the system. It paralyzes the normal functions. Inferiority is an infection which, like leaven, affects the entire system. It dulls ideals, palsies the aspiring faculty, stupefies the ambition, and causes deterioration all along the line.

The human mechanism is so constituted that whatever goes wrong in one part affects the whole structure. There is a very intimate relation between the quality of the work and the quality of the character. Did you ever notice the rapid decline in a young man's character when he began to slight his work, to shirk, to slip in rotten hours, rotten service?

If you should ask the inmates of our penitentiaries what had caused their ruin, many of them could trace the first signs of deterioration to shirking, clipping their hours, deceiving their employers—to indifferent, dishonest work.

We were made to be honest. Honesty is our normal expression, and any departure from it demoralizes and taints the whole character. Honesty means integrity in everything. It not only means reliability in your word, but also carefulness, accuracy, honesty in your work. It does not mean that if only you will not lie with your lips you may lie and defraud in the quality of your work. Honesty means wholeness, completeness; it means truth in everything—in deed and in word. Merely not to steal another's money or goods is not all there is to honesty. You must not steal another's time; you must not steal his goods or ruin his property by half finishing or botching your work, by blundering through carelessness or indifference. Your contract with your employer means that you will give him your best, and not your second-best.

"What a fool you are," said one workman to another, "to take so much pains with that job, when you don't get much pay for it. 'Get the most money for the least work,' is my rule, and I get twice as much money as you do."

"That may be," replied the other, "but I shall like myself better, I shall think more of myself, and that is more important to me than money."

You will like yourself better when you have the approval of your conscience. That will be worth more to you than any amount of money you can pocket through fraudulent, skimped, or botched work. Nothing else can give you the glow of satisfaction, the electric thrill and uplift which comes from a superbly done job. Perfect work harmonizes with the very principles of our being, because we were made for perfection. It fits our very natures.

Someone has said, "It is a race between negligence and ignorance as to which can make the more trouble."

Many a young man is being kept down by what probably seems a small thing to him—negligence, lack of accuracy. He never quite finishes anything he undertakes; he cannot be depended upon to do anything quite right; his work always needs looking over by some one else. Hundreds of clerks and bookkeepers are getting small salaries in poor positions today because they have never learned to do things absolutely right.

A prominent businessman says that the carelessness, inaccuracy, and blundering of employees cost Chicago one million dollars a day. The manager of a large house in that city says that he has to station pickets here and there throughout the establishment in order to neutralize the evils of inaccuracy and the blundering habit. One of John Wanamaker's partners says that unnecessary blunders and mistakes cost that firm twenty-five thousand dollars a year. The dead letter department of the post office in Washington received in one year seven million pieces of undelivered mail. Of these more than eighty thousand bore no address whatever. A great many of them were from business houses. Are the clerks who are responsible for this carelessness likely to win promotion?

Many an employee who would be shocked at the thought of telling his employer a lie with his lips is lying every day in the quality of his work, in his dishonest service, in the rotten hours he is slipping into it, in shirking, in his indifference to his employer's interests. It is just as dishonest to express deception in poor work, in shirking, as to express it with the lips, yet I have known office boys, who could not be induced to tell their employer a direct lie, to steal his time when on an errand, to hide away during working hours to smoke a cigarette or take a nap, not realizing, perhaps, that lies can be acted as well as told and that acting a lie may be even worse than telling one.

The man who botches his work, who lies or cheats in the goods he sells or manufactures, is dishonest with himself as well as with his fellow men, and must pay the price in loss of self-respect, loss of character, of standing in his community.

Yet on every side we see all sorts of things selling for a song because the maker put no character, no thought into them. Articles of clothing that look stylish and attractive when first worn, very quickly get out of shape, and hang and look like old, much-worn garments. Buttons fly off, seams give way at the slightest strain, dropped stitches are everywhere in evidence, and often the entire article goes to pieces before it is worn half a dozen times.

Everywhere we see furniture which looks all right, but which in reality is full of blemishes and weaknesses, covered up with paint and varnish. Glue starts at joints; chairs and bedsteads break down at the slightest provocation; castors come off; handles pull out; many things "go to pieces" altogether, even while practically new.

"Made to sell, not for service," would be a good label for the great mass of manufactured articles in our markets today.

It is difficult to find anything that is well and honestly made, that has character, individuality, and thoroughness wrought into it. Most things are just thrown together. This slipshod, dishonest manufacturing is so general that concerns which turn out products based upon honesty and truth often win for themselves a world-wide reputation and command the highest prices.

There is no other advertisement like a good reputation. Some of the world's greatest manufacturers have regarded their reputation as their most precious possession, and under no circumstances would they allow their names to be put on an imperfect article. Vast sums of money are often paid for the use of a name, because of its great reputation for integrity and square dealing.

There was a time when the names of Graham and Tampion on timepieces were guarantees of the most exquisite workmanship and of unquestioned integrity. Strangers from any part of the world could send their purchase money and order goods from those manufacturers without a doubt that they would be squarely dealt with.

Tampion and Graham lie in Westminster Abbey because of the accuracy of their work—because they refused to manufacture and sell lies.

When you finish a thing you ought to be able to say to yourself: "There, I am willing to stand for that piece of work. It is not pretty well done; it is done as well as I can do it; done to a complete finish. I will stand for that. I am willing to be judged by it."

Never be satisfied with "fairly good," "pretty good," "good enough." Accept nothing short of your best. Put such a quality into your work that anyone who comes across anything you have ever done will see character in it, individuality in it, your trademark of superiority upon it. Your reputation is at stake in everything you do, and your reputation is your capital. You cannot afford to do a poor job, to let botched work or anything that is inferior go out of your hands. Every bit of your work, no matter how unimportant or trivial it may seem, should bear your trademark of excellence; you should regard every task that goes through your hands, every piece of work you touch, as Tampion regarded every watch that went out of his shop. It must be the very best you can do, the best that human skill can produce.

It is just the little difference between the good and the best that makes the difference between the artist and the artisan. It is just the little touches after the average man would quit that make the master's fame.

Regard your work as Stradivarius regarded his violins, which he "made for eternity," and not one of which was ever known to come to pieces or break. Stradivarius did not need any patent on his violins, for no other violin maker would pay such a price for excellence as he paid, would take such pains to put his stamp of superiority upon his instrument. Every "Stradivarius" now in existence is worth from three to ten thousand dollars, or several times its weight in gold.

Think of the value such a reputation for thoroughness as that of Stradivarius or Tampion, such a passion to give quality to your work, would give you! There is nothing like being enamored of accuracy, being grounded in thoroughness as a life-principle, of always striving for excellence.

No other characteristic makes such a strong impression upon an employer as the habit of painstaking, carefulness, accuracy. He knows that if a youth puts his conscience into his work from principle, not from the standpoint of salary or what he can get for it, but because there is something in him which refuses to accept anything from himself but the best, that he is honest and made of good material.

I have known many instances where advancement hinged upon the little overplus of interest, of painstaking an employee put into his work, on his doing a little better than was expected of him. Employers do not say all they think, but they detect very quickly the earmarks of superiority. They keep their eye on the employee who has the stamp of excellence upon him, who takes pains with his work, who does it to a finish. They know he has a future.

John D. Rockefeller, Jr., says that the "secret of success is to do the common duty uncommonly well." The majority of people do not see that the steps which lead to the position above them are constructed, little by little, by the faithful performance of the common, humble, everyday duties of the position they are now filling. The thing which you are now doing will unlock or bar the door to promotion.

Many employees are looking for some great thing to happen that will give them an opportunity to show their mettle. "What can there be," they say to themselves, "in this dry routine, in doing these common, ordinary things, to help me along?" But it is the youth who sees a great opportunity hidden in just these simple services, who sees a very uncommon chance in a common situation, a humble position, who gets on in the world. It is doing things a little better than those about you do them; being a little neater, a little quicker, a little more accurate, a little more observant; it is ingenuity in finding new and more progressive ways of doing old things; it is being a little more polite, a little more obliging, a little more tactful, a little more cheerful, optimistic, a little more energetic, helpful, than those about you that attracts the attention of your employer and other employers also.

Many a person is marked for a higher position by his employer long before he is aware of it himself. It may be months, or it may be a year before the opening comes, but when it does come the one who has appreciated the infinite difference between "good" and "better," between "fairly good" and "excellent," between what others call "good" and the best that can be done, will be likely to get the place.

If there is that in your nature which demands the best and will take nothing less; if you insist on keeping up your standards in everything you do, you will achieve distinction in some line, provided you have the persistence and determination to follow your ideal.

But if you are satisfied with the cheap and shoddy, the botched and slovenly; if you are not particular about quality in your work, or in your environment, or in your personal habits, then you must expect to take second place, to fall back to the rear of the procession.

People who have accomplished work worthwhile have had a very high sense of the way to do things. They have not been content with mediocrity. They have not confined themselves to the beaten tracks; they have never been satisfied to do things just as others do them, but always a little better. They always pushed things that came to their hands a little higher up, a little farther on. It is this little higher up, this little farther on, that counts in the quality of life's work. It is the constant effort to be first-class in everything one attempts that conquers the heights of excellence.

It is said that Daniel Webster made the best chowder in his State on the principle that he would not be second-class in anything. This is a good resolution with which to start out in your career; never to be second-class in anything. No matter what you do, try to do it as well as it can be done. Have nothing to do with the inferior. Do your best in everything; deal with the best; choose the best; live up to your best.

Everywhere we see mediocre or second-class men—perpetual clerks who will never get away from the yardstick; mechanics who will never be anything but bunglers; all sorts of people who will never rise above mediocrity, who will always fill very ordinary positions because they do not take pains, do not put conscience into their work, do not try to be first-class.

Aside from the lack of desire or effort to be first-class, there are other things that help to make second-class men. Dissipation, bad habits, neglect of health, failure to get an education, all make second-class men. A man weakened by dissipation, whose understanding has been dulled, whose growth has been stunted by self-indulgences, is a second-class man, if, indeed, he is not third-class. A man who, through his amusements in his hours of leisure, exhausts his strength and vitality, vitiates his blood, wears his nerves till his limbs tremble like leaves in the wind, is only half a man, and could in no sense be called first-class.

Everybody knows the things that make for second-class characteristics. Boys imitate older boys and smoke cigarettes in order to be "smart." Then they keep on smoking because they have created an appetite as unnatural as it is harmful. Men get drunk for all sorts of reasons; but, whatever the reason, they cannot remain first-class men and drink. Dissipation in other forms is pursued because of pleasure to be derived, but the surest consequence is that of becoming second-class, below the standard of the best men for any purpose.

Every fault you allow to become a habit, to get control over you, helps to make you second-class, and puts you at a disadvantage in the race for honor, position, wealth, and happiness. Carelessness as to health fills the ranks of the inferior. The submerged classes that the economists talk about are those that are below the high-water mark of the best manhood and womanhood. Sometimes they are second-rate or third-rate people because those who are responsible for their being and their care during their minor years were so before them, but more and more is it becoming one's own fault if, all through life, he remains second-class. Education of some sort, and even a pretty good sort, is possible to practically everyone in our land. Failure to get the best education available, whether it be in books or in business training, is sure to relegate one to the ranks of the second-class.

There is no excuse for incompetence in this age of opportunity; no excuse for being second-class when it is possible to be first-class, and when first-class is in demand everywhere.

Second-class things are wanted only when first-class can't be had. You wear first-class clothes if you can pay for them, eat first-class butter, first-class meat, and first-class bread, or, if you don't, you wish you could. Second-class men are no more wanted than any other second-class commodity. They are taken and used when the better article is scarce or is too high-priced for the occasion. For work that really amounts to anything, first-class men are wanted. If you make yourself first-class in anything, no matter what your condition or circumstances, no matter what your race or color, you will be in demand. If you are a king in your calling, no matter how humble it may be, nothing can keep you from success.

The world does not demand that you be a physician, a lawyer, a farmer, or a merchant; but it does demand that whatever you do undertake, you will do it right, will do it with all your might and with all the ability you possess. It demands that you be a master in your line.

When Daniel Webster, who had the best brain of his time, was asked to make a speech on some question at the close of a congressional session, he replied: "I never allow myself to speak on any subject until I have made it my own. I haven't time to do that in this case, hence, I must refuse to speak on the subject."

Dickens would never consent to read before an audience until he had thoroughly prepared his selection.

Balzac, the great French novelist, sometimes worked a week on a single page.

William Macready, when playing before scant audiences in country theaters in England, Ireland, and Scotland, always played as if he were before the most brilliant audiences in the great metropolises of the world.

Thoroughness characterizes all successful men. Genius is the art of taking infinite pains. The trouble with many Americans is that they seem to think they can put any sort of poor, slipshod, half-done work into their careers and get first-class products. They do not realize that all great achievement has been characterized by extreme care, infinite painstaking, even to the minutest detail. No youth can ever hope to accomplish much who does not have thoroughness and accuracy indelibly fixed in his life-habit. Slip-shodness, inaccuracy, the habit of half doing things, would ruin the career of a youth with a Napoleon's mind.

If we were to examine a list of the men who have left their mark on the world, we should find that, as a rule, it is not composed of those who were brilliant in youth, or who gave great promise at the outset of their careers, but rather of the plodding young men who, if they have not dazzled by their brilliancy, have had the power of a day's work in them; who could stay by a task until it was done, and well done; who have had grit, persistence, common sense, and honesty.

The thorough boys are the boys who are heard from, and usually from posts far higher up than those filled by the boys who were too "smart" to be thorough. One such boy is Elihu Root, now United States senator. When he was a boy in the grammar school at Clinton, New York, he made up his mind that anything he had to study he would keep at until he mastered it. Although not considered one of the "bright" boys of the school, his teacher soon found that when Elihu professed to know anything he knew it through and through. He was fond of hard problems requiring application and patience. Sometimes the other boys called him a plodder, but Elihu would only smile pleasantly, for he knew what he was about. On winter evenings, while the other boys were out skating, Elihu frequently remained in his room with his arithmetic or algebra. Mr. Root recently said that if his close application to problems in his boyhood did nothing else for him, it made him careful about jumping at conclusions. To every problem there was only one answer, and patience was the price to be paid for it.

Carrying the principle of "doing everything to a finish" into the law, he became one of the most noted members of the New York bar, intrusted with vast interests, and then a member of the president's cabinet.

William Ellery Channing, the great New England divine, who in his youth was hardly able to buy the clothes he needed, had a passion for self-improvement. "I wanted to make the most of myself," he says; "I was not satisfied with knowing things superficially and by halves, but tried to get comprehensive views of what I studied."

Our great lack is want of thoroughness. How seldom you find a young man or woman who is willing to prepare for his life-work! A little education is all they want, a little smattering of books, and then they are ready for business.

"Can't wait," "Haven't time to be thorough," is characteristic of our country, and is written on everything—on commerce, on schools, on society, on religious institutions. We can't wait for a high school, seminary, or college education. The boy can't wait to become a youth, nor the youth to become a man. Young men rush into business with no great reserve of education or drill; or course, they do poor, feverish work, and break down in middle life, while many die of old age in the forties.

Perhaps there is no other country in the world where so much poor work is done as in America. Half-trained medical students perform bungling operations and butcher their patients, because they are not willing to take time for thorough preparation. Half-trained lawyers stumble through their cases and make their clients pay for experience which the law school should have given. Half-trained clergymen bungle away in the pulpit and disgust their intelligent and cultured parishioners. Many an American youth is willing to stumble through life half prepared for his work and then blame society because he is a failure.

A young man, armed with letters of introduction from prominent men, one day presented himself before Chief Engineer Parsons, of the Rapid Transit Commission of New York, as a candidate for a position. "What can you do? Have you any specialty?" asked Mr. Parsons. "I can do almost anything," answered the young man. "Well," remarked the chief engineer, rising to end the interview, "I have no use for any one who can 'almost' do anything. I prefer some one who can actually do one thing thoroughly."

There is a great crowd of human beings just outside the door of proficiency. They can half do a great many things, but can't do any one thing well, to a finish. They have acquisitions which remain permanently unavailable because they were not carried quite to the point of skill; they stopped just short of efficiency. How many people almost know a language or two, which they can neither write nor speak; a science or two, whose elements they have not fully mastered; an art or two, which they cannot practice with satisfaction or profit!

The Patent Office at Washington contains hundreds—yes, thousands—of inventions which are useless simply because they are not quite practical, because the men who started them lacked the staying quality, the education, or the ability necessary to carry them to the point of practicability.

The world is full of half-finished work—failures which require only a little more persistence, a little finer mechanical training, a little better education, to make them useful to civilization. Think what a loss it would be if such men as Edison and Bell had not come to the front and carried to a successful termination the half-finished work of others!

Make it a life-rule to give your best to whatever passes through your hands. Stamp it with your manhood. Let superiority be your trademark; let it characterize everything you touch. This is what every employer is looking for. It indicates the best kind of brain; it is the best substitute for genius; it is better capital than cash; it is a better promoter than friends, or "pulls" with the influential.

A successful manufacturer says, "If you make a good pin, you will earn more money than if you make a bad steam engine." "If a man can write a better book, preach a better sermon, or make a better mousetrap than his neighbor," says Emerson, "though he build his house in the woods, the world will make a path to his door."

Never allow yourself to dwell too much upon what you are getting for your work. You have something of infinitely greater importance, greater value, at stake. Your honor, your whole career, your future success, will be affected by the way you do your work, by the conscience or lack of it which you put into your job. Character, manhood, and womanhood are at stake, compared with which salary is nothing.

Everything you do is a part of your career. If any work that goes out of your hands is skimped, shirked, bungled, or botched, your character will suffer. If your work is badly done, if it goes to pieces, if there is shoddy or sham in it, if there is dishonesty in it, there is shoddy, sham, dishonesty in your character. We are all of a piece. We cannot have an honest character, a complete, untarnished career, when we are constantly slipping rotten hours, defective material, and slipshod service into our work.

The man who has dealt in shams and inferiority, who has botched his work all his life, must be conscious that he has not been a real man; he cannot help feeling that his career has been a botched one.

To spend a life buying and selling lies, dealing in cheap, shoddy shams, or botching one's work, is demoralizing to every element of nobility.

Beecher said he was never again quite the same man after reading Ruskin. You are never again quite the same man after doing a poor job, after botching your work. You cannot be just to yourself and unjust to the man you are working for in the quality of your work, for, if you slight your work, you not only strike a fatal blow at your efficiency, but also smirch your character. If you would be a full man, a complete man, a just man, you must be honest to the core in the quality of your work.

No one can be really happy who does not believe in his own honesty. We are so constituted that every departure from the right, from principle, causes loss of self-respect and makes us unhappy.

Every time we obey the inward law of doing right we hear an inward approval, the amen of the soul; and every time we disobey it, a protest or condemnation.

There is everything in holding a high ideal of your work; for whatever model the mind holds, the life copies. Whatever your vocation, let quality be your life-slogan.

A famous artist said he would never allow himself to look at an inferior drawing or painting, to do anything that was low or demoralizing, lest familiarity with it should taint his own ideal and thus be communicated to his brush.

Many excuse poor, slipshod work on the plea of lack of time. But in the ordinary situations of life there is plenty of time to do everything as it ought to be done.

There is an indescribable superiority added to the character and fiber of the man who always and everywhere puts quality into his work. There is a sense of wholeness, of satisfaction, of happiness, in his life which is never felt by the man who does not do his level best every time. He is not haunted by the ghosts or tail ends of half-finished tasks, of skipped problems; is not kept awake by a troubled conscience.

When we are trying with all our might to do our level best, our whole nature improves. Everything looks down when we are going downhill. Aspiration lifts the life; groveling lowers it.

Don't think you will never hear from a half-finished job, a neglected or botched piece of work. It will never die. It will bob up farther along in your career at the most unexpected moments, in the most embarrassing situations. It will be sure to mortify you when you least expect it. Like Banquo's ghost, it will arise at the most unexpected moments to mar your happiness.

Thousands of people are held back all their lives and obliged to accept inferior positions because they cannot entirely overcome the handicap of slipshod habits formed early in life; habits of inaccuracy, of slovenliness, of skipping difficult problems in school, of slurring their work, shirking, or half doing it. "Oh, that's good enough, what's the use of being so awfully particular?" has been the beginning of a lifelong handicap in many a career.

I was much impressed by this motto, which I saw recently in a great establishment, WHERE ONLY THE BEST IS GOOD ENOUGH. What a life-motto this would be! How it would revolutionize civilization if everyone were to adopt it and use it; to resolve that, whatever they did only the best they could do would be good enough, would satisfy them!

Adopt this motto as yours. Hang it up in your bedroom, in your office, or place of business; put it into your pocketbook, weave it into the texture of everything you do, and your life-work will be what every one's should be—A MASTERPIECE.

SEMESTER
SEVEN

Nothing will make us so charitable
and tender to the faults of
others, as, by self-examination,
thoroughly to know our own.

François de S. Fénelon

*Criticism of others is futile and if you
indulge in it often you should be
warned that it can be fatal to your career.*

Dale Carnegie

LESSON 31

HOW TO GATHER HONEY INSTEAD
OF BEE STINGS

There is no such being as a "self-made" person.

Those who have truly earned the world's respect and admiration for their outstanding accomplishments are always quick to point out the many helping hands, throughout their life, that helped them reach the pinnacle.

You do not live in a vacuum nor can you harvest the better fruits of life without help and encouragement from others. As members of a wide human society, your growth depends, to a large degree, on how well you handle your contacts with those who cross your path every hour of the day. Without friendship and assistance the successes you enjoy will be few, if any. Even Robinson Crusoe rejoiced when he finally discovered Friday.

Why is it, then, that so many of us go out of our way to offend others with criticism and offensive judgments that so often come back to haunt us? Why do we allow our big mouths to dig ruts in our path so deep that our forward progress is finally nil? Is this more of that "will to fail" that has already been covered? Perhaps.

If your tongue has been busy accumulating enemies for you, enemies you do not need who can harm you, now is as good a time as any to cease and desist. How sad it would be for such a petty habit to destroy your great potential.

This important lesson is from *How to Win Friends and Influence People* which has remained high on best-seller lists for almost fifty years! No one is more capable of teaching you how to deal with people effectively than its famous author, Dale Carnegie . . .

On May 7, 1931, New York City witnessed the most sensational manhunt the old town had ever known. After weeks of search, "Two-Gun" Crowley—the killer, the gunman who didn't smoke or drink—was at bay, trapped in his sweetheart's apartment on West End Avenue.

One hundred and fifty police officers and detectives laid siege to his top-floor hideaway. Chopping holes in the roof, they tried to smoke out Crowley, the "cop killer," with tear gas. Then they mounted their machine guns on surrounding buildings, and for more than an hour one of New York's fine residential sections reverberated with the crack of pistol fire and the rat-tat-tat of machine guns. Crowley, crouching behind an overstuffed chair, fired incessantly at the police. Ten thousand excited people watched the battle. Nothing like it had ever been seen before on the sidewalks of New York.

When Crowley was captured, Police Commissioner Mulrooney declared that the two-gun desperado was one of the most dangerous criminals ever encountered in the history of New York. "He will kill," said the commissioner, "at the drop of a feather."

But how did "Two-Gun" Crowley regard himself? We know, because while the police were firing into his apartment, he wrote a letter addressed "To whom it may concern." And, as he wrote, the blood flowing from his wounds left a crimson trail on the paper. In this letter Crowley said: "Under my coat is a weary heart, but a kind one—one that would do nobody any harm."

A short time before this, Crowley had been having a necking party on a country road out on Long Island. Suddenly a police officer walked up to the parked car and said: "Let me see your license."

Without saying a word, Crowley drew his gun, and cut the police officer down with a shower of lead. As the dying officer fell, Crowley leaped out of the car, grabbed the officer's revolver, and fired another bullet into the prostrate body. And that was the killer who said: "Under my coat is a weary heart, but a kind one—one that would do nobody any harm."

Crowley was sentenced to the electric chair. When he arrived at the death house at Sing Sing, did he say, "This is what I get for killing people?" No, he said: "This is what I get for defending myself."

The point of the story is this: "Two-Gun" Crowley didn't blame himself for anything.

Is that an unusual attitude among criminals? If you think so, listen to this:

"I have spent the best years of my life giving people the lighter pleasures, helping them have a good time, and all I get is abuse, the existence of a hunted man."

That's Al Capone speaking. Yes, America's erstwhile Public Enemy Number One—the most sinister gang leader who ever shot up Chicago. Capone doesn't condemn himself. He actually regards himself as a public benefactor—an unappreciated and misunderstood public benefactor.

And so did Dutch Schultz before he crumpled up under gangster bullets in Newark. Dutch Schultz, one of New York's most notorious rats, said in a newspaper interview that he was a public benefactor. And he believed it.

I have had some interesting correspondence with Warden Lawes of Sing Sing on this subject, and he declares that "few of the criminals in Sing Sing regard themselves as bad men. They are just as human as you and I. So they rationalize, they explain. They can tell you why they had to crack a safe or be quick on the trigger finger. Most of them attempt by a form of reasoning, fallacious or logical, to justify their antisocial acts even to themselves, consequently stoutly maintaining that they should never have been imprisoned at all."

If Al Capone, "Two-Gun" Crowley, Dutch Schultz, the desperate men behind prison walls don't blame themselves for anything—what about the people with whom you and I come in contact?

The late John Wanamaker once confessed: "I learned thirty years ago that it is foolish to scold. I have enough trouble overcoming my own limitations without fretting over the fact that God has not seen fit to distribute evenly the gift of intelligence."

Wanamaker learned this lesson early; but I personally had to blunder through this old world for a third of a century before it even began to dawn upon me that ninety-nine times out of a hundred, no man ever criticizes himself for anything, no matter how wrong he may be.

Criticism is futile because it puts a man on the defensive, and usually makes him strive to justify himself. Criticism is dangerous, because it wounds a man's precious pride, hurts his sense of importance, and arouses his resentment.

The German army won't let a soldier file a complaint and make a criticism immediately after a thing has happened. He has to sleep on his grudge first and cool off. If he files his complaint immediately, he is punished. By the eternals, there ought to be a law like that in civil life too—a law for whining parents and nagging wives and scolding employers and the whole obnoxious parade of faultfinders.

You will find examples of the futility of criticism bristling on a thousand pages of history. Take, for example, the famous quarrel between Theodore Roosevelt and President Taft—a quarrel that split the Republican party, put Woodrow Wilson in the White House, and wrote bold, luminous lines across the World War and altered the flow of history. Let's review the facts quickly: when Theodore Roosevelt stepped out of the White House in 1908, he made Taft President, and then went off to Africa to shoot lions. When he returned, he exploded. He denounced Taft for his conservatism, tried to secure the nomination for a third term himself, formed the Bull Moose party, and all but demolished the GOP. In the election that followed, William Howard Taft and the Republican Party carried only two states—Vermont and Utah. The most disastrous defeat the old party had ever known.

Theodore Roosevelt blamed Taft; but did President Taft blame himself? Of course not. With tears in his eyes, Taft said: "I don't see how I could have done any differently from what I have."

Who was to blame? Roosevelt or Taft? Frankly, I don't know, and I don't care. The point I am trying to make is that all of Theodore Roosevelt's criticism didn't persuade Taft that he was wrong. It merely made Taft strive to justify himself and to reiterate with tears in his eyes: "I don't see how I could have done any differently from what I have."

Or, take the Teapot Dome Oil scandal. Remember it? It kept the newspapers ringing with indignation for years. It rocked the nation! Nothing like it had ever happened before in American public life within the memory of living men. Here are the bare facts of the scandal: Albert Fall, Secretary of the Interior in Harding's cabinet, was entrusted with the leasing of government oil reserves at Elk Hill and Teapot Dome—oil reserves that had been set aside for the future use of the navy. Did Secretary Fall permit competitive bidding? No sir. He handed the fat, juicy contract outright to his friend, Edward L. Doheny. And what did Doheny do? He gave Secretary Fall what he was pleased to call a "loan" of one hundred thousand dollars. Then, in a high-handed manner, Secretary Fall ordered United States marines into the district to drive off competitors whose adjacent wells were sapping oil out of the Elk Hill reserves. These competitors, driven off their ground at the ends of guns and bayonets, rushed into court—and blew the lid off the hundred million dollar Teapot Dome scandal. A stench arose so vile that it ruined the Harding administration, nauseated an entire nation, threatened to wreck the Republican party, and put Albert B. Fall behind prison bars.

Fall was condemned viciously—condemned as few men in public life have ever been. Did he repent? Never! Years later Herbert Hoover intimated in a public speech that President Harding's death had been due to mental anxiety and worry because a friend had betrayed him. When Mrs. Fall heard that, she sprang from her chair, she wept, she shook her fists at fate, and screamed: "What! Harding betrayed by Fall? No! My husband never betrayed anyone. This whole house full of gold would not tempt my husband to do wrong. He is the one who has been betrayed and led to the slaughter and crucified."

There you are; human nature in action, the wrongdoer blaming everybody but himself. We are all like that. So when you and I are tempted to criticize someone tomorrow, let's remember Al Capone, "Two-Gun" Crowley, and Albert Fall. Let's realize that criticisms are like homing pigeons. They always return home. Let's realize that the person we are going to correct and condemn will probably justify himself, and condemn us in return; or, like the gentle Taft, he will say: "I don't see how I could have done any different from what I have."

On Saturday morning, April 15, 1865, Abraham Lincoln lay dying in a hall bedroom of a cheap lodging house directly across the street from Ford's Theater, where Booth had shot him. Lincoln's long body lay stretched diagonally across a sagging bed that was too short for him. A cheap reproduction of Rosa Bonheur's famous painting, "The Horse Fair," hung above the bed, and a dismal gas jet flickered yellow light.

As Lincoln lay dying, Secretary of War Stanton said, "There lies the most perfect ruler of men that the world has ever seen."

What was the secret of Lincoln's success in dealing with men? I studied the life of Abraham Lincoln for ten years, and devoted all of three years to writing and rewriting a book entitled *Lincoln the Unknown*. I believe I have made as detailed and exhaustive a study of Lincoln's personality and home life as it is possible for any human being to make. I made a special study of Lincoln's method of dealing with men. Did he indulge in criticism? Oh, yes. As a young man in the Pigeon Creek Valley of Indiana, he not only criticized, but he wrote letters and poems ridiculing people and dropped these letters on the country roads where they were sure to be found. One of these letters aroused resentments that burned for a lifetime.

Even after Lincoln had become a practicing lawyer in Springfield, Illinois, he attacked his opponents openly in letters published in the newspapers. But he did this just once too often.

In the autumn of 1842, he ridiculed a vain, pugnacious Irish
politician by the name of James Shields. Lincoln lampooned him
through an anonymous letter published in the *Springfield Journal*.
The town roared with laughter. Shields, sensitive and proud,
boiled with indignation. He found out who wrote the letter, leaped
on his horse, started after Lincoln, and challenged him to fight a
duel. Lincoln didn't want to fight. He was opposed to dueling; but
he couldn't get out of it and save his honor. He was given the
choice of weapons. Since he had very long arms, he chose cavalry
broad swords, took lessons in sword fighting from a West Point
graduate; and, on the appointed day, he and Shields met on a sand
bar in the Mississippi River, prepared to fight to the death; but, at
the last minute, their seconds interrupted and stopped the duel.

That was the most lurid personal incident in Lincoln's life. It
taught him an invaluable lesson in the art of dealing with people.
Never again did he write an insulting letter. Never again did he
ridicule anyone. And from that time on, he almost never criticized
anybody for anything.

Time after time, during the Civil War, Lincoln put a new
general at the head of the Army of the Potomac, and each one in
turn—McClellan, Pope, Burnside, Hooker, Meade—blundered trag-
ically, and drove Lincoln to pacing the floor in despair. Half the
nation savagely condemned these incompetent generals, but Lincoln, "with malice towards none, with charity for all," held his
peace. One of his favorite quotations was "Judge not, that ye be
not judged."

And when Mrs. Lincoln and others spoke harshly of the
Southern people, Lincoln replied: "Don't criticize them; they are
just what we would be under similar circumstances."

Yet, if any man ever had occasion to criticize, surely it was
Lincoln. Let's take just one illustration:

The Battle of Gettysburg was fought during the first three
days of July, 1863. During the night of July 4, Lee began to retreat
southward while storm clouds deluged the country with rain.
When Lee reached the Potomac with his defeated army, he found
a swollen, impassable river in front of him, and a victorious Union
army behind him. Lee was in a trap. He couldn't escape. Lincoln
saw that. Here was a golden, heaven-sent opportunity—the opportunity to capture Lee's army and end the war immediately. So,
with a surge of high hope, Lincoln ordered Meade not to call a
council of war but to attack Lee immediately. Lincoln telegraphed

his orders and then sent a special messenger to Meade demanding immediate action.

And what did General Meade do? He did the very opposite of what he was told to do. He called a council of war in direct violation of Lincoln's orders. He hesitated. He procrastinated. He telegraphed all manner of excuses. He refused point-blank to attack Lee. Finally the waters receded and Lee escaped over the Potomac with his forces.

Lincoln was furious. "What does this mean?" Lincoln cried to his son Robert. "Great God! What does this mean? We had them within our grasp, and had only to stretch forth our hands and they were ours; yet nothing that I could say or do could make the army move. Under the circumstances, almost any general could have defeated Lee. If I had gone up there, I could have whipped him myself."

In bitter disappointment, Lincoln sat down and wrote Meade this letter. And remember, at this period of his life he was extremely conservative and restrained in his phraseology. So this letter coming from Lincoln in 1863 was tantamount to the severest rebuke.

My dear General,

"I do not believe you appreciate the magnitude of the misfortune involved in Lee's escape. He was within our easy grasp, and to have closed upon him would, in connection with our other late successes, have ended the war. As it is, the war will be prolonged indefinitely. If you could not safely attack Lee last Monday, how can you possibly do so south of the river, when you can take with you very few—no more than two thirds of the force you then had in hand? It would be unreasonable to expect and I do not expect that you can now effect much. Your golden opportunity is gone, and I am distressed immeasurably because of it.

What do you suppose Meade did when he read that letter?

Meade never saw the letter. Lincoln never mailed it. It was found among Lincoln's papers after his death.

My guess is—and this is only a guess—that after writing that letter, Lincoln looked out of the window and said to himself, "Just a minute. Maybe I ought not to be so hasty. It is easy enough for me to sit here in the quiet of the White House and order Meade to attack; but if I had been up at Gettysburg, and if I had seen as much blood as Meade has seen during the last week, and if my ears had been pierced with the screams and shrieks of the wounded and dying, maybe I wouldn't be so anxious to attack either. If I had Meade's timid temperament, perhaps I would have done just what he has done. Anyhow, it is water under the bridge now. If I send this letter, it will relieve my feelings but it will make Meade try to justify himself. It will make him condemn me. It will arouse hard feelings, impair all his further usefulness as a commander, and perhaps force him to resign from the army."

So, as I have already said, Lincoln put the letter aside, for he had learned by bitter experience that sharp criticisms and rebukes almost invariably end in futility.

Theodore Roosevelt said that when he, as President, was confronted with some perplexing problem, he used to lean back and look up at a large painting of Lincoln that hung above his desk in the White House and ask himself, "What would Lincoln do if he were in my shoes? How would he solve this problem?"

The next time we are tempted to give somebody "hail Columbia," let's pull a five-dollar bill out of our pocket, look at Lincoln's picture on the bill, and ask, "How would Lincoln handle this problem if he had it?"

Do you know someone you would like to change and regulate and improve? Good! That is fine. I am all in favor of it. But why not begin on yourself? From a purely selfish standpoint, that is a lot more profitable than trying to improve others—yes, and a lot less dangerous.

"When a man's fight begins within himself," said Browning, "he is worth something." It will probably take from now until Christmas to perfect yourself. You can then have a nice long rest over the holidays and devote the New Year to regulating and criticizing other people.

But perfect yourself first.

"Don't complain about the snow on your neighbor's roof," said Confucius, "when your own doorstep is unclean."

When I was still young and trying to impress people, I wrote a foolish letter to Richard Harding Davis, an author who once loomed large on the literary horizon of America. I was preparing a magazine article about authors; and I asked Davis to tell me about his method of work. A few weeks earlier, I had received a letter from someone with this notation at the bottom: "Dictated but not read." I was quite impressed. I felt the writer must be very big and busy and important. I wasn't the slightest bit busy; but I was eager to make an impression on Richard Harding Davis so I ended my short note with the words: "Dictated but not read."

He never troubled to answer the letter. He simply returned it to me with this scribbled across the bottom: "Your bad manners are exceeded only by your bad manners." True, I had blundered, and perhaps I deserved his rebuke. But, being human, I resented it. I resented it so sharply that when I read of the death of Richard Harding Davis ten years later, the one thought that still persisted in my mind—I am ashamed to admit—was the hurt he had given me.

If you and I want to stir up a resentment tomorrow that may rankle across the decades and endure until death, just let us indulge in a little stinging criticism—no matter how certain we are that it is justified.

When dealing with people, let us remember we are not dealing with creatures of logic. We are dealing with creatures of emotion, creatures bristling with prejudices and motivated by pride and vanity.

And criticism is a dangerous spark—a spark that is liable to cause an explosion in the powder magazine of pride—an explosion that sometimes hastens death. For example, General Leonard Wood was criticized and not allowed to go with the army to France. That blow to his pride probably shortened his life.

Bitter criticism caused the sensitive Thomas Hardy, one of the finest novelists that ever enriched English literature, to give up the writing of fiction forever. Criticism drove Thomas Chatterton, the English poet, to suicide.

Benjamin Franklin, tactless in his youth, became so diplomatic, so adroit at handling people that he was made United States Ambassador to France. The secret of his success? "I will speak ill of no man," he said, ". . . and speak all the good I know of everybody."

Any fool can criticize, condemn, and complain—and most fools do.

But it takes character and self-control to be understanding and forgiving.

"A great man shows his greatness," said Thomas Carlyle, "by the way he treats little men."

Instead of condemning people, let's try to understand them. Let's try to figure out why they do what they do. That's a lot more profitable and intriguing than criticism; and it breeds sympathy, tolerance, and kindness. "To know all is to forgive all."

As Dr. Johnson said: "God Himself, sir, does not propose to judge man until the end of his days."

Why should you and I?

*Once you learn this valuable
principle of success, and use it,
the results will amaze you.*

Robert Conklin

LESSON 32

HOW TO GET PEOPLE TO
HELP YOU SUCCEED

You have just learned the value and importance of not criticizing others.

Individuals wounded by your careless words or acts, working and conspiring against you, will contribute nothing but harm to you and your career.

Now—how do you get others to pull *with* you instead of against you? How do you get them into your corner, cheering you on, urging you to victory? How do you get them to give you what you want without the use of force, fear, or manipulation? As a matter of fact, how do you get people to do *anything?*

Like all other great truths the answer is simple, so simple that we overlook it in our search for more sophisticated and complex answers to this problem of inducing others to give us what we want or to move in the direction that we desire. Coaches, sales managers, executives, negotiaters, supervisors, teachers, religious leaders, and yes, parents—all grope for that "hot button" in others that will make their task easier while seminars on motivation abound throughout the land, expensive seminars, dispensing over a two- or three-day period a technique which you will learn from a master in the next few minutes.

Robert Conklin is an author, teacher, nationally known speaker, and chairman of the board of two companies. Thousands each year benefit from his many motivational programs and this revealing lesson, taken from his excellent book, *How to Get People to Do Things,* can be worth several thousand times whatever you have

329

expended to attend this university, provided you grasp the concept and use it every day.

The achievement of success is never a "solo" performance, as those who have tried that route will confess. There is an easier and far better way to travel and how far you go will depend, to a large degree, on how well you take this lesson to heart.

"So, to the degree you give others what they want, they will give you what you want."

It was Bill Stilwell from the Management Institute, University of Wisconsin, summing up a two-day conference on motivation and persuasion.

I seized a pencil and wrote down his statement. It was one of those rare, precious, profound chunks of insight that can change the course of one's existence.

I wished I had learned its meaning years before.

To the degree you give others what they want, they will give you what you want!

That is the key to persuading, leading, motivating, selling, supervising, influencing, guiding others—getting people to do things for you.

You can read all the books, take all the courses, spend thousands of hours pursuing the secrets of affecting the thoughts and behavior of others, and you will discover it can all be compressed into that one sentence.

To the degree you give others what they want, they will give you what you want!

It seems incredibly simple. Perhaps it is, if you really understand it. But few do. For there are some implications of the rule that you must know and apply before you can make it work for you. Otherwise, the principle seems to work in reverse: people resist you, act against you, do the things you do not want them to do.

For instance, you must *first* give others what they want. Then they give you the things you want. Most people have that twisted around.

A man says to himself, "I would give my wife a box of candy if she would show me more affection."

An employer feels that an employee should get praise and recognition after putting forth some extra effort.

"I'll start having confidence in my kids when they get some decent grades in school," mutters a parent.

"I could be a lot warmer toward George if he weren't so cold and grouchy," Maude silently thinks.

A salesman tells a manager, "Wow! Would I ever be excited if I cracked the Flanex account!"

These people have the formula backward.

- The man has to bring his wife the candy *first*; then he will get more affection.
- The employer must give praise and recognition *first* in order to bring forth the extra effort from the employee.
- The parent has to express confidence in the kids *first*; then they will start coming through with better grades.
- Maude has to warm up to George *first*; then the indifference and grumpiness of George will melt away.
- The salesman must generate excitement *first*; then the big, juicy sales will fall into place.

So that's the way the law works. You *first* give others what they want; then they will give you what you want.

Of course, it takes patience. And a few other things.

Like knowing *what* it is people want. (We'll get to that later.)

And knowing *how* to give them the things they want. (We'll get to that later, too.) And knowing what it is *you* want and what you're willing to give in order to get it. We'll get to that right now.

Because if you want to manipulate and shuffle people around for your own satisfaction, if you want to inflate your own ego by gaining power over those who are vulnerable, if you are looking for tricky ways to maneuver people into buying things they don't need, if you feel the need to dominate or subdue others (perhaps even your own family) and are looking for psychological buttons to push to always get your own way . . . then you are wasting your time with me.

This is not about getting; it's about giving. And loving. And succeeding. In fact, it's about becoming immensely successful. For if you can get things done with people in joy and harmony, helping them grow and become more than they ever have been before, then you have one of the most treasured talents anyone can possess. The world needs you. It is waiting to reward you highly in material or emotional benefits, to give *you* the things *you* want.

PEOPLE GO IN THE WRONG DIRECTIONS

With a pathway so open and available, why don't more people get on it to go where they want to go? It's probably because of a fork in the road. People are going to go in one of two directions. They are going to be concerned only with what they want or else with what others want. One or the other. Their wants or those of others. Many are so blinded by their personal wants that they give very little thought to filling the needs of others.

- Mary knows what she wants from her husband, but what he wants never fully gets through to her.
- The foreman knows he wants those lug bolts tightened as the body frame comes through the assembly line, but what does the one doing the tightening want?
- The parents know the way they want their children to grow up, but do they show as much concern for what the children want (emotionally, that is)?
- The salesman has a strong desire to sell the stove but is almost afraid to ask about the prospect's wants, for fear the product won't fit.
- Paul feels that Jane does not love him the way he wants to be loved. Maybe it's because he has been blind to her wants and needs.
- The teacher wants that dull, sleepy-eyed teenager to be more attentive, but what does the gawky young stalk of humanity want? Has enough regard been invested in that?

And so it goes. Everyone wants something from someone else and becomes frustrated when it is not forthcoming.

Do you know what often happens then? They start applying an upside-down version of the rule. They try punishing people, just what people do *not* want, in an effort to get what they want.

The air gets chilly when Mary doesn't get what she wants from Frank. The foreman chews out the lug bolt tightener. The parents scold, spank, and threaten when the children do not fit the mold. The salesman jabbers on desperately when it appears the prospect is lukewarm. "Maybe Jane will shape up if I make her a little jealous," Paul reasons. And the teacher threatens, shames, and disciplines, in futile attempts to shake off the teenager's lethargy.

So that's the story of the human being in a highly individualized society. Divorces, splits in families, high job turnover, heavy hearts, wasted careers, crumbled dreams, lonely lives—all haunted by ineffective efforts to relate to other people.

Find out what people want.

Then help them get it.

That's the way to reverse most of those distressing situations!

It's another way of describing the rule. Or the first part of it, that is: "To the degree you give others what they want . . ."

CHANGE "WANT" TO "NEED"

I have observed this process functioning successfully for a number of years. I am more dedicated to it and enthusiastic about it now than when I first heard it. The joys of my personal life have flowered from the use of it. The barren, rocky moments have resulted when my emotions got in the way of my using the rule.

I would make only one change in the formula. Replace the word *want* with *need*.

Wants and needs are separate substances. Wants are frivolous, itchy, plundering, often greedy forces that are never satisfied. Meet one want, and there are two more to replace it.

But needs are the deeper currents of one's existence. They are meaningful, worthy, and not as capricious as wants.

- People want sympathy; they need empathy.
- People want riches; they need fulfillment.
- People want big cars and expensive homes; they need transportation and shelter.
- People want fame; they need recognition.
- People want power; they need support and cooperation.
- People want to dominate; they need influence and guide.
- People want prestige; they need respect.
- Children want freedom and permissiveness; they need discipline.
- People want make-believe relationships; they need honesty and reality.
- People want ease and comfort; they need achievement and work.
- People want adoration; they need love.

So let's say, "To the degree you give others what they need, they will give you what you need."

Let's think about that. What do people really need? What do you and I really need? To discover that, we must become rather close. But we can do that.

For there are few relationships more intimate than that of author and reader. The relationship is silent—no verbal interruptions, no detours. It's a very private conversation between two people, never more. The author, if sincere, is speaking from the heart in a way most understandable to the reader. The reader can reject, accept, pause, ponder, reread, react in any way he or she chooses, without any of the risks accompanying other types of communication.

It's a warm and wonderful association. I, for one, am going to enjoy every word of it. I hope you do, too. I would like to be your friend. That means I must open up and disclose myself to you. When I do that, you will not only know me, but you will also get to know yourself a lot better. And others. This is called "relating."

That's how you will discover what others need so that you can apply our formula: "To the degree you give others what they need, they will give you what you need." Relate. Open up. Remove your mask, and others will remove theirs.

KNOWING ME IS KNOWING YOU

Let me remove my mask. You will see what I mean. For as I talk of myself and the things I need, you will discover that I am also talking about you and the things you need. I'll begin by saying:

"Love me!

"Give me someone, as I wander through life, who cares about me—someone who picks me out of the crowd, notices me, remembers me, makes me believe I'm special."

This is the plea churning about within every human being. It is the greatest hunger of life.

Love is the mainspring of the heart. It is the meaning, the joy, the valleys and the mountains of being.

Love freshens the body, nourishes the soul, shapes the spirit, and glorifies the mind. It is the laughter of the heart, the sunrise of each moment.

Above all else, love is an emotion. That's why it is so vital to the pulse of life. For people are emotional beings. Everything they do is shaped by their emotions.

I wish I could tell you more about emotions, classify them, establish them in the order of their intensity, and find words to make them completely understandable. But that would be a little like trying to describe what a mushroom tastes like. It is impossible.

I only know about *my* feelings. Not yours. We can never know exactly how another person feels. I can laugh with you in your laughter, cry with you in your sorrow, rejoice with you in your happiness, or fret with you in your despair. That is empathy. But neither of us can feel exactly the same way the other feels.

Only you know about your feelings. And only I know about mine. And neither of us are even too clear about that.

But if we can talk to each other about our inner selves, we'll be able to compare, understand, and accept who we are significantly better. And that will help us in getting along with each other—and the people close to us.

So I'll tell you about my feelings, and maybe that will aid you to see yours more clearly.

WE NEVER REALLY GROW UP

A large part of my emotional direction was established very early in life. The longer I live, the more impressed I am about that. Now that I am a seasoned adult, it seems I should have outgrown my childhood nature. But I haven't. I know now I won't.

My childhood was a struggle to receive friendship, acceptance, love, and recognition. Just like chickens, a pecking order was established in the flock of children. Who was the smartest, funniest, strongest, cutest, or more popular? Who could run the fastest, throw a stone the farthest, hold their breath the longest, or win the most marbles?

I sure didn't end up on top. But the great mass of other kids were there with me, reacting about as I did. At that age one doesn't talk about feelings of inadequacy or inferiority. So at times it seemed as though I were alone, separated from the whole world.

Like striking an already bruised muscle, criticism, rejection, failure, or rebuke intensified this conviction. I would not let this be found out, because it seemed shameful, a sign of weakness—proof, perhaps, that I didn't deserve to be on the top of the heap.

I hung on dearly to every indication of love or recognition. Like the comment of Jennie Murphy, my eighth-grade English teacher, who suggested I could write.

"You're a little like Abraham Lincoln," she said. "You say a lot in a few words." A moment later she revealed that she knew I was one of the boys who had tipped over her outhouse on Halloween. What a magnificent person! She was the only teacher throughout my sixteen years of school who said anything good about my academic ability.

Little wonder that at times I had a complex about being a bit backward and dumb, without question quite average intellectually.

I suppose the acorn never stops needing the earth, the moisture, and the air, even after it becomes a grown tree. So, here I am, an adult, and find I have changed so very little in my needs since those long-ago days.

I still seek recognition and acceptance.

I still flourish with praise and crumble with criticism and rejection.

At times I still feel lonely—not when I'm alone or with someone I know well, but when I am surrounded by strangers. In a crowded shopping center, for instance, I feel awkward, distant from everyone else. People stare at me not as a human being, it seems, but as a thing. I want a friendly face to look into, want to meet eyes that say "Hello" rather than "Don't come near me." Perhaps that is why a warm welcome and a smile is so pleasing from one who serves me in a store. It relieves, for a moment, a loneliness.

There are short spaces when I have a strong yearning to be loved. I do not mean physical love, although that is important. I refer to the communication of emotional love. These spans of longing usually come after I have been heavily involved with people for long periods of time. It is almost like wanting a recess, a coffee break, a point of surrender from the process of living. I want to know that all the effort, the trying to be loved, gets some results. I must go to someone who cares about me and merely be in that person's presence quietly and effortlessly and be fulfilled with the sense of being loved.

So I have found that most of the things I want from living I must get from people. It would simplify life to be able to say that I don't need others, that I can exist only with my God, my work, running in the morning, paddling my canoe among the water lilies in the bay, looking at mountain peaks, or just being alone.

I enjoy those things deeply and peacefully, but my life would be shallow if that were all I had. I want to tell someone about my experiences. I must share myself with people.

I have much yet to accomplish with my life. This requires the help of others. I need people to notice me, encourage me, accept me, praise me, and care about me.

You might say, "But you have all of those. Don't you know that?"

And I would respond, "Yes, I know that, logically. You've been around a long time, so I know you are my friend. You married me, you work with me, you fill my car with gas, or you play golf with me. So I know you must be my friend.

"But I do not know it emotionally unless you communicate it and I experience it. If you love me, touch me. If you like being with me, smile at me. If you miss me, write to me. Then my feelings as well as my mind will know of our love and friendship. You will be helping me. For the energy of my life is my emotion.

That is the substance that stimulates me to achieve, grow, work, progress, and become more than I was yesterday.

"And when you do this for me, then I'm a little like a puppy dog. Stroke me, show me affection, and I'll wag my tail, jump up and down, follow you around, and do the things you ask me to do. But your strokes and affection must be real. For, like the little dog, I can tell if it is. If your attention is a false device to manipulate me, I'll find you out and resist you."

ARE WE SIMILAR?

It is not easy for me to disclose myself this way. We are alike, you and I, in that respect. We hide our real selves from the world. We keep our insecurities, doubts, weaknesses, and needs under cover. Perhaps we are saying, "I don't want you to give me the things I need because I have asked for them. I don't want your pity and charity. I want your love and respect." So we conceal our deepest longings, making sure we earn that which we hope for from others. Maybe that's all right. At any rate, that's the way it is.

So why do I bother going through this unnatural process?

Because I don't believe you are very much different from me. We may have traveled separate paths to get this way. Our emotional temperatures might vary. But beneath the surface we are really quite alike.

We yearn to be needed, wanted, and loved. We want to be important to someone. We need appreciation, satisfaction, recognition, acceptance, fulfillment, and a whole lot of other things that we reach out for from within.

Most others are like you and me. Remember, to the degree you give others what they need, they will give you what you need.

What do others need? Look well within yourself, and you will find that which exists in others. What you need, they need. What is closest to your heart, emotionally, is also closest to theirs. You are your own barometer, your own measuring device, of what you need to give in order to get what you need from life.

YOU TAKE OUT WHAT YOU PUT IN

You now have the key for getting people to do things for you. It's simple isn't it? That's as it should be. It resembles the natural course of life. You were born into a sea of life, existing in harmony with all others. You usually do things best when you do them with others, in cooperation, mutual trust, joy, and satisfaction.

The principles are so easy that a child can use them. Regardless of your personality, you have the capacity to get along better with people—but only by giving and sharing of yourself.

This calls to mind the man in a desolate mountain region who was a laborer six days a week and a preacher on the seventh. He served a small rural congregation tucked far up in the hills. The only monetary compensation he got came from the morning offering. One Sunday his six-year-old daughter went along with him to the service. Just inside the door of a small frame church was a table, and on it rested a collection basket. As they entered, the daughter saw her father place a half-dollar in the wicker basket before any of the people arrived.

When the service had ended and the last member had departed, the parson and his daughter started to leave. As they reached the door, both peered expectantly into the collection basket and found that the only "take" was the half-dollar he had donated.

After a short silence the little girl said, "You know, Daddy, if you had put more in, you'd have gotten more out!"

Nena & George O'Neil

LESSON 33

HOW TO TAKE CHARGE
OF YOUR LIFE

You have only one life to live.

Are you living it with self-respect, with purpose, with a strategy for continued growth—or are you little more than a live marionette with others pulling your strings?

Sheep, for self-preservation, always remain with their herd. Any desire for adventure or exploration, or even food and water is instinctively suppressed by the knowledge that danger lurks beyond the protective circle of the group.

Why do so many of us act as if we were sheep? Why do we abandon the management of our lives to others while we stumble forlornly through each day waiting only for the next command to jump or bow or perform for our supper?

Whenever we allow others to control our lives we place our future in their hands, we abdicate our right to make choices beneficial to us, and we stifle all opportunity for growth. With no goals, no priorities, no life strategy of our own, we drift with the herd through an endless meadow of mediocrity, unable to break loose, to achieve even a small part of the dreams we once cherished.

Such a condition is bleak but curable. You *can* learn how to manage your own life, to establish and then pursue your own goals, to leave the herd far behind. You *can* learn how to take a stand for yourself, to say "no" instead of "yes," to act instead of being acted upon.

You are not a sheep, nor are you lost. Any control over yourself that you have relinquished can be retrieved so that you are in command of your own destiny again. Pay close attention. Two distinguished authors and anthropologists, Nena and George O'Neil, are about to help you restore your dignity and your individuality in this provocative lesson from their book, *Shifting Gears* . . .

If we do not rise to the challenge of our unique capacity to shape our own lives, to seek the kinds of growth that we find individually fulfilling, then we can have no security: we will live in a world of sham, in which our selves are determined by the will of others, in which we will be constantly buffeted and increasingly insolated by the changes around us. Without choice we can have no direction; without a life strategy that is our own we lose our sense of self (or never find it) and become a cipher, a nothing. As Jules Henry, the anthropologist, has commented: "For when a man is nothing, he lives only by impacts from the outer world; he is a creature external to himself, a surface of fear moved by the winds of circumstance: one circumstance colliding with another—that is the ebb and flow of thought. Or he is a cyclone of fear in which impulses from the outer world collide at random." When we live a life of sham, Jules Henry goes on to say, we do not consider reality but only try to defeat it.

The reality of the world around us, including the impact of change, is something we must meet if we are to grow—we cannot capitulate to it; we cannot abdicate the making of choices. The only way we can prevent ourselves from being overwhelmed and counteract the forces around us is to find our own center, to believe in ourselves, to ignore the conflicting voices around us and listen to our inner voices. It is only then that we can truly interact with the outside world with courage, conviction, and meaning.

The consequence of letting change happen without our active involvement is abdication to the tyranny of external control, both in a societal and an individual sense. When we lose our individual autonomy and our freedom of choice, then frustration, isolation, aggression, and violence are the result. If you do not manage yourself, then by default either circumstances or other people will manage you. "What modern man needs is not 'faith' in the traditional sense of that term," as philosopher Maurice Friedman has said, "but a *life-stance* [our italics]—a ground on which to stand and from which to go out to meet the ever changing realities and absurdities of a tectronic age." Our life-stance is ". . . that personal and social ground that might enable us to withstand bureaucratization and surveillance—the innumerable incursions of military, industrial, ecological, economic, and political forces into our personal lives."

In order to clarify our individual life stance, to find ourselves and what we believe in and stand for, we need to know not only about the guidelines to a life strategy for change and growth, but also how to integrate those guidelines and put them to work for us. And an understanding of self-management can help us to carry out this integration of the life strategy.

TAKING A STAND FOR YOURSELF

Taking a stand in life, a stand for yourself, is integral to shifting gears, to growing through self-directed change. There are seven keys to creative self-management that can help you to develop a stand in life:

1. Don't ask permission.   Do it.
2. Don't report.   Check things out with yourself, not others.
3. Don't apologize unnecessarily.   This is telling others you are a self-diminisher.
4. Don't recriminate yourself.   The missed-opportunity syndrome keeps you from moving forward.
5. Don't say "I should" or "I shouldn't."   Ask "Why?" or "Why not?"
6. Don't be afraid to say *no* or *yes*.   Act on what you think and feel.
7. Don't put yourself completely in the hands of another.   Be a self-determiner.

Each of these keys is a negative because it is necessary to counteract our too frequent capitulation to cultural and social dicta that insist upon our conformity, that tells us security lies in being like other people instead of fulfilling our individual needs through continuing growth. But this negative cast doesn't mean that we must forsake others or fail to take others into account. The truth is that we can have understanding and consideration for others only to the extent that we ourselves are strong. If we are ciphers, ruled by others, then we have nothing to give others. It is only when we begin to manage our own change that we can truly give ourselves in a caring and sharing way—we give to another or to a project or situation out of our feelings of independence, self-reliance, and security, not out of self-diminishment and weakness. A corollary to these keys is: be kind to yourself. Few of us can reach a compassionate kindness for others unless we can be kind to ourselves first.

These keys make it possible for us to change and grow creatively. It is true, of course, that by saying *no,* by not asking permission, we may lose old friends—but if our friendships are based upon our weaknesses rather than our strengths, how good are they for us? With new strength we will make new friends who are themselves strong. If we find it necessary to "hurt" someone else in order to determine our own lives, what it really means is that we are no longer willing to let them hurt us, no longer willing to let them prevent us from realizing ourselves. Once we stop letting others hurt us, it becomes possible out of our new strength to give and to help them because we care. We can then more easily accept without feeling hurt or rejected when others say no to us.

When we have begun to take charge of our lives, to own ourselves, there is no longer any need to ask permission of someone. If there is another person who will be affected by what you are going to do, then you can ask how the other feels about what you intend to do. Ask for feedback from him or her and then utilize this new information in your decision making. Listening to these feelings and taking them into consideration is important, but it is not the same thing as asking permission. To ask permission is to give someone else veto power over your life; on the other hand, to ask for feedback is to gather information that can be balanced against your own needs, your own values.

Knowing your values and acting upon them means that you have become your own person, your own boss, your own mentor. It does not, however, mean a lack of concern about others and your responsibilities to them or for them. We can explain to others the *why* of our decisions and actions—or our impulsive and thoughtless mistakes—but we should do it because we care for others, not because we feel controlled by them. When we explain to them we are in fact complimenting them, treating them as people of a maturity equal to our own. If other people do not or cannot accept our authentic explanations of our decisions or actions because of problems of their own, they do not deserve an apology in the first place. Explanations, yes, but apologies, no. If they measure our worth only by how closely we conform to what they want us to do, they are really asking us to be worth nothing to ourselves. Such people are not themselves mature and their objections to our steps toward maturity simply are not valid.

Once you are able to accept responsibility for your actions, and can explain your reasons for these actions to other people, once you are able to examine the positive and negative aspects of yourself and by so doing begin to find your path toward change, then other people must also accept your authenticity in this regard; otherwise they show themselves to be diminishers, people whose sense of their own worth is dependent on your being less mature, less sure of your worth than they are of theirs. You can demonstrate no higher regard for other people, in the end, than by caring for them enough to tell them the truth about your needs.

Some people will undoubtedly misuse the rules for self-management we have outlined, misapplying them in the service of what currently but erroneously passes for being true to oneself—letting it all hang out, doing one's own thing without regard for others. You don't owe an explanation to others; but if you are unable and unwilling to give one, you are not moving toward mature and creative change but simply trying to escape from reality into a private fantasy in which it is no longer necessary for you to interact with the world and with the people around you. The psychologist Robert W. White notes that ". . . it is tempting to believe that we can change simply by opening a door and letting out 'true' unsullied impulses." But to misuse our keys for self-management in this way does not lead to change. To quote again from White:

> Change is never so simple. What is really involved is not the releasing of a true self but the making of a new self, one that gradually transcends the limitations and pettiness of the old. This can only be done by behaving differently when interacting with other people. New strategies have to be evolved that express the new intentions and encourage others to take their reciprocal part in finer human relations.

The keys for self-management we have developed are a tool, then, a new strategy for dealing with others that allows us to express our own needs despite the cultural inhibitions against doing so. These keys express a new intention, and when they are accompanied by a compassionate explanation for our actions, they can indeed encourage others to take their reciprocal part in creative change.

But just as it is important that you don't ask permission, that you check things out with yourself rather than reporting to others for instruction, and that you don't apologize unnecessarily, it is also important not to recriminate yourself about past failures. Apologies to yourself are really the basis of the self-diminishment that leads to apologizing to others; if you spend time in self-recrimination, full of remorse over the past and the missed opportunities in your life, you are not managing yourself, but letting the past manage you. Your past holds as many potential half-steps toward the future as it does missed opportunities. Mine your past for what is useful; learn from your mistakes and remember that nothing is wasted.

When you say, "I should do this," or "I shouldn't do that," you are also in many cases allowing yourself to be trapped by the past, following rules set down by parents, teachers, or other mentors that may no longer have real meaning for you in our crisis culture. Many of our society's traditional mores, the *shoulds* and *shouldn'ts* that have been handed down from one generation to another, are eminently worth preserving; but many others make sense only in terms of a kind of society that no longer exists. In order to live in the present, to move into the future and to make the most of ourselves as individuals, we have to begin to make distinctions between the *shoulds* and *shouldn'ts* that make sense in terms of today's world and those that do not. When you find yourself saying, "I should," ask yourself, "Why?" When you find yourself saying, "I shouldn't," ask yourself, "Why not?" If you can't come up with an answer that makes sense in terms of you and your needs for growth and fulfillment, then it is obviously time to discard that rule from the past.

It may also be time to say *no*. You can say *no* to a rule from the past that no longer applies. You can also say *no* to a new development in our society that you personally find unfruitful and not in tune with your inner self. You can even say *no* to change if that is what you want. Just as there are holdovers from the past that make no sense to us as individuals, so will there be current changes that make no sense. The same woman may find herself in the position of saying *no* to her mother's dictum that abortions are sinful, and also saying *no* to the neighboring couple who are into group sex.

But as she says *no* to her mother and to her neighbors, this woman will also be defining more exactly the things she can say *yes* to. Once we have learned to say *no* we can give ourselves permission to say *yes* to the things we really want. In dealing successfully with the option glut, you will want to say *no* quite often—to extraneous diversions, false expectations, to excessive demands from others, to the people, the circumstances, the obligations that give you a sense of being trapped and frustrated. But the other side of that coin is to be able to say *yes*, fully and openly, to the people and circumstances that count for you.

The final key to creative self-management is the cardinal one: never put yourself completely into the hands of another. All of us need advice, support, encouragement, and help from others—but only as a means of strengthening our own self-support. The responsible therapist does not manage his patient's life, but is there only to act as a significant and caring catalyst in the discovery of self, and in implementing positive change. In a complex existence one needs the help of others who have expertise in their own specialities. We must depend upon airline pilots and surgeons and presidents for our very existence at certain times, but the ultimate control of our life management should and can be ours as individuals. The difference between putting ourselves completely in the hands of others and retaining some personal control is the difference between the woman who says *yes* immediately to a major operation (which may later turn out to have been unnecessary), and the woman who, in the face of this major decision, checks one doctor's opinion with a few others, considers the risks, gets all the revelant information and *then* makes her decision, a decision she feels is right for her based on the information she has acquired. You can't sit up on the operating table and give the doctor instructions, but you can make sure beforehand that you are following the wisest possible course of action. That is the essence of self-management.

The development of self-management techniques allows you to have self-control—but control of your self in relation to the world should not be confused with holding things under control. The rigidly conforming person who fears anything new, who insists upon making his decisions according to preset patterns and who fears losing control is not managing himself. He does not have self-control, but rather is being controlled by all the external forces, edicts, and expectations which he has internalized. You cannot control circumstance or other people, but you can control yourself; you can manage and direct behavior in response to circumstance and other people. Self-management leads to the finding of new directions, to a fresh sense of freedom within the limits of responsibility that true freedom entails.

The person who tries to hold things under control in a negative way, who tries to make circumstance and other people fit a preformed mold, is like the man who goes into a Chinese restaurant and always orders all his dishes from Column A. The person who practices self-management, who retains the power of decision in himself, who asks why and why not, who acts on what he really thinks and feels, has the choice of ordering not only from Column A but from Columns B and C as well—or entirely from one column if that is what he wants and finds best for himself at any given point. Or he can choose to walk out of the restaurant without ordering, too. The person who tries to hold things under control in a negative way is taking a prepackaged tour of life: this "if it's Tuesday it must be Belgium" syndrome leads him to say, "if I'm forty-five I must be home safe." But if the tour bus breaks down, or he finds that he is not home safe at forty-five, he is completely at the mercy of circumstance, as well as having missed out on much of life's varied excitement and much of his own potential. When things don't go as expected for the person who practices self-management, on the other hand, that individual has the resources to adjust his plans, to take the new circumstances into account and move forward from there. All kinds of adversities can be turned into advantage if we are willing to take our integral part in making them so.

By managing ourselves we come to know more completely what *we* want for ourselves; we come to know our priorities, our needs, our wants far more clearly, and this knowledge inevitably brings a greater sense not only of freedom but of security. The person who knows himself or herself, and manages his or her life, can tolerate a higher level of ambiguity than before, can deal more successfully with anxiety and conflict because he is sure of his own capabilities. Such people can enjoy change, can improvise confidently in unknown situations. As the psychologist Abraham Maslow suggests, such people can face tomorrow without fear because, whatever it may bring, they have the confidence of self-belief. Self-belief is eroded every time we put ourselves completely in another's hands, every time we ask permission, or report to others, or apologize unnecessarily. Self-belief is increased every time we ask ourselves, rather than others, what we should do with our lives. Self-management bolsters the meaning and the value of the self—and a fuller sense of self-worth and of self-competence is the result.

*If your energy is as boundless as your
ambition, total commitment may be a
way of life you should seriously consider.*

Dr. Joyce Brothers

LESSON 34

HOW TO FIND SUCCESS
IN THE FAST LANE

Let's face it. Whenever a very successful individual is asked for the secret of his or her success and that person replies, "Hard work!" we usually can't help wondering what the *real secret* is behind their good fortune.

Was it a lucky break, a rich relative, some crafty manipulation perhaps, which accounts for that man or woman's great wealth, fame, or power? Questions such as this may comfort our own sagging ego but they also blind us to the truth—and the truth, in most cases, is that when high achievers say they accomplished their objectives with hard work, *they mean it!*

But you work hard, too, don't you? And yet you don't drive a Rolls or have a summer home in Acapulco. However, your definition of work is probably forty to fifty hours of your best effort, each week, with dinners at home and weekends spent in fun and relaxation.

When high achievers use the term "hard work" they mean working at top capacity for *seventy* or *eighty hours,* or more, *every week,* loving their work until it becomes a driving passion, and devoting all their waking hours to thinking, planning, and striving toward goals which others consider impossible. *Total commitment!*

Total commitment is not a recommended life-style for everyone. For many, the price it extracts is much too high, but there are also countless thousands who know exactly what they want and are willing to give as much of themselves as necessary in order to succeed. If you feel that way, more power to you, and Dr. Brothers, in this lesson from her book, *How to Get Whatever You Want Out of Life,* will provide you with invaluable information on how to play the game of "total commitment" as skillfully as anyone . . .

Are you willing to work hard in order to succeed? To go all out? To sacrifice certain pleasures because your time and energy must be devoted to your goal? Will you be happy to make these sacrifices?

If the answer is yes, you want to go all out, then you are right on target. You have found the right goal for the inner you. If, however, you think you will begrudge giving up evenings to work and resent having to pass up weekend fun, then think again. You may not want to climb to the top of the ladder, just partway. Your true goal probably lies elsewhere.

People who succeed in business have the single-minded devotion to their goal that is best described as total commitment. Some people refer to these over-achievers as workaholics. But that implies illness, and if you are doing what you want to do more than anything else in the world, why should you punish yourself by cutting down on the things that make you happy?

Success in business does not necessarily preclude a happy marriage, but those men and women who want to go to the very top, who play for the highest stakes, often find that their total commitment leaves no room for marriage. On the other hand, those men (not women) who want what I call "corporate success" rather than "entrepreneurial success" should know that they will probably advance faster if they are married than if they are not.

Psychologists retained by large corporations to test men and women being considered for promotion to executive ranks look for one quality more than any other. If the candidate has it, that clinches the promotion. If he doesn't, then he's out of the running. This pivotal quality is total commitment, the ability and desire to work to top capacity. They want people who scoff at 40-hour weeks, who work 60-, 80-, and 100-hour weeks because they find their work exciting and rewarding and they are seeking success. Total commitment is the common denominator among successful men and women. Its importance cannot be overestimated.

Take Joe, for instance. Joe is an insurance salesman. He has been called "the greatest insurance salesman in the business."

His secret?

"I put every ounce of energy into my work," he says. "Right from the start, I worked ten to twelve hours a day, seven days a week. There just wasn't anything else that mattered. Everything that I do is associated with selling life insurance.

"When I started out," Joe says, "I was told that if I called seventy-five people, I could expect to get twenty-five appointments. And that ten of those twenty-five appointments would probably fall through, leaving me about fifteen. And I should be able to see three of those fifteen. And that would be a good week's work, they told me.

"I changed the numbers," he says. "I call seventy-five people a day, not a week. I spend five and six hours on the phone. And I spend another five or six seeing people. The law of averages works. The more calls I make, the more sales I make."

Successful men and women must have good health and boundless energy. Climbing to the top demands strength, whether it's to the top of Mount Everest or to the top of the XYZ Corporation. People are born with differing energy reserves. And the man or woman who tires fast, burns out easily would do well to reset his or her goals. Or limit them. Instead of aiming to be chairman of an international multiconglomerate, settle for being president of a small bakery chain or even owner of a neighborhood bakery. For the lower-energy individual, succeeding in business could very well take the form of making it to department chief instead of president. These lesser goals are honorable and satisfying. The men and women who are content with a smaller degree of business success will have richer lives. They are the ones who have time to read and go to the theater, to go hiking with their children, to build strong family ties, to indulge in the joys of friendship, to nurture human values. But the others, those with boundless energy and ambition who want to soar to the top, do not see their total commitment as a sacrifice. To their way of thinking, they are gaining. They feel fulfilled and happy.

Sarah Caldwell, the famed director of the Opera Company of Boston, is one of these. "I love what I do," she says. "I can work for days without sleep because I get so caught up with every detail of producing and conducting an opera. Once in awhile, when everything is just right, there's a moment of magic. People can live on moments of magic."

She was referring to moments of magic on the stage, when everything comes together. Her business happens to be opera, and she is one of the handful of people who have made it to the pinnacle. But in every business there are moments of magic that people with total commitment experience, moments of magic that are the result of what psychologists refer to as flow. And flow is such a peak experience that it is a very strong argument for not resisting the seduction of total commitment.

To most of the world, total commitment is a sign of misplaced values or even disease, and its practitioners are workaholics, but as I said at the beginning, these men and women are doing exactly what they want to do and loving every minute of it. They are a breed apart. They are strivers. They are always reaching—higher than the next person, higher than the last time. And while their marriages may not be spectacularly successful, they find the rewards of their drive staggering. Money. Influence. Power. Prestige. And the joys of flow.

Just what is flow? And what are these joys? Sarah Caldwell described it very well as "moments of magic." It is analogous to the high that joggers experience. A researcher has defined flow as "a sensation present when we act with total involvement." During flow, action follows on action according to an internal logic that seems to need no conscious intervention on the part of the participant. There is no hurry; there are no distracting demands on attention. Moment flows into moment. Past and future disappear. So does the distinction between oneself and the activity.

There was a report in one of the psychological journals several years ago about a surgeon who was so deeply involved in the surgery he was performing that he was completely unaware that part of the operating-room ceiling collapsed. It was only after the last stitch was taken in the last incision that he took a deep breath, stretched, look around—and asked in surprise, "What's all that plaster on the floor?" He had been in a state of flow.

One of the pioneering studies on flow came about because a researcher wanted to know why some people play so hard. What do activities as different as chess and backgammon, tennis and handball, volleyball and football have in common that makes people give their all without any thought of reward? Plato asked this question centuries ago—and never came up with a satisfactory answer. Freud asked the same question—and never came up with an answer either. But Dr. Mihaly Czikazentmihalyi of the University of Chicago isolated the common denominator. He questioned 175 people—30 rock climbers, 30 basketball players, 30 modern dancers, 30 male chess players, 25 female chess players, 30 composers of modern music. What was it, he asked, that they enjoyed so much about composing music or playing chess or climbing steep rock faces? Was it the prestige? The glamour? The prospect of winning? It turned out that the chief attraction was the altered state of being they enjoyed while deeply involved in chess or basketball or whatever.

When people achieve the state that we call flow, they are relaxed, but at the same time feel energetic and fresh. Their ability to concentrate increases markedly. They feel very much in control of themselves and their world. Like happiness, flow is a by-product. The first requirement is to work as hard as you can at something that presents a challenge. Not an overwhelming challenge, but the kind that stretches you just a little, makes you realize that you are doing something better today than you did it yesterday or the last time you tried to do it. Another preprequisite is a significant span of uninterrupted time. It is virtually impossible to switch into a flow state in less than half an hour. And it is absolutely impossible if you are bedeviled by interruptions.

It is possible, with practice, to switch yourself into flow by using a conditioning device in much the same way that you condition yourself to learn effectively. The secret is to analyze previous occasions when you enjoyed those magic moments. Was there any common denominator? Once you have isolated the common denominator, you can set the stage for flow.

Margaret learned how to do this. She was a lobbyist based in Washington D.C., working for a Western conservation group. One night she leaned back in her chair and stretched. It felt good. She had been working hard, pulling together a report on a bill before Congress that would set up new standards for the disposal of wastes from paper mills—a bill that, if passed, would have a direct and adverse effect on the lumber and pulp companies.

She had outlined the present status of the bill, the lobbying efforts of the lumber and pulp interests, and her own activities and had suggested certain steps to bring the situation to the attention of the public, whose sure-to-be-indignant response might sway the legislators into placing conservation above corporate profits.

Now she glanced at the clock. And then took a closer look. Four o'clock! In the morning! She checked her watch. The clock was right. She had been working on the report ever since she had finished supper the previous evening—and she could have sworn that she had been at her desk for no more than two or three hours. She had been so engrossed in what she was doing that the time had raced by.

Margaret had experienced this before. There had been days at the office now and again when she had looked up to find it empty and to realize that it was way after quitting time. On those days, she had always been so much caught up in whatever she was doing that the lunch hour slipped by without her even being conscious that she was hungry.

By analyzing these episodes, she realized that they were similar, each triggered by the near-completion of a project or a phase of a project when she had gathered all the necessary data and was ready to start summing up the problem, outlining the positions taken by opposing interests and making her recommendations for action. She also realized that it happened on days that were relatively quiet in the office—no crises, no important meetings, no out-of-town VIP's.

Once she had this clear in her mind, Margaret made a point of arranging her work so that she could take advantage of flow more frequently. Whenever she reached the trigger stage, she took her work home so that she could count on a stretch of uninterrupted time. And when she sat down at her desk on those days, she also used a verbal conditioning device, saying, "Now I am going to concentrate as hard as I can." It did not always work. There were times when she labored through her reports. But more and more often, she was able to glide into flow, where her concentration increased significantly.

No one can—or should—remain in a constant state of flow. It would be too draining. Like an orgasm prolonged past endurance. The sexual analogy is not a frivolous one, for flow is not confined to work. The potential is inherent in everything we do that demands concentration—playing games, painting, writing, learning, and, of course, sex. It is a truly euphoric state, the ecstasy peak of total commitment.

It is also a stressful state, because the whole organism is at a high pitch, but this is healthy stress. Researchers have found that successful people are healthier than those who are unsuccessful or only middlingly so. One study of very successful men showed that their mortality rate was one third less than that of men in comparable age groups who had not achieved great success. And stress, so often considered to be debilitating, is a positive factor in their health. Some stress, of course, is debilitating, but it is important to realize that it can be healthful as well. Successful people enjoy the stress of coping with difficulties. They are attracted to what one researcher refers to as "the call of controlled risk." They seek it because they are full of energy. They feel more vital when they are active. The active person's brain functions better than the sedentary person's brain, just as the active body functions better than the sedentary body. So flow stress makes for health. Just as physical exertion does. Just as change does. And, just as all of these stress factors are dangerous in excess, so is flow. But don't worry about it. Your system is self-protective. You will not be able to switch yourself into a flow state often enough to cause undue, unhealthy stress.

"It is all very well to talk about total commitment and the euphoria of flow," a businessman objected, "but I know men and women who work like donkeys and never get anywhere."

"So do I," I agreed with him. "And it's because they work like donkeys. Hard work is not enough. You have to have a goal. And you have to know how to make your hard work pay off."

Total commitment is not just hard work: it is total involvement. Building a rock wall is backbreaking work. There are some people who build rock walls all their lives. And when they die, there are miles of walls, mute testimonials to how hard these people worked. But there are other men who build rock walls and all the time that they are placing one rock on top of another they have a vision in their minds, a goal. It may be a terrace with roses climbing over the rock walls and chairs set out for lazy summer days. Or the rock wall may enclose an apple orchard or mark a boundary. When they have finished, they have more than a wall. It is the goal that makes the difference, as Beth's and Trudy's experiences show.

Both got jobs as stewardesses. Both wanted to see the world. But Trudy wanted something more. She wanted to go into business. She thought she might like to have her own travel agency or perhaps work for a hotel chain—something that involved travel. She was not sure exactly what. This job was her first step toward her goal. She would be traveling and learning about the world's great cities and about the kinds of people who traveled—where they liked to go and why. She had a marvelous time and soaked up knowledge like the proverbial sponge. When passengers asked her questions about where they were going, she had all kinds of advice. "I was just there two weeks ago," she would say, recommending a restaurant, "and the food was really terribly good. I must have gained five pounds." She kept a notebook of her favorite places and loved to tell people about special shops and off-the-tourist-track restaurants.

An airline executive who was flying incognito to check out service and personnel watched Trudy at work. She was quick and competent, always helpful. When she was not serving meals, Trudy would be holding a baby so its mother could stretch her legs or answering passengers' questions about their destination.

"That girl's too good to waste as a stewardess," the inspector said when he returned from the trip. "She's a walking encyclopedia of what to do and see in every city we fly to. And she works her head off." A few weeks later, Trudy was offered a promotion. Her new job was working on a series of city-by-city travel pamphlets. Today, ten years later, she is head of her own travel agency, one of the most successful small agencies in the business.

And what about Beth? Beth loved her job. Becoming a stewardess had been her goal. But in time she became disenchanted. It was just plain hard work—rushing up and down the aisles serving meals and taking trays away, answering questions, coping with drunks and bores and airsick passengers. Ten years later, Beth is still a stewardess. A very hardworking, conscientious one. She now has another goal: marriage. She figures that is the only way out of her dead-end job.

In most respects, Beth worked just as hard as Trudy did. But Beth had no goal. And people who do not know where they want to go usually end up going nowhere.

If you know what it is you want out of life and you are totally committed to working for it, then all sorts of opportunities open up. Many of them open up because of inertia. Other people's inertia, not yours. Everyone is basically lazy. Even the men and women who are blessed with boundless energy and burning to be successful. The secret is to understand this and promise yourself that you will not give in to your laziness—and will make it easy for the other fellow to give in to his. The way to do this is to maximize the possibility of success for the other person—minimize the amount of effort he or she will have to make to achieve that success.

Erich worked for a large accounting firm, which had a reputation for getting every last penny's worth out of its employees. "We're being asked to do too much," Erich's colleagues would complain. "This business of working late every night is crazy. They should hire more people."

Erich listened and worked just a little harder. He decided that the only way to stand out from the other accountants was to do more work and to do it better. Searching for ways to do it better, he came up with a plan for reorganizing the work flow that would result in increased productivity. He worked out a table of reorganization, put it in memo form, and gave it to his boss.

He had thought it out very carefully. His memo was neatly typed, but personal. Erich had done the typing himself, not asked one of the girls from the typing pool. He wanted it to be clear that this memo was for his boss alone, that the boss did not have to worry that Erich would go over his head and show it to someone higher up.

More than that, Erich had not just outlined his plan for reorganization; he had indicated just how to achieve the reorganization. If the boss liked the plan, all he would have to do would be say okay. Erich would take care of the rest. The boss liked the plan. He and Erich talked about it over sandwiches one night when they were working late. Erich indicated that if the office were reorganized, the increased productivity would make the boss look good to his superiors. He made it easy for the boss to say yes. Erich had done all the work. He had taken advantage of the boss's inertia. Erich's plan worked so well that the boss got a promotion. And who got promoted right along with him? Erich, of course. The boss needed someone who would make him look good. Erich is now on the executive level where he can talk to the other executives as an equal. And he got there several years ahead of the normal promotion schedule because he took advantage of the power of inertia.

This is very important for the man or woman on the way up. The person who succeeds fastest is the one who does the "too much" and gets credit for it where it counts.

The moral is—don't think of total commitment as a disease; think of it as the only way of life that will result in your attaining your goal of being fabulously successful in business. You will find that the sacrifices are insignificant in view of the fact that you are doing just what you want to do most. So when it comes to the seduction of total commitment, yield.

The image you project, in many circumstances,
is far more valuable than your skills
or your record of past accomplishments.

Michael Korda

LESSON 35

HOW TO LOOK LIKE A WINNER

You knew we'd get around to it, sooner or later, didn't you?

What do people see when they glance in your direction? An obvious success? Or a more obvious loser in life? And by what means, what value system, do they dare pass judgment on you, a stranger in some cases, so swiftly?

You already know the answer: *by how you look!*

Like it or not, since success is what you're after, that outer image of you that is viewed by the world is nearly as important to your upward progress as that inner self-image you have already learned so much about in past lessons. Daniel Webster was correct when he said, "The world is governed more by appearances than by realities."

Fortunately you can improve your outer image in much less time than it takes to change your inner one for the better. In this lesson from his book, *Success!* author and publishing executive, Michael Korda, will begin at the top of your head and teach you, step-by-step, how you can acquire what he calls "the look of a winner" and "the accoutrements of success."

The world is filled with expensive status symbols, any of which can be purchased, provided you have the funds and the need for such ornaments in order to prove to yourself, and others, that you have "arrived." But there is one symbol you can acquire, with a small investment of time, money, and common sense, that will provide you with more satisfaction than any other—*the sweet look of success that you show the world*—and that acquisition need not wait until you have your first million or been moved upstairs to "executive row."

You can, and you should, start dressing for maximum success today. And when you do, the rewards will amaze you . . .

It may be true that beauty is only skin-deep, but the fact remains that the world judges you on your appearance a great deal of the time. It will hardly help your rise to success if you look like a loser. If you're going to be a winner, you may as well begin by *looking* like one.

Obviously, a great deal depends on the field in which you want to gain success. An ambitious rock-guitar player may feel called upon to achieve some kind of distinction by striving for extreme eccentricity of dress and appearance, while someone whose ambition to rise within the ranks of IBM would be well advised to buy some white shirts and get a haircut. Only you can be sure of what standards are most likely to apply in your profession or job. In general, you cannot go very far wrong by adopting those of the more senior and successful people in your own organization.

IF YOU'RE NOT PAUL NEWMAN, THEN . . .

Your face, of course, is what people see most of the time. There isn't a great deal you can do about *that*, nor do I believe that most men are willing to use makeup or resort to plastic surgery to correct any defects in this area. On the other hand, you can make the best of what you've got, even if you're not Paul Newman. A surprising number of men, for example, shave badly. This is odd, but I suspect that it's natural. Nobody ever *teaches* us how to shave. A great many otherwise well-turned-out men begin the day with patches of stubble that they've missed in shaving, and end the day with a heavy growth of fresh beard. This is not the way successful people ought to look. Learn to shave yourself carefully and well, switch razors and shaving cream until you find a combination that works. If you have a heavy beard, keep an electric razor in your desk drawer and use it.

The healthy outdoors look, which is perhaps the greatest success symbol of all, does not necessarily have to be acquired on a forty-foot racing sloop in Hobe Sound. Pouches under your eyes, as well as bloodshot eyes, will respond quickly to fresh air, exercise, and a reasonable reduction in the amount you smoke and drink. Your face should project energy, not fatigue and dissipation, and given the fact that most of us work indoors, it needs all the help it can get.

Try to look at your face as if it were that of a stranger—which should be easy in the early morning—and ask yourself if you've really done the best you can with it. Would you look better if your hair were slightly longer? Do you part your hair on the left side because your mother always parted it that way, or is it really the best choice for your face? If your ears stick out, would it help to let your hair grow fuller at the sides? It may be a good idea to spend some money on having your hair "styled." But remember that the aim is a simple, natural appearance. If you end up with a hairstyle that requires hot-air combing, spray, and antihumidity cream, you will not only get bored with the process, but it will almost certainly look artificial.

Understandably, those whose problem is baldness may want to give some thought to wearing a wig. But a word of warning is in order here. Wigs are not only objects of mirth to a lot of people, but also represent a kind of dishonesty, since you are pretending to have more hair than is in fact the case. If there is the slightest chance that your wig will be noticed, or even suspected, don't do it. Once you have been caught out as a wig wearer, nobody is likely to trust you about anything else. It will be the only thing that most people will remember about you. My own personal opinion is that it is usually better to accept fate and go frankly bald into the world. After all, you have plenty of company.

Fate may not have handed you a perfect set of teeth, and you may not want to go to the expense and pain of having them capped, unless you're an actor. But there is no reason not to have them professionally cleaned as often as is necessary. If you're a heavy smoker, the more often they're "scaled" by your dentist, the better. Yellow teeth turn people off. As far as nails go, I do not think that most men want a professional manicure, and I am myself inclined to distrust men whose fingernails are buffed and polished. But they should at least be short, trim, and clean, and surprisingly often they're not.

GLASSES

It is worthwhile paying some attention to the glasses you select, not only because they serve as a useful prop or cueing device, but because it's one of the few areas in which you can legitimately develop a personal style or trademark of your own. Get a pair that does something for your face. Simple gold frames are usually best. However, the latest status symbol is the large Ray-Ban® aviator goggles. Fashionable as these are, beware: if you have a small face, they tend to make you look like a chipmunk. Avoid colored plastic frames—after gold, real or imitation tortoise-shell is next best. One exception: in the world of high-WASP academia, the proper frame is made of transparent flesh-colored plastic, with very small lenses and very narrow sidepieces. Glasses with metal decorations or decorative inserts are out. Do not go to purchase a pair of frames without first clipping a few photographs of people wearing the kind of glasses that you think would look good on you. Unless you know what you're looking for, you are likely to walk out of the shop in a daze. The variety of styles available now is bewildering.

CLOTHES

Most business people worry a lot about their clothing. And looking at the average business convention, one can easily see why—the number of men who genuinely manage to dress for success is very small. If you want to be successful, you can speed up the process by dressing the right way. And it needn't cost you a great deal of money. Remember: *how you wear your clothes is almost as important as what you wear*.

One of the peculiarities of people's attitudes' toward clothing is that they start to dress for success when they become successful. This is a mistake. Dress for maximum success *now*. Your object is to set yourself apart from other people, in a quiet, dignified but unmistakable manner, and to show that you are a winner.

If you look at the senior members of your organization or profession, you will almost always find that they wear plain dark blue or dark gray suits, with or without a muted pattern or a stripe. It costs no more to buy a blue suit than one in brown or green or some nubbly tweed pattern that looks as if it had been designed as an upholstery fabric for a chain of cheap motels. There is no occasion during the business day (or evening) when a dark blue or dark gray suit is inappropriate. In anything else, you have at least a fifty percent chance of looking out of place.

At the upper level of success a certain status is attached to such tailors as Morty Sills, Dunhill's, or Roland Meledandri, in New York, and Huntsman or Hawes and Curtis, Ltd., in London. It is possible to spend nearly a thousand dollars on a plain suit, and if you can afford to, why not? The pleasure of having it made, and the fact that you're wearing a visible status symbol may make it seem like a worthwhile investment. However, this kind of perfection is only recognizable to a small number of people (most of them attired at similar expense), and is beyond the reach of the average person. You can spend whatever you normally spend, but make sure it is simple, single-breasted and either dark blue (the darker, the better) or dark gray. The cloth should not have any fancy textured pattern. It is also important to avoid contrasting stitching or piping, pockets with buttons on them and lapels so wide that they come out to your shoulders. Look for the kind of suit you would expect a banker or a clergyman to wear.

When you have found it, be ruthless about alterations. It is not all that important how much the suit costs, *but it must fit*. Nothing makes a man look more like a failure than a poorly fitted suit. If you are thin, have the jacket waist taken in to produce a slightly flared look. If you are not thin, adopt the old-fashioned "Brooks Brothers," look, in which the sides of the jacket hang more or less straight down. Do not go in for exaggeratedly suppressed waists (the so-called "Continental Look") unless you want to be mistaken for a bookie or a gigolo.

The left lapel of your suit should have a buttonhole. It is correct, it is traditional, and it belongs there. There should be at least three buttons on the sleeve cuffs of a suit, and if possible four. If the suit only has two, ask for a third one to be sewn on, or get it done yourself. Ideally, the sleeve buttons should be real—that is, you should be able to button and unbutton them—but to get this small, correct touch you have to go to a tailor.

Another thing to beware of in having a jacket altered is the collar at the neck. It is vital that the collar be raised high enough so that it's close to the back of the neck, rather than hanging away from it, as most do. This is the kind of thing you have to be firm about. Insist on putting down a partial payment on your suit, the balance to be paid when you are satisfied with the alterations, and make *sure* you're satisfied.

Trousers are almost always worn too short. Nothing looks worse than a man whose ankles show when he's standing up. You must insist that the trousers be long enough to "break" gently over the shoes. Whether they have cuffs or not doesn't matter, though in fact cuffs make the trousers hang better by adding a bit of weight to the bottoms. If the trousers are cuffless, have them cut at an angle so that they come down lower over the heels of your shoes than they do at front. Any alterations tailor can do this.

Beware of trousers that are too long or baggy at the bottoms, since this tends to give your legs a certain elephantine gracelessness. It is difficult to avoid trousers that have a mild "bell-bottom" these days, but try. It is not a flattering look for most men, and should only be worn by people who have long, thin legs. For short people, it is a disaster, since there is seldom enough length between the jacket bottom and the knees to give the long, sweeping flared look that seems so striking when the trousers are worn by a six-foot-tall model.

A carefully fitted suit is worth the time and trouble it takes, even if it means a certain amount of argument. "Off the rack" doesn't mean it has to fit like a sack.

A little bit of care goes a long way too. Successful people seldom appear rumpled and sweaty, and there's no reason why you should either. A sudden downpour can make your suit look like something an Arab camel driver wouldn't wear. It's useful to keep a freshly pressed suit in your office, ready for emergencies. In general, you should own enough suits so that you don't have to continue wearing them after the trouser crease has gone. If you suffer from dandruff, go see a dermatologist, but in the meantime, keep a clothes brush in your desk drawer and use it. Your object is to appear cool, unruffled, and self-confident at all times. Dress as if you expected to be promoted to the board of directors at any minute, and perhaps you will be.

One way to appear cool is to avoid heavy fabrics. Most offices are overheated to begin with; don't compound the problem by wearing a "winter suit" that brings you out in a sweat. Buy the heaviest overcoat you can find, and wear the same lightweight suits year-round. It's a good way to save money, and you'll increase your comfort at the same time.

Double-knit fabrics have the immense advantage of holding their shape, and are particularly good for travel. On the other hand, they never seem to look quite as crisp as ordinary fabrics, and most of them are manufactured in strange and unappealing colors. If you can find one in gray or dark blue, add it to your wardrobe, and use it for traveling. If it comes with fancy buttons, as many seem to, have them removed and replaced with ordinary black ones.

Blazers should be dark blue, single-breasted, with plain gold buttons. They should never, *never* have a badge on the right breast, and should always be worn with dark gray trousers. If you're in the kind of business where you can get away with a sports jacket from time to time, pick a very lightweight tweed in a subdued and *small* check, and have the leather buttons replaced with plain bone ones. Personally, I think it's OK to have suede patches on the sleeves if you've owned the sports jacket for a decade or so and the sleeves are giving out. But it's ridiculous to buy a *new* sports jacket with suede patches on the elbows.

THE ACCOUTREMENTS OF SUCCESS

Shirts

Despite much that is said to the contrary, a simple white shirt looks better than anything else when worn with a suit. If you can find plain white, one hundred percent cotton shirts with button-down collars, you have it made. (The Orvis Company sells just such a shirt by mail, made of pure cotton with no artificial fibers.) There is a cult of fancy shirts, but my own experience is that men look best in plain ones, and that most successful people either wear white shirts or blue shirts, with an occasional very narrow, understated stripe in a muted color.

One basic rule: *short sleeves are out*. A man who doesn't have a good inch of shirt cuff showing when he's wearing his suit jacket looks naked.

It is also a mistake to put anything in your shirt pocket (if there is one). Shirt pockets are purely decorative, and a row of ball-point pens and pencils clipped in one merely makes you look like a filing clerk.

Despite the contemporary passion for shirt collars that look like the wings of some giant bird, the successful look demands restraint and common sense in this area. The shirt collar should look natural and feel comfortable, and if it comes with little slots for plastic collar stays, use them, and keep a good supply. A crumpled shirt collar looks messy and unkempt.

I suspect that most men are happier with buttons on their cuffs than with cuff links. But remember: *if you are going to wear cuff links, they should be as simple and inconspicuous as possible*. It doesn't matter how much they cost, they shouldn't draw attention to themselves. Plain gold ones are probably best, though these are usually worn by people who inherited them.

During the Nixon years, there was a great deal of status attached to the small, enameled cuff links bearing the seal of the President of the United States that Mr. Nixon gave away to White House visitors. These were kept in what John Ehrlichman referred to as "the Mickey Mouse" drawer of the President's desk, and can still be seen on the cuffs of Nixon loyalists. A number of organizations put out similar cuff links with small enameled devices on them. Any of these is likely to be more suitable than a pair of gold (gold-plated) nuggets, a vast imitation gem or anything similarly clunky in appearance. You can even buy buttons made up as cuff links, in case you're sorry that you bought shirts with French cuffs in the first place.

Ties

Restraint is equally important in ties. For those who have put on weight, a very wide tie has certain advantages. Noel Coward used to say that his ties got wider as he grew older, since they tended to conceal his stomach from view. In general, I would suggest not buying ties that are very thin or very wide. As to color and pattern, the less conspicuous and flashy, the better. Subdued stripes, checks, polka dots, and paisley patterns are fine. But no tie should ever look as if you were wearing a neon sign on your chest. Color is OK, but in moderation, and the design should be quiet— no sprawling geometric shapes, and no sunbursts.

I rather doubt that anybody really needs a tie clip, especially given the width of modern ties, but if you feel it necessary, it should be absolutely plain and inconspicuous, and worn well down on the tie, close to the belt, so that it doesn't show when your jacket is buttoned.

Handkerchiefs, and so Forth

The pocket of your jacket should contain a handkerchief and nothing else. It should be plain white linen, or just possibly a muted silk paisley square, which should never match the tie. Very little of the handkerchief should be visible. It should be unfolded and slightly crushed, rather than arranged in neat little triangles or folded straight.

Under no circumstances carry pencils, pens, or glasses in clip cases in your jacket pocket. As with a crammed shirt pocket, this is a very unsuccessful look. In general, it helps to cut down on the number and weight of things you carry, many of which can be put in a briefcase anyway. Don't start off the day loading your pockets with a pen, a pencil, a thick wallet, keys, coins, a checkbook, cigarettes, a lighter, and a pair of glasses. Eliminate anything you don't actually need, and whatever you must carry with you, put in your pants pockets, not your breast pocket.

Suspenders and Belts

Many successful people wear suspenders instead of a belt.

This is an OK thing to do, but never wear suspenders *and* a belt, which is a sign of real anxiety. As for belts, the lighter and plainer they are, the better. Heavy tooled belts with fancy buckles are fine on cowboys, and look great with blue jeans, but serve no purpose when worn with a business suit—unless, of course, you're a Westerner, and combine them with cowboy boots and a Stetson hat.

Shoes

Assuming you don't wear cowboy boots, take a good look at your shoes. Successful people are fussy about shoes, and you should be too. There's no point in dressing carefully if you wear heavy-soled shoes that make your feet look like King Kong's. One of the purposes of shoes is to indicate that the wearer doesn't need to plod through the muck and rain like ordinary people. This is an age-old function of shoes. The extreme form of cowboy boots, with their pointed toes and heels, was designed to make it evident that the wearer never had to walk, like a farmer or yokel, but went everywhere on horseback. Spanish grandees wore boots of such thin and supple leather that they were obliged to mount their horses directly from the marble steps of their houses, since they were unable to walk in the mud or dust. A simple rule about shoes: *the successful look is the absolute minimum of shoe*.

On rainy, snowy days—until you become one of those very successful people we are trying to emulate who are driven in limousines and never get their feet wet—wear a good, stout pair of hiking boots to work, and keep your success shoes in the office. I have a pair of patent-leather Gucci loafers which seem to me ideal, since they never need polishing and always look elegant. But while Gucci has become a kind of success status symbol, any well-made, neat, light shoe is fine, so long as it's well shined and not run-down at the heels.

On the whole, I think black shoes are more useful for the success look than brown ones. You can wear black with gray and blue and almost anything else, which is not true of brown. And black is always correct, while brown is frowned upon by purists for evening wear. Avoid shoes with very pointed toes or heavy, square toes. They should look as much like your foot as possible, and should be free from welts, fancy stitching, patterns, and ornamental straps. High heels are definitely out, and have no place in the success look. So are thick soles, "space shoes," "earth shoes," sandals, and shoes made out of braided leather, like those of Mexican peasants.

Socks

Apart from showing several inches of ankle by having your trousers hung at half mast, few things look worse than short socks, or socks that fall down in rolls around your ankles. Luckily, this is an area where the solution is simple and will free you from any further thought—buy black stretch full-length socks. Black looks good everywhere and with everything, and takes at least one of the day's decisions off your mind. Stretch socks, particularly the ones made by Supp-hose®, never fall down.

Hats, and so Forth

Personally, I am anti-hat. But I can see that in certain climates a hat makes sense. Very successful people don't need one— (they have limos)—and seldom wear one, but if you feel it's a necessity, don't get one with a very narrow brim, particularly if you have a full face. Avoid any hat that looks funny.

On some people, of course, *all* hats look funny. If you are in this category, buy a good umbrella, black with a plain handle. Remember that dressing for business success means looking your best even if it's five o'clock on a humid day, when everything has gone wrong, and you got caught in the rain on your way back from lunch. What you have to do is to project the appearance of someone who is never affected by the elements, and always manages to appear fresh, energetic, and ready for anything. Most people work their way up to some kind of clothes sense by painful experience as they rise in the world. You don't have to. Stand in front of the mirror and take the first step today!

DRESSING FOR MS. ACHIEVEMENT

Women have far greater problems in deciding what to wear for success, if only because there are fewer guidelines and models for them to use. The women's clothing industry has not yet faced up to the fact that women need solid, reassuring, and businesslike clothes as much as men do. However, women have one advantage over men in that men have no real idea of what a successful woman *should* wear, and are therefore in a poor position to criticize. Furthermore, their cultural background makes it difficult for them to express open criticism of any woman's clothes, though not of course impossible. In other words, if you're an ambitious woman in business and your immediate superiors are men, you can probably get away with a lot more than a man in your position could. That's not to say it's necessarily a good idea to take advantage of the fact, but it's worth remembering that a man who could quickly judge whether or not a male executive was appropriately dressed would find it hard to define just what *would* be appropriate for you.

So much of the clothing made for women is based on fantasy that it is hard to draw up any reliable set of guidelines. Most successful women, however, make a determined effort to find a simple style of dress that both suits them and seems appropriate to the business they're in and unlikely to arouse comment from men. Obviously, a lot depends on the business. An advertising agency or a magazine publisher would be very different from a bank or a government agency. But in general, successful women avoid extremes of dress.

Some years ago, my own bank abandoned its dress code and allowed its personnel to wear pretty much whatever they wanted to. Well, not exactly. In a burst of reverse sexism, they demanded that male personnel wear a suit and a tie, but allowed the women more or less total freedom. I notice that many of the women tellers wear skintight blue jeans, T-shirts, and even halter tops, which is fine (I'm all for freedom). But the women who rise to become supervisors and vice-presidents are those who wear a simple, rather formal dress suit. And I think there is a lesson here: *by and large, women can wear what they want to, within obvious limits; but the women who get ahead take great care to dress unobtrusively and conservatively*.

Perhaps the best thing that has appeared for ambitious women is the Diane von Furstenberg shirt-dress. It looks good on almost every figure, is acceptable under almost any social or business circumstance, is a recognizable status symbol, and is available almost anywhere in the country. It doesn't crease, it doesn't go out of style, its patterns are distinctive and "feminine" without being garish, and it can be worn in any skirt length, from knee-covering conservative to mid-thigh shocking.

If I were a woman in business, I'd buy a dozen of them. I'd also think it worthwhile investing in a few classic, simple suits in dark colors, particularly grays and blues. The real classic seems to me the Chanel suit. But there are many imitations of it that will do just as well, and worn with a simple white blouse it not only looks good, but will seem perfectly appropriate at even the stuffiest business meeting.

Feminists may rebel at the suggestion, but I think a woman who wants to be a success could do a lot worse than to make a careful study of the women's fashion magazines, particularly *Vogue* and *Bazaar*, but also *Glamour* and *Mademoiselle* when they're doing a "working women" issue. You may pick up some ideas that will enable you to create your own "success look." You need all the help you can get, and it's a great advantage to see what other women are wearing in more or less comparable professions.

Avoid: very bright colors, "fussy" clothes, very tight pants suits, skirts so short they make you look like a high school cheerleader, plunging necklines and blue jeans.

Men naturally resent it when women take greater liberties in dress than men are allowed. They are also made uncomfortable in business situations by clothing that has an overtly sexual appeal. There may be occasions on which women can use an alluring outfit to their advantage, but generally speaking it's a *short-term gain* that will be paid for by a *long-term loss*. You will have problems enough in making your way to the top as a woman, without increasing them by the way you dress and present yourself.

For several thousand years, women have been dressed to answer the fantasy needs of men, and to prove that no woman could compete on physically equal terms. The vast dresses and wigs of the eighteenth century, the crinolines and bustles and hats of the nineteenth century, the eccentric "looks" of the great French couturiers in our own era, all made women into more or less decorative and static objects, in some cases hardly even capable of movement from point *A* to point *B* without the assistance of a man. There has been a natural and proper rebellion against this tradition and all that it implies in terms of constriction and role-playing.

Now, the main thing is for you to concentrate on putting men at their ease. You will rise faster this way. For this reason, the extremes of high-fashion makeup and hairstyling are usually a mistake. It is important to make the best of yourself, but not to the extent of obscuring your natural identity and appearance. I can't help noticing, for example, that almost every successful woman I've met uses clear, natural nail polish, rather than the bright or dark colors. It makes sense. Many men feel threatened by the sight of long scarlet fingernails, even though this may be exciting to them as a sexual signal in other contexts. What is more, women with long, lacquered fingernails generally look as if they're incapable of performing any real work. Once again, they represent a male-imposed symbol of sexual possession—the proof that a woman is being kept and therefore doesn't *need* to work. It's a small point, but the kind of thing that gets noticed.

Women have one great advantage over men—their clothes are more comfortable. It is perfectly possible for a woman to wear a simple dress, minimal underwear, and a pair of shoes that are hardly more than a strap with heels, and still look respectably dressed for a business meeting. These days, very few people will notice or care whether you wear pantyhose or not. Bare legs are not likely to cause a scandal, or even be noticed. When you consider that many men, in comparable circumstances, are wearing underwear, socks, a heavy pair of shoes, trousers, a shirt, a tie, and a lined suit jacket, you will realize that not everything in life is in the man's favor.

CARRYING THINGS

OK: A successful woman carries a handbag.
OK: A successful woman carries a briefcase.
Not OK: A successful woman does not carry both.

Personally, I think a woman in business is better off with a good, solid briefcase. It looks professional, and establishes her serious intent. Anything you would normally carry in a handbag can be carried just as easily in a briefcase, and a good deal more besides.

I have the distinct impression that in a working situation men are made nervous by a woman's handbag when it is placed on their desk or in the immediate vicinity. Perhaps it's because the handbag is, in men's mind, a symbol of femininity, and contains God knows what intimate feminine possessions. In certain cases, a woman can use this to her advantage. If you have to negotiate a deal with a man, place your handbag on his desk as you sit down. It will almost certainly distract him and keep him off balance. On the other hand, if you're looking for promotion and success in the business world, never put a handbag on a man's desk or on a conference table. It strikes the wrong image, and will almost certainly be resented, even if unconsciously.

If you carry a briefcase, pick one that's large and solid, as much like a man's as possible. It's effective to have your initials stamped on it. The sight of a woman with a Crouch & Fitzgerald attaché case strikes terror into the hearts of many older men, and this is something you can put to good use in negotiating.

SEMESTER EIGHT

Our greatest glory is
not in never falling, but in
rising every time we fall.

Confucius

Your body is an amazing creation,
capable of performing great wonders, but
you can destroy that miraculous machine's
potential with an overdose of stress.

Dr. Harry J. Johnson

LESSON 36

HOW TO LIVE WITH TENSION

Today, with all of our complex ways of making a living and our infinite possibilities for entertainment, millions of people no longer have the capacity to be "merry." Many of these people are tense and jittery. Others are dragging at the heels, always tired no matter how little they do. Many can't sleep at night. And, to a sizable number, the so-called increase in leisure time has provided only worry and unhappiness.

Those are the words of Dr. Harry Johnson, chairman of the medical board of the *Life Extension Institute,* and he is describing some of the symptoms of a serious ailment which effects many of us—excessive tension. If you are under constant tension, or ever have been, you know how grim life can become.

And yet, Dr. Johnson claims that a certain amount of tension is beneficial to you. You will learn why, and much more about this little-understood subject, in this lesson from his fact-filled book, *Eat, Drink, Be Merry, and Live Longer.*

Success, peace of mind, freedom from money worries, a sense of accomplishment—these are all worthwhile goals only if you are in the proper mental and physical state to enjoy the fruits of your efforts as you pick them. And, of course, you won't enjoy them at all if you apply so much stress to yourself that your mind and body decide they have had enough—and break down.

Let one of the wisest men in the medical profession prescribe ways for you to avoid trouble you don't need—and also show you how to cure yourself if you're already suffering from some of tension's nasty symptoms.

Success is to enjoy ...

The stereotype of the business executive—in fact the way many foreigners think of most Americans—is of a person under constant tension. He swallows tranquilizers by the bushel, and he drinks gallons of black coffee as he sits late at night at his desk, working himself to death. And to watch certain TV commercials, it seems evident that the entire population suffers from the jitters, raw nerves, headaches, indigestion, and complete inability to sleep.

It is certainly true that many of the people who seek medical advice these days have complaints that can be attributed to excessive tension.

At the same time, working hours are much shorter than they were—coffee breaks are an established routine, vacations are longer and more frequent—and we are constantly reminded that we have more leisure than ever before.

Why, then, do we hear so much about tension and pressure? Part of it is the age in which we live. Instantaneous communication has brought the complexities of the world into every home. Constant crises, transmitted to us in solemn voices and big black headlines, provide an atmosphere of anxiety. Because we experience only the present, the perils of today seem worse than anything that has come before. Yet, as we review the advance of the human race, we have never been more secure.

Without at the moment trying to reconcile these seemingly contradictory facts, let us recognize that people who suffer from symptoms caused by tension are faced with a very real and very disturbing condition. Excessive tension can bring about physical ailments, such as indigestion, headache, pain in almost any part of the body, and for people under constant tension, life can be a torture.

However, what is a tension-producing situation for one person, is taken in stride by another. Everyone should learn whether his threshold for tension is high or low.

STRESS AND TENSION—
SIMILAR BUT NOT THE SAME

The human body has been designed to resist an infinite number of changes and attacks brought about by its environment. The secret of good health lies in successful adjustment to changing stresses on the body.

STRESS is the rate of wear and tear on the body. In simplest terms, whatever you do that seems strenuous or wearing is stress. Going out into the cold or the heat produces stress. There is stress on the body from disease, physical or mental effort, crossing the street, or being exposed to a draft. Any emotion, any activity causes stress.

The feelings of being tired, jittery, or ill are subjective symptoms of stress. It is how we react to stress that makes the difference between pleasant healthful living and suffering from a variety of unpleasant symptoms.

Again, stress represents a direct physical attack on the body, and excessive tension is one such stress-producing agent.

What, then, is TENSION? First of all, tension is normal and beneficial. It is part of the normal functioning body—in fact, we cannot live healthfully without it. Tension has been defined as "psychic energy that needs to be released." Tension is that inner drive which is usually considered the mark of a successful person, whether he is a top athlete, a bishop, a business leader, a general. Tension is what makes people "go."

By contrast, many psychotics, such as schizophrenics, experience no tension whatsoever. They live in another world, in almost complete tranquillity.

For some reason, there seems to be a popular notion that tension is bad. This isn't so. Like so many other things in life, tension is only harmful in large doses. A watch spring, for example, cannot perform its function without being under constant tension, but we all know the results of overwinding the watch. It is the same with the human body. Tension that keeps us interested and alert is good and necessary. When we move over the fine borderline where we become apprehensive and anxious and fearful, only then is it bad.

Tension, then, like seasoning in food, gives zest and effectiveness to life. Life without tension is like soup without salt. When we participate in sports or watch a football game, we all become tense.

Under circumstances such as the football game, people aren't conscious of being tense. They only realize it when the grip of tension loosens and they experience a feeling of relief.

Doubtless you can recall many situations when you have been tense and then began to unwind. Perhaps you drove the last hour of a long trip through heavy traffic, then checked into a comfortable hotel room. Gradually you realized that you no longer had to be on the alert and you felt contented and relaxed. These are the good moments of living. But imagine if instead you just couldn't unwind; you couldn't relax even in the comfort of your room, and you lay awake reliving the perils of your trip. This is EXCESSIVE TENSION.

The serious thing about excessive tension is that it can bring about very real changes in the body itself if it persists over a period of time. That is why it is essential, if you have any of the symptoms of excessive tension, to find the causes of the tension as quickly as possible.

THE SYMPTOMS OF EXCESSIVE TENSION

The physical symptoms of excessive tension include headaches, fatigue, irritability, indigestion, back pains, insomnia, muscular rigidity.

Any one of these symptoms can, of course, arise from an organic disorder or a disease. But this can be determined by a physical examination. This is why the annual health audit is so important.

We also know that many of these symptoms can arise from an emotional disorder. This is a complicated situation involving a person's entire pattern of emotional stability. It is not as likely a cause as many people seem to think. Excessive tension is more likely to be the culprit.

Our experience at the Life Extension Institute in examining nearly three million persons since 1914 has confirmed that the most common single symptom of excessive tension is fatigue. A feeling of exhaustion may be present during the entire day, yet the person has difficulty in sleeping at night.

Another common symptom is a feeling of chronic restlessness and inability to concentrate. I recall one executive in a large company who told me, "No matter how hard I work, I can't seem to get anything done. I hurry through the day at top speed, but I accomplish little." The layman has a phrase for this: "wheel spinning."

Then there is the so-called tension headache, which people describe as a tightness and pulling and aching in the back of the neck and head. Tension is probably the commonest cause of head-ache among businessmen. It develops regularly late in the day, but X-ray and examination will not reveal any organic cause.

There are also many characteristic symptoms from the gastro-intestinal tract—"indigestion," gas, constipation, and lower abdom-inal cramps—which may be caused by tension.

Finally, palpitation of the heart accompanied by a sensation of tightness in the chest around the heart can be the result of tension.

Every one of these symptoms is unpleasant, to say the least. They are also a warning that you may be headed for serious trouble.

While excessive tension can disturb people in all walks of life, we think of it most commonly as an "executive disease." It is fashionable to refer to "the rat race" as the villain, and the ulcer is supposedly the Madison Avenue badge of honor.

HOW WIDESPREAD IS EXCESSIVE TENSION?

To find out how widespread tension really is among execu-tives we made a study of six thousand businessmen. Our purpose was to determine the prevalence and degrees of tension, as well as the effects of kinds of jobs upon tension. The results, which were widely publicized, were gratifying: excessive tension among execu-tives is not nearly as prevalent as is commonly supposed.

For instance, 78 percent of the businessmen reported that they were not working too hard.

Eighty-one percent said that they liked their jobs very much.

Only 1 percent reported serious personality conflicts with their business associates.

The great majority reported good health habits as sleeping, recreation, eating, drinking, and smoking.

What it boiled down to was this: only 13 percent of the executives complained of excessive tension, that they worked under constant tension.

This was most encouraging and corrected an important mis-understanding about executive life. However, 13 percent of all executives in the country is still a sizable number of persons to be suffering from excessive tension. We should do our best to under-stand the cause of this excessive tension to reduce the number of sufferers. The effect on the economy, to say nothing of the human misery among a family of a tension-ridden executive, is such that we should make every effort to eradicate tension diseases.

SOME TENSION CASE HISTORIES

Several cases come immediately to mind. I recall John Jones, an extremely successful executive with a large corporation. John is what is known as a "hard-running" executive. He has an inner drive that has propelled him to the top and that makes him impatient for results.

This is an example of the good effects of tension. However, when John came to us for an annual physical, he complained of painful headaches, trouble in sleeping, and increasing irritability with his associates and with his family. It didn't take long to determine that John was now a victim of excessive tension. And it didn't take long either to find out the cause, once we had talked over his usual business day.

John had recently taken over a new division of his company which had a poor profit picture. Even though he worked long and hard, he couldn't seem to make a dent in all of the multiple problems involved. He began to think he was the only person "carrying the load." As his tension built up, he increased the pressure on his staff with resulting ill will and loss of cooperation.

Gnawing away at him also was a fear that his superiors were not happy with his progress. His president was a type who was sparing in his praise and John didn't know where he stood. We suggested to John that he settle this matter immediately with his superiors, even if it meant getting another job.

In a week John came in to see me and already he was beginning to be like his old self. His confrontation with his president had revealed that the company's officers were more than happy with what he was accomplishing, in fact, thought it was "miraculous." The president was so fearful, in fact, that John might leave that he insisted that John take an extra vacation immediately and promised meanwhile to give him some additional staff to help him.

This case has two lessons: I. If you feel you're getting out of depth on your job, find out exactly where you stand. Face up to it regardless of the consequences. 2. And if you have a conscientious man like John Jones on your staff, tell him occasionally that you're pleased with his efforts.

You don't have to be a business executive to suffer from excessive tension. I remember a housewife, who had always been contented with her home and social life. Now she was "tensed up" all the time and given to unpredictable outbursts of temper. Often she would wander through her house in the middle of the night completely incapable of sleep. A brief discussion revealed that she was worried about the lack of progress of her teenage son, who was more interested in mechanics than in preparing for a law career, as his fond mother wanted. Once she faced up to the fact that both law and industry would be better off if her son headed for mechanical engineering, her symptoms vanished.

DON'T BLAME THE "RAT RACE"

Many people who complain of excessive tension brush it off with a reference to the old "rat race"—and obtain a certain perverse pleasure in the illusion that they are working too hard.

I think I can state categorically that few people these days are really working too hard. Rarely do we hear of symptoms that can be traced directly to overwork. Only fifty years ago people worked much longer hours and there were few cases of "tension" and "nerves." Let us recognize that people today spend only 20 percent of their time at work. The rest of the time—80 percent—is spent outside the office or shop. More often that not, the causes of excessive tension are to be found in the pattern of life in the nonworking hours.

Sociologists have long been commenting on the problems of leisure time. As a medical man, I can testify that leisure time and "affluence" do produce health problems. Most people are not victims of the rat race. They have created a rat race of their own. They have not learned to deal with their environment.

• Because it is easier to ride or drive than walk, most people don't get enough exercise.

• Because food and drink are readily available, most people have a weight problem.

• Because of built-in entertainment provided by TV, too many people have become passive in their leisure time activities. They do not receive the mental stimulus that active games and lively conversation provide.

• Because more and more people travel long distances between home and work, they often neglect their sleep in an effort to spend more time with their families.

In solving the causes of excessive tension, then, it is not enough to examine the job situation. You should examine your whole living pattern to find where you may have strayed.

ESTABLISHING YOUR TENSION THRESHOLD

Most people understand their physical limitations. However, many do not seem to realize that the degree of tension one can withstand is highly personal. One person can take a great deal of pressure without an ill effect. The same pressure to another would be incapacitating. If your job or your home environment creates more tension than you can tolerate, don't fight it. Instead, try to change your way of life.

At the same time, you should reexamine your health habits.

In our survey on tension among executives, for instance, this is what we found about the health habits of the 13 percent who complained of excessive tension.

- When they eat:
  they eat breakfast on the fly (under five minutes).
  they bolt their lunch (under fifteen minutes).
  they hurry through their dinner (under thirty minutes).
  and a high percentage are on diets, nursing gastric disorders.
- In their recreation:
  few of those complaining of tension get some form of regular exercise.
  few have extracurricular interests (religious, civic, and so forth).
  many have no hobby at all.
  and one out of five gets no recreation whatsoever.
- For their rest:
  many average six or less hours of sleep at night.
  few have weekends free for family and self.
  and their vacation time is 20 percent less than the overall average.
- In their smoking and drinking:
  most are heavy cigarette smokers.
  most have cocktails for lunch, and many drink more than two.
  many have more than two cocktails before dinner.
- In the drugs they take:
  most of them use sleep-inducing sedatives.
  most of them quiet their nerves with tranquilizers.

If the overly tense person can make a shift in his health habits, this may be all that is needed. If this is not possible, however, then psychiatric help may be indicated.

CONCLUSIONS

We have talked primarily about the persons who already are the victims of excessive stress and tension. These people were not born into the world with these symptoms or, necessarily, with a predisposition to them. Somewhere along the line they acquired habits or failed to face certain situations which brought about these symptoms. If you want to avoid acquiring these symptoms, here are a few guidelines:

- If you have doubts about the ability to do your job well, take steps to find out that you are in the proper line of work, and switch if it seems indicated.
- Face up to the facts of the affluent life and leisure time that most of us now enjoy. Remember that what you do between 9:00 A.M. and 5:00 P.M. is not as harmful as what you do between 5:00 P.M. and 9:00 A.M.
- Live within your income. Don't worry about "keeping up with the Joneses." This advice may seem out of my field as a physician. However, we know that conflicts in everyday living build up tension and hence affect your physical well-being.
- If you have trouble getting on with people, socially or on the job, better get some professional help.
- Every desk-bound worker should leave his chair at least once every two hours and walk about the office for a few minutes.
- Chairmen should call for occasional ten-minute intermissions during meetings, breaking up both tension and boredom.
- If you are always tired, you may actually need more physical activity—or you may be bored with what you're doing. Better find out which it is.
- Relaxation in small and large doses is the antidote to excessive tension. This does not mean rest; it means a change of scene, a change of activity.
- The best cure for tension fatigue is exercise, and the best exercise is walking.
- Finally, learn your tension threshold and live within it.

*If you have always believed that being
a highly competitive person is a habit necessary
for success, you are in for quite a surprise.*

Willard & Marguerite Beecher

LESSON 37

HOW TO AVOID THE TRAP
OF COMPETITION

This lesson may open your eyes to truths about yourself and others that you have never considered before. Taken from Willard and Marguerite Beecher's insightful book *Beyond Success and Failure*, it attacks a concept that most of us have taken for granted since our early youth—the belief that competition is good for us.

All our lives we have been told that we must compete in order to succeed and if we outrun, or outsell, or outmaneuver others, we will be praised for our victories and rewarded with all the trappings of success. From Little League diamonds to corporate sales headquarters, the war cry is exactly the same across the land, "Beat the other guys!" And rarely will a day pass in our lives, no matter what our age or status may be, when we don't find ourselves competing for something, be it a newly created position in our firm or that last parking place at the shopping center.

Is there a better way to live than in the tension-filled hell of constant competition? You can bet your report card there is and the operational word is *initiative*. Initiative is everything that competition is not. Every challenge you accept, every problem you resolve, calls for personal initiative. Initiative produces self-reliance with *you* setting *your* standards, whereas competing with others means that *you* allow *them* to set *your* goals, *your* values, *your* rewards.

Read this lesson slowly, please. Be prepared to underline every statement that seems contradictory to what you have previously been led to believe. Think about the discoveries you make here and what they can mean to how you conduct yourself in the future.

Remember, competition will always place your life in the hands of others, while initiative gives you the freedom to choose your own destiny ...

Competition enslaves and degrades the mind. It is one of the most prevalent and certainly the most destructive of all the many forms of psychological dependence. Eventually, if not overcome, it produces a dull, imitative, insensitive, mediocre, burned-out, stereotyped individual who is devoid of initiative, imagination, originality, and spontaneity. He is humanly dead. Competition produces zombies! Nonentities!

Competition is a process or variety of habitual behavior that grows out of a habit of mind. It originates from our need to imitate others during early childhood. But it is a sign of persisting infantilism if it is still dominating us after adolescence. It is a sign of retarded psychological development, a persisting childishness of "Monkey see—monkey do." We are trapped in imitation.

Once established in orbit, as an habitual way of looking at interpersonal relationships, it contaminates all our relationships. It becomes a way of relating to the world, to other people, and to confronting situations. Competition is a *killer* because it deprives the individual of personal initiative and responsibility.

The habit of competing is so widespread that many people firmly believe that it is a law of nature. Competition is frequently praised as a great virtue to be developed by everyone. This is a costly misunderstanding, since human skills develop adequately only in cooperation, a condition of reinforcement. Competition always lies at cross-purposes with cooperation and thus frustrates individual human initiative.

This unfortunate misunderstanding arises from the fact that people seem to see a superficial resemblance between initiative and competition. Many even regard them as identical like mistaking toadstools for mushrooms. Unless we clearly see the difference between the two, we cannot hope to avoid the evils attendant on competition. It tries in every way to imitate initiative. But the sad reality remains: we compete with others only in those situations *in which we are afraid and defective in initiative*. Those who can, do! Those who cannot, or dare not, imitate.

Initiative is the most highly prized of virtues. It is a vital necessity for everyone, since all human problems demand activity. Human problems do not get solved *where personal initiative* is lacking. Self-reliance is not possible without initiative, and one cannot fulfill his own potentialities unless he is both emotionally and physically self-reliant. *Nothing can take the place of personal initiative* in the life of an individual. It is for this reason that we place such high value on initiative and on the individual who has developed it.

Initiative is the opposite of competition, and *one is the death of the other*. Initiative is a natural quality of a *free mind*. It is wholly spontaneous and intuitive in its response to confronting situations as they arise like the thrusts of a swordsman. The free mind allows one to be an *inner-directed* person whose responses in action are automatic. Competition, on the contrary, is merely an *imitative response* that *lags behind* while it waits for its direction from someone whose head appears to us to be taller and who has been chosen by us to set the pace and direction of our activity. In short, initiative produces spontaneous action, whereas competition produces only delayed *reaction* to stimuli from a pacemaker!

Competition grows out of dependence. It imitates initiative in a deceptive way and thus clouds our understanding. The competitive individual trains himself to outrun his pacemaker, and we may imagine from the result that he is enjoying the fruits of initiative. He often develops much skill so that he appears masterful and competent. As a result of his success, he is often put in a key position where he must originate and organize policy in an unstructured situation that demands independent, imaginative, original planning or activity. In such situations, he cannot function inventively, since he has trained himself only to outrun or imitate *existing patterns;* he has no freedom of mind to create or improvise new forms. He spends his working days in a bind or trap.

To free the mind from the habit of competition, we must see in detail the process by which the mind is ensnared by competition. The way out of a trap is to know the way the trap is built. Only then will it cease being a trap. The release from the stranglehold of competition lies in the increase of self-reliance, since competition can only arise out of a lack of self-reliance! It is that simple. Self-dependence accomplishes that which competition can never touch.

As we have said, the competitive person makes pacemakers out of those he sees around him and puts their heads higher than his own. He abdicates his own birthright doing so. Having abdicated his own initiative, he then begins the struggle to surpass those *he places higher* than himself. Thus he grows blind to his own inner potentialities and in time, is fully under the hypnotic influence of his self-elected pacemakers. He feels hypnotized by them. He enters into a condition of total dependence on outside direction in the sense that he uses others as if they were seeing-eye dogs to guide him. He dares not use his own intuition or spontaneity. Thus, he is in a state of continual irresponsibility, exercising no mind of his own and merely reacting to others. If they take snuff, it is he who sneezes.

An old Zen monk, named Rinzai, summarized his impatience with such individuals by saying:

> If on your way you meet the Buddha, kill him. . . . O disciples of the truth, make an effort to free yourselves from every object. . . . O you, with eyes of moles! I say to you: No Buddha, no teaching, no discipline! What are you ceaselessly looking for in your neighbor's house? Don't you understand that you are putting a head higher than your own? What then is lacking to you in yourselves? That which you have at this moment does not differ from that of which the Buddha is made.

It is evident that the habit of competition is based on, or linked to, another habit—the habit of *making comparisons!* We either compare ourselves as above or below others. We fear those we imagine are above us because we regard them as authority figures who are in a position to block our progress or punish us. We fear those we fancy are below us lest they somehow displace us in an effort to get above us. Thus life appears to us as just one big, dangerous game of one upmanship in which we always stand amidst enemies against whom we must somehow rise and triumph. Or so we imagine it to be.

The built-in hell of the competitive person is that he stamps himself in his own mind as second-class, lacking initiative and originality. A follower! It is exactly that feeling which relentlessly drives him to compete. The self-reliant person feels no desire to compete or otherwise prove himself, either to himself or to others. In short, all competition is second-class or derivative behavior; a back without a brain, incapable of finding its own way or choosing its own objective. It must lean and depend on the pacemaker of its own envious selection.

Comparison breeds fear, and fear breeds competition and one upmanship. We believe our safety depends on killing off the one above us by outrunning him at his own game. We have no time to enjoy any game of our own making lest we lose ground in our race against others for status and preferment. And we may not rest lest those below us steal ahead in the night when we are not aware. The higher we rise, the greater will be our fear of falling. And so we are fearful regardless of *whether we win or lose* the daily skirmishes.

This type of hypnosis is a form of monomania in which one subordinates himself to the commands of someone he accepts as an authority figure. In short, our total dependence on him leads us to total ignoring of all other signals from our environment. *We lose the ability to see and hear* that which is plainly visible around us. We cling to the traditional forms of the game he induces us to play. We thereby sacrifice all our inborn ability to respond spontaneously to the confronting realities of life. We can see, hear, or respond only *vicariously* through the eyes and judgments of the pacemaker whom we imitate or obey. This loss of ability—to see, hear, or respond to emerging reality—*is the most damaging factor* of competition and its wasteful, dominance-submission struggle.

The desire for preferment above others and for personal status leads to the degrading dependence on the opinion of other people and a *pathetic craving for words of praise from them*. The desire for praise carries with it a terror lest others disapprove. Thus the mind is enslaved by the craving for the good opinion of those around us. And so, one can say that the need for personal recognition is merely childish.

The ambitious, competitive individual, then, is an unfortunate who is still trapped in the childhood desire to become the favored child. He stands with his begging bowl before others and pleads for their approval. He will run, jump, steal, lie, murder, or do anything he feels is necessary to do in order to win the praise he seeks. He must somehow impress and thus possess the head that he puts above his own. Since he still views life as a child or as a second-class citizen, all his efforts to get ahead only serve to confirm his habitual way of regarding others and tie him to them. He continues on this path until someone can help him to break the hypnotic spell that binds him by showing him what he has been, and is, doing.

One of the basic, emotional attitudes that underlies competition is the feeling of hostility; there is no such thing as friendly competition. All competition is hostile. It grows out of a desire to achieve a position of dominance and to enforce submission over others. The desire for dominance, in turn, arises from a desire to use and exploit the other person, either phychologically or physically.

This desire to exploit others puts us at cross-purposes with others. We disrupt cooperation and disturb others by either active or passive means. We insist on changing the rules of the game to put them at a disadvantage and to give us a preferred position. We are easily irritated if things happen in any way but the way we want them. Those we cannot find use for, appear only as boring, and we want to ignore or belittle them. We feel comfortable with others only when we have a favorable situation and others look up to us.

The competitive individual is always a poor sport. He cannot stand any situation long in which he is not ahead of others. If he feels he cannot win, he becomes a spoilsport and wants to ruin the game for others. Or he loses courage and interest in the game, so that he retires from it. Or he will only play those games or function in those situations in which he stands a good chance of dominating.

The spirit of competition is the opposite of the spirit of play. The competitive person is incapable of play for the sake of play because he must win or make a good impression. This is easy to see with those who play cards. The competitive cardplayer always wants to win. He groans or is in misery if he is given a bad hand in a deal. He becomes bitter and filled with self-pity every time he loses a trick and blames others for his bad luck. If he gets a good hand, he gloats in a superior way and tries to make others envious of his good fortune. For him, the whole game is only an exercise in hate; he will cheat to win if he dares. With him, winning, not playing, is all that counts.

It has been said that the world is divided into haters and creators. Watching people play cards makes this easy to see. The competitive player in cards—or, in the game of life—has no joy. He lives in fear that he will be put down. But the emotionally self-reliant person plays cards in the "spirit of the picnic." There is no such thing as a bad hand to him, because he does not care whether he wins or loses in the game. The process of playing is his joy. One hand is just as interesting to him as another, since none is like the other. His pleasure is to see exactly what fascinating patterns emerge as the game is played and where he can fit his cards into this changing, developing flux of circumstance. He plays intuitively and without any fear at all, since he is free of any need to win or lose. His whole mind is free to enjoy whatever happens, and he can take any risks he likes with his plays or follow any hunch he may have as to how to play his hand. His only goal is to see what happens—to explore and discover potentialities, not to prove himself.

In summary, the competitive person operates out of constant fear. Fear always limits and degrades us. We can never achieve our potential ability in the climate of fear that competition breeds. Dependence leads to fear; fear leads to comparisons; comparisons lead to competition, and competition eventually destroys us by degrading us to imitation, conformity, infantilism, or mediocrity. Dependence and imitation never lead to creativity and independence. Freedom comes only when we put no head higher than our own.

*If you're waiting for good fortune
to smile on you, that first social security
check might arrive at your door first.*

Lord Beaverbrook

LESSON 38

HOW TO MAKE YOUR OWN LUCK

As you have just learned, competition means placing yourself under the control of others.

Just as harmful to your potential is expecting outside circumstances, usually called "fate" or "luck," to produce that golden opportunity that will mean the difference between your success or failure.

Emerson said,

Only shallow people believe in luck, believe in circumstances. It was somebody's name, or he happened to be there at the right time, or it was so then, but another day it would have been otherwise. Strong men believe that things are not by luck, but by law, and there is not a weak or cracked link in the chain that joins the first and the last of things—the *cause* and the *effect.*

Cause and effect? As you sow, so shall you reap? As you do *not* sow, so shall you *not* reap? "Exactly!" insists William Maxwell Aitken, Great Britain's famed newspaper publisher, Lord Beaverbrook, in this brief and powerful lesson from his book, *The Three Keys to Success.* Lord Beaverbrook's great success as chief of the Aircraft Ministry in England, during her darkest hours of World War II, won the gratitude of the free world. Doubling the aircraft production of his faltering nation within a short period of time had nothing to do with luck.

Again and again, we seem to return to another four-letter word as one of the basic pillars for a life worth living—and that word is *work.*

"Lucky" is what others will call you after your hard work produces results . . .

There is one attitude against which I warn the person who would do well in life. It is summed up in the phrase: "Trust to luck."

No attitude is more hostile to success, and no phrase more foolish.

The phrase is foolish because in a universe governed by the law of cause and effect, strictly speaking, there can be no such thing as luck. There is much in the saying: "Mrs. Harris's pies are not always good by chance." In other words, Mrs. Harris was a good cook.

So with the consistently "lucky" man. It is a fair assumption that he is a consistently industrious and able man.

What we really mean when we say "Trust to luck" is "Trust to circumstances outside our own control." But as long as there is any chance whatever of controlling those factors, it is, of course, folly not to bring them under control.

As the years pass, I become increasingly reluctant to believe in any kind of luck. I once wrote that "It is luckier to be born heir to half a million dollars than to be born in the slums." Even that no longer is true. Being born to poverty may be a spur, whereas being born to riches may lead to ruin.

If a disaster should destroy a man's fortune, something he has labored many years to build, we naturally think that he has had bad luck. But it may be that the disaster was caused by factors that he neglected to control. Or it may be that the disaster was a blessing in disguise, forcing him to exercise intellectual muscles endangered by atrophy, or to strengthen his character at some hitherto-unsuspected weak point.

So I will not dogmatize about the existence of luck except to say this—do not trust in it.

The idea that some are born lucky and some unlucky, in the same way that some are born to be tall and some born to be short, is just nonsense.

Most "good luck" may be explained by industry and judgment, most "bad luck" by a lack of these qualities.

The gambler's creed has been defined as a belief in the imagined tendencies of chance to produce events continuously favorable or continuously unfavorable. To live in this sort of mental atmosphere is to live in a nightmare. It seems to drive some people nearly insane. They constantly consult oracles of one sort or another or perform compulsive actions in a ceaseless endeavor to propitiate Fortune.

Fortune cannot be flattered by such fetish worship. But she can be wooed and won by hard work.

The law of some games of chance is inexorable. It is inevitable, for instance, in card games such as canasta or cribbage, that in the long run a skillful player will beat a player less skilled. So with the great game of life. He who succeeds will be he who, through the totality of his qualities, *deserves* to succeed. He who fails will be he who deserves to fail, and nowhere more than in this—that he has trusted to luck where he should have trusted to himself.

It may be that most of us have something of the gambler in us. We achieve real success, however, only when we have got the better of that imp or demon. In business, the gambler is doomed before he begins to play.

Consider the young man who stakes everything on the hope that some magic key to success will be placed before him on a golden plate. Pathetic is his plight. He consistently refuses good offers or even small chances of work because they are not good enough for him. He expects that Luck will suddenly bestow on him a ready-made position or a gorgeous chance suitable to the high opinion he holds of his own capacities. After a time people tire of giving him any openings at all.

In wooing Luck this young man has neglected Opportunity.

Such men, in middle age, fall into a well-known class. They can be seen waylaying their more industrious and successful associates to pour out a sorry tale of the misfortune that has dogged them throughout life and prevented them reaping the rewards which ought to have been theirs. They develop that terrible disease known as "the genius of the untried."

Far different is the attitude of the person who really means to succeed.

Such a man will banish the idea of luck from his mind. He will accept every opportunity, however small it may appear, which seems to lead to the possibility of greater things. He will not wait on the airy-fairy concept called Luck to launch him royally on his career. He will make his own opportunity and develop its chances by his industry. Here and there he may go wrong, where judgment or experience is lacking. But out of his very defeats he will learn to do better in the future, and in the maturity of his knowledge he will attain success.

At least he will not be found sitting down and whining that Luck has been against him.

There remains to be considered a more subtle argument in favor of a belief in Luck. It is that certain men possess a kind of sixth sense, so that they know by instinct what enterprise will succeed or fail, or whether the market will rise or fall. These men are supposed to make their way to success by what might be called a series of "psychic bids."

Do not believe any of this mystical rubbish.

The real explanation is very different.

Eminent men who are closely in touch with the great affairs of politics or business often act on what appears to be instinct. But in truth they have absorbed, through a careful and continuous study of events, so much knowledge that they appear to reach a conclusion "without stopping to think," just as the heart beats without any conscious stimulus from the brain. Ask for the reasons of their decision, and they can say no more than, "Just a hunch." But their conscious minds do not take into account the long-hoarded experience beneath the level of their conscious thinking.

When these men prove right in their forecasts, the world exclaims: "What Luck!" The world would do better to exclaim: "What judgment! What a wealth of experience!"

The "lucky" speculator is a very different kind of person. He makes a brilliant coup or so and then disappears in some overwhelming disaster. He is as quick in losing his fortune as he is in making it.

Nothing except Judgment and Industry, backed by Health, will insure real and permanent success. The rest is sheer superstition.

It is natural for youth to hope, but if hope turns to a belief in Luck, it becomes poisonous and debilitating.

Youth today has before it a splendid opportunity, but let it always remember that nothing but work and brains count, and that a man can even work himself into brains.

No fairy godmother will waft a person to success. He or she can attain to that goal only by his or her own sense of direction and relentless work.

There is no substitute for work. He who is work-shy will never achieve a permanent success. At best he will eke out a bare subsistence.

*Learn this mighty law which can produce either
success or failure, wealth or poverty, happiness
or heartbreak, and once you fully understand
it you will be able to control your destiny.*

Ralph Waldo Emerson

LESSON 39

HOW TO USE LIFE'S OPTIONS WISELY

There is a very special quality, as you may have noticed, in those extraordinary individuals who have honored this university with their presence and their wise advice. To them, striving for success is only a part of living; it is never the entire apple. Nor are you some experimental human guinea pig on which they are willing to try some new and untested method of climbing to the top. As a group, their premise is simple—you are more than a human being; *you are a human becoming!*

Some lessons back, when Napoleon Hill was urging you to always render more and better service than you were being paid to deliver, he also gave you some valuable reading advice. He said, "Perhaps you have read *Compensation* before. Read it again! One of the strange phenomena that you will observe about this essay may be found in the fact that every time you read it you will discover new truths that you did not notice during previous readings."

Your life is a precious jewel and no one ever defined its true value better than Ralph Waldo Emerson. Among his greatest works was *Compensation,* from which this lesson is taken, and in this classic you will learn the very essence of what it means to "pay a price" for your actions, good or bad. Once you accept the fact, and many cannot, that there is a Law of Compensation which governs all your thoughts and deeds, you will have uncovered the secret of directing your life in any direction you choose.

Just remember—the Law of Compensation has never been repealed. You must live with it whether you like it or not so you may as well use it wisely and to your advantage. You'll be happy you did ...

Ever since I was a boy I have wished to write a discourse on Compensation; for it seemed to me when very young that on this subject Life was ahead of theology and the people knew more than the preachers taught. The documents too from which the doctrine is to be drawn, charmed my fancy by their endless variety, and lay always before me, even in sleep; for they are the tools in our hands, the bread in our basket, the transactions of the street, the farm and the dwelling-house; the greetings, the relations, the debts and credits, the influence of character, the nature and endowment of all men. It seemed to me also that in it might be shown men a ray of divinity, the present action of the Soul of this world, clean from all vestige of tradition; and so the heart of man might be bathed by an inundation of eternal love, conversing with that which he knows was always and always must be, because it really is now. It appeared moreover that if this doctrine could be stated in terms with any resemblance to those bright intuitions in which this truth is sometimes revealed to us, it would be a star in many dark hours and crooked passages in our journey, that would not suffer us to lose our way.

I was lately confirmed in these desires by hearing a sermon at church. The preacher, a man esteemed for his orthodoxy, unfolded in the ordinary manner the doctrine of the Last Judgment. He assumed that judgment is not executed in this world; that the wicked are successful; that the good are miserable; and then urged from reason and from Scripture a compensation to be made to both parties in the next life. No offence appeared to be taken by the congregation at this doctrine. As far as I could observe when the meeting broke up they separated without remark on the sermon.

Yet what was the import of this teaching? What did the preacher mean by saying that the good are miserable in the present life? Was it that houses and lands, offices, wine, dress, luxury, are had by unprincipled men, while the saints are poor and despised; and that a compensation is to be made to these last hereafter, by giving them the like gratifications another day,—bank-stock and doubloons, venison and champagne? This must be the compensation intended for what else? Is it that they are to have leave to pray and praise, to love and serve men? Why, that they can do now. The legitimate inference the disciple would draw was, "We are to have *such* a good time as the sinners have now";—or, to push it to its extreme import,—"You sin now, we shall sin by-and-by; we would sin now, if we could; not being successful we expect our revenge tomorrow."

The fallacy lay in the immense concession that the bad are successful; that justice is not done now. The blindness of the preacher consisted in deferring to the base estimate of the market of what constitutes success, instead of confronting and convicting the world from the truth; announcing the Presence of the Soul; the omnipotence of the Will; and so establishing the standard of good and ill, of success and falsehood, and summoning the dead to its present tribunal.

I find a similar base tone in the popular religious works of the day and the same doctrines assumed by the literary men when occasionally they treat the related topics. I think that our popular theology has gained in decorum, and not in principle, over the superstitions it has displaced. But men are better than this theology. Their daily life gives it the lie. Every ingenuous and aspiring soul leaves the doctrine behind him in his own experience, and all men feel sometimes the falsehood which they cannot demonstrate. For men are wiser than they know. That which they hear in schools and pulpits without afterthought, if said in conversation would probably be questioned in silence. If a man dogmatize in a mixed company on Providence and the divine laws, he is answered by a silence which conveys well enough to an observer the dissatisfaction of the hearer, but his incapacity to make his own statement.

I shall attempt to record some facts that indicate the path of the law of Compensation; happy beyond my expectation if I shall truly draw the smallest arc of this circle.

Polarity, or action and reaction, we meet in every part of nature; in darkness and light, in heat and cold; in the ebb and flow of waters; in male and female; in the inspiration and expiration of plants and animals; in the systole and diastole of the heart; in the undulations of fluids and of sound; in the centrifugal and centripetal gravity; in electricity, galvanism, and chemical affinity. Superinduce magnetism at one end of a needle; the opposite magnetism takes place at the other end. If the south attracts, the north repels. To empty here, you must condense there. An inevitable dualism bisects nature, so that each thing is a half, and suggests another thing to make it whole; as, spirit, matter; man, woman; subjective, objective; in, out; upper, under; motion, rest; yea, nay.

While the world is thus dual, so is every one of its parts. The entire system of things gets represented in every particle. There is somewhat that resembles the ebb and flow of the sea, day and night, man and woman in a single needle of the pine, in a kernel of corn, in each individual of every animal tribe. The reaction, so grand in the elements, is repeated within these small boundaries. For example, in the animal kingdom the physiologist has observed that no creatures are favorites, but a certain compensation balances every gift and every defect. A surplusage given to one part is paid out of a reduction from another part of the same creature. If the head and neck are enlarged, the trunk and extremities are cut short.

The theory of the mechanic forces is another example. What we gain in power is lost in time, and the converse. The periodic or compensating errors of the planets is another instance. The influences of climate and soil in political history are another. The cold climate invigorates. The barren soil does not breed fevers, crocodiles, tigers, or scorpions.

The same dualism underlies the nature and condition of man. Every excess causes a defect; every defect an excess. Every sweet hath its sour; every evil its good. Every faculty which is a receiver of pleasure has an equal penalty put on its abuse. It is to answer for its moderation with its life. For every grain of wit there is a grain of folly. For everything you have missed, you have gained something else; and for everything you gain, you lose something. If riches increase, they are increased that use them. If the gatherer gathers too much, nature takes out of the man what she puts into his chest; swells the estate, but kills the owner. Nature hates monopolies and exceptions. The waves of the sea do not more speedily seek a level from their loftiest tossing than the varieties of condition tend to equalize themselves. There is always some leveling circumstance that puts down the overbearing, the strong, the rich, the fortunate, substantially on the same ground with all others. Is a man too strong and fierce for society and by temper and position a bad citizen,—a morose ruffian, with a dash of the pirate in him?—nature sends him a troop of pretty sons and daughters who are getting along in their classes in school, and love and fear for them smooths his grim scowl to courtesy. Thus she contrives to intenerate the granite and felspar, takes the boar out and puts the lamb in and keeps her balance true.

The farmer imagines power and place are fine things. But the President has paid dear for his White House. It has commonly cost him all his peace, and the best of his human attributes. To preserve for a short time so conspicuous an appearance before the world, he is content to eat dust before the real masters who stand erect behind the throne. Or do men desire the more substantial and permanent grandeur of genius? Neither has this an immunity. He who by force of will or of thought is great and overlooks thousands, has the responsibility of overlooking. With every influx of light comes new danger. Has he light? He must bear witness to the light, and always outrun that sympathy which gives him such keen satisfaction, by his fidelity to new revelations of the incessant soul. He must hate father and mother, wife and child. Has he all that the world loves and admires and covets?—he must cast behind him their admiration and afflict them by faithfulness to his truth and become a byword and a hissing.

This Law writes the laws of the cities and nations. It will not be baulked of its end in the smallest iota. It is in vain to build or plot or combine against it. Things refuse to be mismanaged long. Though no checks to a new evil appear, the checks exist, and will appear. If the government is cruel, the governor's life is not safe. If you tax too high, the revenue will yield nothing. If you make the criminal code sanguinary, juries will not convict. Nothing arbitrary, nothing artificial can endure. The true life and satisfactions of man seem to elude the utmost rigors or felicities of condition and to establish themselves with great indifferency under all varieties of circumstance. Under all governments the influence of character remains the same,—in Turkey and New England about alike. Under the primeval despots of Egypt, history honestly confesses that man must have been as free as culture could make him.

These appearances indicate the fact that the universe is represented in every one of its particles. Everything in nature contains all the powers of nature. Everything is made of one hidden stuff; as the naturalist sees one type under every metamorphosis, and regards a horse as a running man, a fish as a swimming man, a bird as a flying man, a tree as a rooted man. Each new form repeats not only the main character of the type, but part for part all the details, all the aims, furtherances, hindrances, energies, and whole system of every other. Every occupation, trade, art, transaction, is a compend of the world and a correlative of every other. Each one is an entire emblem of human life; of its good and ill, its trials, its enemies, its course, and its end. And each one must somehow accommodate the whole man and recite all his destiny.

The world globes itself in a drop of dew. The microscope cannot find the animalcule which is less perfect for being little. Eyes, ears, taste, smell, motion, resistance, appetite, and organs of reproduction that take hold on eternity,—all find room to consist in the small creature. So do we put our life into every act. The true doctrine of omnipresence is that God reappears with all His parts in every moss and cobweb. The value of the universe contrives to throw itself into every point. If the good is there, so is the evil; if the affinity, so the repulsion; if the force, so the limitation.

Thus is the universe alive. All things are moral. That soul which within us is a sentiment, outside of us is a law. We feel its inspirations; out there in history we can see its fatal strength. It is almighty. All nature feels its grasp. "It is in the world, and the world was made by it." It is eternal but it enacts itself in time and space. Justice is not postponed. A perfect equity adjusts its balance in all parts of life. The dice of God are always loaded. The world looks like a multiplication-table, or a mathematical equation, which, turn it how you will, balances itself. Take what figure you will, its exact value, nor more nor less, still returns to you. Every secret is told; every crime is punished; every virtue rewarded; every wrong redressed, in silence and certainty. What we call retribution is the universal necessity by which the whole appears wherever a part appears. If you see smoke, there must be fire. If you see a hand or a limb, you know that the trunk to which it belongs is there behind.

Every act rewards itself, or in other words integrates itself, in a twofold manner: first in the thing, or in real nature; and secondly in the circumstance, or in apparent nature. Men call the circumstance the retribution. The casual retribution is in the thing and is seen by the soul. The retribution in the circumstance is seen by the understanding; it is inseparable from the thing, but is often spread over a long time and so does not become distinct until after many years. The specific stripes may follow late after the offence, but they follow because they accompany it. Crime and punishment grow out of one stem. Punishment is a fruit that unsuspected ripens within the flower of the pleasure which concealed it. Cause and effect, means and ends, seed and fruit, cannot be severed; for the effect already blooms in the cause, the end preëxists in the means, the fruit in the seed.

While thus the world will be whole and refuses to be disparted, we seek to act partially, to sunder, to appropriate; for example,—to gratify the senses we sever the pleasure of the senses from the needs of the character. The ingenuity of man has been dedicated to the solution of one problem,—how to detach the sensual sweet, the sensual strong, the sensual bright, and so forth from the moral sweet, the moral deep, the moral fair; that is, again, to contrive to cut clean off this upper surface so thin as to leave it bottomless; to get a *one end,* without an *other end.* The soul says, Eat; the body would feast. The soul says, The man and woman shall be one flesh and one soul; the body would join the flesh only. The soul says, Have dominion over all things to the ends of virtue; the body would have the power over things to its own ends.

The soul strives amain to live and work through all things. It would be the only fact. All things shall be added unto it,—power, pleasure, knowledge, beauty. The particular man aims to be somebody; to set up for himself; to truck and higgle for a private good; and, in particulars, to ride that he may ride; to dress that he may be dressed; to eat that he may eat; and to govern, that he may be seen. Men seek to be great; they would have offices, wealth, power, and fame. They think that to be great is to get only one side of nature,—the sweet, without the other side,—the bitter.

Steadily is this dividing and detaching counteracted. Up to this day it must be owned no projector has had the smallest success. The parted water reunites behind our hand. Pleasure is taken out of pleasant things, profit out of profitable things, power out of strong things, the moment we seek to separate them from the whole. We can no more halve things and get the sensual good, by itself, than we can get an inside that shall have no outside, or a light without a shadow. "Drive out nature with a fork, she comes running back."

All things are double, one against another.—Tit for tat; an eye for an eye; a tooth for a tooth; blood for blood; measure for measure; love for love.—Give, and it shall be given you.—He who watereth shall be watered himself.—What will you have? quoth God; pay for it and take it.—Nothing venture, nothing have.—Thou shalt be paid exactly for what thou hast done, no more, no less. —Who does not work shall not eat.—Harm watch, harm catch. —Curses always recoil on the head of him who imprecates them.—If you put a chain around the neck of a slave, the other end fastens itself around your own.—Bad counsel confounds the adviser.—The devil is an ass.

It is thus written, because it is thus in life. Our action is overmastered and characterized above our will by the law of nature. We aim at a petty end quite aside from the public good, but our act arranges itself by irresistible magnetism in a line with the poles of the world.

A man cannot speak but he judges himself. With his will or against his will he draws his portrait to the eye of his companions by every word. Every opinion reacts on him who utters it. It is a thread-ball thrown at a mark, but the other end remains in the thrower's bag. Or, rather, it is a harpoon thrown at the whale, unwinding, as it flies, a coil of cord in the boat, and, if the harpoon is not good, or not well thrown, it will go nigh to cut the steersman in twain or to sink the boat.

You cannot do wrong without suffering wrong. "No man had ever a point of pride that was not injurious to him," said Edmund Burke. The exclusive in fashionable life does not see that he excludes himself from enjoyment, in the attempt to appropriate it. The exclusionist in religion does not see that he shuts the door of heaven on himself, in striving to shut out others. Treat men as pawns and ninepins and you shall suffer as well as they. If you leave out their heart, you shall lose your own. The senses would make things of all persons; of women, of children, of the poor. The vulgar proverb, "I will get it from his purse or get it from his skin," is sound philosophy.

All infractions of love and equity in our social relations are speedily punished. They are punished by Fear. While I stand in simple relations to my fellowman, I have no displeasure in meeting him. We meet as water meets water, or as two currents of air mix, with perfect diffusion and interpenetration of nature. But as soon as there is any departure from simplicity and attempt at halfness, or good for me that is not good for him, my neighbor feels the wrong; he shrinks from me as far as I have shrunk from him; his eyes no longer seek mine; there is war between us; there is hate in him and fear in me.

Experienced men of the world know very well that it is best to pay scot and lot as they go along, and that a man often pays dear for a small frugality. The borrower runs in his own debt. Has a man gained anything who has received a hundred favors and rendered none? Has he gained by borrowing, through indolence or cunning, his neighbor's wares, or horses, or money? There arises on the deed the instant acknowledgment of benefit on the one part and of debt on the other; that is, of superiority and inferiority. The transaction remains in the memory of himself and his neighbor; and every new transaction alters according to its nature their relation to each other. He may soon come to see that he had better have broken his own bones than to have ridden in his neighbor's coach, and that "the highest price he can pay for a thing is to ask for it."

A wise man will extend this lesson to all parts of life, and know that it is always the part of prudence to face every claimant and pay every just demand on your time, your talents, or your heart. Always pay; for first or last you must pay your entire debt. Persons and events may stand for a time between you and justice, but it is only a postponement. You must pay at last your own debt.

If you are wise you will dread a prosperity which only loads you with more. Benefit is the end of nature. But for every benefit which you receive, a tax is levied. He is great who confers the most benefits. He is base,—and that is the one base thing in the universe,—to receive favors and render none. In the order of nature we cannot render benefits to those from whom we receive them, or only seldom. But the benefit we receive must be rendered again, line for line, deed for deed, cent for cent, to somebody. Beware of too much good staying in your hand. It will fast corrupt and worm worms. Pay it away quickly in some sort.

Labor is watched over by the same pitiless laws. Cheapest, says the prudent, is the dearest labor. What we buy in a broom, a mat, a wagon, a knife, is some application of good sense to a common want. It is best to pay in your land a skillful gardener, or to buy good sense applied to gardening; in your sailor, good sense applied to navigation; in the house, good sense applied to cooking, sewing, serving; in your agent, good sense applied to accounts and affairs. So do you multiply your presence, or spread yourself throughout your estate. But because of the dual constitution of things, in labor as in life there can be no cheating. The thief steals from himself. The swindler swindles from himself. For the real price of labor is knowledge and virtue, whereof wealth and credit are signs. These signs, like paper money, may be counterfeited or stolen, but that which they represent, namely, knowledge and virtue, cannot be counterfeited or stolen. These ends of labor cannot be answered but by real exertions of the mind, and in obedience to pure motives. The cheat, the defaulter, the gambler, cannot extort the benefit, cannot extort the knowledge of material and moral nature which his honest care and pains yield to the operative. The law of nature is, Do the thing, and you shall have the power; but they who do not the thing have not the power.

Human labor, through all its forms, from the sharpening of a stake to the construction of a city or an epic, is one immense illustration of the perfect compensation of the universe. Everywhere and always this law is sublime. The absolute balance of Give and Take, the doctrine that everything has its price, and if that price is not paid, not that thing but something else is obtained, and that it is impossible to get anything without its price, is not less sublime in the columns of a ledger than in the budgets of states, in the laws of light and darkness, in all the action and reaction of nature. I cannot doubt that the high laws which each man sees ever implicated in those processes with which he is conversant, the stern ethics which sparkle on his chisel-edge, which are measured out by his plumb and foot-rule, which stand as manifest in the footing of the shop-bill as in the history of a state,—do recommend to him his trade, and though seldom named, exalt his business to his imagination.

The league between virtue and nature engages all things to assume a hostile front to vice. The beautiful laws and substances of the world persecute and whip the traitor. He finds that things are arranged for truth and benefit, but there is no den in the wide world to hide a rogue. Commit a crime, and the earth is made of glass. There is no such thing as concealment. Commit a crime, and it seems as if a coat of snow fell on the ground, such as reveals in the woods the track of every partridge and fox and squirrel and mole. You cannot recall the spoken word, you cannot wipe out the foot-track; you cannot draw up the ladder, so as to leave no inlet or clew. Always some damning circumstance transpires. The laws and substances of nature, water, snow, wind, gravitation, become penalties to the thief.

On the other hand the law holds with equal sureness for all right action. Love, and you shall be loved. All love is mathematically just, as much as the two sides of an algebraic equation. The good man has absolute good, which like fire turns everything to its own nature, so that you cannot do him any harm; but as the royal armies sent against Napoleon, when he approached cast down their colors and from enemies became friends, so do disasters of all kinds, as sickness, offence, poverty, prove benefactors.

The good are befriended even by weakness and defect. As no man had ever a point of pride that was not injurious to him, so no man had ever a defect that was not somewhat made useful to him. The stag in the fable admired his horns and blamed his feet, but when the hunter came, his feet saved him, and afterward, caught in the thicket, his horns destroyed him. Every man in his lifetime needs to thank his faults. As no man thoroughly understands a truth until first he has contended against it, so no man has a thorough acquaintance with the hindrances or talents of men until he has suffered from the one and seen the triumph of the other over his own want of the same. Has he a defect of temper that unfits him to live in society? Thereby he is driven to entertain himself alone and acquire habits of self-help; and thus, like the wounded oyster, he mends his shell with pearl.

Our strength grows out of our weakness. Not until we are pricked and stung and sorely shot at, awakens the indignation which arms itself with secret forces. A great man is always willing to be little. While he sits on the cushion of advantages, he goes to sleep. When he is pushed, tormented, defeated, he has a chance to learn something; he has been put on his wits, on his manhood;

he has gained facts; learns his ignorance; is cured of the insanity of conceit; has got moderation and real skill. The wise man always throws himself on the side of his assailants. It is more his interest than it is theirs to find his weak point. The wound cicatrizes and falls off from him like a dead skin and when they would triumph, lo he has passed on invulnerable! Blame is safer than praise. I hate to be defended in a newspaper. As long as all that is said is said against me, I feel a certain assurance of success. But as soon as honied words of praise are spoken for me I feel as one that lies unprotected before his enemies. In general, every evil to which we do not succumb is a benefactor. As the Sandwich Islander believes that the strength and valor of the enemy he kills passes into himself, so we gain the strength of the temptation we resist.

The same guards which protect us from disaster, defect, and enmity, defend us, if we will, from selfishness and fraud. Bolts and bars are not the best of our institutions, nor is shrewdness in trade a mark of wisdom. Men suffer all their life long under the foolish superstition that they can be cheated. But it is as impossible for a man to be cheated by anyone but himself, as for a thing to be and not to be at the same time. There is a third silent party to all our bargains. The nature and soul of things takes on itself the guaranty of the fulfilment of every contract, so that honest service cannot come to loss. If you serve an ungrateful master, serve him the more. Put God in your debt. Every stroke shall be repaid. The longer the payment is withholden, the better for you; for compound interest on compound interest is the rate and usage of this exchequer.

Man's life is a progress, and not a station. His instinct is trust. Our instinct uses "more" and "less" in application to man, always of the *presence of the soul*, and not of its absence; the brave man is greater than the coward; the true, the benevolent, the wise, is more a man and not less, than the fool and knave. There is therefore no tax on the good of virtue, for that is the incoming of God himself, or absolute existence, without any comparative. All external good has its tax, and if it came without desert or sweat, has no root in me, and the next wind will blow it away. But all the good of nature is the soul's, and may be had if paid for in nature's lawful coin, that is, by labor which the heart and the head allow. I no longer wish to meet good I do not earn, for example to find a pot of buried gold, knowing that it brings with it new responsibility. I do not wish more external goods,—neither possessions, nor honors, nor powers, nor persons. The gain is apparent; the tax is certain. But there is no tax on the knowledge that the compensation exists and that it is not desirable to dig up treasure. Herein I rejoice with a serene eternal peace. I contract the boundaries of possible mischief. I learn the wisdom of St. Bernard, "Nothing can work me damage except myself; the harm that I sustain I carry about with me, and never am a real sufferer but by my own fault."

*There are many ways you can get out
of the ruts of boredom and mediocrity
before you run out of road.*

Auren Uris & Jack Tarrant

LESSON 40

HOW TO SWAP
A LOSING STRATEGY

A rolling stone gathers no moss.
You've heard that all of your life, haven't you?

It's not true! A rolling stone can gather plenty of moss, whereas a stationary boulder, stuck in its own depression, can sit motionless for eternity without acquiring even a hint of green fuzz.

Hopefully you have already adopted and are using several of the success secrets that have been shared with you in these lessons. But making changes, even small ones, in your old method of doing things is difficult, isn't it? Remember how hard Benjamin Franklin had to work at it?

And yet we must change if our present course has us floundering just off life's shore long after we have left the docks. Bacon said, "He that will not apply new remedies must expect new evils." and Thomas Carlyle wrote, "Today is not yesterday. We ourselves change. How then, can our works and thoughts, if they are always to be the fittest, continue always the same? Change, indeed, is painful, yet ever needful; and if memory has its force and worth, so also has hope."

Change need not be traumatic or loaded with self-imposed crises. There is much that you can do, to increase your productivity and value, right where you are, and two business experts, Auren Uris and Jack Tarrant, will provide you with many helpful suggestions in this lesson from their book, *Getting to the Top Fast.* Pay special attention to their comments on habits as they emphasize and reinforce what you learned earlier from Franklin.

Scientists tell us that every single cell of our body is replaced at least once, every seven years. If there is eventually going to be a different you, anyway, let's cooperate with Mother Nature and make it a *successful you* . . .

When your present approach to the top isn't getting you there, it's time to do things differently. Note that we said *do* things. We aren't suggesting that you sit down and conduct a protracted self-review of your whole life and career. This kind of advice is easy to give. It is also easy to start on, but it is quite difficult to finish.

Few of us are lucky enough to experience a blinding flash of insight that says, "What you've been doing so far is wrong. Here's the way to go from now on." Apart from Saul of Tarsus, who saw the blinding flash that converted him into Saint Paul, this sort of thing hasn't really happened to many human beings.

The knowledge that our life or career strategy is not working usually steals on us gradually. We feel vaguely dissatisfied, without knowing why. We don't get much fun out of what we're doing, and we can't see clearly where we're going.

Then it's time for a change. Such a change does not emerge full-blown from your mind. You have to prepare yourself for the change, review your strategy by asking yourself some questions, start to do things differently, decide on new goals or better ways of attaining the old goals, and then replace losing habits with winning ones.

Here are some brief observations on how this can be done. No single recommendation requires extensive soul-searching or tremendous effort. By using some common sense and making some simple moves, you can manage the transition from a strategy that's getting you nowhere, to one that will take you where you want to go.

SHAKE THINGS UP

Suppose your present approach isn't working. You know you're going to have to do something different, but what that different thing will be you haven't yet figured out.

One thing is sure: your revised approach will involve *change*.

You'll have to be ready to accept changes and to make them, but the longer you go on the way you're going now, the harder it will be to change. And it will become increasingly difficult to examine your present strategy with any objectivity. You can wear the rut so deep that one day you're unable to see over the sides. If that day comes, you may be stuck in the rut for all time.

So even if you haven't yet mapped out your fresh strategy, start making changes. Shake up the way you're living and working now.

There are several ways to do it. One method calls upon you to change not the things you do, but the order in which you do them.

The Daily Routine

Look over your daily routine. You're probably doing the same things at the same times, day after day. A manager starts his morning by going through the mail. He calls in his secretary and dictates answers. He confers with some subordinates. He makes some phone calls. This takes him up to lunch. He has lunch in a restaurant—a cocktail, salad, main course, coffee—with one or two colleagues. In the afternoon there's probably a meeting, and more phone calls. Then, in the time remaining, he tries to work on an important report he's drafting. When he leaves for home—well after quitting time—he carries a fat bag of papers and trade magazines.

This manager is getting nowhere on the one project that has most to do with his ascent to the top, the report. His best bet is to rearrange the order of his day without changing its content. Under the new schedule, he comes into the office early, glances at the mail to see if there's anything urgent, then settles down to work on his report. After working on the report for awhile he conducts a meeting and then makes some key phone calls. At lunchtime he orders a sandwich, eats at his desk, works on the report, and reads memos and trade magazines. During the afternoon he talks with subordinates; toward the end of the day he cleans up the routine correspondence.

This altered routine lets him look at every task from a somewhat different perspective. It also has the advantage of placing the more demanding creative tasks earlier in the day, when the manager is freshest, while the things he does by rote are clustered near the end.

The Theme Change

Another way of introducing change is to adopt one basic

theme for doing things differently. For example, Jerry Travers talks with people all day long, in meetings, on the phone, in casual get-togethers. Travers likes people and enjoys talking, but he doesn't seem to be getting anywhere in his pursuit of long-range goals.

So Travers determines, not to rework the details of his day, but to adopt a principle and try to stick to it for awhile. The principle should be one that's the opposite of a major theme of his present routine. Jerry's currently heavily involved with people, so he decides to try talking with as *few* people as possible. He avoids conversations where he can. He doesn't turn himself into a Trappist—he continues to attend meetings and conduct necessary exchanges—but other contacts he eliminates. He works with his door shut. When people drop by he tells them, with a smile, that he's busy.

At first Travers is aware of nothing but the novelty of the new approach. But gradually he finds that he's doing things with a basic difference. He's talking less and thinking more. He ponders problems in solitude, and discovers that his mind functions well with the audio shut off. Travers has still not made basic alterations in his strategy—those will come—but he's preparing the way by changing his routine.

An important principle in changing your pattern can be that of *consolidation* of what Peter Drucker calls discretionary time. For example, Marge Hewitt has for many years pursued the career of housewife. She's getting tired of it. The kids are growing and need her less. She'd like to do something else with her life—but what? She never seems to have a chance to think about it.

Marge Hewitt has fallen into the pattern of spacing her tasks evenly through the day. She makes the beds, sweeps, dusts, puts out garbage, washes dishes, shops, cooks, and so on. To the extent that one chore diminishes in its demands, she expands others to maintain the even load throughout the day. Marge is operating according to Parkinson's Law—that work expands to fill the time available—and she's not accomplishing much.

So Hewitt consolidates her time. She crowds all her work into as small a space of time as possible. By early afternoon all the essential tasks are done, and she has a solid block of discretionary time. This time Marge chooses to use in trips to the public library. There she reads about careers for older women, finds ways to brush up her skills, looks into opportunities for adult education. She hasn't yet formed her strategy, but she's made the change that prepares her to do so.

Shake up your pattern. Don't wait until you have the new

strategy; change your way of doing things first. After the change you'll be more ready to work out a good strategy. And in changing your pattern, make sure you consolidate tasks to give yourself the discretionary time you need to tackle the project of reordering your life.

TAKE A FRESH LOOK AT THE TOP

In replacing a losing strategy with a winning one, begin with a clear focus on the objectives. When you started out, what was your goal? Have you changed your goal? How often?

How long has it been since you thought about getting to the top? Does the top still look as good as it did? At this point, do you really know where you're headed?

Whether you feel you're still determined to reach the pinnacle you first set out for or you think that some other goal would now be more appropriate, it's time to consider alternatives. How close are you to your original top? How much progress have you made? Does progress get easier or harder with time?

Are there distinct obstacles in the way? Can they be overcome? Do you feel like making the effort to overcome them? If the barriers between you and your goal seem very great, if they are not diminishing, if you find it difficult to contemplate making the effort to get over them—then maybe it's time to look for a new top.

If you can't reach your original goal, what goal would you substitute for it? Something in the same line, but lower? Something in an entirely different line? Naturally, if you're choosing new objectives, you don't want all the efforts you've made so far to go to waste.

Is there a goal—not considered before—toward which you'd like to climb? Would you be happy to achieve the new goal? Or would you still wish you'd kept on struggling toward the original top?

How much do you know about the problems involved in the new objective? Can you handle them? Would you enjoy handling them?

There comes a point in thinking about a change in strategy, or a shift in objectives, when the "rut" mentality struggles to take over. One part of your psyche is telling you that it's time for a change; another part is saying it would be easier to keep on doing the same thing.

Do you like what you're doing now? Do you enjoy the struggle as much as you did a year ago? Do you enjoy meeting a new challenge, or would you rather avoid it? Where's the fun in your present routine?

Whether you stick to your original goal or choose a new one, you should take this opportunity to spell out the nature of the objective.

Now what is your goal? What are your advantages in striving toward it? What are your disadvantages? How long do you think it will take to get there? Is the goal clear-cut—will you know when you've arrived?

Are you ready to do the things necessary for a fresh assault on your objective, whether it's old or new?

After a thorough reexamination of objectives, you will have reaffirmed your original aims or substituted new ones. This is a necessary step in getting out from under a losing strategy and assuming a new and more effective one—which will be more fun to execute.

DO SOMETHING DOABLE

Some days it seems impossible to make the big picture seem brighter. The goal is so far away; the complications are so great; your personal weaknesses loom so large.

You're having a bad day. We all have them. But sometimes that one bad day can stretch out into another, and another; and pretty soon they're all bad. You're in a losing rut.

Some people think that this is the moment to sit back and review your whole life. That could be the very *worst* thing you can do. You're discouraged; problems appear insurmountable. Thinking about the whole dismal scene will just push you further down into the dumps.

Instead, try—just for the moment—a *minimum accomplishment* plan. Pick out something you're sure you *can* do—and do it. It doesn't have to be something big. Accomplishing something that lies within your limited scope can give you a lift and fuel the fires for more ambitious undertakings tomorrow.

Pick a project that fits these requirements: it should be doable within a brief space of time. It should be relatively mechanical, not requiring much thought or a lot of decisions. And it' should be a project on which you can see results right away.

That last point is the most important. Psychologists talk about the value of *reinforcement*. We are reinforced when we do something and see immediate positive results.

This principle is one of the bases of the new approaches to education. The student takes some simple action and instantly sees how he made out. The procedure is structured so that a simple action usually achieves a positive result. Impelled by a slight but perceptible lift, the student moves ahead to the next step. If you've ever taken or seen a "programmed instruction" course you've seen the idea in practice. The course is broken up into tiny chunks. You answer an easy question and see immediately that your answer is right. By this means you're led to more difficult questions and answers.

Start with something easy. For instance, Len Barnum is sitting behind his desk wondering how he can cope with a major project coming up next week. The more he thinks about it the harder it seems. He feels lousy. If he continues this way, pretty soon he'll be in such poor mental shape that he can't do anything.

So Len turns instead to a simple task. For some time he's been telling himself that he should get his desk straightened out. He undertakes the task. He sorts the stuff on top of the desk into neat piles. He organizes the material in the drawers. He finds some out-of-date papers that can be thrown away. True, this involves a rudimentary kind of decision making; if Len finds that even these decisions are too much for him, he should stop and turn to an even simpler task, or maybe just take a walk.

Before long the desk is organized. Len Barnum sits there feeling good about a job well done. It didn't take long. He can see what he's accomplished. And he feels better about the bigger project.

Easy mechanical tasks are the most doable: sorting, cleaning, straightening, routine mailing, purchases of little items you've run out of, scheduling. Paying the bills (unless you're strapped, making it a traumatic experience) can be a neat, self-contained, easily accomplished project.

When the major challenges seem too vast, take on some minor ones. Do the doable. You'll find yourself enjoying a small but distinct feeling of satisfaction. You'll be more ready to go about the job of improving your strategy in a positive frame of mind.

FORMING THE HABIT OF SUCCESS

In devising a winning strategy, pick effective tactics and make them a habit. We are all creatures of habit; we have "bad" habits and "good" ones. We're not interested in making moral judgments on habits. We're interested in figuring out how you can form habits that will get you close to where you want to go.

It shouldn't always be a major effort to do the thing you know you should do because it fits your strategy for getting to the top. The effective action should become a part of your pattern—a habit. You have certain habits now that help you. You want to keep these. You have other habits that hinder you. These you want to break.

This is a subject in which knowledge is all important. So here are some facts you should know.

We don't necessarily form habits by doing things over and over again. If the action does not answer a *need*, it does not become part of our makeup. The schematic pattern of a habit works this way. We feel a need, often an unconscious need. We take an action. That action satisfies the need; we feel a reward. So when we feel the need again we repeat the action, and so on until it becomes ingrained, a habit. Smoking is a good example.

The habit has no strength of its own. We sometimes think of habits as if they were independent entities, potent spirits that exist around us and seize some of us in their grip. Not at all. The habit—and its strength—always comes from inside. We provide the need, and we do the thing that satisfies the need. Enjoying the satisfaction, we reinforce the habit and increase its hold on us.

Even the "worst" habit satisfies. X drinks too much. Y smokes like a chimney. Z picks his nose. Why would anyone have such a disgusting, and perhaps harmful habit? The answer is that awful as the habit appears to the outsider and even to the person afflicted with it, it nevertheless satisfies a need. We may not like to admit this, but it's true.

However, in that last fact lies one of the major hopes for breaking bad habits. The bad habit is the best available way to satisfy a recurring need. We don't have to eliminate the need by involved probing of the labyrinthine passages of the mind; we need to find a better means of satisfying the need.

So we don't "get rid of" bad habits; we replace them. And we don't just consciously choose to contract good habits; we acquire them in the same way that bad habits are acquired, as a recurringly satisfying response to a need.

Replacing the Losers

You'll want to form winning habits to execute your new strategy. But first you'll want to replace losing ones. The first rule is, *one at a time*. You can't take a shotgun approach to curing bad habits.

Pick the habit you'd like to break. Denny Foster has a habit of talking too much at meetings. He knows he does it. He is determined to keep his mouth shut; and yet, at the next meeting he realizes he's doing it again, hogging the air waves while people glower, fidget, or doze.

One method Denny can use is a modification of something called "negative practice." Negative practice means that you force yourself to *deliberately* repeat a bad habit until you become so fed up with it you abandon it. This seems to work with habits you can practice on in private. However, Denny can't bring himself to *deliberately* commandeer the meeting.

But he doesn't have to go that far. Sitting in the meeting, listening to somebody else say something, Denny deliberately *thinks* to himself, "I'm going to take over in a minute. I have a lot to say on this subject and they're going to hear me out. I'll cover the history of the thing, and alternatives, and give my opinions, and criticize other opinions. If it takes me an hour I'll say what I have to say." Just *thinking* this way, Denny is able to so appall himself with the idea of shooting off his mouth that he doesn't do it in practice.

Finding the Winners

The negative approach is the first part of getting rid of bad habits. But the process won't "take" unless you substitute a good habit for the bad one.

Remember the pattern. The good habit should satisfy a need, just as the bad one did. You don't have to psychoanalyze yourself to probe to the basis of the need; you just have to come up with a more positive and useful action that satisfies it. So obviously the good substitute has to lie in the same general area as the harmful practice it's replacing. Denny can't use, as a substitute for talking too much, the practice of doing energetic push-ups until he's out of breath. Apart from being inappropriate and nonpositive, this action would probably not satisfy the need that gives rise to his habit of talking.

A combination of common sense and trial and error is a likely road to follow in coming up with the substitute. In Denny's case, he now takes copious notes on what others are saying at the meeting, and then tries to analyze his notes in writing, coming up with new combinations and better answers. This cuts down on the time available for talking.

More to the point, it fills his need, which is to feel that he's in control of what's going on. Previously he was "controlling" things by holding the floor; now he remains in control by making notes that keep him one step ahead of the others. Best of all, this new habit is a positive one; when Denny is called on for a contribution, he's ready with a good one.

Once you've hit on an action that's positive and that fills the need that gives rise to a habit, make it a part of you as fast as possible. Sell and resell yourself on the benefits of the new approach. Reinforcement is needed at the conscious level as well as at the unconscious. Write down what the new action accomplishes; observe its good effects. Keep reminding yourself that it works.

If possible, commit yourself to a change in habit. One of the vital things in getting people to give up cigarettes is making them say publicly that they're going to do so. When we put ourselves in a position where we'll look bad if we don't follow through, we're all the more likely to keep going.

Denny doesn't have to make an announcement to the whole organization that he's going to keep his lip buttoned henceforth. But he should make the commitment to just one good friend, or to his immediate boss. That way he's on record and gives himself a greater incentive to do things right.

Provide yourself with rewards for success and penalties for failure. Set these up strictly with yourself—and stick to them. When Denny manages to keep his cool at meetings for two weeks running, he buys himself the new putter he's been wanting. But if he backslides and tries to filibuster a meeting again, he denies himself a round of golf for two consecutive weekends.

Go all-out. Don't taper off bad habits and start good ones gradually. Make the break a clean one. Work on one habit at a time, but work on it intensively and wholeheartedly. By replacing harmful habits with good ones, you're replacing a losing strategy with a winning one.

SEMESTER
NINE

No life is so hard that you can't
make it easier by the way you take it.

Ellen Glasgow

Dr. Norman Vincent Peale

LESSON 41

HOW TO ENJOY
THE BEST THINGS IN LIFE

How many days has it been since you began *The University of Success* ... 20, 30, 50?

It doesn't matter. What does matter is that you should feel very proud of what you have already accomplished. At your own pace you have persevered and managed to absorb eight semesters of concentrated material on success by the very best teachers on that subject. Be patient and the rewards for your effort are certain to come because you are undoubtedly a far wiser and more competent individual than when you began this study.

Of course, with eight satisfactorily completed semesters in any other college or university you'd be preparing to enjoy the pomp and excitement of a commencement ritual where you would be informed, in usually dull rhetoric, that you are now prepared to go out into the world and contribute your acquired knowledge and talents in order to make this a better place for all of us.

That won't happen here *because you are not ready yet!* Eight semesters in this university may have furnished you with invaluable information on how to succeed *but that is not enough.* Success is a fickle and difficult taskmaster. Achieving it is not the climax, the finish line, the final gun. You must also learn, for your own benefit and for those who love and depend on you, how to deal with success once you have it. And this is usually a far more difficult challenge than any you faced while you were struggling to reach the pinnacle.

During these final two semesters, at *The University of Success,* you will engage in graduate study, study that will help you to become a much wiser and more adaptable member of the human race as you strive to become, for want of a better term, "a master of success." Those words are also a fitting description of Norman Vincent Peale whose philosophy of "positive thinking" continues to influence the lives of millions, throughout the world. In this lesson, from his inspirational masterpiece, *The New Art of Living,* Dr. Peale implores you to slow down and take the time to live because success, without the joy of living, is a game for fools. Even wise old Solomon didn't learn that truth until it was too late ...

W hen Mrs. Ramsay MacDonald, wife of a former British prime minister, was dying, she called her husband to her bedside for a last word. "Keep romance in the lives of our children," she admonished him. It was an impressive parting message which, as we reflect upon it, is deep with wisdom.

This mother knew, as all who meditate seriously upon life must know, that the passing years make a terrific assault upon the zest of man's spirit, and unless he exercises care, will steal from him the romance of life. Napoleon said, "Men grow old quickly on the battlefield"—they do in life also unless they are vigilant.

Charles Lamb once declared, "Our spirits grow gray before our hairs." One starts out in youth with anticipation. Excitedly he looks down the approaching years with the spirit of an adventurer, but before he has traveled far, life starts blowing its cold winds upon him. He tries his wings, perhaps they fail him; and some, sadly enough, having been disillusioned a time or two, give over the dreams and plod wearily on over a pathway from which the romance has fled. That is one of the saddest things that can happen to anyone, to lose the thrill and zest of living.

There is one certain way to decide whether you are old— namely, what is your attitude of mind when you arise in the morning? The person who is young awakes with a strange feeling of excitement, a feeling which he may not be able to explain but which is as if to say, "This is the great day; this is the day on which the wonderful thing will happen." The individual who is old, regardless of age, arises with the spirit unresponsive, not expecting any great thing to happen. This day will be just about like all the rest. They may hope it will be no worse. Some people retain the spirit of expectation at threescore and ten; some lose it early in life. The measure of one's age is actually how well he retains the romance of life.

Perhaps William Wordsworth gave us the best description of the sad process that takes place in many:

> Heaven lies about us in our infancy
> Shades of the prison-house begin to close
>   Upon the growing boy,
> But he beholds the light, and whence it flows,
>   He sees it in his joy;
> The youth, who daily farther from the east
>   Must travel, still is Nature's priest
>   And by the vision splendid
>   Is on his way attended;
> At length the man perceives it die away,
> And fade into the light of common day.

The romance of life is so priceless a possession that it is a supreme tragedy to lose it. Though one may acquire much in wealth, fame, or honor, the real joy of life does not lie there but, rather, in keeping the romance of living going. Nothing gives such complete and profound happiness as the perpetually fresh wonder and mystery of exciting life.

TRAIN WHISTLES AMONG THE HILLS

When I was a small boy, I lay in bed at night and heard the long, low whistle of the train among the hills of southern Ohio. I could see in imagination the speeding train, with its brightly lighted cars, whisking through the night. I always used to love a train and to me there was no more thrilling sight than a big express train speeding over a countryside brightly silhouetted against the darkness. The chief ambition of my boyhood days was to be a railroad engineer. I am thankful that such things still thrill me. When these thrills pass, the romance of life is on the way out.

How quickly for some people the freshness of life passes away! The work to which we set ourselves with high hopes and intense interest is allowed to degenerate into dreary monotony. The marriage begun with such bliss becomes commonplace in the steady round of day-by-day living. The hopes and ambitions which once stirred us become lifeless. Far horizons no longer beckon. The joy of life has fled, leaving our days hollow and our activity meaningless. What shall we do?

What do people generally do when they discover that the excitement of life is going or is gone? Many turn completely to material things as the possible source of its recovery. They think that if they can just possess more things, have more money, enjoy more privileges, go more places, the old joy in life will return. Others turn to a pleasure program when they find the romance of life growing dull. By new sensations, they argue, they will regain life's thrill. They forget that one thrill calls for another in endless succession until a person loses his sensitive appreciation of the beautiful and becomes calloused and cynical.

Still others hope to recapture it by casting aside all restraint and ideals. The trouble with that method is that sensations wear out and become jaded. Also, bypass it as we will, everyone has a troublesome little affair in him called the conscience, which is easily hurt, and a pain in that area is hard to cure. Moreover, in every man, given him by nature, is an innate self-respect which, while it may not prevent him from doing evil, will keep him from ever having peace after he succumbs to evil.

HOW TO KEEP ROMANCE IN LIVING

There are others—honest, wholesome people—who just bravely accept the dreariness of life's hardships. They have too much sense to seek departed romance in things and also too much honor and wisdom to turn to sensual pleasure. But some fortunate people have found the true method of keeping romance in life. There was Robert Louis Stevenson, confined to a bed of pain through long years, yet able to write such happy, lilting little verses that children everywhere have been made joyous by them.

> The children sing in far Japan;
> The children sing in Spain;
> The organ and the organ man
> Are singing in the rain.

Stevenson himself knew how to sing in the rain.

All of which brings us to the fact we want to emphasize, that the secret of a successful and happy life consists in taking time to live. Life is an art, and to be successful in any art it is necessary to know the real from the imitation and to be content only with fineness of quality. The tragic fact is that many people are content with imitation life when they could just as easily possess the genuine.

In *The Barretts of Wimpole Street* Elizabeth Barrett Browning thoughtfully protests, "What frightens me is that men are content with what is not life at all." She is right about many of us. We pass hastily through restless, hurried, anxious days and call it living, thinking if we capture a vagrant thrill now and then that it is life. Deep in our hearts, however, we know that real life is better than that; it is a great and wonderful experience which is to be fervently desired.

DON'T LET BUSYNESS GET YOU

The time in which we live has made real life difficult, but as we shall see, far from impossible. We are a generation busy with things. Stevenson wrote, "The world is so full of a number of things; I am sure we should all be as happy as kings." The world has many more things than in Stevenson's day but there is grave doubt if their possession has really solved the problem of happiness. I can push buttons all over my house and have light, music, and heat. My grandfather had no buttons to push, but just the same he knew the art of living. He was a happy man. The increase of things, instead of providing leisure to be enjoyed, in all too many cases has but multiplied our confusion.

If William Wordsworth, in the quiet of the English Lake Country, could say years ago, "The world is too much with us," what would he say now in modern America? We are also a generation of busyness. Hurry and speed drive us on. A large billboard near the outskirts of a Middle Western city proclaims, "This is a city of wings and wheels." So is most every city. We have the green-light psychology—not that we must make the green light, but how terrible to wait through the red! Watch people waiting for the light to change. Notice that tense expression. That is one thing wrong with us.

All of this has had unfortunate physical effects. It has made nerves and high blood pressure and heart trouble widespread. In speaking of the physical and nervous effects of hurry, William James said, "Neither the nature nor the amount of our work is accountable for the frequency and severity of our breakdowns. But their cause lies, rather, in that absurd feeling of hurry and having no time, in breathlessness and tension and anxiety."

This has done something even more serious to modern people. I refer to its deep psychological and cultural effects. It has had a tendency to make us superficial and thus incapable of appreciating the deeper and more subtle values. This hectic, hasty, hurrying age of ours has left the average man bewildered and out of breath. It has made him think that the chief virtue is to keep up with the flying clock. We seem to have the idea that everyone must be constantly doing something. One must be driving a car or dancing or playing bridge or golf or going to the theater or doing something. The American people—and that means you and me—greatly need to learn to reduce life's tempo unless we are to allow this hurly-burly space age to rob us of life's deepest meaning and happiness.

TAKE IT EASY

A story is told of some Americans who were making their way through Africa. They had employed a group of natives at the seaport and had told them they were in a great hurry, as Americans usually are. The first day they went with rapid progress through the jungle. They continued the relentless pace the second day. The third morning, when they were hurriedly preparing for another day of rapid travel, they found the savages squatting under the trees and refusing to move. When their bewildered and helpless employers asked them why they were not ready to start, they said simply, "We shall rest today to let our souls catch up with our bodies."

Our failure to take time to live actually prevents us from deriving the best from life. Man assuredly was never meant by the good God to beat out his life in hurry and tumult, wearing out his nervous system and making his inner life shabby. We are given this world to live in happily and reflectively. Let us take time to live. Many of us were brought up on the books of Horatio Alger. One bore the title: *Strive and Succeed.* That point of view has been carried to an extreme. Good, hard work is one of man's greatest boons, and a lazy man is to be pitied. But perhaps we will succeed better if we strive less or, at least, reduce the tension of our effort. What good is it anyway to succeed if one cannot enjoy life in the process? We are missing the secret of happy life in this modern American spirit of hurry.

Taking time to live means to realize that the supreme values of this world are spiritual things like music, art, literature, nature, and religion. Many people, especially hard-pressed businessmen, feel mistakenly that music and art and books and religion are not as pressingly important as the mass of details with which their lives are filled. Such men will find themselves becoming a mere machine, whereas God designed each one to be a man. It is well to remember that we do not primarily live to work. We work to live. A person who spends his life with details as the chief concern misses the mark and dies a failure no matter what success he attains. He never learned the skill of life organization.

STOP STARVING YOUR SPIRIT

Do not be a slave to life's machinery; get a song, a lovely poem, and the whisper of God's voice into your mind. You may not know it, but I will tell you honestly that you are starved for these things, and the worst kind of hunger is the longing of man's soul for the things that are more nourishing than bread. No wiser thing was ever said than that statement of the great Thinker, Jesus: "Man does not live by bread alone." He lives, instead, by the beauty of nature, by music and art, and supremely by the presence of the eternal.

I, a city dweller, once had a summer place on a cedar-crested bluff overlooking a lovely bay down by the sea. The salt breezes off the mighty ocean swept cares away; the soft sunlight falling on the grass taught the quiet repose of earth; the unhurried sounds of the natural world, so different in quality from strident city noises. These quieted me as a mother soothes her troubled child; and at night when the stars came out, blossoming one by one in the infinite meadows of heaven, and a hush fell over land and sea, I could hear the friendly voice of Mother Nature, which is the voice of God, saying: "My child, this is life. Take time to live it."

MAKE GOOD FRIENDS

Taking time to live also means to cultivate friendships. Shakespeare advised us to bind our friends to us as with hoops of steel. Mark Twain reminded us that good books and good friends make up the ideal life. We are less than smart to permit the business of life to keep us from the happiness of creative friendships.

I learned a good lesson once from a happy Irishman. It was in Dublin, Ireland, where I called to see a leading merchant of that city. I found a large and very busy department store, and surrounded with all the details of its administration was the man I had come to see. Seeing he was busy, I tried after a brief greeting, to excuse myself, but he asked me to wait and in a few minutes reappeared with his hat. Soon we were seated in his car and he was enthusiastically showing me the sights of the city. When I remarked at his courtesy in leaving his work to be so gracious to me, he said in his big voice, "Not a bit of it, not a bit of it; I never overlook the chance to make a new friend, and, besides"—and this struck me—"I am running the store; the store isn't running me." This man knew how to live and his spirit showed it.

The business of cultivating friends also suggests the thought that God intended us to find interest and fellowship in people. We are unfortunately so excessively taken up with ourselves and the technique of our days that we miss the rare delight of learning to know better all sorts and conditions of men. It is rewarding to cultivate the habit of looking for the interesting qualities in people. There is something interesting in every person.

Look at the man across from you on the bus or subway—ordinary looking enough, isn't he? Yes, but if you only knew the drama, the tragedy, the comedy, even the glory and heroism in that man's life, he would be full of interest to you. Some of the greatest books ever written are about simple, everyday people and simple, everyday happenings. The genius of Charles Dickens, and other enduring writers, is to be found in their ability to see the dramatic quality in what is often mistakenly called commonplace life. There is no such thing as commonplace life.

PAINTING ON A BARREL HEAD

In Florence, Italy, I saw the painting by Raphael called "The Madonna of the Barrel." The outline of the head of a barrel in lieu of canvas is plainly discernible. The story is that Raphael was walking one day through the marketplace of Florence when he saw a mother, evidently a very poor woman, sitting in the street with her child at her breast. She was dressed in shabby attire but her face was the ineffable expression of mother love. Raphael was so charmed by her appearance that nothing would do but that he must paint her at once and where she sat.

Accordingly, he took for his canvas the head of an old barrel which was conveniently nearby, and using color and brushes which were in his pocket painted on the barrel head a picture which today hangs in one of the galleries of Florence, a masterpiece. Raphael was an immortal artist by reason of his native gifts, but more than that because of his capacity to see the beautiful and the romantic in everyday people, even a poor woman in a marketplace.

How can we dully complain that life has lost interest? Look upon the face of that dear one near you; hear the happy laughter of that little child; really know your fellow men. Life will never lose its romance for the person who, unselfishly, does good for people. Those who do lose the thrill of living are the ones who develop the habit of thinking exclusively about themselves, who are constantly concerned with their own interests or their own pleasures, or, what is more common, their own troubles. Start the habit of doing good to the people nearest you. This policy will make you so happy that you will sing inside, and the whole world about you will take on richer color. The grass will be greener; the songs of the birds will be sweeter; the stars will be brighter; the skies bluer; and even if the bank account is low and things are tough, the dreariness of life will depart if you learn the secret of finding your happiness in human service.

I have often heard my father relate the following incident, of which he was an eyewitness, as illustrating how human kindliness and helpfulness can develop a happy and exciting life. The man about whom this story is told was a great expert in the art of living and by his personality impressively showed the technique of that art to his students, who have not forgotten it after many years.

JOHNNY THE NEWSBOY

In a mid-Western city some years ago was a great surgeon who was also a professor in the medical school. This surgeon was a true physician in that he not only had superlative skills but also loved people and went about doing good. He became deeply interested in the little crippled newsboy at the corner, where the doctor regularly bought his paper. He was a bright little fellow, this newsboy, and the famous surgeon said to him one day, "Johnny, would you like to have me cure that leg of yours so that you could run and play like other boys?" "Oh, Doctor," said the little lad, "that would make me so happy!"

Accordingly, the surgeon arranged to operate upon the boy and explained to him that he wanted to perform the operation in the presence of his class of medical students to teach the students how to help other little boys when they became doctors. Johnny agreed. He was placed before the surgeon and the students were arranged in tiers as in an amphitheater so that they could witness the operation. The doctor explained the disease and operative procedure he was to follow.

When all was ready, he said, "Now, Johnny, we are going to fix that leg of yours," and attendants started to administer the anaesthetic. Johnny raised his head and said in a voice that could be heard all over the room, "God bless you, Doctor Dawson, for you have been so good to me." The surgeon looked down at him. Tears came into his eyes. He put his hand on the head of the little fellow and said, "Thank you, Johnny." After the successful operation the surgeon said to the students, "I have operated on many great and prominent men, upon millionaires, senators, governors, and have received many large fees, but what that little boy said was the greatest fee I ever received in my life." Can you imagine romance leaving the life of a man like that? Love people and help them. That will keep life always fresh and interesting.

WHAT MEN MISS

As we miss the fascination in people, so do the charm and delight of things escape us in our busyness. John Ruskin, shrewd observer of men's foibles as well as their greatness, once sadly commented, "I am not surprised at what men suffer, but I am surprised at what men miss." A whole world of beauty and fascination is spread about us, but we are blind to much of it, not because of any fundamental lack of the quality of appreciation within ourselves, but simply because we do not take time to let this beauty affect us.

Consider the pleasure we miss in books, pictures, and music because we do not take time for them. Every night there stretches over us the inimitable and awe-inspiring canopy of the heavens. Sometimes we are caught by it and brought to a stop, especially in a country place, and we see it again with a sense of newness as one who looks upon something once familiar and it becomes fresh again because of long absence. This glory is for our inspiration nightly, but we are too much in a hurry and we bypass it. Life was meant to be enjoyed. Life was made for man, not man for life. It was never intended that one should beat his life out on a treadmill, losing his very personality in the rattle and roar of an artificial civilization.

If one should come into a beautiful room with fine paintings on the wall, a fireplace ablaze, easy chairs to rest in, and beautiful rugs on the floor, he would conclude that the place had been prepared for his pleasure and happiness. Accordingly, as we look about us in this world with its exquisite beauty and obvious delights, we must surely feel it is good and that life itself is good. Let us take time to live and enjoy it all. He who learns to do so is master of the art of living.

Elbert Hubbard

LESSON 42

HOW TO HANDLE
EVERY ASSIGNMENT

This lesson is one of two venerable jewels of self-help literature that you will discover in this first graduate semester. No matter
what your profession or occupation may be, you are certain to
perform it better, tomorrow, just for having read it.

To celebrate a little-known act of heroism in the Spanish-
American War, Elbert Hubbard, in 1899, wrote a short article of
inspiration entitled "A Message to Garcia" and published it in his
magazine, *The Philistine*. That issue was completely sold within
days and soon the presses at Hubbard's plant were running night
and day in order to supply all the requests for reprints of that piece.
The New York Central Railroad ordered more than a million copies
to promote the dependability of their trains and soon every member of the U.S. Marine Corps received a copy as well as every Boy
Scout in the country.

Later, *A Message to Garcia* was translated into Russian and
copies were presented to every railway worker in that nation. During the Russo-Japanese conflict, the Japanese were unable to
understand the significance of the reprints that were found on so
many Russian prisoners but after it was translated into Japanese
and brought to the attention of the Mikado, he immediately directed
that copies be supplied to every member of his Imperial Army and
to all government employees.

Eventually translated into twenty languages, Hubbard's inspired

429

words have probably been read by more individuals than any other single article in history.

A Message to Garcia taught an entire generation some very important values, values that will always apply for those who seek true success ...

In all this Cuban business there is one man stands out on the horizon of my memory like Mars at perihelion.

When war broke out between Spain and the United States, it was very necessary to communicate quickly with the leader of the Insurgents. Garcia was somewhere in the mountain fastnesses of Cuba—no one knew where. No mail or telegraph message could reach him. The President must secure his cooperation, and quickly.

What to do!

Someone said to the President, "There is a fellow by the name of Rowan will find Garcia for you, if anybody can."

Rowan was sent for and given a letter to be delivered to Garcia. How the "fellow by the name of Rowan" took the letter, sealed it up in an oilskin pouch, strapped it over his heart, in four days landed by night off the Coast of Cuba from an open boat, disappeared into the jungle, and in three weeks came out on the other side of the island, having traversed a hostile country on foot, and delivered his letter to Garcia—are things I have no special desire now to tell in detail. The point that I wish to make is this: McKinley gave Rowan a letter to be delivered to Garcia; Rowan took the letter and did not ask, "Where is he at?"

By the Eternal! there is a man whose form should be cast in deathless bronze and the statue placed in every college of the land. It is not book-learning young men need, nor instruction about this and that, but a stiffening of the vertebrae which will cause them to be loyal to a trust, to act promptly, concentrate their energies: do the thing—"Carry a message to Garcia."

General Garcia is dead now, but there are other Garcias. No man who has endeavored to carry out an enterprise where many hands were needed, but has been well-nigh appalled at times by the imbecility of the average man—the inability or unwillingness to concentrate on a thing and do it.

Slipshod assistance, foolish inattention, dowdy indifference, and halfhearted work seem the rule; and no man succeeds, unless by hook or crook or threat he forces or bribes other men to assist him; or mayhap, God in His goodness performs a miracle, and sends him an Angel of Light for an assistant.

You, reader, put this matter to a test: you are sitting now in your office—six clerks are within call. Summon any one and make this request: "Please look in the encyclopedia and make a brief memorandum for me concerning the life of Correggio."

Will the clerk quietly say, "Yes, sir," and go do the task?

On your life he will not. He will look at you out of a fishy eye and ask one or more of the following questions:

- Who was he?
- Which encyclopedia?
- Where is the encyclopedia?
- Was I hired for that?
- Don't you mean Bismarck?
- What's the matter with Charlie doing it?
- Is he dead?
- Is there any hurry?
- Sha'n't I bring you the book and let you look it up yourself?
- What do you want to know for?

And I will lay you ten to one that after you have answered the questions, and explained how to find the information, and why you want it, the clerk will go off and get one of the other clerks to help him try to find Garcia—and then come back and tell you there is no such man. Of course I may lose my bet, but according to the Law of Average I will not.

Now, if you are wise, you will not bother to explain to your "assistant" that Correggio is indexed under the C's, not in the K's, but you will smile very sweetly and say, "Never mind," and go look it up yourself. And this incapacity for independent action, this moral stupidity, this infirmity of the will, this unwillingness to cheerfully catch hold and lift—these are the things that put pure Socialism so far into the future. If men will not act for themselves, what will they do when the benefit of their effort is for all?

A first mate with knotted club seems necessary; and the dread of getting "the bounce" Saturday night holds many a worker to his place. Advertise for a stenographer, and nine out of ten who apply can neither spell nor punctuate—and do not think it necessary to.

Can such a one write a letter to Garcia?

"You see that bookkeeper," said the foreman to me in a large factory.

"Yes; what about him?"

"Well, he's a fine accountant, but if I'd send him uptown on an errand, he might accomplish the errand all right, and on the other hand, might stop at four saloons on the way, and when he got to Main Street would forget what he had been sent for."

Can such a man be entrusted to carry a message to Garcia?

We have recently been hearing much maudlin sympathy expressed for the "downtrodden denizens of the sweatshop" and the "homeless wanderer searching for honest employment," and with it all often go many hard words for the men in power.

Nothing is said about the employer who grows old before his time in a vain attempt to get frowsy ne'er-do-wells to do intelligent work; and his long, patient striving after "help" that does nothing but loaf when his back is turned. In every store and factory there is a constant weeding out process going on. The employer is constantly sending away "help" who have shown their incapacity to further the interests of the business, and others are being taken on. No matter how good times are, this sorting continues: only, if times are hard and work is scarce, the sorting is done finer—but out and forever out the incompetent and unworthy go. It is the survival of the fittest. Self-interest prompts every employer to keep the best—those who can carry a message to Garcia.

I know one man of really brilliant parts who has not the ability to manage a business of his own, and yet who is absolutely worthless to anyone else, because he carries with him constantly the insane suspicion that his employer is oppressing, or intending to oppress, him. He cannot give orders, and he will not receive them. Should a message be given him to take to Garcia, his answer would probably be, "Take it yourself!"

Tonight this man walks the streets looking for work, the wind whistling through his threadbare coat. No one who knows him dare employ him, for he is a regular firebrand of discontent. He is impervious to reason, and the only thing that can impress him is the toe of a thick-soled Number Nine boot.

Of course, I know that one so morally deformed is no less to be pitied than a physical cripple; but in our pitying let us drop a tear, too, for the men who are striving to carry on a great enterprise, whose working hours are not limited by the whistle, and whose hair is fast turning white through the struggle to hold in line dowdy indifference, slipshod imbecility, and the heartless ingratitude which, but for their enterprise, would be both hungry and homeless.

Have I put the matter too strongly? Possibly I have; but when all the world has gone a-slumming I wish to speak a word of sympathy for the man who succeeds—the man who, against great odds, has directed the efforts of others, and having succeeded, find there's nothing in it: nothing but bare board and clothes. I have carried a dinner-pail and worked for day's wages, and I have also been an employer of labor, and I know there is something to be said on both sides. There is no excellence, per se, in poverty; rags are no recommendation; and all employers are not rapacious and high-handed, any more than all poor men are virtuous. My heart goes out to the man who does his work when the "boss" is away, as well as when he is at home. And the man who, when given a letter to Garcia, quietly takes the missive, without asking any idiotic questions, and with no lurking intention of chucking it into the nearest sewer, or of doing aught else but deliver it, never gets "laid off," nor has to go on a strike for higher wages. Civilization is one long, anxious search for just such individuals. Anything such a man asks shall be granted. He is wanted in every city, town, and village—in every office, shop, store, and factory. The world cries out for such; he is needed and needed badly—the man who can "carry a message to Garcia."

Six simple questions that will always
keep you from getting into any
situation that may be over your head.

J. Paul Getty

LESSON 43

HOW TO SEPARATE THE POSSIBLE
FROM THE IMPOSSIBLE

It has happened to nearly all of us at one time or another. An opportunity suddenly arises which seems to present great promise of financial gain or career advancement. Swept up by the excitement and enthusiasm of the situation we leap into the opening with little prior thought or evaluation on the chances of our succeeding— and we fall flat on our face! Sometimes we can look back on our disaster, if it was minor, and shrug it all off with a good laugh. But more often than not, the results of our ill-considered venture can leave scars of failure that remain with us throughout our life.

To accept new challenges and to constantly raise the horizon of your ambitions has been one of the basic premises of this university, primarily because it has long ago been established that all of us are utilizing only a small percentage of our talent. However most of us cannot, without some help and guidance, learn how to distinguish that fine line that divides the realm of possible from that of the impossible, and so we often stumble and fall, chastised and beaten, by undertakings we should have avoided.

J. Paul Getty had accumulated his first million dollars by the age of twenty-four. Four decades later he was being acclaimed as the richest man on earth, having built his fortune, worth more than a billion dollars, through his much-envied ability to evaluate any situation thoroughly before he invested either his time or money.

In this important lesson from his book, *The Golden Age,* Mr. Getty will teach you a simple technique that will enable you to weigh any opportunity that presents itself, against the resources

435

you have on hand so that you can increase your odds of making
the correct decision *before* you leap.

When was the last time you had a billionaire lecture you?

Unfortunately, even after the major initial obstacles and barriers
have been removed from the starting line, the route to a full and
happy life is still not a glassy-smooth superhighway. It still has its
detours, blind curves, crossroads, toll stations and, especially, its
regulatory restrictions.

Precious few individuals—be they philosophers or fools, mag-
nates or mendicants—are free to traverse the thoroughfare as they
please. At least, not as long as they encounter other traffic along
the road and find it necessary to coexist and interact with other
human beings.

True, here as ever there are some exceptions to the rule that
people must obey rules. One *can* take a cutoff to some remote
mountain fastness and there enjoy "total freedom"—but only at a
Stone Age level and only as long as one remains completely isolated
and self-sufficient. For at the moment the anchorite needs to
obtain so much as a crust, a scrap of cloth, or a nail from another
human being, he automatically surrenders a degree of his freedom
by making himself subject to terms and conditions set by another
person or by society as a whole.

Since there are not many among us harboring cravings for a
diet of roots and berries, a wardrobe of primitively cured animal
pelts, or an abode in a cave, it remains for the overwhelming
majority to acknowledge and respect the regulations, rules, and
realities of civilization. In order to qualify as functioning members
of our society, people therefore need to tolerate certain encroach-
ments on their individual liberties by that society. Failure to do so
results in penalties being exacted.

For instance, a citizen is forbidden—under pain of punishment—to commit burglary or bigamy, cheat or choke his neighbor,
fight a duel, or forge a deed. And, for that matter, the average
citizen is not even allowed absolute discretion in disposing of his
own personal earnings; appreciable portions of these are automatically deducted by, or must be handed over to, an array of tax
authorities.

Yes, certainly these and similar restrictions and regulations are intended to protect the safety and welfare of the citizenry and protect and preserve our social system and fabric. Nonetheless, in pure theory if naught else, these *are* infringements on the concept of Absolute Individual Freedom.

In all fairness, it must be admitted that the average person is aware of such circumscriptions and by and large submits to and abides by them without undue protest. But, paradoxically, he conforms even more voluntarily to many other less conspicuous, more sweeping, and decisive limitations which are imposed on us all, even though their very existence—to say nothing of their operative effects—are consciously recognized by only an insignificant minority.

As an example, while the average American enjoys great freedom of choice and decision in most areas of his activity, he is by no means an entirely free agent when it comes to setting the course of his life. He is subject to a profusion of forces, factors, and circumstances to which he must react and respond. And he barely, if at all, realizes that they obtain and operate, even though they frequently impel or compel his more important decisions and actions.

Those who might consider this debatable had best begin by recognizing that, in the course of their lifetimes, it is necessary for them to make many greater or lesser allowances and adjustments, compromises, and concessions merely to survive, and even more if they hope to rise above the faceless mass. Often, when confronted with a choice of options, they are forced to forego what would normally be their first selection and settle for, or on, alternatives or mediums—and only then may they proceed to make the most of them.

I know this all too well from my experience. As a youth, it was my ambition and desire to enter the United States Diplomatic Service and—when, as and if my career therein permitted—engage in a secondary vocation as a writer. I probably would have done so, too, had it not been for the seeming irrelevancy that I was an only child.

This made all—the decisive—difference. Someone would have to carry on the business my father, George F. Getty, had built up over many decades of hard and dedicated work. It wasn't that I was the best-suited or even logical candidate; it just so happened that I was the only one available.

I assure you, the idea of managing a fair-size and successful business was not only a far cry from my original ambitions, but a formidable and perturbing prospect. The attendant responsibilities and problems loomed large, heavy, and ominously burdensome.

But there were no emergency exits through which I could in good conscience evade them, particularly since my mother's security and welfare were also involved and at stake.

Consequently, I abandoned my cherished plans and made my career in the business world rather than in the Diplomatic Service. Once my decision was made, I allowed myself no masochistic luxuries of lingering regrets. I could ill have afforded them in view of the tasks that had to be undertaken.

Admittedly, the "game" was not my first choice, but one into which I had been sent as a substitute player by circumstances over which I had scant control. Nevertheless—and regardless of how I got there—I *was* in the game, and the starting whistle had blown. From then on, it behooved me to participate in it energetically and actively, and keep the ball in play.

Lest there be any misunderstandings, I hasten to disavow any intention of boasting or making claim to any virtues. I am merely using myself as a convenient example to support two contentions. First, that while an individual cannot always have or do what he wants most, he can nonetheless and assuredly adjust and acclimate himself to a reasonable alternative or rational medium. Second, he can still derive pleasure and satisfaction from his occupation and enjoyment from life and living.

Experience has shown me there is nothing more futile or senseless than to waste energy bemoaning and fulminating against the necessity for making compromises and concessions in life. One might just as well rant and rave against the laws prohibiting mayhem and murder because a weather forecaster wrongly predicted clear skies and a sudden cloudburst ruined a family picnic.

After all, seldom does an individual's acceptance of the inevitable equate with abject and unconditional surrender. Nor does it necessarily imply that he must thenceforth renounce his deep-seated aspirations and ambitions and condemn himself to utter despondency.

On the one hand, imaginative and resourceful individuals will broaden the base and structure of their situations to provide ample room and opportunity for realizing their ambitions and fulfilling their desires within the expanded framework. On the other hand, it's never "too late" for courageous and enterprising men and women to raise themselves out of what they consider ruts and switch to entirely different careers or develop new interests which will satisfy their innermost longings.

However, and in all events, it must be a foremost consideration that, for much of his adult lifetime, the average individual will move in two distinct, yet overlapping and interrelated, spheres of existence: the "vocational" (that which involves his work), and the personal. And, for good, bad or indifferent, any vocational or career situation is bound to exert significant and more or less formative pressures on an individual's overall life philosophy and living patterns.

A person who learns or absorbs nothing from, and remains blindly impervious to, an environment in which he or she spends forty or so hours each week is rare enough to be unique. It is extremely improbable that anyone can blot his or her "job" completely from mind upon leaving the office or passing through the factory gates. Practically everyone "talks shop" away from work; this alone would appear to prove that thoughts and impressions are "carried home." Whether these occupational influences are visibly prepotent or deceptively subtle depends on unnumbered factors, but they do unquestionably have their effects, and I rely on the glaringly simple and obvious for illustration.

An airline pilot flying the transatlantic run and an upper-bracket buyer for a department store are likely to receive comparable incomes, but it isn't very likely their philosophies and private lives will be similar. The night-shift machinist and midnight-to-dawn disc jockey both work odd hours, but each develops his own thinking and living patterns, and these, in turn, will have little resemblance to those of the corner druggist or local supermarket manager. A private secretary and a registered nurse are both women, and presumably both have similar basic feminine instincts and qualities, but I'm inclined to question if their viewpoints and perspectives—and their life patterns—will be anywhere near identical.

And, in my opinion, a goodly portion of these differences may be reasonably ascribed to the influences of work situations and experiences.

All things considered, I think most of us will, if we are honest about it, concede that human beings are not really as much the masters of their destinies and captains of their fate as it pleases them to believe. Yet no one can .deny that, within the limits imposed on them, they possess more than adequate freedom and latitude to make what they will—and are able to make—of themselves, their lives, and their careers.

Some, it is deplorable but true, will make nothing, advance nowhere, and be abject failures in either or both—and usually both—spheres of their existence solely because they refuse to make the requisite effort to do more or better. For these individuals, the rest of us need spare scarcely more than a casual glance, or, if we are so inclined, a glum shake of the head.

Others may make an honest and forceful effort but will fail due to intellectual or other shortcomings or even physical infirmities. These individuals are certainly deserving of understanding, sympathy and, where indicated and justified, a helping hand.

Yet others will achieve success—greater or lesser, depending no less on their own scales of measurement than on their abilities—in one or both spheres (and one hopes for their sake it will be in both). While they are often aided in some measure by others, their successes will still be due in large part to their own talents, efforts, and exertions.

However, it strikes me that before any individual begins striving in all-out earnest to attain his aspirations in life and work, he is entitled to receive a few words of rather unconventional caution.

Basing my opinion on years of observation and experience, I have come to the conclusion that almost as many individuals fail because they try to do too much as fail because they do not do enough.

Yes, I know. This sounds paradoxical and smacks of heresy. But, unfortunately, it is true of numerous people. Their basic weakness can be described very briefly. In whichever—or both—spheres of their existence, "vocational" or personal, they seek to achieve and accomplish, they are simply incapable of determining what is possible, within their capacity to reach, and what is impossible, or beyond their grasp, no matter how far they stretch.

They set their sights too high, and then, to their disappointment, see that their most carefully aimed shots have missed the mark.

All this reminds me of an executive—let us charitably call him by the fictitious name John Jones—who once, rather briefly, worked for one of the companies I control. Intelligent, well educated, with a very pleasant personality, a lovely family, and a good record in lesser executive jobs with other firms, he appeared suited for the responsible position to which he was appointed.

The honeymoon was short-lived. It wasn't long before it became apparent that John Jones was not only failing to move forward, but was falling farther and farther behind, dragging other company executives with him. The entire organization was floundering helplessly in a tidal wave of backlogged work, delayed projects, and customers' furious complaints.

It did not require much searching to locate the trouble. Either friend Jones's new job had gone to his head, or he was trying desperately to prove himself—with the net result that he lost all sense of proportion. He believed that he—and the organi-

zation he managed—could work miracles, do anything and everything in a preposterously short time. Whatever anyone wanted or
asked, he unhesitatingly promised—if not for tomorrow, then by
the day following, without fail. And so, harried and overtaxed
personnel were fighting a losing battle against the impossible.

Now, although I am basically a businessman and business
considerations should come first, I imagine I might have kept John
Jones on the payroll—after shifting him to a less responsible job.
He was in his mid-fifties, and I surmised that, with proper handling, he could still do a good job in some lower executive bracket.

I discarded all such notions quickly when it was revealed that
Jones had not only badly fumbled in his vocational sphere, but had
also made a thorough muddle of his personal life. He'd purchased
a house that cost at least twice what his income would justify—
with only a minimum down payment. He had been politely, but
firmly, asked to resign from the country club to which he belonged
after a series of nasty incidents. He was even deeper in debt than
he was in uncompleted work and, quiet inquiry disclosed, Jones
was a tyrant and terror to his wife and children. John Jones's
resignation was demanded—and accepted even before his inked
signature was dry.

If anything sets this sad and sorry saga apart from its countless counterparts in all fields, it is the contradiction of the accepted—
and generally valid—logic that maturity and seasoning reduce the
chances of such near-catastrophic errors. Having passed the 50
mark, Jones was mature enough, I would say. He'd gone through
the mills of both home life and business life. Married for 22 years,
he had 3 children: 19, 16, and 14. His past employment record was
spotless, reflecting a steady if not spectacular climb. These experiences should have produced a thoroughly seasoned person and
business executive. I suppose there is no entirely satisfactory explanation except that he came, he saw—and he was conquered by his
own weaknesses.

But never fear, there are plenty of other John Joneses about,
and if they serve any constructive purpose, it is as unmistakable
stop-look-and-listen warnings to individuals who desire to enjoy
life and get ahead in their work.

Anyone aspiring to succeed in the personal and vocational
spheres of existence must constantly weigh, measure, gauge, and
evaluate to determine what can—and cannot—be accomplished
under the circumstances that prevail and the resources that are
available. In brief, it is essential to separate the wheat of the
possible from the chaff of the impossible in both spheres.

The ability to distinguish the frequently extremely fine line that divides the realm of the possible from that of the impossible is rarely an innate trait. It is acquired partially by a process of trial and error, but mainly—or so one hopes—through development of the powers of reasoning and judgment. However, the following questions might help some as jumping-off points for thought and consideration:

- What am I trying to accomplish?
- Why do I think what I want to do is possible?
- What causes me to think it might be impossible?
- What do I stand to gain—or to lose?
- Will such factors as my age, stamina, or health have any bearing on the outcome—and, conversely, can I suffer any adverse physical effects by battling the idea (or project or whatever) through?
- Could I utilize my time, efforts, and energies to better advantage in other directions?

These, of course, are only suggestions, offered as potential brain stimulators. The final decision rests with the individual involved.

Apropos of the various matters I've covered, I would like to relate what I regard as a uniquely appropriate and illuminating anecdote.

Some years ago, I was the dinner guest of a man renowned for his broad intellectual and cultural interests and pursuits, boundless energy, *joie de vivre* and financial success. He was then 75, but looked 20 years younger, swam and took long walks daily and positively abhorred the thought of ever going to bed before 2:00 A.M.

After dinner, he—and we who were his guests—went into the drawing room. Among those present was a syndicated newspaper columnist unabashedly eager to combine business with pleasure and obtain "human interest" material for one of his articles. He began chatting with our host, politely complimenting him on his notable accomplishments, high honors, and astonishing vigor, and then deftly transformed the conversation into an interview.

"Sir, you've achieved so many successes, press and public call you a genius. Do you consider yourself to be one?" the journalist asked.

"Good Lord, no!" was the laughing—and indubitably sincere—reply. "That is, not unless the fact that I long ago recognized some fundamental truths—which, by the way, are available to everyone—constitutes 'genius.'"

"And exactly what are those 'fundamental truths'?" came the next—and predictable question.

The answer was straightforward, good-natured and, probably because we'd all finished eating only a few minutes earlier, couched in gastronomically oriented figures of speech.

"I'd say there are four. First, a person isn't always able to find every dish he wants on the menu. Second, he can nonetheless usually find enough of a variety to satisfy both his hunger and his palate. Third, while eating, he should obey the old axiom and never bite off more than he can chew. Fourth, this, however, should not prevent him from taking healthy mouthfuls—for any food worth eating should be *eaten*, not toyed with or nibbled in a finicky fashion."

To my way of thinking, these alimentary metaphors deserve to be committed to memory. At some crucial moment, each will prove to be an invaluable guideline for life and living.

All of them have done so for me.

Many times.

Dr. David Seabury

LESSON 44

HOW TO CONTROL YOUR ENEMIES

There is an old Italian proverb which states, "Have you fifty friends? It is not enough. Have you one enemy? It is too much." No one can dispute the wisdom of those words and yet it is virtually impossible for you to achieve success in any form without acquiring a collection of individuals who would rejoice in your downfall. Even the most loving of achievers such as Jesus, Ghandi, and Lincoln had those who plotted against them.

Enemies, of course, can sometimes be valuable. Usually they will come nearer to the truth in the opinions they form of us than those we carry of ourselves and so we can learn from them. But for the most part they are dangerous to our future and we must learn how to deal with them at the least possible risk to ourselves.

There ought to be something on the human side as efficient as machine guns to defend us against the horde of bothers that crowd us in office, home, and street. We've been oppressed too long. We'd like some way to overcome the odds of a greedy world.

Are there any? None, according to the pessimists. You must bear your burdens, cry the moralists. It's that kind of world, sophisticates maintain.

I'm not convinced, however, that the intelligence which split the atom and is sending man into outer space is incapable of discovering ways to live more easily.

Those are the words of David Seabury in the revised edition of his self-help classic, *The Art of Selfishness,* from which this lesson was taken. A best-seller in 1937, this amazing book has

been in print ever since and it continues to shock and stimulate
thousands each year.

Control your enemies? You can do it, without the use of force.
There's a much more effective technique, insists Dr. Seabury ...

Man is born to survive. Though his end is inevitable, there is no
reason why his life can't be a long and pleasant one. There is only
one thing that gets in his way. He has learned to protect himself
against nature; he is gradually winning the battle against disease
and time; but he has not yet learned how to defend himself against
the envy, greed, malice, and selfishness of other men.

Is it sinful to protect yourself against attack?

To sentimentalists, still imbued with infantile ideals, self-
defense seems selfish. They would have you believe that "fighting
back" is a violation of our hereditary morality (which many preach,
but few practice).

Those of us who disagree with this supine spirit believe that
one of the greatest duties of every living creature is to act in such a
way that evil forces have less and less chance to destroy the good
powers of life. If we let them run rampant, there is no hope.

The problem of enmity goes to the very core of the newer
ethics. Two principles have ruled in the older philosophies. In
one, you used violent means, venting your rage, satisfying your
vindictiveness, conquering by fury. In the other, you allowed evil
to conquer you.

Gandhi once practiced this passive method. I doubt its value
to occidentals. Constructive nonresistance, however, an active cam-
paign to overcome the enemy by positive means, is a third and
middle way of dealing with evil. Let your antagonist destroy himself. Find some means of overpowering him without using force. A
sort of *mental* judo or karate.

Don't fight for the sake of fighting. Don't fight to inflate your
ego. Don't fight to exalt your pride. Don't fight to overcome your
adversary or to punish him. Fight only to win a larger end, and
fight without fighting—incongruous as that seems. Strive for the
positive force, the impelling power that will be invincible in overcoming your trouble. For example, a man once threatened to beat
me in order to change my mind. He meant it, too, but before he
started, I said quietly: "After we are through fighting, my mind

won't be changed. You can kill me; you can't convince me. You'll remember this when resting in jail." My firmness overcame his rage. We didn't fight.

I do not mean to suggest that everyone can eliminate any trouble by constructive nonresistance the first time the method is applied. If practiced until one is skillful in its handling, however, it accomplishes miracles. You seldom need to attack if you use your wits.

It has long been said that if you give a man enough rope he will hang himself. Give an enemy scope and he will cause his own failure. He'll do it by revealing some point for you to use as a checkmating factor.

A woman once had few neighbors that her husband liked, but many she was fond of. He also denied her a servant, though they could afford one. She found her housework hard. Her predicament made her sad until it occurred to her that one ill might cure another.

"Isn't it lovely," she then remarked with regularity. "I don't have to keep my house up as other women do, for we have no one to visit us and so it doesn't matter." Shocked by the slovenly condition of the place, her husband hired a housekeeper and brought the neighbors in, so determined was he not to live in a hovel.

Notice that by this method you *win by yielding*. Give up nonessentials while you strive for your purposes. Maintain your convictions, but not the petty values that hinder their consummation. Only the egotist asks a smooth path.

Franklin Delano Roosevelt knew the secret of controlling his enemies. When a balky senator stood in the way of some vital legislation, he discovered that the senator was a rabid stamp collector, and he used that knowledge to great advantage. One night, when he was working on his own stamp collection, FDR phoned the senator and asked for his help. The senator, flattered, came over that evening; they worked together for awhile—and the next day, when a roll-call vote was taken on the bill, the senator voted for it. The lesson here is an important one. At no time during that philatelic session had either man mentioned their differences over the bill. They had simply gotten to know each other better, and the "enemy" had become a "friend."

Sometimes an enemy is a bully—and needs no more than a show of strength to give him pause. This is as true of individuals as it is of nations. Courage and conviction are powerful weapons against an enemy who depends only on fists or guns. Animals know when you are afraid; a coward knows when you are not.

*Among the greatest of human tragedies
are the wasted lives of those who
fail, after enjoying success, and lose
their desire to ever try again.*

Frederick Van Rensselaer Day

LESSON 45

HOW TO BOUNCE BACK
FROM FAILURE

"The Magic Story" first appeared in the December 1900, issue of the original *Success Magazine*. It created an immediate sensation and after urgent requests were made for its reprint, in book form, a small edition of a little silver-gray book was published.

Divided in two parts, Part One related the story of a down-and-out starving artist named Sturtevant whose life suddenly changed for the better after he purchased an old scrapbook for three cents and found, within its covers, what he called "a magic story" written by an unknown author. After telling the story to many of his friends, who all benefited from its message, Sturtevant dispatched one who had not been included in his many tellings to his apartment so that he could read the story in private.

That friend reported,

I found the book without difficulty. It was a quaint, homemade affair, covered as Sturtevant had said, with rawhide, and bound with leather thongs. The pages formed an odd combination of yellow paper, vellum, and homemade parchment. The story was curiously printed on the last-named material. It was quaint and strange. Evidently the printer had "set" it under the supervision of the writer. The phraseology was an unusual combination of seventeenth- and eighteenth-century manner-isms, and the interpolations of italics and capitals could have originated in no other brain than that of its author.

"In reproducing the following story," the friend wrote, "the peculiarities of type, spelling, and so forth, are eliminated, but in other respects it remains unchanged."

This lesson, Part Two of *The Magic Story,* by Frederick Van Rensselaer Day, contains the entire text of what was printed on those homemade parchment pages. Someday the words may be as important to you as they once were to Sturtevant ...

Inasmuch as I have evolved from my experience the one great secret of success for all worldly undertakings, I deem it wise, now that the number of my days is nearly counted, to give to the generations that are to follow me the benefit of whatsoever knowledge I possess. I do not apologize for the manner of my expression, nor for lack of literary merit, the latter being, I wot, its own apology. Tools much heavier than the pen have been my portion, and, moreover, the weight of years has somewhat palsied hand and brain; nevertheless, the fact I can tell, and that I deem the meat within the nut. What mattereth it, in what manner the shell be broken, so that the meat be obtained and rendered useful? I doubt not that I shall use, in the telling, expressions that have clung to my memory since childhood; for, when men attain the number of my years, happenings of youth are like to be clearer to their perceptions than are events of recent date; nor doth it matter much how a thought is expressed, if it be wholesome and helpful, and findeth the understanding.

Much have I wearied my brain anent the question, how best to describe this recipe for success that I have discovered, and it seemeth advisable to give it as it came to me; that is, if I relate somewhat of the story of my life, the directions for agglomerating the substances, and supplying the seasoning for the accomplishment of the dish, will plainly be perceived. Happen they may; and that men may be born generations after I am dust, who will live to bless me for the words I write.

My father, then, was a seafaring man who, early in life, forsook his vocation, and settled on a plantation in the colony of Virginia, where, some years thereafter, I was born, which event took place in the year 1642; and that was over a hundred years ago. Better for my father had it been, had he hearkened to the wise advice of my mother, that he remain in the calling of his education; but he would not have it so, and the good vessel he captained was bartered for the land I spoke of. Here beginneth the first lesson to be acquired:—

Man should not be blinded to whatsoever merit exists in the opportunity which he hath in hand, remembering that a thousand promises for the future should weigh as naught against the possession of a single piece of silver.

When I had achieved ten years, my mother's soul took flight, and two years thereafter my worthy father followed her. I, being their only begotten, was left alone; howbeit, there were friends who, for a time, cared for me; that is to say, they offered me a home beneath their roof,—a thing which I took advantage of for the space of five months. From my father's estate there came to me naught; but, in the wisdom that came with increasing years, I convinced myself that his friend, under whose roof I lingered for some time, had defrauded him, and therefore me.

Of the time from the age of twelve and a half until I was three and twenty, I will make no recital here, since that time hath naught to do with this tale; but some time after, having in my possession the sum of sixteen guineas, ten, which I had saved from the fruits of my labor, I took ship to Boston town, where I began work first as a cooper, and thereafter as a ship's carpenter, although always after the craft was docked; for the sea was not amongst my desires.

Fortune will sometimes smile upon an intended victim because of pure perversity of temper. Such was one of my experiences. I prospered, and, at seven and twenty, owned the yard wherein, less than four years earlier, I had worked for hire. Fortune, howbeit, is a jade who must be coerced; she will not be coddled. Here beginneth the second lesson to be acquired:

Fortune is ever elusive, and can only be retained by force. Deal with her tenderly and she will forsake you for a stronger man. [In that, methinks, she is not unlike other women of my knowledge.]

About this time, Disaster (which is one of the heralds of broken spirits and lost resolve), paid me a visit. Fire ravaged my yards, leaving nothing in its blackened paths but debts, which I had not the coin wherewith to defray. I labored with my acquaintances, seeking assistance for a new start, but the fire that had burned my competence, seemed also to have consumed their sympathies. So it happened, within a short time, that not only had I lost all, but I was hopelessly indebted to others; and for that they cast me into prison. It is possible that I might have rallied from my losses but for this last indignity, which broke down my spirits so that I became utterly despondent. Upward of a year was I detained within the jail; and, when I did come forth, it was not the same hopeful, happy man, content with his lot, and with confidence in the world and its people, who had entered there.

Life has many pathways, and of them by far the greater number lead downward. Some are precipitous, others are less abrupt; but ultimately, no matter at what inclination the angle may be fixed, they arrive at the same destination,—failure. And here beginneth the third lesson:

Failure exists only in the grave. Man, being alive, hath not yet failed; always he may turn about and ascend by the same path he descended by; and there may be one that is less abrupt (albeit longer of achievement), and more adaptable to his condition.

When I came forth from prison, I was penniless. In all the world I possessed naught beyond the poor garments which covered me, and a walking stick which the turnkey had permitted me to retain, since it was worthless. Being a skilled workman, howbeit, I speedily found employment at good wages; but, having eaten of the fruit of worldly advantage, dissatisfaction possessed me. I became morose and sullen; whereat, to cheer my spirits, and for the sake of forgetting the losses I had sustained, I passed my evenings at the tavern. Not that I drank overmuch of liquor, except on occasion (for I have ever been somewhat abstemious), but that I could laugh and sing, and parry wit and *badinage* with my ne'er-do-well companions; and here might be included the fourth lesson:

Seek comrades among the industrious, for those who are idle will sap your energies from you.

It was my pleasure at that time to relate, upon slight provocation, the tale of my disasters, and to rail against the men whom I deemed to have wronged me, because they had seen fit not to come to my aid. Moreover, I found childish delight in filching from my employer, each day, a few moments of the time for which he paid me. Such a thing is less honest than downright theft.

This habit continued and grew upon me until the day dawned which found me not only without employment, but also without character, which meant that I could not hope to find work with any other employer in Boston town.

It was then that I regarded myself a failure. I can liken my condition at that time for naught more similar than that of a man who, descending the steep side of a mountain, loses his foothold. The farther he slides, the faster he goes. I have also heard this condition described by the word Ishmaelite, which I understand to be a man whose hand is against everybody, and who thinks that

the hands of every other man are against him; and here beginneth
the fifth lesson:

The Ishmaelite and the leper are the same, since both are
abominations in the sight of man,—albeit they differ much, in that
the former may be restored to perfect health. The former is entirely
the result of imagination; the latter has poison in his blood.

I will not discourse at length upon the gradual degeneration
of my energies. It is not meet ever to dwell much upon misfortunes (which saying is also worthy of remembrance). It is enough if
I add that the day came when I possessed naught wherewith to
purchase food and raiment, and I found myself like unto a pauper,
save at infrequent times when I could earn a few pence, or,
mayhap, a shilling. Steady employment I could not secure, so I
became emaciated in body, and naught but a skeleton in spirit.

My condition, then, was deplorable; not so much for the
body, be it said, as for the mental part of me, which was sick unto
death. In my imagination I deemed myself ostracised by the whole
world, for I had sunk very low indeed; and here beginneth the
sixth and final lesson to be acquired, (which cannot be told in one
sentence, nor in one paragraph, but must needs be adapted from
the remainder of this tale).

Well do I remember my awakening, for it came in the night,
when, in truth, I did awake from sleep. My bed was a pile of
shavings in the rear of the cooper shop where once I had worked
for hire; my roof was the pyramid of casks, underneath which I had
established myself. The night was cold, and I was chilled, albeit,
paradoxically, I had been dreaming of light and warmth and of the
repletion of good things. You will say, when I relate the effect the
vision had on me, that my mind was affected. So be it, for it is the
hope that the minds of others might be likewise influenced which
disposes me to undertake the labor of this writing. It was the
dream which converted me to the belief—nay, to the knowledge,
—that I was possessed of two identities; and it was my own better
self that afforded me the assistance for which I had pleaded in vain
from my acquaintances. I have heard this condition described by
the word "double." Nevertheless, that word does not comprehend
my meaning. A double can be naught more than a double, neither
half being possessed of individuality. But I will not philosophize,
since philosophy is naught but a suit of garments for the decoration
of a dummy figure.

Moreover, it was not the dream itself which affected me; it
was the impression made by it, and the influence that it exerted
over me, which accomplished my enfranchisement. In a word,

then, I encouraged my other identity. After toiling through a tempest of snow and wind, I peered into a window and saw that other being. He was rosy with health; before him, on the hearth, blazed a fire of logs; there was conscious power and force in his demeanor; he was physically and mentally muscular. I rapped timidly upon the door, and he bade me enter. There was a not unkindly smile of derision in his eyes as he motioned me to a chair by the fire; but he uttered no word of welcome; and, when I had warmed myself, I went forth again into the tempest, burdened with the shame which the contrast between us had forced upon me. It was then that I awoke; and here cometh the strange part of my tale, for, when I did awake, I was not alone. There was a Presence with me; intangible to others, I discovered later, but real to me.

The Presence was in my likeness, yet was it strikingly unlike. The brow, not more lofty than my own, yet seemed more round and full; the eyes, clear, direct, and filled with purpose, glowed with enthusiasm and resolution; the lips, chin,—ay, the whole contour of face and figure was dominant and determined.

He was calm, steadfast, and self-reliant; I was cowering, filled with nervous trembling, and fearsome of intangible shadows. When the Presence turned away, I followed, and throughout the day I never lost sight of it, save when it disappeared for a time beyond some doorway where I dared not enter; at such places, I awaited its return with trepidation and awe, for I could not help wondering at the temerity of the Presence (so like myself, and yet so unlike), in daring to enter where my own feet feared to tread.

It seemed also as if purposely, I was led to the place and to the men where, and before whom I most dreaded to appear; to offices where once I had transacted business; to men with whom I had financial dealings. Throughout the day I pursued the Presence, and at evening saw it disappear beyond the portals of a hostelry famous for its cheer and good living. I sought the pyramid of casks and shavings.

Not again in my dreams that night did I encounter the Better Self (for that is what I have named it), albeit, when, perchance, I awakened from slumber, it was near to me, ever wearing that calm smile of kindly derision which could not be mistaken for pity, nor for condolence in any form. The contempt of it stung me sorely.

The second day was not unlike the first, being a repetition of its forerunner, and I was again doomed to wait outside during the visits which the Presence paid to places where I fain would have gone had I possessed the requisite courage. It is fear which deporteth a man's soul from his body and rendereth it a thing to be despised.

Many a time I essayed to address it but enunciation rattled in my throat, unintelligible; and the day closed like its predecessor.

This happened many days, one following another, until I ceased to count them; albeit, I discovered that constant association with the Presence was producing an effect upon me; and one night, when I awoke among the casks and discerned that he was present, I made bold to speak, albeit with marked timidity.

"Who are you?" I ventured to ask; and I was startled into an upright posture by the sound of my own voice; and the question seemed to give pleasure to my companion, so that I fancied there was less of derision in his smile when he responded.

"I am that I am," was the reply. "I am he who you have been; I am he who you may be again; wherefore do you hesitate? I am he who you were, and whom you have cast out for other company. I am the man made in the image of God, who once possessed your body. Once we dwelt within it together, not in harmony, for that can never be, nor yet in unity, for that is impossible, but as tenants in common who rarely fought for full possession. Then, you were a puny thing, but you became selfish and exacting until I could no longer abide with you, wherefore I stepped out. There is a plus-entity and a minus-entity in every human body which is born into the world. Whichever one of these is favored by the flesh becomes dominant; then is the other inclined to abandon its habitation, temporarily or for all time. I am the plus-entity of yourself; you are the minus-entity. I own all things; you possess naught. That body which we both inhabited is mine, but it is unclean, and I will not dwell within it. Cleanse it, and I will take possession."

"Why do you pursue me?" I next asked of the Presence.

"You have pursued me, not I you. You can exist without me for a time, but your path leads downward, and the end is death. Now that you approach the end, you debate if it be not politic that you should cleanse your house and invite me to enter. Step aside, then, from the brain and the will; cleanse them of your presence; only on that condition will I ever occupy them again."

"The brain hath lost its power," I faltered. "The will is a weak thing, now; can you repair them?"

"Listen!" said the Presence, and he towered over me while I cowered abjectly at his feet. "To the plus-entity of a man, all things are possible. The world belongs to him,—is his estate. He fears naught, dreads naught, stops at naught; he asks no privileges, but demands them; he *dominates*, and cannot cringe; his requests are orders; opposition flees at his approach; he levels mountains, fills in vales, and travels on an even plane where stumbling is unknown."

Thereafter, I slept again, and, when I awoke, I seemed to be in a different world. The sun was shining and I was conscious that birds twittered above my head. My body, yesterday trembling and uncertain, had become vigorous and filled with energy. I gazed upon the pyramid of casks in amazement that I had so long made use of it for an abiding place, and I was wonderingly conscious that I had passed my last night beneath its shelter.

The events of the night recurred to me, and I looked about me for the Presence. It was not visible, but anon I discovered, cowering in a far corner of my resting place, a puny, abject, shuddering figure, distorted of visage, deformed of shape, disheveled and unkempt of appearance. It tottered as it walked, for it approached me piteously; but I laughed aloud, mercilessly. Perchance I knew then that it was the minus-entity, and that the plus-entity was within me; albeit I did not then realize it. Moreover, I was in haste to get away; I had no time for philosophy. There was much for me to do,—much; strange it was that I had not thought of that yesterday. But yesterday was gone,—today was with me,—it had just begun.

As had once been my daily habit, I turned my steps in the direction of the tavern, where formerly I had partaken of my meals. I nodded cheerily as I entered, and smiled in recognition of returned salutations. Men who had ignored me for months bowed graciously when I passed them on the thoroughfare. I went to the washroom, and from there to the breakfast table; afterward when I passed the taproom, I paused a moment and said to the landlord:

"I will occupy the same room that I formerly used, if, perchance, you have it at disposal. If not, another will do as well, until I can obtain it."

Then I went out and hurried with all haste to the cooperage. There was a huge wain in the yard, and men were loading it with casks for shipment. I asked no questions, but, seizing barrels, began hurling them to the men who worked atop of the load. When this was finished, I entered the shop. There was a vacant bench; I recognized its disuse by the litter on its top. It was the same at which I had once worked. Stripping off my coat, I soon cleared it of *impedimenta*. In a moment more I was seated, with my foot on the vice-lever, shaving staves.

It was an hour later when the master workman entered the room, and he paused in surprise at sight of me; already there was a goodly pile of neatly shaven staves beside me, for in those days I was an excellent workman; there was none better, but, alas! now, age hath deprived me of my skill. I replied to his unasked question with the brief, but comprehensive sentence: "I have returned to work, sir." He nodded his head and passed on, viewing the work of other men, albeit anon he glanced askance in my direction.

Here ends the sixth and last lesson to be acquired, although there is more to be said, since from that moment I was a successful man, and ere long possessed another shipyard, and had acquired a full competence of worldly goods.

I pray you who read, heed well the following admonitions, since upon them depend the word "success" and all that it implies:

Whatsoever you desire of good is yours. You have but to stretch forth your hand and take it.

Learn that the consciousness of dominant power within you is the possession of all things attainable.

Have no fear of any sort or shape, for fear is an adjunct of the minus-entity.

If you have skill, apply it; the world must profit by it, and, therefore, you.

Make a daily and nightly companion of your plus-entity; if you heed its advice, you cannot go wrong.

Remember, philosophy is an argument; the world, which is your property, is an accumulation of facts.

Go, therefore, and do that which is within you to do; take no heed of gestures which would beckon you aside; *ask of no man permission to perform.*

The minus-entity requests favors; the plus-entity grants them. Fortune waits upon every footstep you take; seize her, bind her, hold her, for she is yours; she belongs to you.

Start out now, with these admonitions in your mind. Stretch out your hand, and grasp the plus, which, maybe, you have never made use of, save in grave emergencies. Life is an emergency most grave.

Your plus-entity is beside you now; cleanse your brain, and strengthen your will. It will take possession. It waits upon you.

Start to-night; start now upon this new journey.

Be always on your guard. Whichever entity controls you, the other hovers at your side; beware lest the evil enter, even for a moment.

My task is done. I have written the recipe for "success." If followed, it cannot fail. Wherein I may not be entirely comprehended, the plus-entity of whosoever reads will supply the deficiency; and upon that Better Self of mine, I place the burden of imparting to generations that are to come, the secret of this all-pervading good,—*the secret of being what you have it within you to be.*

SEMESTER TEN

It is not how much we have, but how much
we enjoy, that makes happiness.

Charles Spurgeon

*When you become caught up in the heady pursuit
of success you always run the risk of losing
far more than you gain unless you are careful.*

Dr. Allan Fromme

LESSON 46

HOW TO PREVENT YOUR SUCCESS
FROM TURNING INTO ASHES

In that great winter of discontent—1929—an important meeting was held at Chicago's Edgewater Beach Hotel. Around the conference table sat eight of the world's most important financiers, men whose desires and decisions affected the lives of half the world's population. They were:

- The president of the largest steel company
- The president of the largest utility company
- The president of the largest gas company
- The president of the New York Stock Exchange
- A member of the United States Cabinet
- The greatest speculator on Wall Street
- The chairman of the world's greatest monopoly
- The president of the Bank for International Settlements

Certainly we must admit that gathered here were a group of the world's most successful men, men who obviously had found the "secret" of achieving wealth and power.

Twenty-five years later Charles Schwab was dead, bankrupt. Samuel Insull was a penniless fugitive from justice. Howard Hopson was insane. Richard Whitney served time in Sing Sing. Albert Fall was pardoned from prison so he could die at home. Jesse Livermore was a suicide. Ivan Krueger was a suicide. Leon Fraser—suicide.

Something strange invariably happens to most of us as we approach our goals. Our values become twisted. We become blinded by the gold in our hands. We leave behind us, in our onrushing upward scramble, bodies of spouses and children who had loved

461

and depended on us—and the success we strained to reach with so much of our mind and body becomes little more than ashes.

It need not be that way! In this lesson, taken from his stirring book, *The Ability to Love,* Dr. Allan Fromme, distinguished author and psychotherapist, points out the options that are available to you so that you can be permanently on guard against the traps that have snared so many others who became "successes" in name only . . .

W e all love things—material things that cost money. We love them so much they actually become a significant part of our love life. All we have to do is listen to people to hear them assert this love again and again. "I'd love to have a new car." "I'd love a fur coat." "We love our new home." Are they using the word "love" differently when they speak this way? The answer is an emphatic "no." We may commonly link love with romance, sex, marriage. But love is an attachment and it does not limit itself to an involvement exclusively with people.

In these materialistic reveries, people not only reveal their desires but, because these desires are strong and recurrent, they simultaneously suggest how absorbed they are and how much they might do to obtain these things. This absorption may occupy even more of their time, thought, and energy than their love of a particular person. No one ever says so outright but acquisitiveness and the status many seek to derive from it could become their major love.

We like to think of ourselves as capable of great love in the romantic sense as opposed to this crass acquisitive addiction. And it is true that we are eminently capable of dreams, desires, and even some of the most tender feelings for someone who "walks in beauty like the night." But few of us enjoy enough freedom from nagging forces within us and potent social forces around us not to respond strongly to the attraction of ownership. We see this early in the life of the child when, by the age of four or five, he begins every other sentence with the same phrase, namely, "I want" or "Give me." Many of us never get over this.

WHAT THINGS DO FOR US

The culture of our Western world has, of course, placed a high value on acquisition. Nor is this a recent development. It has been going on for centuries. Possessions held in abundance give us status. And this does something for us psychologically. Most people find it a lot easier to feel secure at the wheel of a gleaming new expensive automobile than they feel in a battered old one. Many a man spends more time on a Sunday polishing and caressing the automobile of which he is so proud than he spends with his wife. Possessions and position do help blunt the sting of anxiety from which we all suffer in varying degree. They even give us the illusion of unconditional love, or if not love, at least approval for which we all unconsciously yearn from early childhood.

To put it simply and directly, things satisfy us and in this satisfaction the largest component is generally self-love. Our first step in learning to love is self-love, and that self-love is the love we know best for the first years of life. We never relinquish our infantile self-love entirely, although we learn to transform it, to sublimate it, in ways that bring us more adult satisfactions.

The drive for wealth and status and the consequent public approval offer direct satisfaction for infantile self-love. It creates no complications, makes no demands on us to consider the needs and wants of another human being. We do not have to consider anybody to win this general approval. We need only to consider ourselves and acquire things. After awhile, our acquisitions become part of us—an indistinguishable part of us—so that we come to feel bigger, more important as a result of them.

Things have a tangibility that makes the ethereal quality of love seem pale and elusive. We are taught to believe that "he who steals my purse steals trash," but we take good care not to be robbed. We use locks and burglar alarms and we take out insurance besides. And we become suspicious of love itself. Many a person wonders whether he is loved for himself or his money.

Love may be inconstant, unreliable. We discovered that as children, and some of us rediscover it as adults. Possessions, on the other hand, are reliable, barring a stock market crash or a business failure. They do not return our love, but neither do they give us harsh words, or run off with someone else.

They also lend themselves to mathematical enumeration. They can be counted, cataloged, and their value added up in cold cash. How do you count or measure love? Elizabeth Barrett tried, in a sonnet that she wrote to Robert Browning:

How do I love thee? Let me count the ways.
I love thee to the depth and breadth and height
My soul can reach . . .

She went on in this vein, and it is a beautiful sonnet, but at the end all we know is that she was very much in love.

We are told, and only half in jest, that we all have problems and money will not cure them, but if we must have problems it is better to worry about them in the back of a Cadillac. They will be much less painful. We are also told that since we must work anyway we may as well do a good job of it and make as much money out of it as we can. There is just enough hard practical sense in all this to be persuasive.

BACK TO THE LOVER

In order to understand love, it is the lover who must be understood. The lover himself is easily shaped by many influences, creating many attachments, which crowd out the love he believes is primary in his life. For many people, the love between a man and a woman gets to be like the book they have been promising themselves to read or the letter they have been meaning to write. Somehow, despite the genuineness of their desires, the goodness of their intentions, things get in the way.

The reasons for this are many. In the first place as members of society it behooves us to act like others. And we do. We spend the greater part of our waking hours engaged in the mechanics of living. This consists of earning a living or cooking, cleaning, saving, and purchasing the things we require for our everyday life. So little time is left for love, entertainment, self-education, or play that we easily become more proficient at work.

Secondly, although we may become attracted to someone for a variety of reasons, the love we develop is one of the ways we reduce the feelings of anxiety we all have. Other ways of anxiety reduction are even more available. Many things which serve as a buffer and protection from what we dread can simply be bought. All we need is the money. And there are countless ways we are spurred on to make money.

THE TIMELESS CONFLICT

These two ways of allaying anxiety have been in conflict from time immemorial. By Jesus's time the conflict was already old, for it was he who emphasized that we love our neighbor as ourselves and that a camel could go through the eye of a needle sooner than a rich man could enter heaven. And Jesus followed his own precept. According to St. Matthew, when Satan led him to a high mountain and promised him the world and all its glories, Jesus turned from it and answered, "Get thee hence, Satan."

Although Jesus succeeded in gaining our confidence on the importance of loving one another, he was less successful in teaching us to abstain from loving material things. John Calvin, a religious leader of far less note, fifteen hundred years later taught a different doctrine. Seeking to strip religion of its panoply and ritual, and simplify it to its essentials, he preached that industry and thrift made a man acceptable in the eyes of the Lord.

In the wealthy city of Geneva where Calvin preached, this was a most appealing precept, and events of the following centuries strengthened its influence. Inherited nobility and power perished in the American and French revolutions, and with the Industrial Revolution of the next century, wealth and status came within reach of everyone. A man could be born a nobody, but if he followed Calvin's teachings, worked hard, and used his earnings prudently, one day he would be rich and respected. He would have the status of an honorable man.

The word "status" is often on our lips today but it is not new. The man who introduced it into American thinking was Thorstein Veblen, a highly original economist of the first quarter of the century. His book, *The Theory of the Leisure Class*, was a searching critique of the drive to acquisition and status, which until then had been respectable beyond question.

He examined the behavior of people who subscribed to the doctrine of working hard and spending prudently, and he discovered that they were not nearly so rational as they believed. They believed that they bought what they needed and what they liked; that is, that the consumption of goods was rationally motivated by physical and aesthetic wants. A man might think he bought an overcoat to keep him warm, thus satisfying a physical want, and that he bought one coat rather than another because it looked better on him, satisfying an aesthetic want. Not so, said Veblen. A man bought his coat and also his house, furniture, horse, carriage, not out of these rational wants but out of the motive of emulation. He was seeking to win the same attention and respect that was accorded to men who already had such possessions.

This pattern of social behavior was not born in the United States, but it was especially easy to trace in a land where many men had begun side by side with an equal lack of resources. Out of a number of men who settled, for example, at the same period on the same rich land in Indiana, one man after a decade might have a flourishing farm, many head of cattle, a fine house and barns, while his neighbors were still only moderately well off and some remained poor and struggling. Naturally the man who had done so well won the respect of the community. People saw in him superior ability. They went to him for advice, listened respectfully to his opinions at the town meeting, voted for him as a church elder and a school trustee. His possessions proved his superiority and he was honored for it.

Once possessions became the basis for popular esteem, by a psychological transition they also became the basis for self-esteem. So far the pattern seems logical and rational. But then Veblen observed a most irrational reversal. Instead of saving thriftily what they had worked so hard to gain so that they could have many possessions and hence much popular and self-esteem, people tended to spend their money in a most reckless fashion.

MONEY: A SHOWCASE FOR THE SELF

Yet this was not so irrational as it seemed. To win attention and esteem, people had *to display* their wealth. If a man lived shabbily and at his death half a million dollars was found stuffed in his mattress, he would not have enjoyed anybody's respect. But if he spent his half million on a palatial mansion and a yacht, even if he went into debt to keep them, people would respect him. The chances are that the business community would not only grant him generous credit, but would put him in the way of earning still more millions.

Having great wealth is not enough, said Veblen. It must be displayed. For this he invented the phrase, "conspicuous consumption," and the companion phrase, "conspicuous leisure."

By conspicuous consumption, Veblen meant a blatant display of wealth. The principle involved is just the opposite of what goes into a search for bargains. Instead of trying to stretch a dollar and get the most for it, the idea is to give the impression that one's dollars are limitless. There was a time during the wild prosperous 1920s when a man who was anxious to establish his social position following the accumulation of wealth would become an art collector. What he bought was not nearly so important as the price he paid for it—because it made news, front-page news. If an old bathtub of Louis XIV was expensive enough, it was worth buying.

This becomes a way of saying, "I am so able, so ingenious, and consequently so wealthy that I can afford to indulge my every whim without in the least threatening the substantiality of my wealth." Wealth so huge certainly commands notice, envy, respect and its possessor becomes the inevitable subject of our attention. Additionally, if what he collects shows good taste, he grows in stature and, to some degree, this is bound to happen merely as a result of the facilities available to help him choose. Something has to rub off; even people who fall asleep regularly at the opera cannot escape becoming somewhat familiar with a libretto or aria or two.

Despite the depression at the end of the twenties, the practice continues. In fact there has lately been a resurgence of interest in the purchase of art. This is not to doubt that many art collectors like the paintings they buy, but the monetary value of a painting frequently usurps their thought and discussion of it.

Although our democratic society is abandoning more and more of the ritual and formality it inherited from its monarchical forbears, many occasions remain to display wealth. The first night at the opera is one of these, not only in New York but in Paris, London, Rome. The choice seats are not those from which one can best see the opera, but from which one can best be seen by the audience. The newspapers the next morning publish photographs and descriptions of what each celebrated woman wore. This consists of two things straight out of what Veblen called the man's "unremitting demonstration of the ability to pay": jewels and a dress by a famous couturier. Like a painting, she is signed with the artist's name.

Women are constantly used, perhaps not altogether reluctantly, by men to put their wealth in evidence. Even as a girl approaches womanhood, the process begins. Even today, the father of a debutante would think nothing of spending many thousands of dollars just on the flowers to decorate the ballroom for her coming-out party, flowers that would have faded by the last waltz of the evening. This conspicuous consumption is frequently matched later on, as these girls marry, by the conspicuous leisure their husbands make possible for them. These women are seen and photographed at social events, on shipboard, at expensive resorts, always magnificently dressed and magnificently doing nothing.

Aside from a merely decorative and deliberately unproductive wife, a man can collect many other things of status value for himself. The longest or most expensive automobile, membership in costly even if seldom used clubs, fine homes, servants, the best seats and first nights at theaters, dinners at fine restaurants, prominently placed tables at such restaurants and nightclubs, costly recreations such as polo, yachting, fox hunting—all these things confer position in society worthy of emulation. The quest for status along these lines occasionally reaches such humorous extremes as the need to have an indoor dog and an outdoor dog.

For most of us, who cannot afford such extravagance, Veblen described the imitative elements in our own behavior as consumers. "Pecuniary emulation" was the phrase he used to mark the nonrational purchase of goods for the purpose of satisfying not our physical wants, but rather our desire to be thought well of by others.

We buy a new coat not because the old one is frayed or no longer warm, but because the style has changed and we feel poor and sorry for ourselves if we do not keep up with others. The purchase may be a modest one and yet it bears the stamp of emulation. The mass-produced clothes most women have to settle for are generally copied down versions of costly designers' clothes worn in their original form by the wealthy. Similarly, women who cultivate long, polished fingernails are generally unaware that this high-style manicure originated as a symbol of wealth, for obviously such hands did not have to do housework.

Although we are cautioned that "clothes do not make the man," we are just as often and realistically reminded of the importance of the impression we make. And this, in turn, leaves us impressionable. Advertisements sell us again and again by associating things with the wealthy. The implication is that their product is either popular with rich people or that it is indistinguishable from the real thing. In either case, such a purchase will allow us to enjoy the status conferred by wealth.

No doubt an unsympathetic exaggeration of Veblen's thesis can easily reduce it to absurdity. On the other hand, it is true that many of our dreams have a material, monetary quality. And dreaming is little more than an extension of everyday thinking. It is naive to believe that we do not act on our dreams. We do, perhaps more often than we like to admit. And, as Veblen helps us to recognize, there are strong social forces which aid and abet the process.

THE TROUBLE WITH PEOPLE

From a purely psychological point of view, our love of things is frequently easier to satisfy than our love of people. Our individual shortcomings give us much less trouble in making money than they do in achieving satisfying relationships with others.

There are many men who believe that the only sane part of their day is the time they spend in the office. They say, "It's impossible at home—everybody is always in a state. I can't get along with my wife; nobody can control the children; nothing makes any sense. In my office, even if things do not go the way you expect them to, you can work them out. There are procedures, forms, principles by which we abide most of the time. At home we all love each other but things get out of hand, nothing goes the way you expect it to go. It's a mess."

So the man says. And from his point of view he is quite right. The vicissitudes of business and the stock market are more predictable to him than people. Many men feel that women anyway are hopelessly unpredictable, that they are full of moods, as variable as the weather.

We might note that the men who feel this most strongly are usually the very men who give all or most of their time and attention to business and the acquisition of things, and have little to spare for becoming familiar with the needs or wants of wives. They study market reports and business newsletters and keep well informed so that the twists and turns of high finance do not surprise them. But it does not occur to them that if they took equal trouble to learn about people they might find the study of human behavior equally valuable.

For many people, not being sure how others will act and feel from one moment to the next is far more threatening than they realize. Even surprises are not so agreeable for many as we tend to think. For most of us a real surprise, one which catches us truly unprepared, can be more disturbing than pleasurable even though it may be a happy piece of news. Remember how you felt the last time you were given a real surprise; remember the behavior of someone to whom you told an important and genuinely unexpected piece of news. The first response is not pleasure but shock. One has to sit down, catch one's breath, get used to the new idea. Some people burst out laughing but it is likely to be shaky laughter. A woman is likely to burst into tears. She may muster a smile but it is a tremulous one.

The fact is, we really do not like surprises as much as we think we do. As children, we certainly did not like them. The reason surprises are more disagreeable than otherwise to children is that a child has a small "apperceptive mass," as psychologists call it, a small backlog or body of experience, to which to relate the new experience. Anything totally new is frightening; it can please only when they have become used to it. Young children generally hang back from even the kindest and gentlest stranger until they have looked him over thoroughly. Every spring, some of the children who have been anticipating their first visit to the circus for weeks go home after the show and have nightmares for months. Many children have the same reaction after their first trip to the zoo, their first movie, or children's play.

Children do not feel safe with the unfamiliar, because it is unpredictable. If a young child is to be exposed to a new experience, it is wise to prepare him for what he is going to see. The child needs to know in advance, so that he can enjoy the fun of the surprise without the shock of strangeness and its accompanying fear.

We do not get over this entirely when we grow up. Even as our apperceptive mass, our background of experience, grows with living, we are still wary of surprises. Experience makes fewer events totally surprising, but experience may also reinforce our basic anxiety, our basic feelings of insecurity about life. A really unexpected turn of events stirs up ripples in this unconscious pool of anxiety; a major surprise can cause a tidal wave. Our first response is one of disturbance. Only secondarily can we assess the meaning of the event and feel pleasure in it.

Yet, we like and seek some new experience. There are those of us who are more adventurous, others less so. Most of us have no desire to see what surprises may be in store at the top of Mt. Everest or under the Arctic ice cap. We will settle for lesser adventures. We like novelty, within reason. We mostly prefer predictability. And people, in a general way, give the impression of being unpredictable. The fear of unpredictability in a relationship with another human being is strong with some people. It may be so strong that it blocks them from the experience of love.

These may be people whose parents displayed extreme swings of mood and behavior. Or the parents may simply have been inconsistent in their handling of the child. The pattern is familiar: a parent is inattentive, perhaps reading the paper or talking to a friend, while the child forages around for something to do. The child finds something, but it is the wrong thing—he is dismantling the new coffee table lighter, perhaps—and the parent pounces on him, furious. "Haven't I told you not to touch things! Why must you take everything apart!"

To a young child, this is unpredictable and very upsetting behavior. One moment all was serene, mother was pleasant or at least indifferent, and the child was permitted to wander about unmolested. The next moment he is seized, shouted at, possibly spanked, and the all-important adult in his life has become hostile and menacing. If this happens often enough, he has good reason to mistrust the behavior of people for the rest of his life. And for the rest of his life, such a person may always feel safer with things than with people.

LOVERS ARE PREDICTABLE

Predictability may seem difficult to develop in a relationship between people, but it is very far from impossible. All of us have at least one friend whom we know well, and whose behavior is reasonably easy to foresee. We all take the trouble to know an employer or colleague whose reactions are likely to be important to us, and we can say in advance, "He isn't going to like that," or "She won't see it that way." We do not expect to be right every time in our prediction of how the boss will react. But neither do we expect to be right every time about the stock market or the sales figures. Our prediction is a guess, but an educated guess.

We can make the same kind of guess about a human being's behavior, if we take the trouble to become educated about that human being. People are not unpredictable; far from it. One might justly complain that they are too predictable, that they fall into habits and patterns of behavior too readily and too inflexibly. We only need to know an individual well enough.

Lovers are not unpredictable to each other. Lovers face few surprises in each other, once they have progressed from romantic love to a relationship based on real knowledge of each other. Some lovers arrive at this relationship before they marry, some not until after several or many years of marriage. There is a peak in the divorce rate at about five years of marriage. These are lovers who either never succeeded in coming to know each other, or else did not accept the reality when they discovered it.

Lovers who succeed in replacing the romantic image of the loved one with the real person are no longer afraid of what they may discover in each other. They learn that they can trust each other. They find security in each other and enjoy their interaction. Social status may remain important to them, but not nearly to the degree of their personal status with each other.

THE VULNERABLE MALE

Since so many more men than women seem to turn to a love of things rather than people, we might ask whether men are in fact more susceptible to this type of love. We must recognize, to begin with, that a man's role in our society is traditionally that of the provider for his family. He is the one who goes out to make a living. His position in the community is a barometer of how well he is performing his role. His status reflects favorably or otherwise on his wife and children. In a very real sense, his public position is part of the provision he succeeds in making for their welfare.

A man is thus more vulnerable to the enticements of wealth and status than a woman, simply because of this traditional role. But there are also deeper psychological forces driving him to these goals.

Early in childhood a boy has the experience of feeling displaced by his father. He is at home with his mother, playing with her or perhaps being fed his supper by her. He has her whole attention, when suddenly his father comes home and the entire household changes. Mother gets up, greets father, talks to him, goes to check the state of father's dinner that she is preparing. Even if she returns, even if Father sits down and the child is again made the center of attention, the constellation has altered. Until that moment the little boy possessed his mother entirely; he had her all to himself. Now he no longer has full possession of her, or of his father either. Each of them also has a share in the other.

Little girls have the same experience, of course. But later the experiences of boys and girls begin to diverge. The boy becomes inextricably involved in a kind of competition with his father. Yet his angry feelings make him uneasy, for he also loves his father and wants the love of this strong protector. So he succeeds in gradually converting his resentful rivalry into emulation, which is both more comfortable and more profitable. He sets out to equal his father and if possible outdo him.

Psychoanalysts make the further point that the boy is sensitive to the difference in size between himself and his father, and that this awareness of size tends to be carried over into other pursuits as the child grows. He soon discovers that in his world of school and sports, physical prowess is a great advantage, and this again involves size as well as physical skill. The heroes of his world are the ones who can run fastest, hit the ball farthest, get on the team, win the game. Being first, making records—these are the standards of excellence for the boy when he thinks about what kind of person he is or would like to be.

By this time the experience of boys and girls has diverged considerably, as a father discovers when his children are old enough to get their drivers' licenses. His insurance rates go up at once when his son begins to drive, for the accident rate for teenage boys is the highest for any drivers. Characteristically, boys drive much faster than girls. They race their cars on the road, make a point of darting away first when the light changes from red to green, and take all sorts of risks to get there first and fastest.

Youths of every era have been preoccupied with being out in front, from the games in ancient Greece, to the playing fields of Eton. The first rule of every game is to try to win. Rewards are not equally distributed. They are distributed only among the winners. Similarly, the satisfaction to be derived from one's performance depends on whether or not one wins. The admiration of others and the admiration one has for oneself both follow the quality of one's performance. This may not be love in its purest or best form, but it is certainly a common substitute.

Women are not entirely exempt. A little girl competes with and then emulates her mother, and later she is competitive about her school grades, about the college that accepts her, about the man she marries. She wants to love her husband, to be sure, but she also wants to make a good marriage, and that means marrying a man of some importance, some distinction, perhaps some wealth and position.

A CONSPIRACY AGAINST LOVE

All this adds up to a considerable psychological force of competitiveness and ambition in each one of us, male and female. Men are still more driven by this force in our society than women, but our society is changing, and women are finding or perhaps seeking increasing opportunities to express their competitive drive. Parents play a part in instilling these drives in their children, and the family by its very relationships stimulates competitive feelings and competitive behavior. There is competition with one parent for the other's love, competition with brothers and sisters for parents' love and even for parents' nonlove in the form of punitive attention. Competition is encouraged in the playground, in school, on the athletic field. The drive for achievement and honors is an inevitable and often an exaggerated force throughout the growing years, and none of us is entirely free of it.

Everything conspires to enhance the power of this drive in our adult lives. Behind it are not only history, tradition, and to some extent the religious influences of Calvinism, but also the most obvious appurtenances of our affluent culture. Advertising plays on our acquisitive desires and uses them to sell products to us. Our newspapers tell us about plain John Doe only if he killed or robbed someone or was killed or robbed, but we read every event in the lives of people of wealth and status the day after it occurs, and when they die we read it all over again at full length in their obituaries. In this respect, our newspapers are like our history books. Of all the people who crossed the Rubicon, only Caesar's crossing is recorded.

We learn business and professional skills to develop our ability to acquire wealth and status, but there are no courses in the ability to love. There is a Harvard School of Business Administration, but so far no Harvard School of Love, and if some eccentric millionaire alumnus were to endow such a school in his will it would put the trustees of the university in a pretty quandary.

The world does not accord us much honor for achievement in loving. When a man is unusually happy in his love, his friends say, "Wasn't he lucky!" When two people achieve noteworthy happiness in their marriage, people say, "How lucky they are!" and "Weren't they lucky to have found each other!" We look upon making good in worldly achievement as a mark of extraordinary ability. But making good in love is an accident of two people's blindly stumbling upon one another and haphazardly coming out all right. There is no notion that perhaps we may choose wisely and well, and that having chosen each other, we invest considerable effort and art in shaping our love to meet our mutual desire for harmony, happiness, and fulfillment with each other.

With so much pressure to turn us the other way, it is remarkable that the love of people, rather than of things, is still one of our major ideals. It might be that things, the acquisition of them and the status they bring, do not really satisfy our loneliness, our anxiety, our need for one another, and our desire to find happiness with one another.

It is extremely difficult to avoid a primary attachment to the accumulation of things in a world where they figure so prominently. Success is important to us and its most common hallmark is financial achievement. Most everything has a price and people come to feel that money is the easiest and most universal measure of value. They see in their store of worldly goods satisfaction, security, status, an enlargement of self, a basic confirmation of their adequacy and worthwhileness. Like little Jack Horner, having gotten the plum, they now think, "What a good boy am I."

THINGS ARE NOT ENOUGH

All this would be fine except for two considerations. First, there is an unabated lingering concern with self which more closely resembles infantile self-love than some of its more mature expressions. Why should someone so secure continue to watch the stock market ticker so feverishly? Why should someone with such status continue to wheel and deal even on weekends and vacations? Security and satisfaction should bring freedom from the recurrent need to prove oneself; it should bring self-assurance and tranquillity.

The second consideration is that we live in a world of people. No matter how much we do for ourselves in the successful accumulation of property, the emotional overtones of our life remain primarily influenced by the people closest to us and how we react to them. True, others may confer honor and status upon us, but our position in our own home is of greater ultimate value in the most deeply personal sense. The members of our family do not respond to us according to sociological principle. Their hair is down and they see us similarly unadorned by our rich socioeconomic achievements. The millionaire and the ordinary man face their six-year-old child—and, for that matter, anyone else close to them—with the same naked ability to love. Sooner or later, the truth emerges. Not everything can be bought. There is no substitute for people.

The love of material goods and the love of people often conflict. Yet there is no law of human nature or society which makes this necessarily so. We all inescapably have many loves and one of the major challenges of life is to make them compatible. The ideal solution does not demand the sacrifice of one for the other. Enough people have combined the benefits of both loves to encourage the conviction that they can exist harmoniously together. Acquisition and achievement need not necessarily be at others' expense. Cooperative effort is not a mere dream. People have been known to achieve more as a result of working with others than against them. Even a business relationship leaves room for dignity, respect, for love. The more our daily behavior manifests this, the more consistent do work and love become. Our relationships with others yield greater satisfaction, we get to be less guarded, and the material symbols of status attract us less than the deeper values we realize people are willing to share with us.

*You, scanning these words, are living proof
that one need not stop learning, or
growing, after some predetermined youthful age.*

John W. Gardner

LESSON 47

HOW TO STRIVE FOR EXCELLENCE

"We want meaning in our lives. When we raise our sights, strive for excellence, dedicate ourselves to the highest goals of our society, we are enrolling in an ancient and meaningful cause—the age-long struggle of a man to realize the best that is in him."

Those are the words of John W. Gardner, founder of *Common Cause* and former president of the Carnegie *Foundation for the Advancement of Teaching.* In this lesson, from his widely read book, *Excellence,* Mr. Gardner will prod you into asking many serious questions about yourself and the society around you.

- What does excellence mean to you?
- Where should self-gratifying individuality end?
- What good is our freedom without a moral commitment?
- Why is it that many of us don't get wiser as we get older?
- What is your company doing to foster your development?

The United States has been, and is, a nation of success. We have certainly been the most successful of all peoples in developing a prosperous economy and a powerful community. And yet despite our applause for winners and our enthusiastic veneration of those who rise from "rags to riches," we still exert our democratic rights, more often than not, to restrict or slow down the rise of those who appear to be more ambitious than ourselves. And if those ploys don't succeed we take away the additional fruits of his or her success through taxation. What can be done to encourage, instead of put down, the ideal of individual fulfillment?

You have already come a long way since you began Lesson

477

1. It's time you began to ponder the future, for you and your children ...

Some years ago I had a memorable conversation with the ten-year-old son of one of my fellow professors. I was walking to class and he was headed for his violin lesson. We fell into conversation, and he complained that he couldn't play any real pieces on the violin yet—only those tiresome exercises. I suggested that this would be remedied as he improved, which led him to respond with melancholy: "But I don't want to improve. I expect I may even get worse."

The idea of excellence is attractive to most people and inspiring to some. But taken alone it is a fairly abstract notion. It is not the universally powerful moving force that one might wish. We must therefore ask ourselves what are the moving and meaningful ideas that will inspire and sustain people as they strive for excellence.

In our own society one does not need to search far for an idea of great vitality and power which can and should serve the cause of excellence. It is our well-established ideal of individual fulfillment. This ideal is implicit in our convictions concerning the worth of the individual. It undergirds our belief in equality of opportunity. It is expressed in our conviction that every individual should be enabled to achieve the best that is in him.

The chief instrument we have devised to further the ideal of individual fulfillment is the educational system. But in our understandable preoccupation with perfecting that instrument, we have tended to forget the broader objectives it was designed to serve. Most Americans honor education; few understand its larger purposes. Our thinking about the aims of education has too often been shallow, constricted, and lacking in reach or perspective. Our educational purposes must be seen in the broader framework of our convictions concerning the worth of the individual and the importance of individual fulfillment.

Education in the formal sense is only a part of the society's larger task of abetting the individual's intellectual, emotional, and moral growth. *What we must reach for is a conception of perpetual self-discovery, perpetual reshaping to realize one's best self, to be the person one could be.*

This is a conception which far exceeds formal education in

scope. It includes not only the intellect but the emotions, character, and personality. It involves not only the surface, but deeper layers of thought and action. It involves adaptability, creativeness, and vitality.

And it involves moral and spiritual growth. We say that we wish the individual to fulfill his potentialities, but obviously we do not wish to develop great criminals or great rascals. Learning for learning's sake isn't enough. Thieves learn cunning, and slaves learn submissiveness. We may learn things that constrict our vision and warp our judgment. We wish to foster fulfillment within the framework of rational and moral strivings which have characterized man at his best. In a world of huge organizations and vast social forces that dwarf and threaten the individual, we must range ourselves whenever possible on the side of individuality; but we cannot applaud an irresponsible, amoral, or wholly self-gratifying individuality.

America's greatness has been the greatness of a free people who shared certain moral commitments. Freedom without moral commitment is aimless and promptly self-destructive. It is an ironic fact that as individuals in our society have moved toward conformity in their outward behavior, they have moved away from any sense of deeply shared purposes. We must restore *both* a vigorous sense of individuality *and* a sense of shared purposes. Either without the other leads to consequences abhorrent to us.

To win our deepest respect the individual must both find himself and lose himself. This is not so contradictory as it sounds. We respect the man who places himself at the service of values which transcend his own individuality—the values of his profession, his people, his heritage, and above all the religious and moral values which nourished the ideal of individual fulfillment in the first place. But this "gift of himself" only wins our admiration if the giver has achieved a mature individuality and if the act of giving does not involve an irreparable crippling of that individuality. We cannot admire faceless, mindless servants of The State or The Cause or The Organization who were never mature individuals and who have sacrificed all individuality to the Corporate Good.

WASTE ON A MASSIVE SCALE

In our society today, large numbers of young people never fulfill their potentialities. Their environment may not be such as to stimulate such fulfillment, or it may actually be such as to stunt growth. The family trapped in poverty and ignorance can rarely provide the stimulus so necessary to individual growth. The neigh-

borhood in which delinquency and social disintegration are universal conditions cannot create an atmosphere in which educational
values hold a commanding place. In such surroundings, the process by which talents are blighted begins long before kindergarten,
and survives long afterward.

The fact that large numbers of American boys and girls fail to
attain their full development must weigh heavily on our national
conscience. And it is not simply a loss to the individual. At a time
when the nation must make the most of its human resources, it is
unthinkable that we should resign ourselves to this waste of potentialities. Recent events have taught us with sledge hammer effectiveness the lesson we should have learned from our own tradition—
that our strength, creativity, and further growth as a society depend
upon our capacity to develop the talents and potentialities of our
people.

Any adequate attack on this problem will reach far beyond
formal educational institutions. It will involve not only the school
but the home, the church or synagogue, the playground, and all
other institutions which shape the individual. The child welfare
society, the adoption service, the foundlings' home, the hospital,
and clinic—all play their part. And so do slum clearance projects
and social welfare programs that seek to create the kind of family
and neighborhood environment which fosters normal growth.

But it is not only in childhood that we face obstacles to
individual fulfillment. Problems of another sort emerge at a later
stage in the life span.

Commencement speakers are fond of saying that education is
a lifelong process. And yet that is something that no young person
with a grain of sense needs to be told. Why do the speakers go on
saying it? It isn't that they love sentiments that are well-worn with
reverent handling (though they do). It isn't that they underestimate their audience. The truth is that they know something their
young listeners do not know—something that can never be fully
communicated. No matter how firm an intellectual grasp the young
person may have on the idea that education is a lifelong process,
he can never know it with the poignancy, with the deeply etched
clarity, with the overtones of satisfaction and regret that an older
person knows it. The younger person has not yet made enough
mistakes that cannot be repaired. He has not yet passed enough
forks in the road that cannot be retraced.

The commencement speaker may give in to the temptation
to make it sound as though the learning experiences of the older
generation were all deliberate and a triumph of character—character
that the younger generation somehow lacks. We can forgive him

that. It is not easy to tell young people how unpurposefully we learn, how life tosses us head over heels into our most vivid learning experiences, how intensely we resist many of the increments in our own growth.

But we cannot forgive him as readily if he leaves out another part of the story. And that part of the story is that the process of learning through life is by no means continuous and by no means universal. If it were, age and wisdom would be perfectly correlated, and there would be no such thing as an old fool—a proposition sharply at odds with common experience. The sad truth is that for many of us the learning process comes to an end very early indeed. And others learn the wrong things.

The differences among people in their capacity for continued growth are so widely recognized that we need not dwell on them. They must not be confused with differences in the degree of success—as the world measures success—which individuals achieve. Many whom the world counts as unsuccessful have continued learning and growing throughout their lives; and some of our most prominent people stopped learning literally decades ago.

We still have a very imperfect understanding of why some people continue to learn and grow while others do not. Sometimes one can point to adverse circumstances as the cause of a leveling off of individual growth. But we cannot identify the conditions which have hindered or fostered development.

Of course, people are never quite as buffeted by circumstances as they appear to be. The man who experiences great personal growth as a result of some accidental circumstance may have been ready to grow in any case. Pasteur said that chance favors the prepared mind. The man defeated by circumstance might have triumphed had he been made of other stuff. We all know individuals whose growth and learning can only be explained in terms of an inner drive, a curiosity, a seeking and exploring element in their personalities. Captain James Cook said, "I . . . had ambition not only to go farther than any man had ever been before, but as far as it was possible for a man to go." Just as Cook's restless seeking led him over the face of the earth, so other men embark on Odysseys of the mind and spirit.

It is a concern both for the individual and for the nation that moves the commencement speaker. Perhaps many men will always fall into ruts. Perhaps many will always let their talents go to waste. But the waste now exists on such a massive scale that sensible people cannot believe that it is all inevitable.

Unfortunately, the conception of individual fulfillment and lifelong learning which animates the commencement speaker finds no adequate reflection in our social institutions. For too long we have paid pious lip service to the idea and trifled with it in practice. Like those who confine their religion to Saturday or Sunday and forget it the rest of the week, we have segregated the idea of individual fulfillment into one compartment of our national life, and neglect it elsewhere. We have set "education" off in a separate category from the main business of life. It is something that happens in schools and colleges. It happens to young people between the ages of six and twenty-one. It is not something—we seem to believe—that need concern the rest of us in our own lives.

This way of thinking is long overdue for a drastic change. If we believe what we profess concerning the worth of the individual, then the idea of individual fulfillment within a framework of moral purpose must become our deepest concern, our national preoccupation, our passion, our obsession. We must think of education as relevant for everyone everywhere—at all ages and in all conditions of life.

Aside from our formal educational system there is little evidence of any such preoccupation. Some religious groups are doing excellent work. Our libraries and museums are a legitimate source of pride. Adult education programs have become increasingly effective. Certain of our organizations concerned with social welfare and with mental health play profoundly important roles.

But what about moving pictures, radio, and television, with their great possibilities for contributing to the growth of the individual? It would be fair to say that these possibilities have not dominated the imagination of the men who control these media. On the contrary, these media have all too often permitted the triumph of cupidity over every educational value. And what about newspapers and magazines, with their obvious potentialities for furthering the intellectual and moral growth of the individual? At best, a small fraction of the publishers accepts such a responsibility. Book publishers are less vulnerable to criticism, but they are not without fault.

Serious pursuit of the goal of individual fulfillment will carry us even farther afield. Unions, lodges, professional organizations, and social clubs can all contribute importantly to individual growth and learning if they are so inclined. Only sporadically have they been so inclined. There are innumerable opportunities open to the employer who is willing to acknowledge his responsibility for furthering the individual development of men and women in his employ. Some forward-looking companies have made a highly significant beginning in accepting that responsibility.

What we are suggesting is that every institution in our

society should contribute to the fulfillment of the individual. Every institution must, of course, have its own purposes and preoccupations, but over and above everything else that it does, it should be prepared to answer this question posed by society: "what is the institution doing to foster the development of the individuals within it?"

Now what does all of this mean? It means that we should very greatly enlarge our ways of thinking about education. We should be painting a vastly greater mural on a vastly more spacious wall. What we are trying to do is nothing less than to build a greater and more creative civilization. We propose that the American people accept as a universal task the fostering of individual development within a framework of rational and moral values. We propose that they accept as an all-encompassing goal the further-ance of individual growth and learning at every age, in every significant situation, in every conceivable way. By doing so we shall keep faith with our ideal of individual fulfillment, and at the same time insure our continued strength and creativity as a society.

If we accept this concern for individual fulfillment as an authentic national preoccupation, the schools and colleges will then be the heart of a national endeavor. They will be committed to the furthering of a national objective and not—as they now often find themselves—swimming upstream against the interests of a public that thinks everything else more urgent. The schools and colleges will be greatly strengthened if their task is undergirded by such a powerful public conception of the goal to be sought.

And both schools and colleges will be faced with a challenge beyond anything they have yet experienced. We have said that much will depend upon the individual's attitude toward learning and toward his own growth. This defines the task of the schools and colleges. Above all they must equip the individual for a never-ending process of learning; they must gird his mind and spirit for the constant reshaping and reexamination of himself. They cannot content themselves with the time-honored process of stuffing students like sausages or even the possibly more accept-able process of training them like seals. It is the sacred obligation of the schools and colleges to instill in their students the attitudes toward growth and learning and creativity which will in turn shape the society. With other institutions at work on other parts of this task, the schools and colleges must of course give particular atten-tion to the intellectual aspects of growth. This is uniquely their responsibility.

If we accept without reservation these implications of our traditional belief in individual fulfillment, we shall have enshrined a highly significant purpose at the heart of our national life—a purpose that will lift all American education to a new level of meaning. We shall have accepted a commitment which promises pervasive consequences for our way of thinking about the purpose of democratic institutions. And we shall have embraced a philosophy which gives a rich personal meaning to the pursuit of excellence.

Dr. Jess Lair

LESSON 48

HOW TO LET YOUR KIDS FIND
THEIR OWN SUCCESS

It was Oscar Wilde who said, "Children begin by loving their parents. After a time they judge them. Rarely, if ever, do they forgive them."

There is no more difficult task in the world than raising a child from infancy to adulthood. Since Adam and Eve's problem with Cain and Abel, parents have struggled with an assignment that calls for more talent, ability, patience, wisdom, and loving than most humans can provide. Still we try, wrestling with an array of child-rearing problems that increases with each century.

This upbeat lesson, from Dr. Jess Lair's book, *I Ain't Well—But I Sure am Better,* deals with a predicament that confronts every loving parent. How much guiding and shaping and leading should be administered to the young one so that he or she grows up to be a success instead of a failure? The dangers and risks involved in this attempt at playing God are rarely considered by even the most well-meaning mother or father.

To have one's children succeed can become an obsession to parents, especially if their own lives have been nonproductive. Their children, at any cost, must redeem the parents. They must be brilliant in school, become wealthy, attain position, marry brilliantly, because their parents never scored in any of these areas.

But suppose the children are not innately equipped to rise higher than their parents? Suppose they would be happier as plain citizens, leading useful but ordinary lives? Thus are many of our youth ruined by authority figures in the home who force them to try to be more than they are or want to be. These parents, instead, make failures of them, failures reflecting their own vanity, greed, and egotism.

Pay attention as a warm and worldly professor, who has counseled thousands, shows you how to help your kids grow and flourish in a garden of their own choice, not yours.

When that happens, both you and they have succeeded!

My wife contends that I was a natural-born bachelor—maybe even a natural-born monk. When I see how hard it is for me to face some of the constant problems I have living with my wife and children, I'm inclined to think there is a lot of truth in what she says.

But I know I'm even more poorly suited for a solitary life than the married life. I crammed into my first twenty-three years practically everything anyone could want to do. I had plenty of fun and hell-raising as I grew up. I went to army college and to the army in a year and a half. I graduated from college with trips out west skiing, mountain climbing, and fishing. I took a long canoe trip into Canada. I worked many jobs to pay for all my activities. I had many friends and the deep love of a few good young women.

In August of 1947 just before I was twenty-one, I was visiting Berkeley after a summer working in the mountains. I was looking for my high school love who had ditched me while I was in the army.

As it got toward dark and the lonesome time of day, I looked out across the bay at the lights of the Golden Gate Bridge. I thought, "Here is one of the most beautiful sights I have ever seen. But I'm alone and don't enjoy seeing this by myself. I'm going home."

I went back to the hotel and checked out that evening and started hitchhiking home. I wasn't in a rush to get married. I was still scared of it. But that was the time I turned my back on the single life.

The point of my story is that I had all the opportunities in the world to stay single and enjoy it. But I chose not to stay that way. I chose to be a family man. If this was my choice and if I believe my family is the most crucial way to satisfy my need for relationships, then why don't I act like it?

All I can say to myself in my defense is that what I'm trying to do is for me one of the two hardest things I've ever tried. One of the hardest is to find God as I understand Him, and make a continuing, conscious contact and give up playing God myself. The other terribly hard thing is to be a husband and a father.

In neither of these two problems can I blame anyone else. I can't blame the troubles I have had trying to find a higher power on the people who taught me about religion. Everyone who taught me religion was as kind and loving as they could be. I was never punished. But because of this awful conspiracy of silence we maintain with the people around us on talking about spiritual matters, I see so many people who think they are all alone in their spiritual quest. They think they are so alone that it takes them quite awhile to admit to their own problems and fears because they think they are so weird and different for having them.

I see a number of driving forces in us. We can do something out of a sense of compulsion, driven by something inside that we don't understand or feel comfortable with. We can do something out of a sense of fear where we are driven by the fear of a punishment. We can do something out of a sense of dedication where we drive ourselves because as near as we can see this is something that is right for us and that we should do.

Dedication is about the best I can say about most of the things I do in the family. I do them because I believe in them for me and I'm dedicated to them.

But there is a higher driving force—the highest of them all. That is when we do something out of love. This force is so powerful yet there is the feeling of no power at all. It is like the perfect golf swing—there is no feeling of strain or effort, just smoothly focused speed in the club head that lifts the ball straight and true. You can feel that near perfect shot in your whole body and you know how good it is the minute your club head makes contact with the ball.

When I do something in my family because I really enjoy it, then my duty has become my pleasure. And it is a pleasure for all the people around me.

When it comes to my children I have to continually fight my tendency to try to raise them—to make them go the way I want them to go so they will make me look good. And I expect more maturity from them than I had when I was their age or even more maturity than I have now at forty-eight.

When I talk to other parents what is so unreal is their horror at some of the things kids are doing today. The only way they can be so horrified is to have forgotten what they did when they were kids. I ran around with every kid my age in Bricelyn, Minnesota. And I knew most of the other kids two and three years older and younger than me. They were all cut from the exact same cloth. The degree of hell that they would raise would be a little bit different, but it just wasn't that much different. Yet, I'm sure that today some of those kids are holding up a level for their kids that they were never able to measure up to themselves.

Recently one of my kids got in some trouble. I was telling him of some similar trouble I was in when I was about his age. Jackie couldn't restrain herself. She said, "Yes, I know you did those things, but I don't want him to turn out like you!" And that's the problem. When we raise kids we know just exactly how we want them to turn out.

I want people to see my kids and marvel at their manners, their poise, and their talent. I wasn't that way, but that's the point. I don't want my kids to start out like me. I don't want them to make the mistakes I made or that anyone else made and I want them to turn out better than me. And I want this exact same thing for all five of them.

There's no freedom for them in that. And no real learning either. How can you learn ballet or life without making mistakes?

When you ask me why I don't want my kids to make mistakes, I'll claim it's because I don't want to see them get hurt. But that's not really why I don't want them to make mistakes. I'm worried about my ego. I don't want people thinking less of me because of what my kids do. I don't want to have to fish my kids out of the police station. I want them on the stage at school winning awards. I want my children to be ornaments for me just like a new Cadillac sitting in the driveway is an ornament.

One of my students claimed that when she was faced with the issue of a kid getting a haircut, or whether they are going to make the honor roll or not, what she was really worried about was that kid. The more I thought about it, the more I thought she was crazy. We like to say what we are worried about is that kid, but I don't think so. I think we are more worried about our own egos. We're using our kids as extensions and instruments of our own egos, to build us up.

If we've got kids that are straight as a string and on the honor roll all of the time, and never give any adult any back talk and don't steal anything, and they are always respectful one hundred percent, and things like that, they are an adornment to us, just like a big diamond ring. They help show us off and we can walk downtown real comfortable knowing that our kid is always just exactly where he is supposed to be and doing just exactly what he is supposed to be doing. Nobody's got kids like that, but that's the pressure we're putting on them to be. Well, what kid can ever live up to that kind of thing? And why should any kid be an ornament for us? They aren't a necklace or a piece of jewelry. If we want ornaments, buy 'em. But again, our tendency is to make our kids into things that will build us up. Any time they threaten to tear us down in any way in the eyes of our neighbors, boy, we really climb right up their frame. We let them know, by God, we ain't taking any of that crap. They are going to get their hair cut short like everybody else so their ears are showing. They're going to do that. Sure we justify it in the name of our concern about them.

Self-justification is the most dangerous thing there is because it blinds us to truth and reality. Sure it is awful to face that I am so mean to my kids because of my fears about what my neighbors will think. I can see this very clearly if I imagine my family was on a desert island. Would the long hair or not studying hard bother me there? No, it wouldn't. Well, that's the answer. If I say that my priorities are my higher power first and my family second, I had better act that way in my family. When I let my fear of what my neighbors might think control me, I'm putting their views of me in first place. And I shatter my commitment to my family.

If my family is my most crucial way of getting my needs met for mutuality, then I break down right in my most important relationships. Commitment means just that—commitment. And it means all the commitment I can muster up—until I can manage a deeper commitment.

"Well, should we as parents teach our kids the values that we have?"

No, we shouldn't try to teach values the way we want to by talking about what we think our values are. I think the only way you can teach them those values is to live them. I think that the saddest thing in the world is when we talk one value and live another. If you want to ask me am I a Christian, I will say, "No. I'm working on it." If a kid wants to ask me, "What do you think about honesty, Dad?" I will say, "Well, just look at the way I run my life, son, and you will know real fast how I really feel about honesty. I could defend honesty as a logical virtue, but what he is going to be most impressed by is what he sees. And I would far rather rest my case on that than run the risk of telling him these things.

I think the danger is we have a set of values that are hopes, for us. We're trying to live up to them, but failing. We want our kids to realize these hopes. Well I'm not realizing them; why should I ask my kids to. I've got a lot more muscle than they have in that area. So I think that we doom our kids to failure by a very unrealistic set of goals for them. We want them to do the things that we can't and didn't do. And the parent who wants to tell me that he can do the things he asks of his kids, just let me follow him around for a day.

We have all of these people who claim they are so law-abiding. There are a lot of you, I'm sure, who don't know how to make a legal turn off of one four-lane street into another four-lane street. If I was a cop, I could camp on your tail and I could arrest you, I bet, within fifteen minutes for something. You say, "Oh, I don't mean that. That's not really illegal." You want to redefine, all of a sudden, legality.

I don't steal anymore. I used to. Well, I steal a little, but I don't steal like I used to. How come I cut down on the amount of stealing I did? Simple. I just found out that it didn't work. It made me feel bad. And I got so nervous that it canceled out any gain. And then there are some other things that entered into it more recently. OK, say I'm going to tell my son, "Don't steal." I argue that is a value I have learned. Well, how did I learn it? I learned it by making mistakes and I got some of it from my father and grandfather, not by what they said, but by their example— what they did. I'm still learning from my father's example and he has been dead twenty years.

I think we are awfully overwhelmed by what we want our kids to represent. We overlook their strengths too much because we have our eyes so strong on their weaknesses.

I talked to you about the idea of valuing a person just as they are. That is the most precious thing that we can do for a human being. If valuing is as good as I say it is, it seems to me that I should do that first for my wife and the next most obvious people are my five kids. If my mind is full of a program for their self-improvement, I'm not valuing them as they are. And they feel it.

My old friend Vince believes you should sponsor a kid as you sponsor an alcoholic. When a guy gets drunk on one of my friends in Alcoholics Anonymous who are sponsoring him, they don't go and yell at him and holler at him and slap him around. They wait until he sleeps off his hangover. They don't come butting in on him when he is feeling bad. They come around the next day and say, "Hey, how are you feeling?" And he says, "Gee, I'm sorry that I let you down and got drunk on you like that." They tell him, "Don't think anything of it. Hell, I've slipped, too."

This is what Vince means when he says, "You don't raise kids; you raise carrots. You sponsor kids." And that drives people up the wall when I even tell them about it. They say, "Oh my

God!" But as near as I can see, my mother and dad did a lot of that with me. And I sure appreciated it. I don't say that I'm a good advertisement for the idea, but I sure appreciate it. They spent a lot of time asking me, "What do you think you're going to do next?" I would say, "Well I think I'm going to do this." And they would say, "Fine. We were just curious as to what you had in mind." I made all my own decisions so my mistakes were all mine, too. There was no one I could blame them on.

"You talk about letting kids assume some responsibility, which I agree with, learn by their own actions, which I agree with, but how, for example, do you teach your kid not to ride a tricycle out in the street when they are only three years old? You can't avoid your responsibility for him. Obviously, you aren't going to let him get killed or hurt."

That's right. It's like trying to teach somebody to float, you have your hand under them for awhile and you take that hand away gradually. As fast as you can. But you don't go so fast that they drown on you. What I think we do is we use this principle to justify pounding hell out of that kid. Like so many parents who have left thousands of temptations in the kid's way and they go around slapping the kid's hands. Gotta teach him. Gotta teach him. The simplest way is to put temptation out of sight.

I don't say you necessarily let a kid reach out and touch a hot stove. But a kid is going to make mistakes. He is going to get hurt some. And the job of a parent is like teaching a person to float. You've got the hand under them real heavy at first; you may even have both hands under them practically holding them out of the water. Then you gradually move your hands away.

Let me tell you a story that has some bearing on this. My friend Vince was in the news store with one of his kids, Charlie. This is Vince's second family. He lost his first family to alcohol. So he is really taking care of the second one. Little Charlie is next to the youngest of five kids. Vince always had his kids ride in his plumbing truck with him until they were old enough to go to school. So they were in the news store together so Vince could buy some Copenhagen tobacco. Charlie says, "Can I have some candy, Dad?" "Yeah, go ahead and help yourself." Charlie came back with some candy in a sack and Vince asked him, "Are you sure you've got enough to last you all day?" And the little guy ran back and got some more candy. He came back and again Vince said, "Are you sure you've got enough? It's a long day." So Charlie went back and took a little more candy. Charlie's important to Vince.

We think that is indulging that kid and that's terrible. But our parents did that for us and it didn't screw us up, especially when it wasn't done in a sick way. It's just an openhanded gift. But I see a lot of times when we will use the idea, "Well, I've got to teach my kids. I've got to protect them from this or that, and I've got to guard them from this or that," and we use that way past where we should. Sure it is impossible to argue with the principle of not letting a three-year-old kid out on a street on their tricycle. There are some things we have to say "No" to. But you can say "Oh, no" to only so many things. So you had better set some priorities and say no to the things that are really important to you as you see it. And then that is it. And there has to be a lot of places where we aren't saying no. If you say no to everything then you're in trouble. And I think a lot of times that's what we fall into. The person who raises the point you have to protect the three-year-old doesn't fool me. The question is too obvious to need an answer. What is probably really bothering her is she wants to keep her eighteen-year-old son from going steady. She wants to protect him from girls.

A lot of people get mad at me when I talk this way. "Well that Jess, he says anything goes." I'm not saying that at all. But I am saying we are stepping in, in a lot of places with our kids where we shouldn't. I can show you kids coming out of our high school here in Bozeman, Montana who are beautiful illustrations of overcontrol. They are so packed into a Brownie box by the time they come to the university, they are just little mechanical men. They are just studying machines, Brownie point makers. It is going to take a lot of hard knocks to teach them anything about life. I have watched some of them go through four years of university trying to live with their fellow students and not learn a thing.

"At some times, don't some children not have enough discipline?"

Yes. You can go off either end. I don't see the kids in the bottom end very much. I see some of them but not so many because most of them don't make it to the university. I *can* see, though, that at least a third to a half of those kids on the high honor roll are really in trouble.

I was reading a biography of Einstein this morning. He took violin lessons from about eight until fourteen. His instructors were very mechanical. It was pretty much play the scales and stuff, no fun. He got ahold of some early records of Mozart's sonatas for the violin. He started studying them all by himself and he really started coming along with his love for the violin. This story in his biography was just another example to me of how we learn so much faster out of love than out of duty.

I was asked to speak at the National Honor Society initiation at Bozeman Senior High. I tried to tell the honor society that some part of their grades came from a love of subject and some part of them came from a sense of fear and competitiveness. I told them how I made the honor society partly because I liked some subjects and partly to get better grades on tests than my friends. Hopefully they would work toward increasing the part of their grades that came out of studying out of a love of something and enjoyment of it, and decrease the part that came out of a sense of fear or sense of competitiveness and destroying the other person.

After my speech, the mother of one of the officers of the honor society came up and said, "Dr. Lair, you don't believe that anybody would ever study anything because they liked it, do you?" What can you say to a woman like that? The mother of an honor society officer? That kid has gone to school with a hot spear prodding him in the back all of his school life.

Most everything I have learned, I have studied because I liked it. Two thirds of my psychology courses I liked, or half of them at least. Sure there is stuff you don't like. I like psychology in general and I liked a good share of the courses I took. That is why I took the Ph.D. in psychology. I have done a lot of studying. I know more things about more out of the way subjects just because I love to study things. I have made a deep study of the ballistics of the 7-mm. magnum. It doesn't make any sense to know all I know about the ballistics of the 7-mm. magnum. It's dumb. But once I get interested and start studying, I'll soon have six books on the subject, and be reading like the dickens. I'll have a pile of note-books full of notes. There's no grade, no nothing prodding me, just love.

When I talk like this about self-direction and doing things out of love, many of my students, young or old, get angry at me. They say, "That Jess, he is really screwed up." Again, we can look at Einstein. Do you realize that the same year that Einstein was coming up with some of his crucial equations there were three other men who were publishing articles that contained most of the basic equations for the theory of relativity? The three of them were just a gnat's eyebrow away from it. In fact, they say you can derive the theory of relativity out of any of those other articles with just the equations that they put down. But I think the one thing that distinguished Einstein from those other three cats was they didn't have the guts to step away from tradition like Einstein did. I think those others would defy tradition up to a point and then they would get frightened. What I think happened was Einstein had been raised in the same orientation toward the past as the other three men. But Einstein had the courage to go past the accepted boundaries. I will grant you this point; you can raise some very mediocre lawyers, doctors, and scientists by this red-hot spear-at-the-back treatment. You can get exceptionally dutiful, high-achieving kids, but they have got an automatic ceiling in their training because their fear stops them from going so far or deep into things because that would be irreverent and disrespectful.

Some of these overtrained kids end up cussing us. "Why in the hell didn't Ma and Pa let me know that there were some other careers than the kind you go to college for?" I heard a dad get the shaft from his son for that back in Minnesota. I thought, "Hey, man, you are paying." He had these kids who were really straight. They had short haircuts and did everything right. For a parent with all my problems, it just makes you sick to your stomach watching kids like that. They have a sense of duty. They are on scholarships. But one of his sons who was in a profession said to him one day, "You know, I wish that I hadn't had so much pressure to go to college. I wish I was a tool and die maker."

I think he is a little frightened by the profession he is in. And he doesn't feel up to it. And yet he doesn't see himself as being free to change. If he really wants to be a tool and die maker, simple. Learn tool and die making at night while he is doing the job that he has got, and five years from now he will be a tool and die maker.

So, you can get anything that you want from your kids. The only thing is you've got to be willing to pay the particular price for whatever it is you want. And the price tag I'm talking about is if you are trying to treat your children and other people like individuals and trying to give them a degree of freedom, you've got to pay the awful price that freedom exacts. Which is, the mistakes are out in the open. All the mistakes are out in the open and you've got to face them straight on.

There isn't anything that doesn't have a price. You can stamp out kids just like cookie cutters; all you've got to use is enough fear and enough pressure and you can have anything that you want, and you pay the price in a different way. But not only do you pay the price for the kids, but you pay a price for yourself. You separate yourself from them. Here are all these old people sitting around saying, "Why won't my kids come to see me?" Well, like I said earlier, why should they? Why would they want to? You see this in families. The minute those kids get married they go as far away as they can. I know all kinds of families where the kids have got jobs in all different corners of the United States and its possessions. Isn't it strange it happens that way? In my grandpa's family most of his seven kids never went more than sixty miles away. It wasn't in a dependent way but in a good way. They wanted to have work so they could stay close by home. I don't think that's an accident either. We still see families who stay together today. That's supposed to be impossible because of mobility and specialized careers. But in northeast Minneapolis where the Poles live, you see kids coming back to the neighborhood. They might come back as doctors or lawyers, even. But so many of them come back. If you want to be close to your family, you don't decide to be an oil engineer and go to North Africa. I think much of the mobility we see today isn't a basic cause of problems as much as it is an effect. A good way to avoid closeness is to run and keep on running. If your family rates a higher priority than work, then you find work that lets you be close to family. If work is most important in your life, then you go anywhere your work takes you. You may say, "Oh, I love my dear old dad and mother. I haven't seen them for ten years, but I sure love them." I don't understand that.

Each spring the trout are in the creek. Each fall the elk are up the Gallatin. Each winter the powder is on the Bridgers. Each day the sun is on the hills. Those of us who want to will be here together enjoying those things.

You can put distance between you and your parents for two reasons. You can go to some far place as a part of your own spiritual quest. Or you can put distance between you and your family because you can't stand to be around them. The person who leaves his family because he can't stand them will be a prisoner of that family. He has unfulfilled hopes and expectations from that family that tie him to them emotionally no matter how far he goes. He is just as tied to them as the one who hangs around forever who is also looking for something he didn't get.

The only way you can ever really leave your family emotionally is to walk away from them seeing they gave you what they could. What they didn't give you, they didn't have to give. The son or daughter who leaves a family this way is free to move away or stay around depending on what's right for them.

It is hard for me being on the other end of this decision. I've watched three of my five children struggle with leaving home with more or less success. And it is sad to see some needs on their parts I couldn't fulfill. And the only thing they can do is see that it wasn't maliciousness on my part, just incompetence. By the time I had learned even a few of the things I learned as a parent, it was too late. Lord Rochester said, "Before I got married I had six theories about bringing up children; now I have six children, and no theories."

Even worse, I'm still not good at some things that are very

important. I'm terrible at listening to my kids when they are trying to talk out some problem. Once in awhile I can do it, but most of the time I can't. Fortunately, Jackie is good at this. She yells at me to listen more, but unless there's a very special problem, I can see I'm not good at it. She says to do it anyway. I try, but it is easy for them to tell my heart isn't in it.

These are my failings as a parent. I see a few things I can do and I'm thankful for them. But I would sure hate to see my kids hanging around me until they were fifty hoping that someday I would finally see the light and start listening to them. I see the light now, but so far the gift of listening to them well hasn't been given me. And I know that thinking positively hasn't worked very well for me. So I'll just have to bear down harder on what I can do and hope for compassion on the part of my kids. So far they have given me far more of that than I ever hoped for.

I think the biggest problem I had as a father is realizing how different each of my children are and learning to respond to each of them as an individual.

My oldest son went with me from his earliest years hunting and fishing. When he got to be fifteen he made close friends and was with them. So I figured, "OK, it's now my second son's time to go hunting and fishing with me." But he didn't care much for hunting and fishing. But my youngest son did. My thought was, "I can't take you, youngest son, because it's your middle brother's turn." Except he didn't need or want his turn.

I finally got that straightened out in my head. Then I realized something even worse. My middle son enjoyed cars and would like to work on them. But I didn't like working on cars. I realized what I had been doing. I had been saying to my sons, "Come on and share my interests with me. If you do that, we will be able to do things together." That's a very limited deal.

I'm now seeing much more clearly how different each of my five children are from Jackie and me and from each other. And I've pretty well reconciled myself to the fact I'm not interested in a lot of things they are interested in and I'm not going to be able to pretend much interest I don't have. So we do together what we are interested in together. On the other things we find what companions we can.

My relationship with my wife was mutual. I chose her and she chose me. But my children just came. Another hard thing to face was that I couldn't change the amount of mutuality there is between me and each of my children. All I could do was accept the differing amounts of mutuality and do with it what I could. This hasn't been easy either. My ego says I'm a groovy parent. I'll have groovy relationships with all my kids. Except it doesn't work that way.

Once I woke up to the reality that I had five separate different relationships things got better fast. Now I can enjoy the wonderful qualities each of the five have and not try to force something artificial. In the process, I've gained what mutuality that is there so I've got five relationships that are valuable to me. They give me lots of good feeling about life and myself. And they hold up a clear mirror so I can see myself better and move along more smoothly on my spiritual quest.

But all this time, the hardest thing to do is let them make their own mistakes. I'm constantly screaming at myself, "What kind of lousy father are you? Don't you care about your children? Why don't you do what you are supposed to do to raise them up the way they should be raised and set their feet upon the paths they should be set upon?"

The only thing that helps me is so far I can't see that anyone did that to me so I'm trying to do the same for my children and not try so hard to raise them, but to do some sponsoring of them.

Louis Binstock

LESSON 49

HOW TO HAVE A HAPPY LIFE

More than a thousand years ago, the mighty Caliph of Cordova wrote,

> I have now reigned above fifty years in victory or peace,
> beloved by my subjects, dreaded by my enemies, and respected
> by my allies. Riches and honors, power and pleasure, have
> waited on my call, nor does any earthly blessing appear to
> have been wanting to my felicity. In this situation I have
> diligently numbered the days of pure and genuine happiness
> which have fallen to my lot. They amount to fourteen.

Philosophers, wise men, and poets are nearly unanimous in
their conclusion that the ultimate goal of life is to be happy and yet
happiness, for most of humanity, is a butterfly which, when pursued, is always just beyond our grasp. Why? What is there about
this condition, free to all, that makes it so rare? And what must we
do, or cease doing, in order to let more sun shine into those
somber days of our lives?

Our nation became the first in the history of the world to
incorporate the word "happiness" into its basic founding documents. It was a praiseworthy effort by some very wise men but two
hundred years of experience have proven that giving us the freedom to enjoy happiness has been no guarantee that we would.

Success and happiness are often coupled as goals, as if the
attainment of the first automatically guaranteed the second. Not so.
All of us know successful individuals who are miserable.

Can you be both successful and happy? Yes! In this lesson
from his book, *The Power of Maturity*, Louis Binstock introduces
you to five spiritual senses which are as important to your life as

the five physical senses of seeing, hearing, smelling, tasting, and feeling. Combine these five important senses with the success secrets you have learned in this university and your life will be filled to the brim with joy, love, and achievement ...

Many of us know the story of *Mutiny on the Bounty*, or have seen it in either of its two motion picture versions. Who can forget Charles Laughton's commanding voice bellowing, "Mr. Christian!" and adding to the injustices that set up the mutiny— led by Clark Gable.

There really was a mutiny on a real ship named *Bounty*. The cause of the mutiny seems to have been the inhumane actions of Captain Bligh; but, between the lines, one can see other factors. Surely one of them was the feeling among the mistreated English sailors that they could find a permanent haven on some beautiful island like Tahiti, where they had been able to stay for an enchanted while. There, in a balmy climate of sunny days and moonlit nights, living at the bounteous breast of nature, they could end their days amid a happy native people, without wants or cares.

As it turned out, the mutineers dared not stay at Tahiti, where other English ships might call. Most of them ended their days on Pitcairn Island, regretting their isolation, and finding life not so easy as they had thought it would be. Yet had they stayed on Tahiti, had they never been molested, would they have been happy? The almost certain answer is *No*.

When you try to escape the world, you can leave behind the gray skies of the northern regions, the responsibilities of your job, your debts, and everyone who ever bothered you, but you take along yourself. What is a civilized man who has escaped to a tropic island? He is someone whose general temperament and thoughts, basic emotions and ambitions, fundamental desires and fears remain the same. He may find he is happy. In that case, however, he is a man who is quite capable of being happy anywhere because he is happy with himself. Basically, happiness depends upon what you are as a person, not upon the place where you live.

As someone put it very well: if Jesus goes in through the door, it is Jesus who will come out. If Judas goes in through the door, it is Judas who will come out.

When Joe E. Brown was starring in the play *Harvey*, I asked him to tell me the line in the script that he liked the most. He knew it instantly—a line said by Harvey's slaphappy friend: "I always have a wonderful time wherever I am and with whomever I am."

Joe E. was one of those people who knows that a man makes his own happiness. He does not have to let his happiness depend on where he is or upon the people around him. His happiness depends, rather, upon his own approach to that place and those people.

Nor will he find it necessarily in the possession or enjoyment of things. I have seen many times that when a man becomes too heavily tied to material matters, he finds it difficult to evoke happy relations with other people. "Uneasy lies the head that wears a crown," for the crown and all its responsibilities and dangers must ever weigh more than the simple pleasures of life. There are many kinds of crowns. Only the other day I lunched with a man of great power in the business world and possessed of enormous fortune. He is on intimate terms with scores of men like himself. None of them, he told me, is happy. He went on to examine the general reason for the millionaires' unhappiness, and I was not surprised to find that it hinged on very personal matters. As a rule, these men seemed to have faulty relationships with their wives and children. Their money had pushed them into a way of life that gave them such faulty relationships—and nothing money could buy could mend the damage that had been done.

It does not follow that money must bring misery, or that poverty—or having just enough money—brings happiness. Nor does it follow that the inevitable truth is the other way around. Happiness always is a personal matter. A truly mature rich man will never let his money sour his life. A truly mature poor or middle-income man is entirely capable of being happy. Ultimately, your life is what *you* yourself make it.

The world's literature and folklore are full of stories that point out how futile it can be to *seek* happiness. Rather, happiness is a blessing that comes to you as you go along; a treasure that you incidentally find.

Count Maurice Maeterlinck's *The Bluebird* tells such a story. A woodcutter's boy and girl, Tyltyl and Mytyl, keep a blackbird in a cage in their home. What they want, however, is the bluebird of happiness. They set forth from their humble hut to find this fabulous bluebird. Since the story is a fantasy, it has the seekers wandering through many lands, even the lands of those who have died and those yet to be born. Eventually they return disappointed and discouraged—only to find that happiness is next door.

Their blackbird, lent to a neighbor's sick child, turns gradually into a bluebird. At last the children realize that the bluebird of happiness was always at home.

Often, a man is convinced he will be happy when he attains a certain goal. Sometimes he is. Often he is not, for one way to avoid being happy is to set conditions on happiness, to say, "Thus I am able to be happy" and "Thus I am not."

You often can see this phenomenon at work among mothers. First they will say, "When Johnny gets out of elementary school, I'll be happy!" And they are for a while. Next you hear them telling their friends, "When Johnny graduates from high school, I'll be so happy!" And they are, at least for the summer. Johnny's graduation from college brings the same result, and so does Johnny's marriage, and so does the birth of Johnny's first child, when Momma becomes an ecstatic grandmother and the feeling may continue until she becomes a baby-sitter. If Momma has not learned how to be happy in between her special blessings, she does not know much about being happy.

Serendipity, a word coined by Horace Walpole, is defined as accidentally finding unexpected things while working on something else. So it often is with happiness. Some people go through life seeking it but never seeing it. Others, engaged in the faithful performance of their daily tasks, or in doing good for their fellow men, find they are also consistently happy.

Let us make the point that happiness is not to be confused with pleasure. Pleasure might be a very gratifying sex experience; but if it were gained as part of a deceitful adulterous relationship, unhappiness waits to move in. One may gain a stunning triumph—some great goal gained after years of trying—but if the winning of the goal leaves scars of physical and emotional damage, no real happiness is attained. Happiness runs deep; it is an undercurrent of life. Pleasure is transient, mere pretty bubbles that rise to the surface, and can be briefly admired before they break.

Contentment is perhaps closer to happiness, yet it is really something else. I am thinking of an old story called *Bontsche the Silent*. Bontsche, from the day of his birth till the day of his death, was the victim of every kind of misfortune. He knew poverty and misery, rejection, and persecution. But he never complained. (My own note on the story: noncomplaining is not always a virtue. It may show only lack of awareness as to what is possible to one in life.) When he died, and appeared before the Heavenly Throne for judgment, a Divine Voice called out that his sojourn on earth had been most exemplary in its saintliness, and that as a reward he might have anything his heart desired. Bontsche hesitated, wondered, finally stammered forth, "Might I please have a buttered roll for breakfast every morning?" So underprivileged had he been that this had become his ultimate idea of happiness.

Happiness should be relevant to you. You should be conscious of your capacity for happiness, and never consider yourself as one "doomed to sorrow" or never-ending depression.

In your further understanding of happiness, however, know that there is animal happiness and human happiness. Animal happiness is essentially physical, and human happiness is primarily mental and emotional. How can you bring happiness to a dog or a cat or a horse? You make sure it has adequate food, comfortable quarters, affectionate attention, and freedom to roam and romp. In short, an animal is made happy by the same factors that make a human child happy.

The surest sign of immaturity in a human being is his contentment with animal happiness. In children, we expect it. We know they are primarily interested in having fun, in stuffing themselves with goodies; in *getting*. Only as maturity begins to arrive does the child show evidence of feelings that are not completely selfish, and that encompass also the joy of giving. Now he can sow the seeds of deep, mature happiness. He need not at any time in his life deny his interest in physical pleasures, although he will observe some sense of balance. He will, however, give a higher degree of the cerebral to his concept of happiness, and so he will find he is more deeply and maturely happy.

Now we shall set down some definite criteria of happiness. You will note again that so many factors that many people regard as being essential for happiness are more closely related to passing pleasure. But nothing can be defined in a completely all black-and-white, pattern. We begin with five criteria that seem very desirable, and yet are not the essence of genuine happiness.

LIFE

Of course, without life, you would not be able to be happy. At the same time just to be alive is not sufficient reason for happiness. The ancient Hebrew toast, "To life!" is not intended to refer only to the counting of one's years. It refers rather to making one's years count. It is a toast to life lived on a plane far higher than the animal.

The ancient sages had a way of speaking that can be puzzling to the uninitiated. Know the true meaning of some of their sayings, however, and you know you are face to face with truth. Thus, they asked, "How shall a man live?" "Die," was the answer. This meant that a man was to slay all that was ugly and mean in himself, and so live truly and worthily.

They asked, too, "How shall a man die?" The answer was, "Live." This meant that if you live in a self-centered, animal-like way, concerned only with your own pleasures, without any thought for real happiness, you will effectively slay all that is worthwhile.

Remember Oscar Wilde's *The Picture of Dorian Gray*. In addition to dealing with a magical picture, it drew a word picture of a man who destroyed himself by the way he lived. His idea of happiness was to fill his life with the satisfaction of all his animal urges; to eat and drink like a glutton; to gratify his sexual passion wherever and whenever possible; to fill each day with the largest possible amount of play and the least possible work.

Thus did Dorian Gray destroy himself. The saddest part of this story is that it is largely autobiographical. Oscar Wilde, despite his great talent, never knew mature happiness. In *De Profundis*, written while he was in Reading Jail, he set down this line to his friend, Lord Douglas: "It was only in the mire we met." Wilde at length saw what he had done to himself by wallowing in mire. It was too late then for him to gain a spiritual mountaintop where the ground is firm and the air is pure and the view is always broad and far and clear.

To have life, then, is to have the opportunity to find true happiness. To say that one is happy merely because one is alive is to beg a vital question.

SUCCESS

I began my book *The Road to Successful Living* with these words:

The most conspicuous failure in our time is success. No age in man's history has been so feverishly occupied with success; no age has been so noisily boastful of it. The reality or the promise of "good things" pervades our view of the world; almost everywhere plenty has replaced or has begun to replace poverty.

But I went on to point out that this same age of ours has beheld:

. . . one of humanity's recurrent disillusionments, one of the great unlearned lessons of history. Success does not create happiness. . . . For half a century it has been taught by both precept and example that material success—distinction

in the acquisition of fame and money, position, and power—
is the most important goal in life. . . . Material success is
what a man has; spiritual success is what he is; and we had
tended to lump them together, to assume that happiness was
the product of wealth. We had been proved wrong.

We spoke earlier of the kind of mother who keeps on making
conditions for happiness, tying those conditions to the life-progress
of her son. The son, himself, if he acquired his mother's point of
view, would have trouble in proving to himself that he ever was
happy and not just waiting for happiness. Being in the lower
grades, he would dream only of high-school-level happiness. Discovering that high school studies made demands upon him, he
would yearn only for college, a golden dream. Finding out that
college life involves something more than song fests and football
games, he would yearn for the happiness of having a job. Once he
had a job . . . But you can see the sequence here.

Let us go back to the question of goals. It is easier to set up a
specific goal, such as making a million dollars or becoming president of a large corporation, than a general goal such as missing no
opportunity to help one's fellow men. I know a man who thought
he would be happy if he accumulated one hundred thousand
dollars by the time he was forty. He had his hundred thousand
before he was forty, and set his goal at a higher level. Reaching it,
he wanted a million; he got his million dollars—and wanted more.
Was he happy? He could not rest; he wanted more, more, and
more. He was another of those men who came to wonder dismally
why he could not master so simple a skill as getting along with his
wife and his children.

Was Alexander the Great ever happy? While we may remember his conquests, we remember him most as the man who died at
thirty-three, unhappy because he had no more worlds to conquer.
Was Napoleon ever happy? He wanted power and he acquired
power; but never enough. There *never* is enough. And he died
frustrated, exiled, and lonely.

Thus, much hinges on one's definition of *success*. In that
sense, the person who knows deep, mature happiness has succeeded in life. Set aside, however, all ordinary definitions of
success when you relate it to happiness.

SECURITY

What kind of security do we mean here? Again we must take
security in its meaning for most people; financial security.

Who has it? We must first rule out the millions who fall asleep every night—if they can sleep—with one last worried thought as to whether they will be able to pay their bills, meet the rent, count on holding their jobs long enough to pay off on the refrigerator . . . and every other thought that goes with chronically not having enough money.

You would assume that those who do have a good supply of money must feel secure! Alas, they do not. To the immature, "financial security" is so relative a term that it hardly can be said to exist. Some of my readers will be able to recall the wave of suicides that ran through Wall Street at the time of the great crash in 1929. The record showed later that many a man who jumped out of his office window was neither penniless nor anywhere near penniless. But to be reduced from a multimillionaire to the ownership of only a few hundred thousand dollars is more than some men can tolerate.

Nor does a rich man have to lose his money in order to show how little it does for him by way of giving him true, inner security. It is not too uncommon for a man with millions to keep his wife on a miserly allowance. A noted multimillionaire—he *succeeded* in making a certain soft drink popular all over the world—would approach hysteria every time he had to write a check to pay his taxes.

I have heard it said, "You either have security or you don't have it." This is true when we talk of the only real security, inner security. Yet those who have it not can seek it and often find it—once they know that security is not measured in money, nor in friendships, nor in anything else that can fade away.

PASSIONATE LOVE

The ancient teachers looked upon our Sacred Scriptures as being primarily concerned with spiritual love, the love of man for God, the love of man for man as his brother.

What then are we to make of *The Song of Songs?* Here is a paean in praise of young, physical love, telling—though in delicate and muted terms—of female charms and sexual urges. How did this somewhat profane book find its way into the Biblical Canon? Among other explanations (rather farfetched), scholars have said that after all it was designed to teach us the meaning of real, mature love. They center their interpretation upon the following lines:

> For love is as strong as death. . . .
> Many waters cannot quench love.

Passionate, youthful love, then, can eventually become mature, deep love. Love can be carried far past youth, and, on its own better terms, last all one's life despite the ravages of time and circumstance. Love can become a maturity; a strength with which to meet all circumstances.

Passionate love has its place. To deny the passions of youth would be to deny human nature. Only remember that this kind of love—to many, the only kind of love—has no firm connection with happiness.

Unfortunately, passionate love is more dramatic than mature love—more visible, more amenable to treatment in song and story. The hit parade is always top-heavy with songs of love at a romantic, if not passionate, level. Love stories last through the ages. Thwarted young love will be a theme for the novelist and poet forever.

Passionate love can be a great wellspring of pleasure. It also can be a source of considerable torture, whether the loving two discover they are different people after all, or the fatal third party enters. The mature person may enjoy passionate love, yet he knows it is passing. And he knows that any passing phenomenon is no fit foundation for happiness. Mature young people can love each other deeply, yet their essential happiness is a factor that strives beyond their passion.

Within a family, there may be deep love and yet constant bickering. I know many children who love their parents but somehow must quarrel with them. Surely this love brings no happiness to either side.

PEACE

Joshua Loth Liebman's *Peace of Mind* was published over twenty years ago. Peace still remains as individual a matter as it did in his portrayal. Certainly there is no general peace, either within or without. Despite our great strides on various fronts of material progress, we are still torn by inner tensions and live now with special terrors, knowing that one false move can depopulate the earth.

With all this, we must realize that there cannot be any such condition as absolute peace on earth—except the peace of the tomb. Again I quote from my book *The Road to Successful Living:*

The peace of life cannot be perfect and it cannot be permanent. The very essence of living is movement, and movement always encounters resistance. And resistance means conflict. Armed warfare may someday cease—and soon, we hope: but the inner conflicts of humanity will never be totally resolved. Peace on earth in the political sense is a distinct possibility—even a necessity—but absolute personal peace of mind for all men everywhere is millenial and a dangerous illusion at that.

The mature man knows that only someone who lives like a vegetable, bereft of the vital processes of thinking, feeling, and aspiring, can ever have peace of mind. But that does not mean that an active man cannot have happiness. Some of the most genuinely happy men and women I know are involved in associations and activities that trouble their days and disturb their nights. In giving of themselves to others, in working eagerly without pay for worthy causes, however unpleasant that work may be, they find a happiness unknown to those who seek only peace.

So long as our minds are active, our hearts sensitive, and our souls searching, we always shall be occupied in refashioning our environment according to our heart's desire. Discontent need not take away our happiness. There is great wisdom in the words *divine discontent*.

We have examined five vital values that many will say are basic to human happiness. We have seen that—in their general conception at any rate—these values are not really the essence of happiness.

What then are the permanent values that do make for happiness? I shall now set them down in a positive program for the attainment of happiness. They are a sense of being, a sense of belonging, a sense of meaning, a sense of growing, and a sense of giving. We may call them the five spiritual senses that correspond to the five well-known physical senses of seeing, hearing, smelling, tasting, and feeling. The physical senses give us great capabilities for pleasure. The spiritual senses can guide us to true happiness.

A SENSE OF *BEING*

In his *The Importance of Living*, Lin Yutang reminds us that the three great religions of China, Confucianism, Taoism, and Buddhism, shared in common a very commonsense earthy approach to the pursuit of happiness. Consequently the mature Chinese was a person who never allowed himself to become so immersed in thought that he drowned out all his emotion or to become so completely wrapped up in any one idea or ideal or philosophy or faith that he failed to appreciate his own entire being—the joy of just being alive. Merely *to be*—to wake up in the morning; to behold the glory and grandeur of this world; to satisfy a healthy appetite; to experience the normal functioning of the body; to talk with friends; to look upon the face of loved ones—that is happiness enough. The mature Chinese, in contrast to his Occidental brother, gives his emotions and instincts much freer reign; he is less subject to inhibitions and restrictions. Like the character in the musical who sings, "I enjoy being a girl," he enjoys just being a man. *To be* is a great privilege even if you are incapable of great thought or great achievement. Read the Bible, particularly some of the Psalms and The Song of Songs and you will find the same approach to life and love.

As anyone who reads Lin Yutang's book will recognize, he is too profound to be opposed to the use of the intellect. He tells us, rather, that our Western world has placed so much emphasis on thinking that it has downgraded feeling. He is not asking man to give up the cerebral processes that make him human, but only to enjoy himself at the same time on a level of *being*, where he can be happy with what he is.

I asked a very brilliant nun of the Catholic Church what happiness is. After some careful thought, she answered in essence, "We are all so restless that we fail to rest; to look inward more than outward; to let our eyes rest on nature as well as man." She went on, "To be happy you must have a sense of being, always knowing you are part of a wonderful world, reflecting upon the joy of your being, physically, mentally, emotionally; meditating upon the mystery of the universe, marveling at the magic of nature and of human nature."

I know people who have developed the art of solitude. When others are trying hard to "find something to do" in leisure hours, these people find happiness in sitting alone in a park to admire the trees and listen to the birds; or in taking long walks, luxuriating in the sun and the wind. This is far more than merely being alive. It is a full tasting of the essence of life; of *being*. It is a communion with one's inner strength and at the same time a "tuning in" of one's own self to forces beyond and above. *Being* is the overall experience, the very foundation of a happy life.

A SENSE OF *BELONGING*

A generation ago, Eugene O'Neill gave us his play *The Hairy Ape*. In it he portrayed a hairy-chested apelike stoker named Yank, who shoveled coal in the boiler room of a transatlantic liner.

I shall attempt in my own words only to approximate Yank's way of speaking. He demands of his fellow stokers: "What's them slobs in the first cabin got to do with us? We're better men than they are, ain't we? Sure! One of us guys could clean up that whole mob with one mitt. Put one of them down here for one watch in the stokehole. What'd happen? They'd carry him off on a stretcher. Them boids don't amount to nothin'. They're just baggage. Who makes dis old tub run? Ain't it us guys? Well den, we belong, don't we? We belong and they don't. Dat's all."

One day, Yank, curious, wanders into the first-class passenger section in the upper part of the ship. Accidentally, he comes face-to-face with a beautiful, aristocratic, well-bred girl. Startled and shocked by his big, brawny, hair-chested, hulking figure and vacuous face, she shrinks back with obvious revulsion and rejection. She shows the kind of fear that one might feel if one were to meet a ferocious hairy ape in a forest.

This is a very painful experience for Yank. Slowly he tries to think his way through it. It tells him in no uncertain terms that he does not really *belong;* he does not really belong to the human race.

In the last scene we find Yank in a zoo, talking through the bars of a cage to a gorilla inside. Says Yank to the real hairy ape, "You're lucky. See? You don't belong wit' 'em and you know it. But me—I belong wit' 'em but I don't, see? They don't belong wit' me. That's what." Yank opens the cage and says to the gorilla, "Step out and shake hands!! I'll take yuh for a walk down Fift' Avenue. We'll knock 'em offn the earth and croak wit' the band playin'. Come on, brother." The gorilla grabs Yank in its enormous arms and crushes him to death. Dying, Yank gasps, "I'm t'rough. Even him don't think I belong." And then the final, despairing cry, so typical of so many lost people, "Christ, where do I get off at? Where do I fit in?"

Man is a gregarious animal, and gregarious in more than the physical sense. Not only does he wish to mingle with others; he also wants to mingle his thoughts with the thoughts of others, to work with others in attaining common aspirations, and to be accepted as a worthy member of human groups such as the family and the community. As regards these groups, we also increase our sense of belonging by joining ourselves to others; we become members of a particular religion, citizens of a particular nation. Most of all, we belong to our fellow men and they belong to us in our sharing of membership in humanity; we are concerned with each other, and that basic concern comes through despite quarrels and misunderstandings.

Yank, a great muscular child, found his belonging only at one level, in the companionship of the stokehold. Most of us find the sense of belonging at many levels. Yet few of us can stand up against a rejection that leaves us without orientation, as though we had been robbed of anyplace to stand in the world. This may happen to a child when he begins his conscious life without a feeling of love around him. He may never quite be able to get over that basic disorientation.

Even those who most value the highly individual sense of *being* know that in joining themselves to others they fit themselves all the better for the enjoyment of life. Belonging is ever a part of happiness, and maturity thrives in one who knows how to share his world; how to belong.

A SENSE OF *MEANING*

To feel one's meaning in the world is closely akin to belonging. More particularly, we connect meaning with purpose and worthy achievement.

Thus, a man is helped to feel he has meaning when his job has meaning. Richard Cabot published a list of seven requirements for a good job, of which the last four are particularly significant:

4. A chance to achieve, to build something, and to recognize what we have done
5. A title and a place which is ours
6. Connection with some institution or some firm or some cause which we can loyally serve
7. Honorable and pleasant relations with our comrades at work

He goes on to say that we all like "to believe that our intentions, our hopes, our plans, our daily food and drink have not passed through us for nothing, for we have funded their worth in some tangible achievement that outlasts them . . . We need something to show for ourselves, something to prove that our dreams are not impotent."

A wife needs to know that her job of household work has great meaning for her family. A child needs to know that he has meaning in his parents' life, and he can be permanently hurt if he is made to feel he is just another mouth to feed, just another nuisance that cannot be avoided. A person whom we help should now and then be given a chance to help us in some manner, so that he feels the meaning of the *giving* side of life.

In *To Let*, one of the several volumes of *The Forsyte Saga*,

John Galsworthy portrays two aging servants whose only work is the care of a very ancient Forsyte. This special job becomes their special pride. In my own experience, I have seen a cook or a maid who has spent years half helping, half annoying a family with her lax, lazy work, suddenly change into an eager, conscientious worker when the family became really dependent upon her.

The meaning of a life may be held so firmly as to transcend life itself. One of the best-known lines from the speeches of the late Martin Luther King is, "If a man doesn't have something worth dying for, he isn't fit to live." Not all will find the happiness of meaning at that transcendent level. Yet all of us can find the meaning of involving ourselves with humanity in matters beyond our daily jobs.

A SENSE OF *GROWING*

One of the greatest misfortunes in human life is to be retarded in growth. This is particularly true of physical retardation because it is always visible. I have been close to the agony of boys and girls who through some defect are doomed never to grow beyond four feet in height—and must be told. And I have watched them develop a mature approach to their plight, put aside self-pity, and become the happiest individuals in a circle of young friends. They even develop a sense of humor about their affliction. They turn a liability into an asset. Maturely, they grow within.

One of the happiest communities I have ever come across was in a school for the mentally and emotionally retarded. Some of the happiest parents I have met have been the mothers and fathers of retarded children. It is true that some retarded children are happy because they are incapable of feeling the trials and tensions that make for unhappiness, yet even with the retarded, the sense of growing is a sense of happiness. Learning the use of a few new words, realizing that one has made a friend, or developing—after many trials—some small but useful skill, are meaningful and delightful growth to these children. It is also the basis of usefulness, of belonging, of meaning. To see their retarded children grow just a little is one of the greatest joys of their parents.

In our time, intellectual growth has become the "in" thing. Acceleration and expansion of learning for normal children now begin in their nursery years. An increasing number of adult classes in many fields is another sign of the educational thrust forward.

To increase our emotional growth, however, still remains a problem difficult to solve. In the midst of a world filled so heavily with injustice and cruelty, hatred and violence, how is one to grow in charity, compassion, mercy, forgiveness, and love? The development of this emotional (and spiritual) growth is the goal of all great religions. It is basic to the growth of maturity, which, as we know, is in itself a constant inward growth.

A SENSE OF *GIVING*

Just what is giving? In the physical sense, it usually amounts to handing over part of one's excess possessions to someone else— usually someone in need. This can be a mechanical motion. Money can do good no matter where it comes from and no matter in what spirit it is given. True giving includes a gift from within. It must be a gift of the heart along with the gift of the hand. Money may be its outward and necessary symbol, but one who really gives knows how to give part of himself.

Anyone who takes part in the management of charity drives knows there are ways in which to get increased donations. In a large city, the Community Chest's board of directors found that a certain prominent and prosperous merchant had donated only $500 to the annual drive. They called on the man.

"Mr. X," they said, "we know you are one of the finest and fairest men in our city. Isn't it part of your responsibility, along with the rest of us, to take care of the indigent, the blind, the aged, and the orphaned?"

"Yes," said Mr. X. "It's not that I don't believe in supporting charitable agencies. But I'm sorry, I am simply not a charitable man. I know others in my position give more, but I give what I give and that's all there is to it."

The directors smiled. Their spokesman said, "We ourselves once felt that way, and we had to learn. Let us help you learn how to become charitable. You will find there is a great happiness in giving. Now, we thought a man like you would give, say, $15,000. Never mind that. Why don't you just make out a check for $5,000 to the Chest, this year, as a beginning. Next year I know you'll want to give more."

Confronted with the sense of *noblesse oblige,* presented with an image of himself that he felt impelled to live up to, the merchant wrote out a check for $5,000. The next year, he gave more. In a few years he became one of the city's biggest and proudest givers. Or, was he truly a *giver*? As his fellow citizens watched, they came to appreciate having his money but somehow they never could appreciate him. They felt he never learned to give himself with his gift. Giving made him proud, gave him status, but never really made him happy.

That strangely gifted, strangely troubled man, Oscar Wilde, wrote a fable, *The Happy Prince,* that begins:

"High above the city on a tall column stood the statue of the Happy Prince. He was gilded all over with thin leaves of fine gold; for eyes he had two sapphires, and a large red ruby glowed on his sword hilt."

There came a swallow who had delayed his winter trip to Egypt and on his hurried way happened to put up for the night between the feet of the statue. The swallow discovered that the Prince was weeping; he wept at the sight of the poverty and misery of the poor people in his city. The swallow was persuaded to stay long enough—too long into the winter—to help the Prince give literally of himself as he distributed riches to the poor. First the swallow took the ruby to a mother tending a sick child so that his health could be restored. Then the swallow carried one sapphire eye to a starving writer in a cold attic. The other sapphire eye was flown to a little match girl. Then, one by one, the swallow carried all the leaves of gold that covered the Prince's body to give aid to undernourished, emaciated children.

Now the Prince had given himself away. In the cold of the winter, his leaden heart cracked. So too did the swallow die in the cold.

" 'Bring me the two most precious things in the city,' said God to one of his angels, and the angel brought him the leaden heart and the dead bird."

Long ago it was said, "It is more blessed to give than to receive." One who has not learned how to give can learn; and perhaps he will learn more easily if he does not have excess money. Or if he lacks any money to give, he truly gives himself— in attention, in service, and in time taken from mere pleasures and so transformed into happiness because it is time used for *giving*.

Thoreau once said that most men lead lives of quiet desperation. This probably is an exaggerated statement, but it is certainly worth remembering and using as a measure against one's own state of mind.

At best, most of us make a compromise with contentment. We have pleasures, and from time to time we feel real joy. But also we experience many misfortunes. Sometimes all we can see and feel is the sorrow that rains upon us. And so we may conclude that happiness is only a will-o'-the-wisp, an empty dream. It is not to be found in the here and now. Perhaps it is waiting in the sweet bye and bye.

For that reason, most religions provide the concept of an

afterlife. With it may come the vision of a Messiah who will at length deliver humanity from its vale of tears.

The concept is comforting. As with the concept of God, there is no way of proving or disproving it. I trust we have learned, however, that real, deep-down happiness *is* attainable in this life, on this earth. Happiness need not be considered as a permanent, unflawed state, but rather exists as a bedrock foundation of living, sensed and felt and trusted no matter what storms may arrive.

You can find happiness. You can find happiness no matter who you are or where you live or what your age may be. Happiness is always close by. In fact, you carry the seeds within yourself right now.

Howard Whitman

LESSON 50

HOW TO KEEP THE FLAME OF SUCCESS SHINING BRIGHTLY

Benjamin Franklin, toward the end of his illustrious life, wrote words that would give anyone pause. "When I reflect, as I frequently do, upon the felicity I have enjoyed, I sometimes say to myself, that were the offer made me, I would engage to run again, from beginning to end, the same career of life. All I would ask, should be the privilege of an author to correct in a second edition, certain errors of the first."

The goal of this university, which you have attended so faithfully since the first lesson, has been to help you reduce the number of errors you have been making in your life and thus light a path for you, however dim on occasions, that would guide you toward the treasures that really matter—pride, peace of mind, contentment, and a sense of accomplishment.

Certainly you have not failed to notice two parallel themes coursing their way through all ten semesters. The first was that you can achieve as much success and wealth as you desire, providing you are willing to combine your natural God-given talents with your newly acquired knowledge and determine to pay the price in time and effort. The second theme, as important as the first, is that success without happiness is a worthless state of being.

Is success, true success, worth the struggle? Make up your own mind, with the help of this parting lesson, taken from Howard Whitman's book, *Success Is Within You.*

And ask yourself one final question as you take leave of that fabulous faculty who have willingly shared so much of their wisdom with you:

"Where will I be, five years from today, if I apply all that I have learned here?"

Recently I saw an advertisement in the newspaper which began, "You can stop smoking in exactly forty-three days—no will power needed!" How typical of the day in which the common virtues— will power for one—have become not only uncommon but unpopular. We have somehow, in the late twentieth century, come to the belief that in our spectacular age we have learned so much more than all of humanity before us, that we can jettison the past, shelve the verities, and regard the virtues as interesting but useless antiques.

In our attitude toward success we have all but turned the virtues into vices. We have looked down our twentieth-century noses at such qualities as hard work, perseverance, thoroughness, diligence, conscientiousness, aspiration, and ambition. Some of these we even have considered neurotic. In the workaday world, instead of looking for young men burning with ambition, we have labeled this type the "eager beaver" and we have chalked his eagerness up as a demerit against him.

A few years ago a young man, whom I had known when he was a boy out in Ohio, came to New York to try his hand at journalism. He got a job on a large New York paper. Regarding me as a kind of Dutch uncle, he came to see me occasionally to ask advice and report on his progress. From my acquaintance with this young man as a boy (I had been his camp counselor) I knew that he was a conscientious fellow with a high-powered desire to make his mark in the world. So I was not surprised when, in his first progress reports, he told how well he was getting along and of numerous pats on the back he had received. But after a few months the picture changed. He came to me disconsolately to report that he wasn't getting on too well. Then one day he called, in bleak spirits, to say that he had been fired. I asked why. And all he could tell me was what an older man on the copy desk, who had befriended him, had explained: "Don't worry about it, kid. You did fine. The only trouble was you worked too hard. They were afraid you wanted to be editor."

There is no question that hard work, if it doesn't always get you fired, at least can make you mighty unpopular in the day of the enthronement of mediocre effort. You are just not supposed to be an eager beaver. You are not supposed to race so fast, to be so ambitious in pursuit of that old-fashioned, outworn prize called success.

And yet it is a strange phenomenon that the very individuals who scoff at success seem desperately to want it for themselves. The author of a book condemning materialism is no less interested in his royalty statements than any other author. The educator who doesn't want students to buck for grades or honors is nonetheless bucking as hard as he can for that advancement to a superintendency with its additional two thousand dollars a year. The young parents who, in their twenties and full of modern psychology, do not want their children to be materialistic or ambitious, have a way of growing on into parents of forty who hope their children will make "good" marriages, live in "nice" homes in the suburbs, and—in short—be successful.

There is a reason for the inconsistency between what many of us pay lip service to and what we truly believe. The smashing attack upon success in recent decades should never have been directed against success at all, but against false notions of success. Not only have we thrown the baby out with the bath water; we haven't even known the difference between the two. Much has been said about unhealthy, unproductive living which passes in the dark as "success." It is, of course, nothing but failure in a masquerade costume. But success itself, real success, remains as true as ever, just as the good law remains good no matter how many times it is violated. Success has been violated, to be sure; yet it is no less authentic a goal because many have followed false trails and failed to reach it.

When the American Psychological Association met in the fall of 1955, the customary search was made for a truly comprehensive definition of mental health. One was advanced by Dr. Frank Barron of the University of California, a definition which, as one observer remarked, "was unusual because it sounded so usual."

Dr. Barron's fourfold ingredients of mental health were:
1. *character and integrity;*
2. *intelligence;*
3. *ability to set a goal, keep it in sight, work toward it persistently and efficiently;*
4. *good judgment in appraising reality, likability, and self-knowledge.*

Mental health, like so many of the explorations of modern man, had, in this definition, come full circle. The definition made no mention of "maladjustment," "compulsiveness," or "perfectionism." Instead it listed time-honored virtues which were recommended to the young as guides for living long before Freud was born, and certainly before mental health became a national movement. One review of the psychologists' meeting pointed out, "The factors listed by psychologist Barron as indicating good mental health might have been cited by any old-fashioned moral philosopher."

There is something built into the nature of man (put there by the Creator and beyond the power of any theorist to remove) which spurs him on toward the expression of his best effort, toward exertions and striving, and rewards him with the satisfaction of a job well done. We tend to measure our own value and gear our self-respect to how much we achieve and how good we are at our jobs. Were it not so, the world might still be plodding along with oxcarts, plowing the ground with crooked sticks, and dressing in the stripped-off hides of animals. Inner satisfaction is our built-in reward for accomplishment and it spurs us to do our best whether that is the fashion of the social seers or not.

The twentieth century has been called the century of the common man. The appellation flowed quite logically out of the wars, depression, and social reorganization that marked the first half of the century. But let us hope that some part of the second half will enthrone the competent man along with the common one. Competence is a quality which gravitates to neither social position nor privilege; it is not one of the appurtenances of wealth, nor can it be bought. It is where you find it, innate in the man. It shines in him whether he springs from a mansion on Beacon Hill or a slum in Kingsbury Run. It is, thus, one of the qualities most in tune with democracy, for the highest have no greater claim to it than the humblest. In seeking for it all men are equal. It holds forth opportunity to every man with incorruptible parity.

We have shunned success, virtually conspired against it, to the peril of our times and civilization. We have mistaken democracy for "mediocracy," trying to strike a dead level of middleness as a cultural ideal. Now it must be growing clear to many that we thus lose the finest fruit of democracy: the freedom and opportunity of each individual to release the best that is in him, to achieve the most he can—and to be recognized for it.

The French writer-philosopher André Malraux, after exploring the tanglewoods of modern intellectualism, offers, as a new yardstick for our time, the simple dictum, "Man is what he achieves."

Indeed, the forward motion of achievement is life demonstrating its aliveness. If we can select the goals we truly want to pursue, for our own good and honest reasons, and have both the courage and the competence to go on pursuing them, then we have the kind of success one describes as "real." We can, for a fact, be rich—with or without money.

Once the poet Carl Sandburg said, "Before you go to sleep, say to yourself, 'I haven't reached my goal yet, whatever it is, and I'm going to be uncomfortable and in a degree unhappy until I do.' When you do reach it, find another."

This is the forward motion of life. It is the cadence of success.

Success is no exclusive club. It is open to each individual who has the courage to choose his own goal and go after it. It is from this forward motion that human growth springs, and out of it comes the human essence known as character.

Perhaps the ultimate purpose of life itself is the testing of the human spirit, to develop out of it something better, more nearly perfect. The ultimate success of the individual, then, is not to be found in the material results of his labors, for whole civilizations have already been buried in the sands and the dust, and undoubtedly more civilizations will crumble on top of them in a never-ending heap. But after them what is added to the human spirit? This is the heart of the matter, for after the sands and the dust only the human spirit is left to go on. Each individual in his lifetime is entrusted with a fragment of that human essence, to be the spark of his own existence from birth to death.

Is he rich? Has he enriched the life spirit which was given him?

Is he successful? Has he made the spark glow more brightly?

THE FACULTY

ABOUT THE AUTHOR

University of Success is Og Mandino's tenth book. His first nine, with multi-million copy sales, make him, without doubt, the most widely read inspirational and self-help author in the world during the past decade.

In 1976, at the age of fifty-two, he shocked the publishing industry by resigning his presidency of *Success Unlimited* magazine to devote all his time to writing and lecturing and he is now one of the most sought-after speakers in the country.

Countless thousands in seventeen nations, from American corporate executives to Japanese factory workers, from Mexican prison convicts to Dutch housewives, from National Football League coaches to nuns in the Philippines, have acknowledged, in their letters, the great debt they owe Og Mandino for the miracle his words have wrought in their lives.